AFTER SATURDAY COMES SUNDAY

I dedicate this book to those priests, pastors, nuns and countless lay workers who struggle against overwhelming odds as they shepherd Christ's precious flock through dark and dangerous days. I honor you.

May the Lord supply your every need (Phil 4:19).

Isaiah 40:31; Romans 8:31–39;
2 Corinthians 4:7–18; Ephesians 3:20–21.

Contents

Acknowledgments | viii
List of Abbreviations | ix
Introduction | xiii

1. "After Saturday Comes Sunday" (First the Jews, then the Christians) | 1
2. The Sunni-Shia Divide | 24
3. "Hasten to Success" | 36
4. Islamic Revival, 1979 | 61
5. The Shia Crescent | 81
6. The "Arab Spring" | 108
7. Myth Busting the Syrian Crisis | 123
8. The Evolution of a War | 143
9. The Return of the Caliphate | 166
10. "A Message Signed in Blood to the Nation of the Cross" | 190
11. A House Divided | 201
12. "After Saturday Comes Sunday" for the Nation of the Cross | 227

Appendix 1. Christian Solidarity: The Sound of Silence | 241
Appendix 2: God's Human Instruments: Just Do It! | 248
Bibliography | 257

Acknowledgments

I want to acknowledge and thank Christian Faith and Freedom (Canberra) for its support, without which this book might not have been written.

Abbreviations

AH	after Hijra
AQI	al-Qaeda in Iraq
AQIM	al-Qaeda in the Islamic Maghreb
AUA	Assyrian Universal Alliance
BBC	British Broadcasting Corporation
BP	British Petroleum
BTC	Baku-Tibilisi-Ceyhan
CIA	Central Intelligence Agency
CNS	Catholic News Service
CPR	Critical Prayer Requests
DI'ISH	Al-Dawlah Al-Islamiyah fe Al-Iraq wa Al-Sham
EFHR	Egyptian Federation of Human Rights
ESV	English Standard Version
FSA	Free Syrian Army
GCC	Gulf Co-operation Council
ICG	International Crisis Group
IDOP	International Day of Prayer
IDP	internally displaced person
IED	improvised explosive device
IOCC	International Orthodox Christian Charities
IRGC	Iranian Revolutionary Guards Corp
IS	Islamic State (previously ISIS/ISIL)
ISF	Iraqi Security Force

ISI	Islamic State of Iraq	
ISIS	Islamic State of Iraq and al-Sham/Greater Syria (aka ISIL; later IS)	
ISIL	Islamic State of Iraq and the Levant (aka ISIS; later IS)	
ISW	Institute for the Study of War	
JV	junior varsity	
LIFG	Libyan Islamic Fighting Group	
MB	Muslim Brotherhood	
MP	member of parliament	
MSN	Morning Star News	
NATO	North Atlantic Treaty Organization	
NDP	National Democratic Party	
NIE	National Intelligence Estimate	
PKK	Kurdistan Workers' Party	
PLO	Palestinian Liberation Organization	
RLPB	Religious Liberty Prayer Bulletin	
RNSC	Russian National Security Council	
ROC	Russian Orthodox Church	
SCAF	Supreme Council of the Armed Forces	
SAA	Syrian Arab Army	
TOW	tube-launched, optically tracked, wire-guided	
UK	United Kingdom	
UN	United Nations	
UNPO	Unrepresented Nations and Peoples Organisation	
US	United States	
USSR	Union of Soviet Socialist Republics	
YPG	Kurdish People's Protection Units	
WCC	World Council of Churches	
WMD	weapons of mass destruction	

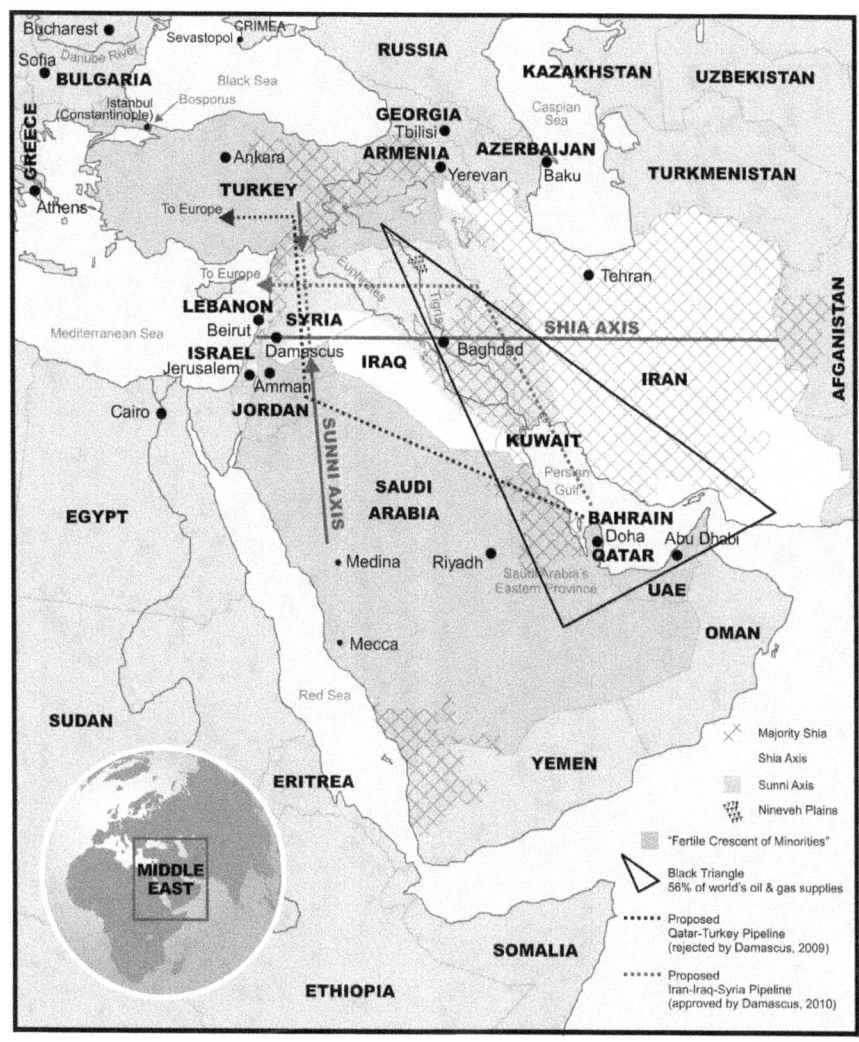

Figure 1. Geostrategic map of the Middle East.
Full color map available at www.ElizabethKendal.com

Introduction

GENOCIDE IS UNFOLDING IN the ancient Christian heartland of Mesopotamia.[1] Yet across the West, Christians and non-Christians alike remain disengaged from the Christian crisis in the Middle East primarily because it doesn't make sense; they can't get their heads around it.

Cognitive dissonance rings in our heads as foreign correspondents on the Syrian frontline describe the bushy-bearded, black-flag waving, "*Allahu Akbar*"-shouting, heavily armed Islamic militants behind them as "moderate rebels" fighting for freedom, democracy, and human rights. Confusion reigns as leaked news of sectarian massacres and ethnic-religious cleansing is whitewashed by Western politicians who assure us "Islam is peace" and then send the "rebels" more guns.

The first casualty of war is truth. The media is awash with propaganda and conflicting narratives abound. And because the narrative of Middle Eastern Christians conflicts with the narrative of Western governments, the Christians—along with their inconvenient and politically incorrect narrative of Islamic persecution and genocidal jihad—are airbrushed out of the picture and silenced, pushed ever deeper into the fog of war, which for most observers is pea-soup thick.

Cognizant of that "fog" and the need to dispel it, and cognizant that every incident of persecution is but a vignette—a single scene within a great drama, I have resisted the temptation to write a dramatic running commentary on, or an emotional patchwork quilt of stories from, the war zone (although this book does contain both commentary and stories). Rather, I determined from the outset to write a book that exposes the persecution within its context, to help people *understand* the Christian crisis in the Middle East. Understanding has long-term value and is a very powerful thing,

---

1. Mesopotamia (from the Greek, meaning "between two rivers") lies within the Fertile Crescent and covers much of Iraq and northern Syria. Fed and watered by the Euphrates and Tigris Rivers, the region is often referred to as the cradle of civilization.

for it can enable discernment—which is essential if we are resist manipulation and exploitation—and propel people into action.

Of course, there are people for whom the only thing necessary to be propelled into action is the knowledge that people are in need. But for most, this is not the case. If it doesn't make sense, if they can't get their heads around it, they will struggle with motivation and may resist any involvement. But when the penny drops, when the light bulb goes on, when they can finally say "Now I get it! Now it all makes sense," I find that in unravelling the confusion we have leaped a hurdle, opening the way to passionate, committed active engagement with and for the persecuted. As such, I have developed a deep appreciation of the link between understanding and active engagement.

With that in mind, chapter 1 takes the Arabic war cry—"After Saturday comes Sunday" (which essentially means "After we [Muslims] get rid of the Jews we'll get rid of the Christians")—and shows how this threat has been playing out on the ground, specifically in the historic Christian heartland of Mesopotamia.

Chapters 2 and 3 then take the reader back to the very beginning, where the foundations of geography, history, and ideology are laid. We look at the Sunni–Shi'ite divide, to see why these sects are such implacable foes. We look at Islamic ideology and worldview, in order to understand why Islam has, throughout the ages, been such a threat to non-Muslims (and dissident Muslims) in its path and under its rule.

Chapters 4, 5, and 6 build the framework and establish the context by detailing what I believe are the most significant and relevant stage-setting trends and events leading into the current crisis: the Islamic uprisings of 1979, the rise of the "Shia Crescent", and the eruption of the "Arab Spring."

I am firmly of the opinion that the Christian crisis in the Middle East cannot be separated from any of the issues, events or trends covered in chapters 2 through 6, nor can it be understood without them.

Chapters 7, 8, and 9 track the evolution of the current crisis: from the outbreak of civil war in Syria, through its evolution into a regional imbroglio and the principle theatre of international Islamic jihad, to the return of the caliphate.

Entitled "A Message Signed in Blood to the Nation of the Cross," chapter 10 stands apart as a brief vignette, zooming in on a single episode: the Islamic State's mass execution of twenty-one Christian martyrs (twenty Copts and one Ghanaian) on a beach in Libya. That incident, along with the Coptic Church's response to it, in many ways encapsulates the Christian crisis in the Middle East.

Chapter 11 is a call to solidarity in the face of resurgent Islam: a call for Christian solidarity across denominational lines with the suffering and existentially imperilled church in the Middle East, and a call for operational solidarity within the Dar al harb ("House of war"—i.e., all those outside the Dar al Islam, or "House of Islam") in what is destined to be a long war in defense of civilization.

Returning to the Arabic war cry—"After Saturday Comes Sunday", chapter 12 essentially serves as a "bookend," complementing chapter 1. Here, however, the Arabic threat is turned on its head as it is translated through a theology of the cross. "Sunday" need hold no terror for the "Nation of the Cross."

It is my fervent prayer that this book will go a long way towards eliminating the ignorance, unraveling the confusion, and dispelling the hopelessness that culminate in bad policy and hinder active engagement. For in this time of darkness, as we await the dawn, the Christians of the Middle East need all the help they can get.

— 1 —

"After Saturday Comes Sunday"

(First the Jews, then the Christians)

THERE IS A POPULAR Arabic war cry which never fails to make the blood of Middle Eastern Christians run cold. Whether Muslims are spray-painting it on walls, whispering it in ears, or chanting it in the streets, "*Ba'd as-sabt biji yom al-ahad*" ("After Saturday comes Sunday") is issued as a threat, meaning: As sure as Saturday (the day of Jewish worship) is followed by Sunday (the day of Christian worship), first we'll kill the Jews, then we'll kill the Christians.

It should be clear by now that this is no idle threat.

Iraq

In 605 BC, Nebuchadnezzar, king of Babylon, invaded Judah. To save Jerusalem, Jehoiakim, king of Judah, pledged allegiance to Nebuchadnezzar. A deal was brokered, and Nebuchadnezzar returned to Babylonia with tribute monies secured from the king, valuable artifacts looted from the temple, and captives taken from the cream of Judean society.

In 598 BC, King Jehoiakim rebelled, refusing to pay tribute. Nebuchadnezzar responded, laying siege to Jerusalem and taking Jehoiakim captive.

Jerusalem fell in 596 BC, her starving, decimated and devastated citizens no longer able to resist. After being ravaged and looted, the city was razed and an estimated 10,000 Judeans—all but the poorest of peasants—were taken captive to Babylonia. There, in historic Babylon, some 85 km south of modern-day Baghdad on the banks of the Euphrates, the Jews lamented: "By the waters of Babylon, there we sat down and wept, when we remembered Zion" (Ps 137:1).

But empires come and go: in 539 BC, Babylon was eclipsed and conquered by the Persians, whose king—the great King Cyrus—decreed that

Jews could return to Judah. The Jews who journeyed back with Zerubbabel in 538 BC rebuilt the altar and then the temple, and the Jews who returned with Ezra and Nehemiah rebuilt the city the walls. For those who chose to return, it was a dream come true: "When the Lord restored the fortunes of Zion, we were like those who dream" (Psalm 126:1).

However, not all of Babylonia's Jews wanted to "return" to the land of their ancestors. Many Jews—who by now were second- and third-generation Babylonians—preferred to remain in Babylonia where they had put down roots, assimilated, and were leading comfortable lives.

Meanwhile, to the north of Babylonia in the upper reaches of the Fertile Crescent was the nation of Assyria. Once the regional superpower, Assyria had been eclipsed by Babylonia, which had conquered Assyria and sacked its capital Nineveh in 612 BC before invading Judah.

Tradition has it that the Assyrians began worshipping Yahweh, the God of Israel, after the Hebrew prophet Jonah preached in Nineveh sometime between 780 and 755 BC.[1] Subsequently, the Assyrians developed close relations with Jerusalem and watched with interest as the scandal of Jesus of Nazareth, who claimed to be the Christ (the Messiah), played out. When news arrived in Nineveh that Jesus, though crucified, killed and buried, had risen from the dead (just as he said he would) and was seen by many before ascending to heaven, the Assyrians believed that Jesus was indeed the Messiah of whom the Jewish Scriptures spoke.

The Assyrian Church of the East—also known as the Nestorian, Persian, or Syriac Church—was established in Edessa[2] (now in southeastern Turkey), in the first century of the Christian era.

The Assyrians had great missionary vision. By the end of the second century, the church in Edessa had four Gospels in Aramaic and was spreading Christianity east through the Persian Empire. In around AD 280, the Assyrian Church of the East established its headquarters at the metropolitan seat of Seleucia, 32 km southeast of modern-day Baghdad. And all the while, Christian refugees fleeing violent persecution in Europe were streaming east, seeking sanctuary in Mesopotamia and Persia.[3]

The Assyrian church's legendary missionary work continued for centuries, as historian R. G. Tiedemann explains: "As Nestorian Christianity spread eastward from Persia among the Turkic nomads of Central Asia and

---

1. Mackay, *Jonah, Micah, Nahum, Habakkuk, Zephaniah*, 15.

2. Historic Edessa is in the vicinity of modern-day Urfa, Sanliurfa Province, southern Turkey, which is contiguous with and due north of Syria's Raqqa.

3. "History of the Nestorian Church."

along well-established trade routes, it eventually came into contact with Chinese civilization, probably sometime in the sixth century."[4]

In the early seventh century, the Arabs swept through Mesopotamia and Persia, severing the Assyrian Church from her missions in the Far East. At that time, some twenty-one Nestorian monks were active in China, where the first Christian church and monastery had already been built and *The Sutra of Jesus the Messiah* had already been translated into Chinese.[5]

"Just as the rivers flowed out of Eden," writes historian Philip Jenkins, "so the other patriarchs flowed forth from Mesopotamia . . . The natural home of Christianity was in Mesopotamia and points east."[6]

Friday: Islamic Conquest and Colonization

Arabs from the Arabian Peninsula had been migrating to the greener pastures of Mesopotamia for centuries before the Muhammadian armies invaded in AD 633. The Arab Muslim armies comprised mostly nomadic tribes from Yemen, the Hejaz and other regions of Arabia, and their arrival in Mesopotamia caused a split in the settler community. While some Arab settlers remained loyal to the state that had become their home, others switched allegiances and turned on their Christian neighbors in pursuit of booty and status.

Historian Bat Ye'or elaborates: "The conquest extended over a decade and comprised some decisive armed confrontations, but mainly *razzias* [raids] and the pillage of both villages and rural areas. This conquest was facilitated by support from Arab tribes who had infiltrated the Mesopotamian and Syro-Palestinian borders of Arabia during the previous two centuries, occasionally settling there. Some of these tribes had become Christianized . . . As vassals of these states, they assumed responsibility for defending their frontiers and protecting towns and villages against the raids of the nomadic Bedouins who roamed through the adjacent deserts."[7]

Concerning the invasion and conquest of Mesopotamia, Ye'or writes:

> The attack on Babylonia took place on two fronts which corresponded precisely to the densest Arab settlements . . . Large numbers of Christian Arab tribes fought on the Persian side, but others, long settled in the regions and attracted by booty, went over to the Muslims . . .

4. Tiedmann, "China and its neighbours", 369–70.
5. Ibid., 370.
6. Jenkins, *The Lost History of Christianity*, 14.
7. Ye'or, *The Decline of Eastern Christianity Under Islam*, 43–44.

> Helped by local Arab support—particularly active in the central region and the lower Euphrates—and by troop reinforcements sent from Arabia, the Muslims extended their raids on the countryside and villages to the south and centre of Iraq . . . These raids were supported by [Caliph] Umar who sent reinforcements from Medina. The monasteries were pillaged, the monks killed, and Monophysite [Christian] Arabs massacred, enslaved, or Islamized by force; in Elam [east of Basra, in modern-day southern Iran] the population was also decimated, and in Susa [city] the notables were put to the sword. The conquest of Mesopotamia took place between 635 and 642. Like the conquest of Syria, it seems to have been a joint operation between the Muslim armies and Arabs already settled in the region.[8]

And so it was, that over time, Iraq came to be dominated by Arabs and Islam.

Saturday

Muslim anti-Semitism intensified across Arab lands from the 1920s onwards, fuelled mostly by the vehement anti-Semite Mohammed Effendi Amin el-Husseini, the Grand Mufti of Jerusalem.[9] Consequently, violence against Jews also escalated.

In 1906, an Ottoman census counted 256,000 Jews in the Ottoman *villayets* (provinces) of Basra, Baghdad and Mosul (which together comprise modern-day Iraq).[10] By 1949, only around 130,000 remained. "An estimated 130,000 Jews lived in the Iraq of 1949," writes journalist and author Edwin Black,

> half of whom resided in Baghdad. The Baghdad Chamber of Commerce listed 2,430 member companies. A third were Jewish, and, in fact, a third of the Chamber's board and almost all of its employees were Jewish. Jewish firms transacted 45 percent of the exports and nearly 75 percent of the imports. A quarter of all Iraqi Jews worked in transportation, such as railways and port administration. The controller of the budget was Jewish; a director of the Iraqi National Bank was Jewish; the Currency Office Board was all Jewish; the Foreign Currency Committee was

---

8. Ibid., 46.

9. For more on the influence of el-Husseini, the Grand Mufti of Jerusalem, see Rubin and Schwanitz, *Nazis, Islamists, and the Making of the Modern Middle East.*

10. Black, *Banking on Baghdad*, 337.

about 95 percent Jewish. Over the centuries, Jews had become essential to the economy.[11]

As the anti-Jewish pogroms reached their peak in the early 1950s, the newborn state of Israel rescued some 120,000 Iraqi Jews—most secretly airlifted out of Iraq in Operation Ezra and Nehemiah. The Iraqi Jews arrived in Israel penniless, having been stripped of their wealth by the Iraqi government of Nuri Said.[12]

Black writes, "Between January 1950 and December 1951, Israel airlifted, bussed, or otherwise smuggled out 119,788 Iraqi Jews—all but a few thousand. Within those two years, Iraq—to its national detriment—had excised one of its most commercially, industrially, and intellectually viable groups, a group that for 2,600 years had loyally seen the three provinces of Mesopotamia as their chosen place on earth. This dispossessed group, who arrived in Israel with nothing but their memories, rose to become some of the Jewish state's most productive citizens."[13]

By 2004 only thirty-five Jews remained in Iraq; by 2008 there were ten,[14] with eight living in Baghdad under the care of Rev. Canon Andrew White who described their situation as "more than desperate."[15] In 2011, WikiLeaks published diplomatic cables from Baghdad, which Iraq's last seven surviving Jews feared could hasten their demise, should they be identified.[16]

In October 2014, Canon White was evacuated at the request of the archbishop of Canterbury, Justin Welby, who rightly assessed that White's high profile had made him a highly desirable target. Six Jews remained.[17]

After Saturday comes Sunday

Iraq's last official census (1987) counted 1.4 million Assyrians—the indigenous people of Iraq, who now are Christian. However, as Islamic zeal rose in the wake of Gulf War I (1991), Christians with means emigrated. By the time of the March 2003 US-led invasion, Iraq's Assyrian population had declined to between 800,000 and 1.2 million.

11. Ibid., 348.
12. Ibid., 338–52.
13. Ibid., 352.
14 "Jews in Islamic Countries: Iraq."
15. Van Biema, "The Last Jews of Baghdad."
16. Satherley, "The Last Jews of Baghdad."
17. Friedson, "Vicar of Baghdad."

The US-led regime-change operation liberated Iraq's long-repressed Shi'ites, whose most senior cleric, the Grand Ayatollah al-Sistani, vilifies Christians as *kafir* (infidels) and *najis* (unclean), equal to "Urine, Faeces, Semen, Dead body, Blood, Dog, Pig . . ."[18] It also triggered Sunni resistance, providing fertile ground for al-Qaeda. In September 2006, the Mujahedeen Shura Council, an umbrella organization of Sunni Arab extremist groups that included al-Qaeda in Iraq (AQI), vowed on its website to "destroy the cross and to slash the throats of those who believe in the cross."[19]

Deemed subversive by the "resistance" and *infidel* or *kafir* by Muslims (Sunnis and Shi'ites), Christians were easy picking for criminals and other hostile elements who exploited the cover of conflict to rape, loot, persecute, and kill Christians with impunity.

Christians fleeing persecution, war, and insecurity in Basra and Baghdad headed for Lebanon or Jordan, but mostly for northern Iraq, where they hunkered down in the ancient Assyrian heartland and homeland of the Nineveh Plain, mostly around the cities of Mosul (the capital of Nineveh province and Iraq's second-largest city) and nearby Bakhdida (also known as Qaraqosh or Hamadaniya), Iraq's largest Assyrian city.

In subsequent years, thousands of Islamic State of Iraq (ISI) jihadists would also relocate north. Driven out of the Anbar, Baghdad and Diyala provinces in 2006–2007 by the US "Surge", ISI regrouped in Mosul where they subjugated, extorted [demanded *jizya* (protection money)], murdered, and terrorized the city's Christians and assassinated the Christian leadership.

Father Boulos Iskander (59), a Syrian Orthodox priest, was kidnapped by ISI in Mosul on 9 October 2006. Two days later his decapitated and dismembered body was found dumped on the outskirts of the city.[20]

On April 2007, Fr. Ragheed Ganni (35) and three sub-deacons—Basman Yousef Daud, Wahid Hanna Isho and Gassan Isam Bidawed—were ambushed and assassinated by ISI jihadists as they left Mosul's Church of the Holy Spirit after leading a celebration of the mass. Archbishop Paulos Faraj Rahho, the bishop of Mosul, oversaw their funerals.[21]

---

18. Kendal, 'Iraq: Can Sovereignty Guarantee Security?' This post cites the website of the Grand Ayatollah Al-Sistani (which has not changed). On his website, Iraq's most senior Shia leader gives a list of those things Muslims are to consider *najis* (unclean): "The following ten things are essentially najis: Urine, Faeces, Semen, Dead body, Blood, Dog, Pig, Kafir, Alcoholic liquors, The sweat of an animal who persistently eats najasat." Christians are included under "kafir" (see Al-Sistani's official website, http://www.sistani.org/english/book/48/2132/, accessed August 2015).

19. "Iraq's al-Qaida Threatens To 'Destroy the Cross'."

20. "Kidnappers Behead Priest in Mosul."

21. "The Chaldean Church Mourns Fr. Ragheed Ganni and His Martyrs."

In February 2008, Archbishop Rahho (65) was ambushed, shot in the leg, and kidnapped by ISI fighters as he left the Church of the Holy Spirit after leading a celebration of the mass. His driver and bodyguards were shot dead. Allegedly kidnapped for his refusal to pay *jizya*, the head of Mosul's Chaldean (Catholic) community died in captivity. His body was later found in a shallow grave.[22]

As the persecution and targeted killings of Assyrian Christians did not threaten the volatile, all-important Arab versus Persian, Sunni versus Shi'ite, ethnic-sectarian situation in Baghdad—because Mosul's Christians refused to retaliate and repay evil with evil,[23] it was deemed to be of no strategic significance and so was generally ignored by all but Christian media. As persecution escalated, so too did the Assyrian exodus, with multitudes fleeing across the border into the safe haven of Assad's Syria.

For security purposes, most Christian women in Iraq took to wearing the *hijab* (head scarf), or even the *niqab* (full covering), to hide their Christian identity, for increasingly the harassment, intimidation, and threats were coming not only from al-Qaeda, but from local Muslims—even long-time friends and neighbors. While some local Sunnis genuinely supported the jihad, others simply turned on their Christian neighbors in pursuit of booty and status.

By 2010, after seven years of war, sectarian killings, church bombings, ethnic-religious cleansing, and targeted terrorism, an estimated 400,000 Christians remained.

Distressed by the sight of rapidly emptying churches, Iraq's church leaders pleaded for Christians to return, but to no avail. Speaking from his place of refuge in Damascus, Syria, in April 2010, Christian refugee Toma Georgees told Catholic News Service (CNS): "It's . . . impossible to turn back to Iraq. Our problem is not with the Iraqi government. Our problem is with Iraqi people . . . who want to kill us, who want to kill all the Christians . . . Those people are ignorant, and they just want to drink our blood as Christians."[24]

---

22. Malek-Yonan, "Genocide Unfolding: Death of a Catholic Assyrian Archbishop in Iraq."

23. Christians follow a unique creed that teaches "love your enemies and pray for those who persecute you" (Jesus, in Matt 5:43–48) and "do not repay evil with evil" (Prov 20:22; Rom 12:17; 1 Pet 3:9). It is precisely because attacks on Christians tend not to trigger a violent destabilizing response, that their suffering is routinely ignored. Yet as a peaceable people, they are surely worthy of our attention.

24. "Despite Pleas from Iraqi Leaders, Christians Say They Won't Go Home."

On 25 April 2010, the BBC's *Heart and Soul* program aired a report titled "Iraq's forgotten conflict", which described the systematic persecution of Iraq's religious minorities as "a campaign of liquidation":

> Untold until now is the story of "a campaign of liquidation" against Iraq's religious minorities who, post invasion, have had to endure torture, killings, forced conversions and exile.
>
> As troops move out of Iraq, and in the wake of elections, US and British politicians refer to "the emergence of a pluralistic democracy."
>
> Chaldean Catholic Patriarch Louis Sako, of Kirkuk, begs to differ: "200,000 Christians fleeing Mosul alone, in fear of their lives, and 1,000 murdered, is not much of a basis for pluralism or democracy."
>
> It's not just Christians who suffer. Both Mandaeans, who speak Aramaic—the language of Christ—and the Yazidis, goldsmiths with a history going back further than Christianity or Islam, are fast disappearing, too.
>
> "Does nobody care about what is going on here?" asks Patriarch Sako. "It's nothing less than the destruction of our ancient and honoured heritage, and our religious and cultural traditions."
>
> The Archbishop of Canterbury, Dr Rowan Williams, does. He tells the BBC that he fears it heralds the disappearance of Christianity from the Middle East . . . [25]

At the time of the BBC broadcast, Christians were so endangered in Northern Iraq that Assyrian students were travelling to university in convoys under Iraqi military escort. On Sunday May 2, 2010, two bombs ripped through a convoy of buses transporting Assyrian college students from the Assyrian town of Bakhdida (Qaraqosh) to the University of Mosul. As the first buses had passed through the Kokjali checkpoint (manned at the time by US, Iraqi, and Kurdish soldiers), a car bomb parked on the shoulder of the highway exploded in their path, followed moments later by a roadside bomb. A local shopkeeper was killed and more than one hundred people, including some seventy of the targeted Christian college students, were wounded; seventeen critically.[26]

Jamil Salahuddin Jamil (25), a geography major who was on the first bus, told reporters that one of his classmates lost her leg in the attack and two others were blinded. "We were going for our education and they

---

25. "Iraq's Forgotten Conflict."

26. Kendal, "The Insufferable Plight and Bleak Future of Iraq's Indigenous Assyrian-Chaldean Christians."

presented us with bombs," he said. "I still do not know what they want from Christians."[27]

The answer is obvious, yet unthinkable and unutterable: the jihadists and all who support them want Christians out of Iraq.

Then, on Sunday evening, October 31, 2010, Christians in Baghdad experienced the worst attack on a Baghdad church to date. At 5:30 p.m., an ISI suicide bomber blew himself up in his car at the fortified gate of Our Lady of Salvation Chaldean Catholic Church in the inner-city suburb of Karrada. How he even got there through multiple checkpoints is a matter of contention; most believe he was waved through by Islamic sympathizers in the security forces.

Alerted to the impending danger, the church's priests, who had been preparing to celebrate mass, ushered at least half of the 120-strong congregation into a back room. There they barricaded the believers behind bookshelves in a bid to protect them.

A terrorist then burst through the front door, gunned down the young priest standing before him, and hurled an explosive device into the sanctuary. The path now cleared, a group of ISI jihadists dressed in military uniforms stormed the church, mercilessly and indiscriminately shooting the worshippers whom they abused as "infidels."[28]

The streets of Karrada were closed off and the electricity cut. Helicopters circled above, periodically illuminating the chaotic scene with the occasional flare. As Iraqi security forces closed in, the militants inside the church detonated several large bombs. At 8:30 p.m., eight US soldiers arrived to assist the Iraqi counter-terror squad. Fierce gunfire erupted and three militants inside the sanctuary detonated their explosive suicide vests. Another round of shooting ensued—before silence descended over the cathedral like a shroud. That silence was soon shattered by the howl of ambulance sirens.

Reporting for *The Guardian*, Martin Chulov described the scene:

> For the next forty minutes, a cacophony of screeching ambulances carried away the dead and injured. Walking wounded and survivors without injuries stumbled past them through the mayhem.
>
> "They killed people, they injured people," cried Bassam, before collapsing on the road outside the church. "Where is our father?" he screamed, referring to his priest. "Where is our father?"

---

27. Dagher, "Bombs Hit School Buses in Northern Iraq."

28. Chulov, "Baghdad Church Siege Survivors Speak of Taunts, Killings and Explosions."

Among [the walking wounded] were two elderly ladies in their blood-stained Sunday best, several children trembling too much to walk and a traumatised elderly couple searching in vain for their priest.

Bewildered and frantic, the survivors collapsed onto a median strip crying for telephones to call their families.

"I am going to leave Iraq with my family tomorrow," said Bassam, an employee of an internet company. "Why am I here?" he wailed. "Look at this – this is Iraq."[29]

The next Sunday, November 7, 2010, around 100 survivors and mourners gathered at the cathedral. They lit candles in the shape of a cross on the now pockmarked and bloodstained marble floor next to the names of more than fifty dead. At the top they placed photographs of their martyred priests, Father Wissam (27) and Father Tha'ir (32). Another priest, aged seventy, was also killed, while a fourth priest, Father Rafael, survived with serious injuries. Many youths were amongst the dead; the youngest fatality was only four months old.

"They kill us not because we are Iraqi but because we are Christian," said Fr. Douglas Bazi, who has permanent injuries after being kidnapped and tortured four years ago. His own Chaldean Catholic parish in the working-class neighbourhood of New Baghdad had dwindled from 2,500 families in the 1990s to less than 300 by 2010.

"We are singing the hymns we couldn't finish [last] Sunday," said Ms. Riyadh, who was in the choir on the previous Sunday when the gunmen stormed the church and was shot in the leg. Fortunately, she was amongst more than fifty wounded to be flown out of Iraq to receive medical treatment in hospitals in France and beyond. At the time, Ms. Riyadh did not know if she would ever return to Iraq.

"I was one of the ones who wanted to come back," said another member who did not want his name revealed, "but now we're all leaving. What's happening to us is what happened to the Jews."[30]

In March 2013—on the ten-year anniversary of the US invasion—Canon Andrew White estimated that a mere 200,000 Christians remained in Iraq, most hunkered down in northern Iraq's Nineveh Plains.[31]

On June 9, 2014, the Islamic State of Iraq and al-Sham/Greater Syria or the Levant (ISIS/ISIL) flooded into Nineveh province, capturing its capital

---

29. Chulov, "Christian Worshippers Killed in Baghdad Church Raid."
30. Arraf, "The Oct. 31 Attack on a Baghdad Church."
31. Blair, "Iraq Invasion Anniversary."

Mosul in a blitzkrieg. Half a million people, including some one thousand Christian families, fled for their lives.[32]

On June 29, ISIS declared its caliphate and changed its name to Islamic State (IS). On July 18, it delivered an ultimatum to Mosul's remnant Christians: convert to Islam, submit and pay *jizya* (protection money/tribute), leave, or "face the sword." And so Mosul's remnant Christians departed, their homes and possessions forfeit to IS. They were met at checkpoints on the roads out of the city by IS militants, who robbed them of their cash, gold jewellery, and passports—essentially everything but the clothes on their backs.

Not so long ago, Mosul had been home to some 60,000 Christians. By July 19, 2014, only the most disabled and infirm remained—but not for long. Unwilling to convert and unable to pay *jizya*, they would soon be shot and killed.

"Christian families are on their way to Dohuk and Irbil [in Iraqi Kurdistan]," cried Patriarch Louis Sako. "For the first time in the history of Iraq, Mosul is now empty of Christians."[33]

"Our people are disappearing," lamented Canon Andrew White. "Are we seeing the end of Christianity? We are committed come what may, we will keep going to the end, but it looks as though the end could be very near."[34]

On August 6, 2014, IS forces overran Bakhdida (Qaraqosh), Iraq's largest Assyrian city.

Patriarch Louis Sako, the Iraq-based leader of the Chaldean Catholic Church, issued a statement on August 10, 2014, through the Catholic charity Aid to the Church in Need, in which he warned that Iraqi Christians "are facing a human catastrophe and risk a real genocide."[35] Noting that all the churches from Mosul to the border of Iraqi Kurdistan were now deserted and desecrated, the patriarch lamented, "The level of disaster is extreme."

Syria

Christianity has existed in Syria since its inception two thousand years ago, pre-existing Islam by more than six hundred years. In fact, it was in Antioch

---

32. Kendal, "Upper Mesopotamia: Christians at the Mercy of ISIS"; "ISIS Issues New Rules for Mosul" (includes photograph of document).

33. "Iraqi Christians Flee after Isis Issue Mosul Ultimatum."

34. "What is the future for Iraq's Christians?"

35. "Christians in Iraq on the Run"; Kendal, "IRAQ: Christians Flee the Killing Fields."

in Syria—Rome's "capital of the East"; a city with a "considerable and well-established Jewish community" [36]—that the "disciples" (followers of Jesus Christ) were first called Christians (Acts 11:26).

Yet, as Bloomberg diplomatic correspondent Flavia Krause-Jackson has ominously noted, "a history that predates Islam won't guarantee the communities' survival."[37]

It certainly didn't help the Jews.

Friday: Islamic Conquest and Colonization

After Muhammad's death, the first caliph, Abu Bakr, organized the invasion of the Levant, which Muhammad had already envisaged. The whole region from Gaza to Caesarea was sacked and plundered in the campaign of AD 634. "Four thousand Jewish, Christian, and Samaritan peasants who defended their land were massacred," writes historian Bat Ye'or, who goes on to describe how the villages of the Negev were plundered, the countryside was overrun, and Jerusalem was besieged.[38]

In Syria, Arab settlers sided with the invading Muslim Arabs, leaving Greek Christians to bewail the destruction of churches and monasteries, the sacking of towns, and the burning of fields. Whole villages were totally eliminated; cattle and people were carried off as booty. Thousands subsequently perished due to conflict-related famine and disease.

"The Arabs," writes Ye'or, "continued to launch successive raids on Palestine, Syria, Mesopotamia, Persia, and Armenia. The countryside suffered constant razzias [raids], while those who escaped the sword swelled the contingents of enslaved women and children, shared out amongst the soldiers after the deduction of the fifth reserved for the caliph. According to Michael the Syrian, the land taken from the Greeks was systematically pillaged. 'The Taiyaye [Arabs] grew rich, increased and overran (the lands) which they took from the Romans [Byzantines] and which were given over to pillage.'"[39]

And so it was, that over time, Syria came to be dominated by Arabs and Islam.

36. Witherington, *The Acts of the Apostles*, 366–67. Withington notes concerning Antioch (founded 300 BC) that, "Jews played a significant part in this city from its earliest days, and there was a considerable and well-established Jewish community in Antioch in the middle of the first century A.D."

37. Krause-Jackson, "Syrian Christians Say 'Arab Spring' Changes Could Hasten Extinction."

38. Ye'or, *The Decline of Eastern Christianity Under Islam*, 44.

39. Ibid., 47.

Saturday

"In the 1930s," writes Professor Harold Troper, "during the French colonial administration, Syria emerged as a center of Arab anti-Zionist sentiment." Violent attacks on Jews were commonplace, and because French authorities did not want Syrian nationalist leaders to support the Nazis and foment insurrection, they turned a blind eye to the persecution. "In 1944," writes Troper, "the Jewish quarter of Damascus was twice sacked by mobs."[40]

In 1947, Syria was home to some 40,000 Jews.[41] On November 29, 1947, when the United Nations voted to partition Palestine to create the Jewish state of Israel, Arab mobs responded with riots and pogroms. In Aleppo, the 2,500-year-old Jewish community was violently attacked and devastated. Scores of Jews were killed and more than two hundred homes, shops, and synagogues were destroyed. Thousands of Jews fled Syria for refuge in Israel.

When Israel declared independence on May 14, 1948, Muslims responded with violence yet again. Syrian Jews were beaten and killed while their homes were looted and burned. Jewish institutions were closed, holy books were burned, businesses were boycotted, and properties were seized. Syria's Jews were left destitute.

To prevent Jews escaping to Israel where they could strengthen the Israeli state and even become Israeli soldiers, Syria closed the borders and banned Jewish emigration. That period was so chaotic however, and the Syrian regime so unstable, that many Jews still managed to escape illegally into Lebanon or Turkey. By the time the doors were sealed shut in 1958, only around five thousands Jews remained—"approximately three thousand in Damascus, fifteen hundred in Aleppo, and another five hundred or so in the north-eastern town of Qamishli, near Syria's border with Turkey."[42]

Not only were Syrian Jews prevented from leaving, they were marginalized, segregated, repressed and persecuted. Their mail was censored and their phones monitored. Confined to Jewish neighborhoods in Damascus, Aleppo, and Qamishli, they were not even afforded freedom of local movement; they had to request permission to travel more than 3 km from their homes.

In 1967, the Arab states were decisively routed in what came to be known as the Six-Day War [against Israel], and Syrian Jews paid the price.

---

40. Troper, *The Rescuer*, 1–2.
41. "Jews in Islamic Countries: Syria."
42. Troper, *The Rescuer*, 2.

Faced with wholesale vigilante and state terror, the only way to survive was to pay an exorbitant *jizya*. Even then, security was tenuous.

During that time, Canadian Jewish couple Rubin and Judy Feld started wondering why the plight of Soviet Jews attracted so much more attention than the plight of Jews in Arab lands.

> Then, as now, realpolitik and "vital interests" determine whose suffering matters and whose crimes will be tolerated. The West ignored the plight of Jews in Arab lands so as not to jeopardize its "vital interests" with the Arabs. Meanwhile, the West exploited the plight of Jews in Soviet lands to criticize communism and punish the revolutionary soviet regime. The same selective indignation occurs today—"There is nothing new under the sun" (Eccl 1:9).

The Felds took up the cause of Syrian Jewry, and by late 1972 were in regular communication with a Rabbi in Damascus, sending coded messages and secret notes hidden in religious books.

When Rubin Feld (40) died of a heart attack in June 1973, the Felds' cause might have died with him except for the fact that Judy—a formidable woman—was so passionate about it herself. After her husband's death, Judy Feld devoted herself to speaking and fundraising on behalf of Syria's beleaguered and imperiled Jews.

In October 1973, when the Arabs failed (yet again) to eradicate the state of Israel—this time in the Yom Kippur War (also known as the Ramadan War)—the situation for Syrian Jews deteriorated further. In the first week after the war, Judy received the news that all Jewish males in Aleppo had been arrested. The fate of Jews in Damascus and Qamishli was unclear. Gradually, stories emerged of Jews dying while trying to flee. Judy knew that the remaining Syrian Jews needed to be rescued.

"I took my first person out of Syria by ransom—a rabbi from Aleppo—in 1977," she tells.[43] Eventually she gave up her career as a musicologist to devote herself full time to running clandestine operations to rescue Jews out of Syria.

In April 1992, the Syrian regime of President Hafez al-Assad lifted the travel ban imposed on the country's remnant Jews. At that point, the New York Syrian Jewish community organized a rescue operation through which hundreds of Jews were secretly airlifted out of Syria en masse.

Judy, who re-married and now goes by the name Feld-Carr, continued rescuing Syrian Jews until September 2001, by which time all the Jews who

---

43. Linde, "Judy Feld Carr Secretly Rescued Syrian Jews."

wanted to leave had left. By then, despite raising six children of her own, Judy had been involved in the rescue of 3,228 Syrian Jews. How did she do it? "Slowly, slowly, slowly," she says, "with a great deal of difficulty; it was not an easy thing to do, and I am not from Syria—I am an Ashkenazi [a Jew with Eastern European ancestry] from northern Canada originally—I figured out the system." [44]

In September 2013, as war raged in Syria, Sam Sokol reported for *The Jerusalem Post* that Syria's remnant Jews—numbering about fifty—were living in central Damascus under the protection of President Bashar al-Assad. "The average age there is around 45 or 50," he said. "There are no more youths under that age to my knowledge. No youths, no children." [45] In other words, the end of the Jewish existence in Syria was in sight, and all but guaranteed.

By 2014 there were as few as eleven Jews left in Syria.[46] These were Jews who had chosen to stay and die in their homeland.

Watching the carnage of the Syrian conflict, Judy Feld-Carr commented in March 2014, that she was actually glad there were virtually no Jews left in Syria. "If they were there now . . . I know what would have happened. It would have been the slaughter of the Syrian Jewish community, that is for sure . . . I know there would be a slaughter."[47]

After Saturday comes Sunday

In April 2008, Elias Khoury (65) reminisced to *The New York Times* that he could still remember the days when the people who lived in his cliff-side village of Maaloula (around 55 km northeast of Damascus) were virtually all Christian and the elderly spoke only Aramaic, the language of Jesus. Mr. Khoury lamented the loss of culture. Not only had the government's Arabization policies hurt, but as Assyrian (also known as Chaldean or Syriac) youths emigrated seeking better lives in the West, Arab Muslims flowed in to take their place. By 2008, Maaloula—which not so long ago had been entirely Christian and Aramaic-speaking—was almost 50 percent Muslim.[48] It would not be long before loss of culture would be the least of Mr. Khoury's worries.

---

44. Ibid.
45. Sokol, "Amid Civil War."
46. "The Woman Who Saved Syria's Jews."
47. Ibid.
48. Worth, "In Syrian Villages."

International jihadists flooded into Syria throughout 2012, mostly over the Turkish border with the tacit approval and even aid of Turkish authorities, to wage jihad against the "infidel regime" of Bashar al-Assad. In March 2013, the northern city of Raqqa became the first provincial capital to fall under full rebel control. Divisions emerged in the rebel ranks, and within months Jabhat al-Nusra (the main al-Qaeda affiliate in Syria) had split between those loyal to al-Qaeda and those loyal to a new group: ISIS/ISIL. The Syrian government was being seriously challenged on multiple fronts.

Maaloula

The war had turned Maaloula into highly strategic territory. Located on high ground just off the main highway between Damascus and the then-rebel-capital of Homs, Maaloula would be an ideal place from where rebels could launch attacks on the strategic M5 highway critical to the government's supply lines.

Early on the morning of Wednesday September 4, 2013, jihadists from al-Qaeda's al-Nusrah Front, Ahrar al Sham (another hard-line al-Qaeda-linked, Salafist/Wahhabi, puritanical Sunni outfit), and a supposedly "moderate" US-allied Free Syrian Army brigade from Homs, seized control of Maaloula.[49]

True to the al-Qaeda modus operandi, the attacked commenced with a suicide bomber blowing himself up at the regime checkpoint at the entrance to the village. After seizing the checkpoint, the jihadists disabled two tanks and an armored personnel carrier. Eight Syrian soldiers were killed defending the historic Christian town. After seizing control of the Safir Hotel high on the hilltop, and the nearby caves that overlook the town, the jihadists began shelling the residents below. Some eighty terrified locals took shelter in a convent already home to thirteen nuns and twenty-seven orphans. Others managed to escape the town.

From her refuge in Damascus, Maaloula refugee "Marie" lamented: "They arrived in our town at dawn on Wednesday and shouted, 'We are from the Al-Nusra Front and have come to make lives miserable for the Crusaders [i.e. Christians].'"[50]

Another Maaloula refugee, Adnan Nasrallah (62) told reporters: "I saw people wearing Al-Nusra headbands who started shooting at crosses," adding that one of them "put a pistol to the head of my neighbour and forced

---

49. Joscelyn, "Videos Show Joint Al Nusrah, Free Syrian Army Attacks."
50. "Jihadists 'Killed, Threatened Christians' in Syrian Town of Maalula."

him to convert to Islam by obliging him to repeat 'there is no God but God'. Afterwards they joked, 'he's one of ours now.'"

Mr. Nasrallah told reporters that he had spent forty-two years running a restaurant in the US state of Washington—a restaurant he had named after his hometown, Maaloula. "I had a great dream," he told reporters. "I came back to my country to promote tourism. I built a guesthouse and spent $2000 installing a windmill to provide electricity in the town. My dream has gone up in smoke. Forty-two years of work for nothing."

But for Mr. Nasrallah, the worst thing of all was the reaction he witnessed from his Muslim neighbors when the jihadists entered the town: "Women came out on their balconies shouting with joy, and children . . . did the same. I discovered that our friendship was superficial."

Maaloula refugee Rasha recounted how the jihadists seized her fiancé Atef, who belonged to the town's defence militia, and brutally murdered him:

> "I rang his mobile phone," said Rasha, "and one of them answered."
>
> "Good morning, Rash rush," the voice said, using her nickname. "We are from the Free Syrian Army. Do you know your fiance was a member of the shabiha (pro-regime militia) . . . we have slit his throat."
>
> The man on the phone told Rasha that Atef had been given the option of converting to Islam, but had refused.
>
> "Jesus didn't come to save him," he taunted.[51]

Kessab

In the early hours of Friday March 21, 2014, jihadists from al-Qaeda affiliates al-Nusra Front, Sham al-Islam, and Ansar al-Sham crossed into Syria from Turkey via the Kessab border crossing.

Located in Syria's far northwest, Kessab is a historic Christian Armenian town in the coastal province Latakia. Kessab's population had swelled in recent years as Armenian refugees had flooded in from Aleppo, Raqqa, and other Syrian war zones.

As the jihadists advanced, most of the 3,500 Armenians living in Kessab (some 670 families) either fled into the hills or were evacuated to the port city of Latakia.[52] Only the frail, infirm, and disabled remained. By the

---

51. Ibid.
52. "Two Thousand Kessab Armenians Find Safety in Latakia."

end of the day, Kessab, the border crossing, and the strategic hill known as Observatory 45 were all under rebel control.

The next day, the Syrian Arab Army (SAA) launched a counteroffensive. Its jets attacked rebel positions and drove the jihadists back. On Sunday March 23, however, jihadist reinforcements arrived and homes were looted, churches were desecrated, and the remnant Armenians were taken hostage. According to Armenian media, at least eighty Armenians were killed in the rebel assault in which Kessab was ethnically cleansed of its Armenian Christian community in a jihadist operation facilitated by Turkey.

In a written statement, the Armenian National Committee–International condemned the attacks along with Turkey's active role in aiding and abetting extremist groups in their targeted attacks against the Christian and minority populations in Syria:

> For months, we have warned the international community of the imminent threat posed by extremist foreign fighters against the Christian minority population in Syria. These vicious and unprompted attacks against the Armenian-populated town and villages of Kesab are the latest examples of this violence, actively encouraged by neighboring Turkey. We call upon all states with any influence in the Syrian conflict to use all available means to stop these attacks against the peaceful civilian population of Kesab, to allow them to return to their homes in safety and security. In the last one hundred years, this is the third time that the Armenians are being forced to leave Kesab and in all three cases, Turkey is the aggressor or on the side of the aggressors.[53]

Understanding the Christian crisis in the Middle East

A massive firestorm is devouring the Middle East. It is a highly complex storm with many elements to it, many factors driving it, numerous trends fueling it, and decades—even centuries—of pent-up momentum behind it. Contributing elements include apocalyptic politico-religious ideology and tortured history. Contributing factors include international geopolitics and strategic realpolitik. Contributing trends include urbanization, economic stress, Islamic radicalization, heightened sectarianism, globalization, the growth in communication technologies, and the decline of the West.

---

53. "Kessab Targeted by Al-Qaeda Front Groups."

Most of these contributing trends have converged to create what strategic analyst Gregory R. Copley describes as a "perfect strategic storm."[54] Two trends, however— decline of the West and the rise of Islam—could better be described as having passed each other, like travelers on adjacent escalators heading in opposite directions.

A century of Western hegemony has come to an end, and the West, having overturned the balance-of-power dynamic that existed through much of the twentieth century, is now in the process of departing the arena. It leaves behind a complex and multi-layered struggle through which regional forces are staking their claims, securing their interests, and advancing their agendas.

One layer of this struggle involves the region's three imperialistic powers which are competing for territory and influence: ascendant Iran *versus* the Arabs (led by Saudi Arabia) *versus* neo-Ottoman[55] Turkey.

Another layer involves the seemingly eternal struggle between region's two Islamic sects: the Sunnis *versus* the Shi'ites.

Yet another layer involves the region's two political axes: the east-west, Iran-led, Shi'ite-dominated Shia Axis or Axis of Resistance (comprising Tehran, Baghdad, and Damascus, along with Lebanon's Hezbollah and other "resistance" groups such as Hamas) *versus* the north-south, Turkey-Arab-Sunni Axis (which itself is split between pro- and anti-Muslim Brotherhood [MB] factions). The fact that Russia backs Damascus while the US backs its Sunni allies merely adds fuel to the fire.

Rising up like a mushroom cloud in the midst of the chaos—indeed, exploiting and feeding on the chaos to advance its own ends (as is its modus operandi)—is the global movement of transnational jihadism. This movement—which is committed to establishing a caliphate in the heart of the Middle East from where it will wage jihad against the West—has now split into two mutually hostile factions: the pragmatic, pro-resistance al-Qaeda *versus* the inflexible, anti-Shi'ite IS. While the transnational jihadist element adds another layer to the conflict, it also transcends it while infecting every other layer.

Of all the groups operating in the Mesopotamian theatre, only the US lacks clear goals. Consequently, US policy has been inconsistent and contradictory, confounding its allies, and causing dismay and despair amongst the region's existentially imperilled Christians who, in their heart of hearts, had truly believed that the West, particularly the US, might actually help them.

54. Copley, "Early Warning. Here Comes the Cavalry."

55. Neo-Ottomanism is a political ideology that aspires to empire and promotes greater political influence in and ties between Turkey and the regions formerly part of the Ottoman Empire.

Instead, it is as if the West can't even see them; although maybe it is just that the West is quite prepared to sacrifice them.

The struggle for hegemony will be furious, for the stakes are high. These groups are not merely fighting for hegemony over fertile, oil-rich Mesopotamia. They are fighting for hegemony over the whole Middle East; indeed, for hegemony over Muslims—for the right to claim leadership of the Muslim *ummah* (nation). None will accept the pacification of Mesopotamia until their interests have been secured.

In the eye of the storm, in the buffer zone between the region's three imperialistic powers, on the sectarian fault line between the region's two principle Islamic sects, at the flashpoint where the two political axes intersect, is the ancient Christian heartland where the disciples of Jesus were first called Christians—where the first Christian denomination (the Assyrian Church of the East) was established, from where the gospel spread west into Europe and east into Persia and China, and to where persecuted "early church" Christians once fled for refuge.

Egypt

Even in Egypt, home to the Middle East's largest Christian community, escalating persecution is driving a new exodus.

The Copts are the indigenous people of Egypt, the true descendents of the pharaohs. Tradition has it that Mark the Evangelist took Christianity to Egypt in the first century, becoming the first bishop of Alexandria. Tradition also has it that he was martyred there, burned alive during the reign of the emperor Trajan.[56]

When the Arabs invaded Egypt in the December of AD 639, Coptic Egypt was predominantly Christian and part of Byzantium (the Greek Church). According to historian Bat Ye'or, the invading Muslim army, which comprised "four thousand men," overran al-Arish (on the Mediterranean in North Sinai) and seized Pelusium in the Delta region after a month-long siege before advancing on Old Cairo. The Arabs simultaneously sent a force against the Fayyum oasis. "Behnesa, a town further south, was seized by the Muslims, who exterminated its inhabitants, while the Fayyum and Asboit suffered the same fate. The whole population of Nikious was put to the sword. Amr continued the conquest of Egypt, pillaging and massacring . . ."[57]

---

56. Foxe, *Foxe's Book of Martyrs*, 7.
57. Bat Ye'or, *The Decline of Eastern Christianity*, 46–47.

The situation did not improve with time, as Philip Jenkins notes: "Although Egypt's Christians had often been subjected to outbreaks of persecution, the events of 1354 reached an alarming new intensity. Mobs demanded that Christians and Jews recite the Muslim profession of faith upon threat of being burned alive. The government struck at churches and confiscated monasteries, destroying the financial basis of the Coptic Church."

According to Jenkins, the persecution of 1354 was systematic, nationwide, and so acute that many converted to Islam just to survive. He describes it as a "catastrophic time", not only for the Copts in Egypt, but also the Christians right across the Middle East where the Seljuk Turks were expanding their empire, bringing added pressure and more conflict. "So disastrous, in fact, were the cumulative blows against the churches in these years that we can properly see the fourteenth century as marking the decisive collapse of Christianity in the Middle East, across Asia and in much of Africa."

"The story of religious change," concludes Jenkins, "involves far more active persecution and massacre at the hands of Muslim authorities than would be suggested by modern believers in Islamic tolerance."[58]

And so it was that over time, Egypt came to be dominated by Arabs and Islam.

In September 2011, the Egyptian Federation of Human Rights (EFHR) released a report revealing that some 93,000 Coptic Christians had fled Egypt since the March 2011 "Arab Spring" toppling of President Hosni Mubarak. Naguib Gabriel, the head of the EFHR, estimated that the figure could increase to 250,000 by the end of 2011.[59]

Just weeks later, on the evening of Sunday October 9, 2011, some one thousand mostly Coptic Christians, and maybe just as many sympathetic Muslims, rallied outside the Maspero building—the home of Egyptian state television and radio, near Tahrir Square in Cairo. The crowd, comprising mostly youths, rallied peacefully in protest of the escalating violent persecution of Copts in the wake of the toppling of Mubarak.[60]

The Egyptian military came out in full force against the protesters. In the ensuing chaos, twenty-four protesters were killed and some 329 injured—run down by tanks and gunned down by soldiers to shouts of "*Allahu Akbar*" (Allah is greater). One soldier was caught on video boasting that he had "killed two of those infidels" (referring to Copts).[61]

---

58. Jenkins, *The Lost History of Christianity*, 97–99.
59. Kamill, "NGO Report: 93,000 Copts Left Egypt Since March."
60. Kendal, "EGYPT: 'more radicalised than we realised.'"
61. Rashwan, "Maspero Survivors Finally Testify."

On October 10, 2011, *The Wall Street Journal* published an article on the Maspero Massacre, which noted:

> Egypt's post-revolutionary political ferment has ushered in a powerful contingent of Muslims who adhere to the fundamentalist Salafi school of Islamic thought widely practiced in Saudi Arabia. The Salafis were largely absent from pre-revolutionary political life, and their rapid ascent to the political mainstream— and widely suspected role in past incidents of sectarian violence— has alarmed liberal Egyptians and religious minorities.
>
> "People are burning churches!" said Nasser Abdel Mohsen, a Muslim who said he had joined the Christian protesters out of solidarity. "That's never happened before. We always used to live peacefully as Copts and Muslims."
>
> Sunday's events began in the early afternoon when thousands of Coptic Christians marched from the Cairo suburb of Shubra to the television building to protest what they said was the reluctance of the interim ruling Supreme Council of the Armed Forces to prosecute radical Islamists who recently attacked two churches in Upper Egypt . . . The attacks occurred even after church officials had acquiesced to demands from local Salafis to remove bells and crosses from the church's facade.
>
> . . . Mr. Mohsen said the military and fewer than a dozen "bearded men" who he said he suspected were Muslim radicals convened a group of men from local neighborhoods to assault the protesters with iron bars.
>
> "It's a stupid thing that the army is coordinating with the thugs and Salafis," said Mr. Mohsen. "These are people who want to burn down the country, which will lead to burning down the region and then the whole world."[62]

An Egyptian Jew by the name of Joseph Wahed from Moraga, California responded to *The Wall Street Journal*'s article via a letter to the editor:

> As an Egyptian Jew, I read with special interest your article "Clashes Between Christians, Police Rock Cairo" World News, Oct. 10, 2011. I was reminded of what our Coptic Christian neighbor told my family as we were being expelled from Egypt in November 1952: "After Saturday comes Sunday." He accurately predicted that the Coptic community also would feel the wrath and hatred of Egyptians, much of it inspired by radical Muslims . . .

---

62. Bradley, "Clashes Between Christians, Police Rock Cairo."

Nowadays, Christians are being victimized by the Muslim community in Iraq, Pakistan, Gaza, Bethlehem, Lebanon, Nigeria and elsewhere. Sadly, just as when Jews were being ethnically cleansed, there's the same stone silence from the U.N., human-rights organizations, religious leaders and the world's Christian community.[63]

Sunday is upon us

The Christian crisis in the Middle East is existential and immediate. Lest we forget: the elimination of an entire ethnic-religious group is not without precedent—the Arab states have already been "cleansed" of Jews.

It *is* possible that Christians and Christianity could be eliminated from the Middle East. The only thing necessary for this to be achieved is that we do nothing.[64]

---

63. "Anyone Notice the Persecution of Mideast Christians?"
64. Paraphrasing Edmund Burke: "The only thing necessary for the triumph of evil is for good men to do nothing."

— 2 —

The Sunni-Shia Divide

Type the word 'Ashura' into a Google image search and what you will get is a screen full of blood. You will see thronging crowds of men and boys taking blades to their foreheads, slapping chains to their chests, and flagellating their backs. You will see open wounds, torn flesh, blood pouring over faces, blood flowing down backs. Ashura is a highly charged event.

Most Westerners totally fail to understand Ashura. Unable to see past its barbarity, they interpret and even despise the event as a grand display of irrational and hysterical tough-guy antics of the "look what I can endure" kind.

However, with Ashura, Shi'ite Muslims are not saying "Look at me" as much as they are saying "Look at them, the Sunnis. This is what the Sunnis did to our people and to our leader Husayn—the Prophet Muhammad's own grandson!"

Ashura reminds the whole world of that fateful day in AD 680 when Husayn, son of Ali, grandson of Muhammad, was martyred at Karbala (southern Iraq) by Sunni jihadists on the orders of an irreligious, intolerant, violent Sunni strongman.

With every Ashura, the Shi'ites are saying: "We are Shi'ites; and the blood of our martyrs is as fresh today as ever. We will never forget. We will never forgive!"

Who Will Lead the Muslims?

When Muhammad died in AD 632, Muslims found themselves divided over the matter of choosing a successor.

Most Muslims believed that while Muhammad was a prophet, he was still just an ordinary man. What's more, they believed that Allah's words were to be taken literally, at face value, and as such could be readily understood by anyone. Consequently, the only thing required of a leader was that he be a strongman capable of maintaining order and guaranteeing security. These Muslims believed they should simply follow the Arab tribal tradition (the *sunna*), whereby a council of elders would elect a leader. These Muslims became known as *Sunnis*.

A *minority* of Muslims, however, believed Allah's appointment of Muhammad was significant and leadership was a matter of divine appointment. They also believed that spiritual knowledge was esoteric—that is, it could only be understood and interpreted by a divinely appointed and gifted select few. Consequently, they maintained that as Allah had divinely appointed Muhammad, then only blood relatives of Muhammad should be appointed to lead the Muslims. These Muslims believed that Ali—Muhammad's cousin and son-in-law—should succeed him as leader. These Muslims became known as *Shi'ites*.

The Four "Rightly Guided Caliphs"

After Muhammad's death, the Muslims convened a gathering at Saqifah Bani Saeda for the purpose of choosing a new leader. The will of the Sunnis (the demographic majority) prevailed, and Muhammad's companion and father-in-law, Abu Bakr, was elected as the first caliph (successor). While the dissenting Muslims (the Shi'ites) believed that Muhammad's cousin and beloved son-in-law, Ali ibn Abi Talib, should succeed him, they respected the majority decision and submitted to the Sunni caliph.

During the reign of the second caliph, Umar ibn Khattab, tensions arose between the Arabs and the Persians. Historian Vali Nasr explains that the Persians particularly disliked Caliph Umar, "because during his caliphate Arab armies conquered Iran. Iranians resented him for his Arab chauvinism and discrimination against Iranian converts: he forbade marriages between Arabs and Persians, for instance. He also stood accused of abusing Ali and his wife, Fatima, the prophet's daughter."[1]

The Persians developed strong ties to the Arab Shi'ites, and as Nasr notes, Muhammad's companion Salman the Persian supported the Shia position that Ali should succeed Muhammad. Sunni Arab intolerance and aggression against Arab Shi'ites (on religious grounds) and Persians (on racist grounds) might have caused a great deal of suffering, but it also forged a strong sense of Arab-Shi'ite-Persian solidarity. Loathed for his cruelty, Caliph Umar was eventually assassinated by a Persian prisoner of war.

In AD 656, the third caliph, Uthman ibn Affan, was also assassinated, allegedly by Muhammad ibn Abu Bakr with the aid of Persian fighters from

---

1. Nasr, *The Shia Revival*, 64.

Kufa (some 170 km due south of Baghdad and 84 km south of Karbala). Subsequently, Ali ibn Abi Talib—Muhammad's beloved son-in-law and the leader of the Shi'ites—was appointed as the fourth caliph.

Like the caliphs before him, Ali faced rebellions, attempted mutinies, betrayals and unrest: the Muslim community was descending into chaos. Critically, Uthman's cousin Muawiya ibn Hudayj—the governor of Damascus—was demanding that Ali avenge Uthman's murder, something Ali was loathed to do as that would involve attacking his own Shi'ite and Persian support base. A power struggle ensued which ultimately evolved into full-blown civil war.

Civil War

At that time, the most important urban centres of the Arab empire were Damascus (in Syria), Makkah (i.e. Mecca) and Medina in Hejaz (in western Saudi Arabia), and Basra and Kufa (in southern Iraq). Ruled by Muawiya, Damascus was the centre of Sunni opposition to Ali. With Makkah and Medina also under the control of opposition forces, Caliph Ali fled to Basra on the Persian frontier where he was assured of strong support.

When rebel forces attacked Basra, Ali sent messengers north to Kufa to appeal for reinforcements. Already well known as a centre of resistance against Sunni Arab dominance, the mostly Persian city of Kufa sent 12,000 warriors to assist Ali in Basra where they defeated the Sunni rebels in the Battle of the Camel.

Ali subsequently transferred the headquarters of his government from Medina in Hejaz to the frontier city of Kufa.[2]

Enter the Khawârij

Compounding Ali's problems was the emergence of a new sect, the Khawârij, a deeply orthodox, puritanical Sunni sect that followed the Qur'an literally and mercilessly. The Khawârij grew their beards as instructed by Muhammad, but distinguished themselves by shaving their heads. They were essentially the ISIS of their day—they were the first *takfiris* (that is, Muslims who engage in *takfir*, the act of excommunicating and even killing Shi'ites

---

2. Vali Nasr notes (p. 40) that in 2004, when the Shia cleric Muqtada al-Sadr symbolically moved his headquarters from Baghdad to Kufa, where he preached wearing a white linen funeral shroud, he was signalling his resolve to follow in the footsteps of Caliph Ali and lead the resistance against the infidel invaders (the US) and their lackeys in Baghdad.

and other "lesser" Muslims they deem *kafir*, or apostate). After a dispute with Ali, a group of Khawârij plotted to kill him.

On the morning of the 19th day of the month of Ramadan in the 40th year on the Islamic calendar[3] (AD 661), a Khawârijite named Abd-al-Rahman ibn Muljam assassinated Caliph Ali—the fourth so-called "Rightly Guided Caliph"—in the Great Mosque of Kufa as he was making the call to prayer. Many believe it was not a coincidence that Ali's assassination took place on the eve of his planned invasion of Syria, and that Ali's implacable enemy Muawiya, the governor of Damascus, was behind the assassination plot.

After the death of Ali, Muawiya assumed the caliphate, becoming the first of the Umayyad caliphs to rule from Damascus in a dynasty that spanned nearly a hundred years. The Sunnis, who were only interested in Muawiya's power, not how he got it, accepted Muawiya's rule. However, the partisans of Ali, the Shi'ites, could not.

Lacking religious authority, Muawiya delegated religious matters to professional religious scholars—the *ulama*—establishing the Sunni tradition wherein a ruler is simply required to maintain order and protect the Muslim community, while religious matters are handled by religious scholars and clerics: the *ulama*.

As far as the Shi'ites were concerned, the violence and chaos wracking the Muslim community only served to prove that the Sunnis had erred in trusting tribal tradition over divine appointment. Convinced of this, the Shi'ites began to separate themselves from the Sunnis. As Shi'ite veneration of Ali grew, so did Shi'ite anger and resistance.

When Husayn, the son of Ali and grandson of Muhammad, married Princess Shahrbanou, the daughter of the last Sassanid[4] king of Persia, he cemented the bond between the Arab Shi'ites and the Persians. Eventually, a defiant Husayn simply refused to acknowledge the Umayyad Caliphate.

Karbala 680

Caliph Yazd I, the second Umayyad caliph in Damascus, grew tired of the rebellions in Kufa. Not only were the Shi'ites rebelling, but so too were the

---

3. The Islamic calendar began the year that Muhammad and his Muslim disciples fled from Mecca to Medina in the Hijra (emigration); that year, AD 622, became year 1 on the Islamic calendar. The year AD 661 on the Gregorian calendar is therefore year 40 AH (after Hijra) on the Islamic calendar.

4. The Sassanid Empire or Sassanian Dynasty ruled Persia from AD 224 to 651.

Persians who were resisting the Arab nature of Umayyad rule. Eventually Yazd I decided to put an end to it once and for all.

In AD 680, he sent a Sunni Arab army from Damascus to Karbala to subjugate Husayn and his Shi'ite followers, along with the restive Persians of Kufa. At Karbala, the army laid siege to Husayn's caravan, whose male members fought for six long days before the Umayyad general, Shimr, managed to separate the Shi'ites from their water supply.

Eventually Husayn's men, their strength spent, had no option other than to surrender to the Sunnis or die fighting. Though clearly outnumbered, they charged the Umayyad army only to be massacred. The Sunni jihadists beheaded the Shi'ites and left the decapitated bodies to rot while they mounted the heads on pikes and paraded them in Kufa before sending them on to the Sunni caliph, Yazd I, in Damascus. Local villagers buried the bodies.

Husayn's sister, Zaynab—an eyewitness to the battle of Karbala—is largely responsible for the narrative. Faithful to the end, Zaynab accompanied the head of her brother to Damascus. She herself is buried there in the Mosque of Sayyida Zaynab (Lady Zaynab), which remains to this day an important site for Shia pilgrims.

After the Battle of Karbala, the surviving Shi'ites fled east into Persia. The martyr Husayn was survived by his young son Ali, the fourth of twelve Shia imams to have descended directly from Muhammad. Tradition has it that the 12th imam, Muhammad al-Mahdi, disappeared down a well in Qom, Iran, in AD 939 before he could produce an heir. According to Shia legend, al-Mahdi did not die, but was taken into a state of occultation—that is, he became unseen, or hidden—and in the last days will reappear as Islam's Messiah.[5]

Al-Mahdi also appears in Sunni eschatology, although not as a Shia. According to Islamic eschatology, Jesus will follow behind al-Mahdi and pray behind him before unleashing the final jihad in which Christianity (a blasphemous falsehood) will be eliminated.

---

5. McRoy, "Shia Eschatology in Contemporary Islamic Politics."

According to Islamic eschatology, when Christians see that Jesus is a Muslim, many will convert to Islam. However, Christians who continue to say that Jesus was crucified will be killed. According to the hadith,[6] "Allah's Apostle said, 'The Hour will not be established until the son of Mary [i.e. Jesus] descends amongst you as a just ruler, he will break the cross [the symbol of Christianity], kill the pigs [the food of Christians], and abolish the Jizya tax [protection money (thereby removing the means of protection)]. Money [loot] will be in abundance so that nobody will accept it (as charitable gifts).'"[7] According to the Qur'an, "They denied the truth and uttered a monstrous falsehood against Mary. They declared: 'We have put to death the Messiah, Jesus son of Mary, the apostle of God.' They did not kill him, nor did they crucify him, but they thought they did . . . There is none among the People of the Book but will believe in him before his death; and on the Day of Resurrection he will bear witness against them."[8]

Who Will Lead the Muslims Today?

The Struggle for the Soul of Islam

Shia historian Vali Nasr explains: "Shi'ism and Sunnism not only understand Islamic history, theology and law differently, but each breathes a distinct ethos of faith and piety that nurtures a particular temperament and a unique approach to the question of what it means to be Muslim."[9]

"The Shia-Sunni conflict is at once a struggle for the soul of Islam," says Nasr,

> a great war of competing theologies and conceptions of sacred history . . . Faith and identity converge in this conflict, and their combined power goes a long way towards explaining why, despite periods of coexistence, the struggle has lasted so long and retains such an urgency and significance. It is not just a hoary religious dispute, a fossilized set piece from the early years of Islam's unfolding, but a contemporary clash of identities. Theological and historical disagreements fuel it, but so do today's

6. The hadith are the collection of traditions recording the actions and sayings of the Prophet Muhammad.

7. *Sahih Bukhari*, Volume 3, Book 43, Number 656.

8. Q.4:156–159 in Dawood, *The Qur'an*, 76–77.

9. Nasr, *The Shia Revival*, 34–35.

concerns with power, subjugation, freedom, and equality, not to mention regional conflicts and foreign intrigues. It is, paradoxically, a very old, very modern conflict.[10]

The Shi'ite assertion that only blood descendents of Muhammad can rightly guide the Muslims challenges the legitimacy not only of the Sunni caliphs, but of today's Sunni dictators and monarchs for whom the stakes are high. Instead of countering this challenge with theological reasoning, Sunni Islam has opted instead to demonize Shi'ism as heresy; vilify Shi'ites as spoilers, dissidents, fanatics, and *rwafida* (rejectionists); and incite and legitimize their persecution.[11]

The struggle for the wealth of Islam

The Arabs were nomads and merchants, as were the Turks, and the nomadic trading culture so prevalent amongst Sunnis saw Sunni Islam taken to distant fields. Consequently, Sunnis now make up around 87 percent[12] of all Muslims worldwide.

What is often overlooked by politicians and media—who tend to think of Islam either as a monolithic bloc or simply as Sunni with a Shi'ite minority—is that while Shi'ites comprise only around 10 percent of Muslims worldwide, they comprise roughly 50 percent of Muslims in the greater Middle East, and (critically) around 80 percent of Muslims around the oil-rich Persian Gulf. So while the Sunni Arabs might dominate the deserts and trade routes, and have control over the two holy mosques, the Shi'ites—backed by Iran with its superior Persian culture and vast military resources—are sitting on virtually all the region's oil and gas, which amounts to 55 percent of the world's proven reserves.[13]

Like most political campaigns today, the struggle for the soul of Islam, which is essentially a struggle for leadership of the Muslim *ummah* (nation), will likely be determined by who has access to the most wealth. There is an awful lot at stake!

---

10. Ibid., 20.

11. Examples of Sunni demonization of and discrimination against Shi'ites, specifically in Saudi Arabia, can be found in the following excellent reports: "The Shiite Question in Saudi Arabia" and "Denied Dignity."

12. "Mapping the Global Muslim Population."

13. "Persian Gulf Oil and Gas Exports Fact Sheet."

Tensions rise

The 1979 Islamic (Shi'ite) Revolution in Iran greatly excited the region's long repressed and persecuted Shi'ites, including the Shi'ite majority in Saudi Arabia's Eastern Province—where virtually all Saudi Arabia's oil fields and refineries are located. While Iran's Ayatollah Khomeini advocated toppling the House of Saud (i.e., the Saudi monarchy ruling Saudi Arabia), more realistic Saudi Shi'ite leaders sought to exploit the tense situation to press for reforms, specifically an end to the religious vilification and systematic discrimination.

On November 25, 1979, some four thousand Saudi Shi'ites defied a government ban and poured out onto the streets of Safwa City, in Eastern Province's Qatif district, to commemorate Ashura. Saudi security forces responded with force, and as protests spread throughout Qatif, the Saudi National Guard cracked down mercilessly. More than twenty Shi'ites were killed, while dozens were arrested and hundreds were forced into exile. The aspirations of Saudi Shi'ites were dashed; as a demographic minority within the kingdom, they stood no chance of effecting revolution—not without the support of foreign aid.

Despite the crackdown, Saudi Shi'ites pressed ahead with efforts to have their grievances addressed, but to no avail. If anything, their situation deteriorated: persecution escalated as Shi'ites were systematically vilified as infidels and promoters of polytheism (*shirk*) for their veneration of Ali and Husayn (amongst others). They are also accused of heresy (*bid'a*)—a sin punishable by death. In Sunni schools, students are taught that the Shi'ites rejected the early caliphs, and that Sunnis should despise this rejection as an act of betrayal and treachery. Consequently, Shi'ites are routinely vilified as *rwafida* (rejectionists).

Fatwas (religious rulings) issued by Saudi clerics since 1979 denounce Shi'ites as the ultimate scum and the principal enemy. These *fatwas* are not just for local consumption, but are intended for Sunni Muslims worldwide.

As International Crisis Group (ICG) reports:

> In 1991, Abdullah bin Abd al-Rahman al-Jibrin, then a member of [Saudi Arabia's] Higher Council of Ulama, issued a *fatwa* designating Shiites as apostates and condoning their killing. In January 1994, responding to a question about the *rawafid* (alternative of *rafida* or *rwafida*) praying in Sunni mosques, he issued a *fatwa* asserting "they are the enemy and may God fight those that lie." In another *fatwa* that year in answer to a question about how to deal with Shiites in the workplace, he stated that, "it is necessary to display abhorrence, loathing, and hatred

[toward them] ... and the priority is to strive to restrict/oppress (*tadayiq*) them."

Some of the most egregious examples abated after September 11, 2001, when the Saudi government clamped down on radical speech more generally and warned clerics on its payroll to tone down their rhetoric. Still, institutions under less direct oversight continue propagating anti-Shiite sentiment in the most vituperative of terms. In 2002, the powerful Jeddah-based International Islamic Relief Organisation (IIRO), a leading Saudi charity, disseminated a book in al-Hasa [Al-Hasa Governorate, Eastern Province], *One Hundred Questions and Answers on Charitable Work*, which claimed it: "was necessary for Sunni Muslims to hate (*baghida*) the people of heresy (*ahl al-bid'a*), to loath them and to scorn them as *rafida*, deniers of God, grave [tomb] visitors [an act of heresy according to Wahhabis], and as apostates. It is incumbent on the Muslim according to his ability ... to get rid of their evil."[14]

Clearly the Wahhabi Islam of Saudi Arabia is a *takfiri* creed, condemning Shi'ites and other "lesser Muslims" as *kafir*, apostates to be killed. While the persecution and the killing is committed in religious zeal, it serves a political purpose, ensuring Shi'ites and Shi'ism cannot threaten the Sunni elite's political and economic interests.

The Iranian Revolution of 1979 stoked sectarian tensions, fueled Islamic zeal, and widened the Sunni-Shia divide. By 2003, Iraq was a tinderbox waiting for a spark.

Karbala 2003

As a Sunni Arab ruling over a majority-Shi'ite population on the Sunni-Shi'ite and Arab-Persian frontier, Iraqi president Saddam Hussein knew it was in his interests to keep Iraqi Shi'ites disempowered, repressed, isolated, fearful, and downtrodden. To that end, Saddam Hussein suppressed Ashura for decades. Consequently, April 22, 2003—the first Ashura Day after regime change and the toppling of Saddam—was an event of unprecedented emotion and profound political significance.

According to terrorism analyst Yossef Bodanksy, after the fall of Saddam, "Iran directly sponsored, through local Shiite networks, the organization of roughly two million people marching to Qarbalah [Karbala] to

---

14. "The Shiite Question in Saudi Arabia."

commemorate the Ashura."[15] Carrying Shi'ite flags, chanting Shi'ite slogans, the great throng of bloodied, highly emotional marchers was an awesome sight.

Shia scholar Vali Nasr was in Pakistan at the time on a research trip. He happened to be in Lahore on that very day, visiting the headquarters of the Sunni fundamentalist political group known as the Jamaat-e Islami (Islamic Party). He writes:

> The office television set was turned on to CNN, as everyone was following news from Iraq. The coverage turned to scenes of young Shia men standing densely packed in the shadow of the golden dome of the Imam Husayn's shrine at Karbala. They wore black shirts and had scarves of green (the universal color of Islam) wrapped around their heads. They chanted a threnody [lament] in Arabic for their beloved saint as they raised their empty hands as if in prayer towards heaven and in unison brought them down to thump on their chests in a rhythmic gesture of mourning, solidarity, and mortification. The image was magnetic, at once jubilant and defiant. The Shia were in the streets, and they were holding their faith and their identity high for all to see. We stared at the television screen. My Sunni hosts were aghast at what they were seeing. A pall descended on the room.[16]

Nasr explains that what Americans saw as Iraqi freedom, his Sunni hosts saw quite differently. "Iraqis were free," he says, "free to be Shias, free to challenge Sunni power and the Sunni conception of what it means to be a true Muslim . . ."

Karbala 2014

Eleven years later, on Friday June 6, 2014, hundreds of jihadists belonging to ISIS/ISIL flooded into northern Iraq's Nineveh province.

ISIS is a *takfiri* outfit. Like the Khawârij who assassinated Ali (the fourth caliph and leader of the Shi'ites), ISIS militants are Sunni purists— fully fledged Wahhabis, following the official doctrine taught in and disseminated by the clerics of Saudi Arabia. They do not tolerate infidels or apostates, which for Wahhabis includes all Shia Muslims.

Now in possession of US-made weapons, tanks, and Humvees, ISIS advanced south towards Baghdad where it claimed to have "unfinished

---

15. Bodansky, *The Secret History of the Iraq War*, 269.
16. Nasr, *The Shia Revival*, 19.

business." On Wednesday June 11, 2014, ISIS captured the mostly Sunni city of Tikrit, along with several districts on the outskirts of Samarra—home to the spectacular gold-domed Askari Shrine, one of the most venerated Shi'ite places of worship in Iraq.[17]

Early on the morning of Thursday June 12, 2014, ISIS spokesman Abu Muhammad al-Adnani uploaded an audio message to his fighters on the group's website: "Continue your march as the battle is not yet raging . . . It will rage in Baghdad and Karbala. So be ready for it."

The message included a grave warning to Shia prime minister Nuri al-Maliki. ISIS, it said, would settle its scores with him and the Shi'ites, not in Baghdad or in the Iraqi shrine city of Samarra, but "in Karbala, the filth-ridden city, and in Najaf, the city of polytheists."[18]

Unable to rely on Iraqi security forces, Iraqi president Nuri al-Maliki offered to arm any citizen who would volunteer to fight the *takfiri* ISIS. His call was supported by Iraq's highest-ranking Shia cleric, Grand Ayatollah Ali al-Sistani. Thousands of Shi'ites responded to al-Sistani's *fatwa*, which called on his followers to defend the holy sites. Soldiers of the Iranian Revolutionary Guards Corp—that is, Persian Shi'ites—crossed over into Iraq to assist the Arab Shi'ites in the defense of Shia holy places.

Many of the Sunni jihadists had come from the Syrian battlefield (via Anbar and Nineveh) determined to take the fight to Baghdad, the seat of government; to Karbala, the site of the Imam Husayn Shrine, the burial place of Imam Husayn who was martyred by Sunni jihadists from Damascus in AD 680; and to Najaf (in the vicinity of Kufa), the site of the Imam Ali Mosque, the burial place of Imam Ali who was assassinated by the Khawârij/*takfiris* in AD 661.

One couldn't help but feel a strong sense of déjà vu.

On June 13, 2014, Shi'ite fighters paraded with their rifles in front of television cameras in Baghdad. As they marched, these Shi'ite warriors chanted "*Labeiki ya Zaynab, labeiki ya Zaynab*"("we will follow you Zaynab"), indicating their willingness to follow in the footsteps of Lady Zaynab, the daughter of Imam Ali, who stayed faithful to her brother Husayn as he resisted Sunni aggression and died fighting for what he believed.

When asked what the men were chanting, the Australian correspondent describing the scene shook his head, shrugged his shoulders, and

---

17. The Askari Shrine houses the remains of the tenth and eleventh Shia imams, along with those of several of Muhammad's other blood relatives. It was the famous gold-domed Askari Shrine that Sunni al-Qaeda insurgents bombed in February 2006, to trigger full-blown civil-sectarian war.

18. Erdbrink, "In the Shadows of Shrines."

answered in a slightly bewildered tone: "I don't know; some sort of Arabic war cry I guess."

And I thought to myself: "O my goodness; you have no idea!"

— 3 —

"Hasten to Success"

DURING AN INTERVIEW ON Egyptian television in February 2013, Yusuf al-Qaradawi (head of the International Union of Muslim Scholars and a leading scholar in the global MB movement) made a most incredible admission. Defending Islam's apostasy law, which mandates death for apostasy (leaving Islam), al-Qaradawi noted: "If they [Muslims] had gotten rid of the punishment [usually death] for apostasy, Islam would not exist today."[1]

Al-Qaradawi's admission confirms what a Coptic missionary working in the Middle East once told me: "If there was ever true religious freedom in the Muslim world, it would not be long before there was barely a Muslim left."

Islam might be so philosophically weak that it can only retain its adherents through threat of death, but what it lacks in philosophy, it makes for up in tactics. For example, by deeming every child born to a Muslim man "Muslim" while making apostasy a capital offence, Islam guarantees perpetual growth, even in the absence of conversions.[2]

Chief amongst its tactics for luring converts and pacifying the repressed Muslim masses is Islam's promise, which is heard five times every day in the call to prayer: the promise of *success*.

---

1. Darwish, "If They [Muslims] Had Gotten Rid of the Punishment for Apostasy, Islam Would Not Exist Today"; "Yusuf al-Qaradawi: Killing Of Apostates Is Essential For Islam To Survive."

2. Further to this, Islamic law mandates that a Muslim woman may only marry a Muslim man, thereby ensuring the fruit of the Muslim womb will be Muslim. Meanwhile, Muslim men are actually encouraged to marry Christian women, so that the fruit of the Christian womb might also be born Muslim and Muslim growth might come at the expense of the Christian community.

"Hasten to Success"

Tradition has it that in AD 622, Muhammad and his little band of Muslim disciples fled rejection and persecution in Mecca in what has come to be known as the Hijra (the Arabic word for migration).[3]

Once settled in Medina (known then as Yathrib), Muhammad decided to establish a means by which the Muslims could be called to prayer. He rejected the horn, for Jews used the horn. He rejected the bell, for that was used by the Christians. Instead, Muhammad opted for a vocal call to be delivered in the most beautiful voice and from the highest rooftop; a call that would carry "on the waves of the air unto all corners of the horizon"; a call that would penetrate "the ear of life itself."[4]

The tradition continues, and five times every day, from mosque minarets all around the world, the *muezzin* sounds out the call to prayer:

(Muezzin: Arabic) *Allahu Akbar, Allahu Akbar.*
(Translation: English) Allah is the Greatest, Allah is the Greatest.

Allahu Akbar, Allahu Akbar.
Allah is the Greatest, Allah is the Greatest.

Ash-hadu alla ilaha illa-llah.
I bear witness that there is none worthy of worship but Allah.

Ash-hadu alla ilaha illa-llah.
I bear witness that there is none worthy of worship but Allah.

Ash-hadu anna Muhammadar-Rasulullah.
I bear witness that Muhammad is the Messenger of Allah.

Ash-hadu anna Muhammadar-Rasulullah.
I bear witness that Muhammad is the Messenger of Allah.

Hayya 'ala-s-Salah, hayya 'ala-s-Salah.
Hasten to the Prayer, hasten to the Prayer.

Hayya 'ala-l-falah, hayya 'ala-l-falah.
Hasten to success, hasten to success.

---

3. The Hijra, not the birth of Muhammad, marks the birth of the Islamic state, the beginning of the Islamic era, and the start of the Islamic calendar.
4. Haykal, *The Life of Muhammad*, 184.

Allahu Akbar, Allahu Akbar.
Allah is the Greatest, Allah is the Greatest.

La ilaha illa-llah.
There is none worthy of worship but Allah.[5]

Islamic historian and biographer, Husein Haykal, writes that when the Muslim exiles heard the call to prayer, "[their] fears were dissipated and they felt secure. Yathrib became Madinah al Nabiy or 'the City of the Prophet.' While the non-Muslim inhabitants began to fear Muslim power . . . the Muslims collected the fruits of their patience and enjoyed their religious freedom."[6]

Known as the Adhan, the call to prayer is, as Haykal notes, "equally a call to Islam." Above all, however, the Adhan is a profession of faith: Allah is the greatest, he alone is worthy of worship, Muhammad is his prophet, and in Islam is *success*.

Understanding the Islamic Worldview

Like everything in Islam, *success* is to be interpreted literally, in worldly, material terms; it is not to be spiritualized. As such, *success* is understood to mean power, privilege, and prosperity. And while Muslim *success* is viewed as evidence of divine blessing and approval, infidel/unbeliever success is viewed only as evidence of Muslim failure and disobedience.

In his book *The Third Choice: Islam Dhimmitude and Freedom*, linguist, Anglican minister, and Islam expert Rev, Dr Mark Durie explains: "According to Islam, the human problem is *ignorance (jahiliyyah)*," the solution to which "is *guidance (huda)*." As Durie notes, guidance is "one of the central concepts of Islam." Ultimately, writes Durie, "For those who submit to Allah and accept his guidance, the intended result is *success (falah)*."[7]

To illustrate, Durie likens the Islamic view of the human situation to that of a slave in their master's house. The slave is *ignorant* of what is required of them. So the master graciously provides them with a written job description, thereby giving them *guidance*. If the slave submits and does what is required, then they will meet with *success*.

"The Quran emphasises the importance of success a great deal," writes Durie. "It teaches that those who submit to Allah will find success in this life and the next. The Quran divides humanity into winners and the rest.

---

5. "Adhan (The Call to Prayer)."
6. Haykal, *Life of Muhammad*, 184.
7. Durie, *The Third Choice*, 16–20.

Those who do not accept Allah's guidance are repeatedly called 'the losers' (*al-khasirin*)."[8]

Christianity, on the other hand, teaches that the human problem is *sin*. And as Rev. Durie explains, sin is not ignorance, but "wrongdoing and rebellion which separates human beings from God, making it impossible for them to be in his holy presence or enjoy right relationship with him. From the point of view of the Bible, while ignorance can contribute to the problem of sin, it is not the root cause of it."[9]

The Bibles teaches that sin is a problem that sinful, corrupted humanity cannot fix. As such, human beings are in need of rescue through a legally just process that secures God's *forgiveness*. A person who has been rescued or *redeemed* from the consequences of their sin (the consequence being eternal death[10]) is thus reconciled to God and "saved" to eternal life. "The traditional term for rescue," writes Rev. Durie, "is *salvation*."[11]

Comparing Christian and Muslim worldviews.

Worldview	Problem	Consequence	Solution	Result
Islam	Ignorance (a failing; a problem in the head)	Failure in life (material)	Humans submit to God's guidance—through works and law keeping	Material success in this life. (Only martyrs are assured of Paradise)
Christianity	Sin (a rebellion; a problem in the heart)	Separation from God (spiritual; results in eternal death)	God forgives those who put their faith in *him*—he rescues the sinner by grace through faith	Salvation, reconciliation with God, and eternal life

---

8. Ibid., 16–17.

9. Ibid., 18.

10. "For the wages of sin is death, but the free gift of God is eternal life in Christ Jesus our Lord" (Rom 6:23).

11. For a wonderful short book that explains the Christian position on sin, forgiveness, and salvation without the use of theological jargon, I would recommend McGrath, *What was GOD doing on the Cross?*

Unsurprisingly, these radically different worldviews produce radically different individuals, values, and cultures. "A rescued person," observes Durie, "is not the same as a successful person. A rescued person is humbled by their experience, but a successful person will tend to feel superior and proud of their success."[12]

Durie quotes Muslim writer Isma'il R al-Faruqi, who notes that salvation is not even in the vocabulary of Islam as Islam teaches that humanity does not need saving. "*Falah* [success]," says al-Faruqi, "or the positive achievement in space and time of the divine will, is the Islamic counterpart of Christian 'deliverance' and 'redemption.'"[13]

Islam and Christianity also work in totally opposite ways, for while Christianity works from the inside out, Islam works from the outside in. Let me explain:

In Christianity, though human beings are recognized as sinners, the Spirit of God graciously works in a sinner's heart—to cleanse, enlighten, and spiritually transform. That inner transformation then works itself out in the form of personal restraint and active righteousness. Christians are called to spread the "good news" of rescue and transformation through Jesus, so that sinners might be saved and nations might be healed. It is precisely because Christianity works from the inside out that Christian cultures are so open, free, and dynamic—less external law is needed.

In contrast, Islam regards human beings as inherently good but simply misguided; they require not inner transformation, but application of the law. Thus Islam works from the outside in. To this end, Muslims are called to establish control over territory so that the law of Allah—Sharia law—might be enforced. Being totalitarian and legalistic, Islamic culture is thus closed, profoundly repressive, and stifling.

Oblivious to Islam's worldview and ignorant of Islam's history, many Westerners have been surprised by the hostile, demanding, violent, repressive nature of resurgent Islam. They are shocked, for this is something they have not seen before. However, while this Islamic aggression might be unprecedented in our lifetime, it is certainly not unprecedented.

> Those who do not remember the past are condemned to repeat it—George Santayana.[14]

---

12. Durie, *Third Choice*, 19.

13. Ibid., 20.

14. Jorge Agustín Nicolás Ruiz de Santayana y Borrás, also known as George Santayana, was a philosopher, essayist, poet, and novelist. He was born in Madrid, Spain, in 1863, and died Rome, Italy, in 1952. He was US educated and received a Nobel Prize in Literature. While this quote has been attributed to various people, including

A Millennium of Islamic Success

The first millennium of Islam might have been fraught—plagued as it was with infighting, civil war, and sectarianism, but it was marked by virtually continuous territorial expansion: *success* upon *success* upon *success*.

Invasion, Conquest, and Colonization

Tradition has it that Sura 9 (i.e., chapter 9) of the Qur'an was revealed in the year AH 9 (AD 630) when Muhammad was fighting the Meccans and other Arabian tribes. Sura 9 (titled *al-Tabwah*, meaning "The Repentance"), contains what is regarded as "the consummate position of Islam towards Jews and Christians."[15] In Q.9:29–33 we find the following:

> Fight those who do not believe in Allah or in the Last Day and who do not consider unlawful what Allah and His Messenger have made unlawful and who do not adopt the religion of truth from those who were given the Scripture—[fight] until they give the jizyah willingly while they are humbled.
>
> The Jews say, "Ezra is the son of Allah"; and the Christians say, "The Messiah is the son of Allah." That is their statement from their mouths; they imitate the saying of those who disbelieved [before them]. May Allah destroy them; how are they deluded?
>
> They have taken their scholars and monks as lords besides Allah, and [also] the Messiah, the son of Mary. And they were not commanded except to worship one God; there is no deity except Him. Exalted is He above whatever they associate with Him.
>
> They want to extinguish the light of Allah with their mouths, but Allah refuses except to perfect His light, although the disbelievers dislike it.
>
> It is He who has sent His Messenger with guidance and the religion of truth to manifest it over all religion, although they who associate others with Allah dislike it.[16]

---

eighteenth-century British statesman Edmund Burke, Santayana is generally regarded as its source.

15. *The Qur'an Dilemma*, 133–142, 501.
16. Sahih International translation, at http://quran.com/9/29-33.

This Sura is replete with incitement to jihad, through which Muslims are called to "fight in the cause of Allah", to "kill" and be "killed."[17]

In the first centuries of the Islamic era, the Arabs, being militarily strong, advanced north through the Levant, northeast into Mesopotamia, Persia and the subcontinent, and west across North Africa and into Spain. This was pure Arab imperialism, legitimized and justified on the pretext of spreading Allah's religion.

Subjugation and Sharia Law

According to Egyptian-born Jewish historian and writer Bat Ye'or, in the early years of Islam, the first four Caliphs were so engrossed in their military campaigns that they left the conquered peoples to administer themselves under the oversight of Arab governors.

As colonization advanced apace, tensions escalated between the settled, mostly agrarian indigenous peoples and the Arab settlers/immigrants who, being nomads, were adverse to agricultural and urban occupations. It was in this context of imperialist expansion and Islamic jihad, conquest, and occupation that Islamic Sharia law developed for the purpose of maintaining order and legitimizing fiscal control of the conquered lands and peoples.

Ye'or explains that the process of the "Arabo-Islamic invasion of the lands bordering Arabia—Palestine, Syria and Iraq—extended over a period of time, taking place at two levels during the crucial phase of conquest."[18] The first level involved nomadic invasion and predatory migration, pillage, and destruction. The second level involved negotiations, which took place between the Arab governors and the representatives of the harassed native populations. "In return for payment of tribute [*jizya*], these representatives—civil governors or religious leaders, such as patriarchs or bishops—obtained the security of life, property, and civil and religious institutions for the vanquished populations."[19]

Subjugated as *dhimmis* (second-class citizens in the worst sense imaginable), Jews and Christians were denied the right to possess arms/weapons, and they were also deprived of legal rights. Consequently, they

17. Q. 9:111, Sahih International translation: "Indeed, Allah has purchased from the believers their lives and their properties [in exchange] for that they will have Paradise. They fight in the cause of Allah, so they kill and are killed. [It is] a true promise [binding] upon Him in the Torah and the Gospel and the Qur'an. And who is truer to his covenant than Allah? So rejoice in your transaction which you have contracted. And it is that which is the great attainment" (http://quran.com/9/111).

18. Ye'or, *The Decline of Eastern Christianity*, 56.

19. Ibid., 58.

lacked effective means of self defense and were not permitted to testify against Muslims in court. Obliged to be lower than Muslims in every way and forced to wear distinctive clothing, the exceedingly vulnerable *dhimmis* were easy prey for rapists, thieves, violent thugs, and all manner of criminals. They were also vulnerable to all kinds of deprivations, humiliations, and violent abuses from Muslims who had been guaranteed impunity.

Furthermore, the Qur'an and the example of Muhammad legitimized systemic slavery and the keeping of concubines. For example, the Qur'an permits a Muslim man to take war captives as slaves and have sexual relations with any woman his "right hand possess" (Q.70:29–30; 23:5–6; 33:50; 4:24).[20] Consequently, when Arab Muslims sacked Ephesus in 781, "7000 Greeks were deported into captivity."[21] When Arab Muslims sacked Thessaloniki in 903, "22,000 Christians were shared between the Arab chiefs or sold into slavery."[22]

If right to life was secured through payment of *jizya*, then right to "peace" (i.e., absence of war or jihad) was secured through *total submission*.[23]

> *What has been is what will be,*
>
> *and what has been done is what will be done,*
>
> *and there is nothing new under the sun.*
>
> *Is there a thing of which it is said, "See, this is new"?*
>
> *It has been already in the ages before us.*
>
> (Eccl 1:9–10)

Understanding the Crusades

Islamic Success in the Holy Land

Since the earliest days of Christianity, Christians had been making pilgrimage to the Holy Land. Roman Emperor Constantine I had a church built in Jerusalem—the Church of the Holy Sepulchre—which he dedicated in

---

20. Khan, *Islamic Jihad*, 270. See also Durie, "Sex Slavery and the Islamic State." For an Islamic defense, see "The Revival of Slavery Before the Hour."

21. Ye'or, *Decline of Eastern Christianity*, 109.

22. Ibid.

23. For a thorough examination of *dhimmitude*, see the works of Bat Ye'or and Mark Durie.

335. The constant flow of pilgrims ensured the Islamic advance did not go unnoticed in Europe. Even after the Arab conquest, European Christian pilgrims continued to travel to the Holy Land, enabled by the fact that as paying tourists, they, unlike local Christians, could generally move around unmolested by the Muslims who knew what was good for business.

Early in the eleventh century, Byzantium (the Greek-speaking, eastern part of the Roman Empire) experienced an economic boom, which in turn facilitated population growth and increased prosperity. As a result, more European Christians found it within their means to make the pilgrimage to the Holy Land. The increased traffic led to increased anxiety amongst Muslims living in the region, who feared these pilgrimages could be a prelude to conquest.

Adding to their anxiety was the fact that the whole region was in a state of flux. Intra-Arab conflict raged between two rival caliphates—the Abbasid caliphate (Sunni) based in Baghdad and the rival Fatimid caliphate (Shi'ite) based in Cairo. As the Abbasid caliphate gradually collapsed, the Fatimids expanded their territory at Abbasid expense. Meanwhile, the Byzantines exploited the power vacuum, seizing the opportunity to liberate their lands. After liberating Antioch in 969, the Byzantines pushed south, deeper into Syria. However, by 1025, intra-Christian factional conflicts had caused the reconquest to grind to a halt.

Enter the Turks

While the Middle East was enmeshed in chaos, a nation of nomadic warriors was rising from the steppes of Central Asia: the Turks. By 1025, the Turks had seized power from the Abbasids in Baghdad. Championing Sunni orthodoxy, the Seljuk Turks moved against the Shi'ite Cairo-based Fatimids and seized control of Jerusalem. From there, Turkish tribes launched raids north into Byzantine (Greek-speaking Christian) Anatolia (modern-day Turkey), conquering territory and enforcing Islamic law, spreading terror and misery everywhere.

In 1071 the Byzantine emperor Romanus IV Diogenes responded to Turkish aggression, launching a reprisal into Turk territory. It was unsuccessful, and at Manzikert (then in Armenia, now in eastern Turkey), the forces of Sultan Alp Arslan thoroughly routed the Byzantine army, causing Byzantium to descend into civil war.

In 1073, Byzantine Emperor Michael VII appealed to Pope Gregory VII for aid against the Seljuk Turks. However, with Byzantium still wracked by civil war and in no position to assist, the appeal was rejected—there would be no military aid. Consequently, Emperor Michael was forced to negotiate. In exchange for peace, the Turks were handed the territory of Anatolia, home to vast numbers of Greek-speaking Christians.

By 1095, Emperor Alexis I Comnenus had stabilized Byzantium and was keen to exploit the chaos in Islamic lands for a reconquest. Lacking troops, he appealed to Pope Urban II for forces to aid the subjugated, persecuted, and imperilled Christians of the East. And so the age of the Crusades began.

Christendom's counter offensive

As noted by Crusade historian Thomas F. Madden, the Crusades were "in every way defensive wars. They were a direct response to Muslim aggression—an attempt to turn back or defend against Muslim conquests of Christian lands." Madden explains:

> Christians in the eleventh century were not paranoid fanatics, Muslims really were gunning for them. While Muslims can be peaceful, Islam was born in war and grew the same way. From the time of Mohammed, the means of Muslim expansion was always the sword. Muslim thought divides the world into two spheres, the Abode of Islam and the Abode of War. Christianity—and for that matter any other non-Muslim religion—has no abode. Christians and Jews can be tolerated within a Muslim state under Muslim rule. But, in traditional Islam, Christian and Jewish states must be destroyed and their lands conquered. When Mohammed was waging war against Mecca in the seventh century, Christianity was the dominant religion of power and wealth. As the faith of the Roman Empire, it spanned the entire Mediterranean, including the Middle East, where it was born. The Christian world, therefore, was a prime target for the earliest caliphs, and it would remain so for Muslim leaders for the next thousand years.
>
> The Crusades were not the brainchild of an ambitious pope or rapacious knights but a response to more than four centuries of conquests in which Muslims had already captured two-thirds of the old Christian world. At some point, Christianity as a faith and a culture had to defend itself or be subsumed by Islam. The Crusades were that defense."[24]

---

24. Madden, "The Real History of the Crusades."

> Thomas F. Madden is a consummate historian, a professor of medieval history, and author of numerous books. His sixty-minute lecture titled "The Crusades: Then and Now," delivered at the Augustine Institute, is freely available online.

Pope Urban II gave the Crusaders two goals, both of which would remain central to the eastern Crusades for centuries: to rescue the Christians of the East and liberate Jerusalem from Muslim rule.

His successor, Pope Innocent III, later wrote this moving appeal for the persecuted:

> How does a man love according to divine precept his neighbor as himself when, knowing that his Christian brothers in faith and in name are held by the perfidious Muslims in strict confinement and weighed down by the yoke of heaviest servitude, he does not devote himself to the task of freeing them? . . . Is it by chance that you do not know that many thousands of Christians are bound in slavery and imprisoned by the Muslims, tortured with innumerable torments?

Madden writes:

> When we think about the Middle Ages, it is easy to view Europe in light of what it became rather than what it was. The colossus of the medieval world was Islam, not Christendom. The Crusades are interesting largely because they were an attempt to counter that trend. But in five centuries of crusading, it was only the First Crusade that significantly rolled back the military progress of Islam. It was downhill from there . . .
>
> By the 15th century, the Crusades were no longer errands of mercy for a distant people but desperate attempts of one of the last remnants of Christendom to survive. Europeans began to ponder the real possibility that Islam would finally achieve its aim of conquering the entire Christian world . . .
>
> Of course, that is not what happened. But it very nearly did. In 1480, Sultan Mehmed II captured Otranto [in south-east Italy] as a beachhead for his invasion of Italy. Rome was evacuated. Yet the sultan died shortly thereafter, and his plan died with him. In 1529, Suleiman the Magnificent laid siege to Vienna. If not for a run of freak rainstorms that delayed his progress and forced him to leave behind much of his artillery, it is virtually

certain that the Turks would have taken the city. Germany, then, would have been at their mercy.[25]

Madden concludes:

> From the safe distance of many centuries, it is easy enough to scowl in disgust at the Crusades ... But we should be mindful that our medieval ancestors would have been equally disgusted by our infinitely more destructive wars fought in the name of political ideologies ... Whether we admire the Crusaders or not, it is a fact that the world we know today would not exist without their efforts. The ancient faith of Christianity, with its respect for women and antipathy toward slavery, not only survived but flourished. Without the Crusades, it might well have followed Zoroastrianism, another of Islam's rivals, into extinction.[26]

History Pivots at the Gates of Vienna

The defeat of the Ottoman Turks at the Gates of Vienna in 1683 is generally regarded as the pivotal moment when, after a millennium of advance, Islam was finally stopped in its tracks. Subsequently, Islamic military and imperialist power began to fade and crumble beneath the expanse of the empire, the corruption of the caliphate, and the rising industrial, military, scientific, technological, and economic power of post-Reformation Europe.

In his lecture at the Augustine Institute, Madden remarks:

> For a thousand years after the death of the prophet, Muslim armies had managed to conquer fully three-quarters of the old Christian world, despite the efforts of generations of Crusaders to halt or turn back this advance. An impartial observer at the time might well have concluded that Christendom was a doomed remnant of the ancient Roman Empire, destined to be supplanted by the more youthful, energetic religion and culture of Islam. Yet that observer would have been wrong. Within Europe, new ideas were brewing that would have dramatic and unprecedented repercussions not just in the Mediterranean, but across the entire world.
>
> Born out of a unique blend of faith, reason, individualism and entrepreneurialism, those ideas produced a rapid increase in scientific experimentation with immediately practical

---

25. Madden, "The Real History of the Crusades."
26. Ibid.

applications. By the seventeenth century, European wealth and power was growing exponentially. Europeans were entering a new and utterly unprecedented age. It is one of the most remarkable events in history, I think, that the Christian West—an eternally divided region, seemingly on the brink of conquest by a powerful empire—suddenly burst forth with amazing new energy, neutralizing its enemies and expanding across the globe—something that no culture or civilization had ever done before.

The spectre of advancing Muslim armies, which for centuries had posed such a danger to the Christian West, no longer constituted a serious threat. Indeed as the gaze of Europeans now spanned new global horizons, they soon *forgot* that such a threat had existed at all.[27]

> Those who do not remember the past are condemned to repeat it—George Santayana.

Europeans might have been quick to forget that Islam had long been the most powerful and dynamic force on the planet, but Muslims were not about to. Islam might have been in retreat and in decline, yet five times a day, day after day, year after year, the call to prayer continued to beckon: "Hasten to success, hasten to success."

So what were Muslims to make of their loss of power and privilege, their lack of *success*? And how would they manage to be successful once again? Historically, they have responded in two ways: Islamic resistance and Islamic reformation. These responses progress side by side, for infidel success must be resisted while the work of Islamic reformation is undertaken. And until such time as Muslims have attained their goal, Islamic resistance and Islamic reformation will continue.

Islamic Resistance

Throughout the nineteenth century, as "the sick man of Europe" (the Ottoman Empire) grew sicker and weaker, Muslim power and privilege was challenged from within (as the subjugated peoples demanded their rights and liberty) and from without (as foreign powers attempted to impose reforms). Unsurprisingly, every attempt to roll back *Islamic success* triggered fierce and exceedingly bloody *Islamic resistance*.

In 1821, a Greek uprising in the Danubian provinces (modern-day Romania) was quickly crushed by 30,000 Turkish troops, who unleashed

---

27. Emphasis added.

reprisals against local Christians. Historian Orlando Figes writes: "Turkish soldiers looted churches, murdered priests, men, women and children and mutilated their bodies, cutting off their noses, ears and heads, while their officers looked on."[28] Thousands of Eastern Christians fled into Bessarabia, presenting the Russians with a massive refugee problem and humanitarian crisis.[29]

"The violence even spread to Constantinople," writes Figes, "where the patriarch and several bishops were publically hanged by a group of janizaries[30] on Easter Sunday 1821." Historian Philip Jenkins elaborates: "The patriarch of Constantinople was hanged outside his cathedral—on Easter Morning!—and other archbishops and patriarchs were hanged or beheaded, at Adrianople and Thessaloniki, and across Cyprus."[31] Russia broke off diplomatic relations in protest, and the Turks responded by seizing and looting Russian ships, taking their crews captive.[32]

In 1822, the Turks crushed a Greek uprising on the island of Chios. Some 20,000 Greeks were hanged, while the remaining population, some 70,000 Greeks, were deported into slavery.[33]

To deny Russia—long-recognized as the protector of Eastern Christians—any pretext to interfere in Ottoman affairs in a way that could threaten Britain's own imperialistic interests, Britain pressed Turkey's sultan to enact reforms. British MPs were of the opinion that all Turkey needed in order to be fixed, rescued, spared collapse, and steered towards enlightenment was a good injection of European civilization. It is a thought not unlike the modern view that all the Muslim world needs today is a good injection of Western-style liberal democracy and free-market capitalism!

> There is nothing new under the sun—Ecclesiastes 1:9.

It never occurred to these British MPs that Muslims might *resist* the imposition of humiliating, un-Islamic reforms with genocidal fury.

Figes writes that in 1839, at the behest of the British,

---

28. Figes, *The Crimean War*, 33.

29. Bessarabia is now part of modern-day Moldova plus Odessa Oblast (southwest Ukraine). It was liberated by Russia in the 1806–1812 Russo-Turkish War.

30. The janizary corps comprised young men who had been taken from Christian families as small children by means of a "tax" on firstborn sons. They were raised as Muslims and trained for the Sultan's service.

31. Jenkins, *The Lost History of Christianity*, 158.

32. Figes, *Crimean War*, 34.

33. Ibid.

the 16-year-old new Sultan Abdülmecid issued a decree, the *Hatt-i Sharif of Gülhane* (Noble Decree of the Rose Chamber), announcing a number of reforms. The *Hatt-i Sharif* was to be the first in a series of reforms also known as the *Tanzimat* (Reorganisation). The goal of the *Tanzimat* was to roll back Sharia (Islamic Law) and extend equal rights to Christians so as to improve their situation.

The Hatt-i Sharif promised everyone in the Sultan's empire security of life, honour, property, regardless of their faith; it stressed the rule of law, religious toleration, the modernization of the empire's institutions, and a just and rational system of centralized taxation and military conscription. In essence, the decree assumed that the commonwealth would be promoted by giving guarantees of personal liberty to the empire's most dynamic elements, the non-Muslim *millets* [nations], whose unfair treatment by the Muslim majority had created instability.[34]

While the Ottoman government was good at talking about reform, it did little to actually implement it, fully aware that *Islamic resistance* would be great. Figes notes that though the sultan renounced the death penalty for apostasy in 1844, local governors continued to execute converts from Islam. Similarly, though Christians gained the right to become members of provincial councils and sit on juries in courts where Western legal principles were applied from the late 1840s, blasphemy was still punishable with death. Moreover, the slave trade continued, "most of it involving the capture of Christian boys and girls from the Caucasus [southern Russia, between the Black and Caspian Seas] for sale in Constantinople [Istanbul]."[35]

The reforms were an affront to Turks, who continued to believe that Muslims were superior to infidels. This belief is unsurprising, considering the Qur'an tells Muslims they are "the best nation produced for mankind" (Q.10:110).[36] Consequently, Muslims *resisted* having their divine rights denied to them.

Furthermore, Muslims were both wary and envious of the fact that Christians, despite having been repressed and persecuted as second-class *dhimmis* for centuries, were emerging as the dominant and most successful economic group in the Ottoman Empire. This too was resisted as totally

---

34. Ibid., 57.

35. Ibid., 58.

36. "You are the best nation produced [as an example] for mankind. You enjoin what is right and forbid what is wrong and believe in Allah. If only the People of the Scripture had believed, it would have been better for them. Among them are believers, but most of them are defiantly disobedient" (Q.3:110).

un-Islamic; after all, the Qur'an clearly says: "Allah will not give the disbelievers any way (of success) against the believers" (Q.4:141).

Figes continues: "Incited by the clergy, Muslims demonstrated against the reforms in many towns: there were acts of violence against Christians; churches were destroyed; and there were even threats to burn the Latin Quarter in Constantinople."[37]

Indeed, violence escalated until Russia was forced to intervene yet again in defense of persecuted Christians. Unlike previous Russian interventions, however, this one would not be successful. Facing certain defeat, the Turks masterfully exploited the geopolitical tension between the imperial European powers of Britain (to the west) and Russia (to the east). To bring Britain into the war, the Turks sent a flotilla into the Black Sea knowing that the Russian Black Sea fleet had orders to fire on any Turkish ships suspected of taking fighters or arms to the Caucasus. Unbeknown to the Russians, the flotilla, though clearly packed with armed soldiers, also had a secret cargo: unarmed civilians. As expected, the flotilla was attacked, civilian women and children were killed, and Britain entered the war to fight the Russians on the pretext of a "humanitarian intervention."[38]

The Crimean War of 1853–1856 was a pivotal war in which Britain and France allied with Islamic forces in pursuit of economic and geostrategic gain at the expense of persecuted Christians. The war was thoroughly politicized, driven by media, fuelled with propaganda, and justified through toxic Russophobia[39] and the vilification of Orthodox Christianity. Protestant church leaders seized upon the war as a righteous struggle and a Christian duty, lauding it as a struggle for religious liberty, and against the impure and idolatrous faith of degenerate Russia.[40]

> There is nothing new under the sun—Ecclesiastes 1:9.

In 1856, the final year of the Crimean War, Britain attempted yet again to impose reforms on the Ottoman Empire.

Historian Bat Ye'or elaborates: "From the time that Sutlan Abd al-Majid promulgated the emancipation edict (*Hatt-i Humayun*) on 18 February

---

37. Figes, *Crimean War*, 59.

38. Figes, *Crimean War*, chapter 5.

39. Russophobia existed long before the "evil" Soviet Empire existed. It is a tool of Western powers used to stir up anti-Russian sentiment whenever any territory between them (i.e., the Middle East, Mesopotamia, the Balkans, Ukraine) is "in play." (Once the issue was territory; today it is usually access to markets.) Skilled in asymmetric warfare, Islam routinely plays competing "Christian" powers off against each other.

40. Figes, *Crimean War*, 162–164.

1856, European consuls in the Ottoman Empire strove to enforce compliance with two major principles: the right for Christians and Jews to give evidence in Islamic courts when a Muslim was a party, and respect for the life and property of non-Muslims . . . In both cases their efforts failed."[41]

Regarding equal rights as decidedly un-Islamic, Muslims resisted the reforms, unwilling to surrender either their superior status or their legal impunity. What's more, because the reforms were being imposed on Muslims by infidel powers at a time of political and military confrontation, Muslims viewed the reforms as a direct attack on Islam designed to humiliate Muslims.[42] Islamic resistance would be bloody indeed.

Syria 1860

In Damascus, Syria, more than 20,000 Christians were slaughtered in the pogroms of 1860 as Muslims resisted the British-imposed reforms. Cyril Graham, an English traveller in Damascus with connections to the British government, wrote a report for London on the massacres of Christians in the districts of Hasbeya and Rasheya, Lebanon. He left Damascus on August 8, 1860, and reached Rasheya the next morning. There he found the Christian remnant in a dire state; most of the men had been killed and the survivors were starving. Gathering them together, he put aid directly into their hands.

That night Graham started out towards Hasbeya, travelling through Kfeir and Mimis, "two villages in which almost all the Christian houses had been burned and some 110 Christians killed." In Hasbeya he repeated his delivery of aid to the remnant Christians. He wrote of his experience:

> The whole number of Christians at that moment was 1,430, there having been three months ago, no less that 3,200[;] some few are in Beyrout and Damascus but I fear that fully 1,300 were slaughtered . . . I visited the Serai [a Christian basilica], which was full of the Corpses of the Christians, none had been buried and strange to say the bodies were well preserved, having been parched by burning Syrian sun. The sight was dreadful, bodies lying in every attitude on the paved court of the Palace . . . but the upper rooms presented even a more horrible spectacle; in almost all of them, the bodies were piled one upon another to the hight [sic] of 5 or 6 feet, and lay just as they had fallen; to add to the horror of this frightful scene the poor women followed

---

41. Ye'or, *Islam and Dhimmitude*, 123–124.
42. Ibid.

me in, and began to howl and mourn over their dead; they led me from corpse to corpse, telling me how they had seen their brothers, fathers, husbands, sons, slaughtered before their eyes, and calling me to witness and to avenge their wrongs.[43]

Bulgaria 1875

In Batak, Bulgaria, in 1875, a Christian uprising in demand of equal rights triggered ferocious *Islamic resistance*. J. A. MacGahan, an American journalist with the *London Daily News*, visited Batak three months after the massacre. His investigation resulted in an article which was published in the *London Daily News* on August 7, 1876. In it he described a scene of utter devastation:

> I counted from the saddle a hundred skulls, picked and licked clean: all of women and children. We entered the town. On every side were skulls and skeletons charred among the ruins, or lying entire where they fell in their clothing. They were skeletons of girls and women with long brown hair hanging to their skulls. We approached the church. There these remains were more frequent, until the ground was literally covered with skeletons, skulls and putrefying bodies in clothing. Between the church and the school, there were heaps. The stench was fearful. We entered the schoolyard. The sight was even more dreadful. The whole churchyard for three feet deep was festering with dead bodies . . . The church was still worse. The floor was covered with rotting bodies quite uncovered. I never imagined anything so fearful. There were three thousand bodies in the churchyard and church . . . In the school, a fine building, two hundred women and children had been burned alive. All over the town there were the same scenes.[44]

Armenia 1895

In Turkish Armenia, as many as 250,000 Armenians were slaughtered in the violent pogroms of 1895–1896; thousands more were spared after being forcibly converted. Whole Armenian villages were razed to the ground, the men killed, and the women taken into captivity. Bat Ye'or notes that

---

43. Ye'or, *The Decline of Eastern Christianity*, 401–403.
44. Fregosi, *JIHAD*, 394.

the massacres started within days of the sultan signing new reforms into law. The British Embassy surmised that the Muslims believed it was their responsibility to resist the reforms by destroying and seizing the lives and property of the Armenians. (Note: this was twenty years *prior* to the Armenian Genocide, which took place under the cover of World War I.] Ye'or writes:

> At Urfa [formerly Edessa, in southern Turkey] in October 1895, again in the last days of December, and then on 16 and 17 January 1896, the mob and the army massacred more than ten thousand Armenians, while women and children were sold in public squares. Those who had taken refuge in the Armenian cathedral were hacked down, or ritually slaughtered, after the recitation of sacred verses by clerics. Everything—human beings and Bibles—was sprinkled with petrol and set alight, while five mullahs gave praise to Allah."[45]

Keen to maintain its pro-Muslim policies, Britain adopted a conspiracy of silence with regards to the killings, while running a highly successful propaganda campaign blending the demonization of Russia with the vilification of Orthodox Christianity.

Then, amidst the chaos of World War I and just as the Anzacs prepared to launch the Gallipoli Campaign (also called the Dardanelles Campaign), the Young Turk government[46] unleashed its *pièce de résistance*: a pre-organized campaign of ethnic-religious cleansing.

Genocide 1915

The Armenian Genocide, which commenced on April 24, 1915, resulted in the deaths of 1.5 million Armenians, some 500,000 Greeks throughout Asia Minor, and up to 750,000 Assyrian Christians throughout Mesopotamia (where Arabs and Kurds joined in the killings). Millions more were either forcibly converted[47] or forced into exile.

---

45. Ye'or, *Islam and Dhimmitude*, 128–129.

46. The Young Turks were a revolutionary movement that rebelled against the sultan in a drive for multi-party democracy. During World War 1 they allied with Germany and plotted the cultural homogenization of Turkey.

47. There is a movement underway amongst the descendants of those forcibly converted by the Turks: many are now discovering and returning to their roots—that is, to Christianity. See: "Forcibly Islamized Armenians get Baptized in Turkey"; Hurtas, "How Some Armenians Are Reclaiming Their Christian Faith."

Thus, the final century of the caliphate was soaked in blood as Christians throughout the unravelling Ottoman Empire suffered massacre, forced deportation, forced Islamization, mass starvation, and genocide at the hands of resistant Muslims who would sooner kill than accommodate those whom they believed were beneath them.[48]

Islamic Reformation

As Europe's and Islam's fortunes reversed, a general consensus developed amongst conservative Muslims that Islam's political and military decline—or lack of *success*—was a direct consequence of religious decline. Consequently, it was believed that what Islam desperately needed in order to be successful again was Islamic Reformation: a return to traditional puritanical Qur'anic Islam.

The most significant Islamic religious reformer of the eighteenth century was Mohammed Ibn Abdel Wahhab. Wahhab maintained that Islam's glory could only be restored through Islamic reformation and attention to right *guidance*. Traditionally, Wahhab's followers—known as Wahhabis—have distinguished themselves by trimming their moustaches while letting their beards grow, just as Muhammad commanded.[49]

One of Wahhab's most influential followers was Mohammed al-Saud, a tribal sheikh from the Nejd (central Arabia). Wahhab and al-Saud formed a pact which married puritanical zeal to military might.

Wahhabis were (and still are) vehemently anti-Shi'ite. In 1802, al-Saud's Wahhabi warriors attacked the Shi'ite holy city of Karbala in the Ottoman *villayet* (province) of Basra (southern Iraq). They torched the mosques and Shi'ite religious academies, mercilessly massacring Shi'ites with unspeakable brutality. According to author Yaroslav Trofimov, some 4,000 camels were needed to carry all the plunder back to the Nejd.[50]

The very next year, 1803, al-Saud's Wahhabi warriors descended on Mecca in the Hejaz (western Arabia). Fully aware of what had taken place in Karbala, the terrified Meccans surrendered without a fight. Al-Saud's Wahhabi warriors subsequently went on to seize Medina, also in the Hejaz. In all

---

48. The killings did not end with the dissolution of the caliphate. In 1933, after the Assyrians put forward a case for autonomy within the state the Iraq—so they might be free to advance their Christian culture and not have to live as persecuted *dhimmis*—the Iraqi government responded with brutal resistance. Some 3,000 Assyrians were slaughtered by the Iraqi Army in the Simele Massacre of 1933, while thousands more were beaten, raped, and looted by local Muslims incited by the military.

49. "Is Growing Beards Mandatory in Islam?"

50. Trofimov, *The Siege of Mecca*, 14.

of the places under their control, the Wahhabis enforced strict Sharia codes and enacted cruel Sharia penalties—without mercy, without compromise. (They were essentially the ISIS of their day.)

Although Egyptian forces subsequently reconquered Mecca, Medina, and al-Saud's capital of Dirraiya on behalf of the Ottoman Turks, World War I saw fortunes reversed again as the Turks were defeated and driven from Arab lands as the Ottoman Empire unraveled.

Despite having fought for the liberation of their lands, and despite promises and assurances from the Allies, the Arabs were betrayed and their lands carved up. Iraq and Palestine (which included Jordan) were placed under a British mandate, while Syria was placed under France. A balance of power was established.

At that point, the West concluded that its problems with Islam were all but over. Nothing could have been further from the truth. For as Islam scholar Mark Durie notes, each Islamic setback merely "triggered a renewed call for Islamic reform, a return to puritanical Qur'anic fundamentalism." [51]

"The urgency of the question 'What went wrong?' drove the Islamic revival, an interconnected network of renewal movements which have as their central tenet that Muslims will once again be 'successful'—achieving political and military domination over non-Muslims—if they are truly devoted to Allah and implement Islamic laws faithfully. These are *reformation* movements in the original (medieval) sense of the Latin word *reformatio*," writes Durie, "for they seek to restore Islam to its former glory by returning to first principles. Durie elaborates:

> Some of the main formative strands of Islamic revivalism have been: the Wahhabi movement which originated in the 18th century; the Deobandi movement in India and Pakistan which dates from 1866; *Jamaat e-Islami*, which was founded 1941 in India; the Muslim Brotherhood, founded 1928 . . .
>
> Out of these have come a myriad of offshoots and branches such as the Taliban (from the Deobandi movement); Al Qaida (a product of the ideology of Muslim Brotherhood theologian Said Qutb); the missionary movement *Tablighi Jamaat*; and *Hizb Ut-Tahrir*.
>
> Even the Organisation of Islamic Cooperation, the 'United Nations' of the Muslim world, is a revivalist organization: this is reflected in its Charter which states that it exists 'to work for revitalizing Islam's pioneering role in the world,' a euphemism for reestablishing Islam's dominant place in world affairs.

---

51. Durie, "Islam's Second Crisis: The Troubles to Come."

> In essence, Islamic revivalist movements aim to restore the greatness of Islam and make it 'successful' again. This hope is embodied, for example, in the Muslim Brotherhood's slogan 'Islam is the solution', implying that when Islam is truly implemented and right guidance followed, then all the problems human beings face—such as poverty, lack of education, corruption, and injustice—will be solved. The flip-side of this slogan is the thesis that all the problems of the Muslim world have been caused through want of genuine Islamic observance: Allah allowed his people to fall into disarray because they were not faithful in obeying his laws. The correction to this spiritual problem should therefore be more sharia compliance.

Not all Muslims were keen to jump on the Islamic Reformation bandwagon. Indeed, the Islamic Reformation merely served to *widen the gap* between the "traditionalists"/"conservatives" (of which the Salafis and Wahhabis were the most prominent) and the "modernizers"/"progressives" (Muslims convinced that Islam's future lay in embracing modernity).

Meanwhile, the seemingly invincible and ascendant West, feeling confident in its ascendancy and comfortable in its supremacy, simply forgot (as Madden notes) that Islam had ever been an existential threat.

> Those who do not remember the past are condemned to repeat it—George Santayana.

Islamic Revival Gets a Helping Hand

Unfortunately, the West not only forgot history, it re-wrote it. Maybe its vain belief in perpetual progress caused it to think the past didn't really matter.

In his lecture at the Augustine Institute, Thomas Madden makes reference to the work of Carol Hillenbrand, a scholar of Islam who uncovered the way in which the West, during the 1920s, reconstructed the history of the Crusades.

Crusading imagery had been used throughout World War I to depict the Allied campaign as "a Great Crusade" to defend freedom and liberate the Holy Land from Germany's Muslim ally, the Ottoman Empire. Madden sights an example: "When Britain's General Allenby took Jerusalem from the Turks in 1917, *Punch* magazine published *The Last Crusade*, a cartoon depicting Richard the Lionheart [a Crusader king] looking down on Jerusalem and saying, 'At last my dream come true.'"[52] The drawing of parallels between World War 1 and the Crusades changed how later generations viewed the Crusades. Rather than being remembered as counteroffensives aimed at halting the advance of imperialistic Islam and liberating subjugated, persecuted Christians, the Crusades were refashioned as glorious Western enterprises aimed at bringing civilization to the Middle East.

Hillenbrand discovered that prior to the West's reconstruction of Crusade history, Muslims had scant interest in the Crusades. They saw the Holy Land as just one of many theatres of jihad, one in which the crusaders were unsuccessful and therefore irrelevant.

Madden explains that the British had long-maintained a great respect for Saladin—the Kurdish caliph who reconquered Jerusalem in 1187—romanticizing him as an oriental warrior of great courage and honour, a worthy opponent for any British knight. In the Middle East however, Saladin had been all but forgotten. To Arabs and Turks, this Kurd—whose successes were short-lived—was of no consequence. When Kaiser Wilhelm II (the German Emperor from 1888 to 1918) visited Damascus in 1889 and asked to see the tomb of the great Saladin, no one had a clue what he was talking about. When Wilhelm did eventually locate the tomb, he was shocked to find it neglected and overgrown. To demonstrate his respect, Wilhelm paid for a new mausoleum to be constructed, which he adorned with a bronze wreath bearing the inscription: "From one great emperor to another."[53]

When Europeans returned to the Middle East after World War 1, they propagated this romanticized view of the Crusades, along with the false narrative that the Crusades were a campaign of European imperial powers to bring civilization to the Arab world. This romanticized false narrative was taught in Muslim schools right across the Middle East, courtesy of the European colonial powers.

Though normally fierce opponents, Arab nationalists and Islamists were united in embracing this narrative; indeed, a better gift could not have been given! Both camps used this false narrative to deflect criticism and establish the *myth* that Muslims suffered poverty and backwardness *not* on account of poor governance or a problematic worldview, but because arrogant European crusaders had swept into peaceful Arab lands leaving carnage in their wake. What's more, they maintained, the Europeans were now repeating the process in the twentieth century.

---

52. Hillenbrand, "Legacy of the Crusades," 204.

53. Madden, "The Crusades: Then and Now," commencing around the thirty-minute mark.

Of course, Muslim dictators and Islamic leaders were not the only ones to embrace and exploit this narrative—so too did the West's leftist intellectual elite who (then as now) leap at every opportunity to apologize for the alleged sins and failings of Christianity.

The West has done much to advance Islam.

Islam is Back!

Today, after centuries of decline and decades of weakness, *Islam is back*, and back with a vengeance.

Islamic expansion is back, and with it, invasion, conquest and colonization, including predatory migration.[54] Subjugation is back, and with it, the repression and persecution of non-Muslims and the inequity and injustice of *dhimmitude* which includes the demand for *jizya* (tribute or protection money as mandated in Q.9:29[55]). Sharia law is back, and with it, barbaric, cruel, and inhumane punishments, including death for blasphemers (be they in Pakistan or Paris) along with lashings, amputations, beheadings, crucifixions, and burnings—all live on Twitter for our entertainment and edification. By July 2014 the Caliphate was back, and with it, the mass slaughter of men, the enslavement of women and children, ethnic-religious cleansing, and even genocide.

Islam is back, which means the sword is back above the necks not only of Christians but of all who will not yield—all who dare stand in the way of Islam's *success*. None of what we are witnessing today is "unprecedented", none of it.

It is sobering to realize however, that the main reason Islam is back in the twenty-first century is because, having forgotten history, having forgotten the threat of Islam, the West has sided with Islam, aided Islam, funded Islam, armed Islam, appeased Islam, romanticized Islam, and protected Islam. All the while, the West has failed to confront the philosophical weakness of Islam, a weakness Islam counters through gross human rights

---

54. Examples of contemporary Islamic predatory migrations include the migration of Fulani Muslims across Nigeria's volatile Middle Belt; the migration of Albanian Muslims into the Serbian province of Kosovo; the organised transmigration of Javanese Muslims into Christian Eastern Indonesia; and the mass migration of Muslims into Europe. None of these mass migrations have been spontaneous or accidental; all have been facilitated by policy and driven by powerful forces.

55. "Fight those who do not believe in Allah or in the Last Day and who do not consider unlawful what Allah and His Messenger have made unlawful and who do not adopt the religion of truth from those who were given the Scripture—[fight] until they give the jizyah willingly while they are humbled" (Q.9:29).

abuses such as the cruel subjugation and persecution of unbelievers, denial of freedoms, and penalties such as death for blasphemy and apostasy.

> Those who do not remember the past are condemned to repeat it—George Santayana.

> Indeed, we are repeating it.

> There is nothing new under the sun—Ecclesiastes 1:9.

After World War 1, many in the West believed the Islamic dragon had been mortally wounded. Then, after Muslims allied with the Nazis during World War II only to suffer yet another crushing defeat, many in the West were convinced that Islam was surely now suffering its death throes and would expire in due course as modernity caught up with it.

Consequently, the West turned its attentions elsewhere. Despite having allied with the soviet communists in World War II, the West devoted all its resources to the Cold War struggle against the soviets and the spread of communist ideology.

All the while, however, five times every day, from mosque minarets all around the world, *muezzins* continued to sound the call: *"hasten to prayer, hasten to success."* And all the while, Islamic reformers such as Sayyid Abu'l A 'la Mawdudi (1903–1979) and Sayyid Qutb (1906–1966) stoked the fires of grievance and victimhood and quietly fanned the flames of puritanical traditional Islamic thought while railing against the West's never-ending "international crusaderism."[56]

Barely noticed and rarely challenged (at least not in the West), Islam's reformers worked tirelessly to ensure the Islamic dragon would not expire. Through their efforts, Islam would not only revive but thrive, outliving and even exploiting Arab, Turkish, and Persian failed experiments with secularism, socialism, nationalism, and despotism. And all the while, the trends of rapid population growth, rapid urbanization, and poor governance were converging to produce mass disaffection.

It would be into this incendiary environment that the fire-breathing dragon of revived Islam would burst. The result: *Islamic Revolution*.

Yes, the dragon would indeed revive to pursue success once again.

---

56. Hillenbrand, "Legacy of the Crusades," 208.

— 4 —

Islamic Revival, 1979

THE EYES OF THE whole world were fixed on Iran in 1979, as a year of protests and rising Shi'ite revolutionary fervor culminated on January 16 in the fall of the US-backed shah (king). Two weeks later, on February 1, the world watched in nervous awe as five million Iranians poured out into the streets to welcome Ayatollah Ruhollah Khomeini into Tehran. After years in exile, Khomeini had returned to establish his version of Islamic government: *velayat-e faqih*, guardianship of (Islamic) jurists. Then on November 4, in a carefully planned and executed assault, revolutionary students seized control of the American embassy in Tehran, taking sixty-four hostages. It was spectacular drama and the world was gripped.

So gripped was the world by events in Tehran, that when revolutionary Sunnis in Saudi Arabia laid siege to Mecca's Grand Mosque on November 20, 1979, the crisis went virtually unnoticed. What's more, because the siege was resolved, it was quickly forgotten. Yet the consequences of the failed Sunni revolution in Saudi Arabia have been just as significant as the consequences of the successful Shi'ite Revolution in Iran, if not more so. For though the Sunni revolutionaries failed in their objective—the overthrow of the Saudi monarchy—they paved the way for Saudi Arabia's fundamentalist Wahhabi clerics to secure a most strategic win; a victory all the more exploitable precisely because the world was so oblivious to it.

These two events of 1979—the successful Shi'ite Revolution in Iran and the failed Sunni Revolution in Saudi Arabia—energized fundamentalist elements and radicalizing forces within both sects of Islam. In each case, fundamentalist clerics were catapulted from the margins of society to the centre of state power where they could dictate policy and gain access to state funds. In Iran, the role of the clerics would be loud and overt as the clerics assumed supreme power. In Saudi Arabia, the role of the clerics would be quiet and covert, exercised from behind the benign facade of the US-allied House of Saud.

The events of 1979 sent the process of *Islamic Reformation* into overdrive, fuelling the acceleration of three critical trends:

- *Widening the gap* between Islam's traditionalists and modernizers (polarization within Islam—with traditionalists increasingly hostile towards modernizers).
- *Widening the gap* between Sunnis and Shi'ites (polarization of the sects—with Sunnis increasingly hostile towards non-Sunnis).
- *Widening the gap* between Islam and non-Islam (polarization of cultures—with Islam increasingly hostile towards non-Islam).

> The trend of polarization of cultures has accelerated at the same time as many Western states have been embracing multiculturalism, adopting cultural relativism, and receiving many hundreds of thousands of Muslim migrants. The tensions in multicultural societies are not imagined. Furthermore, they are not (generally) the product of racism, but of Islamic radicalization which widens the gap between the cultures, with Islam increasingly hostile towards non-Islam. The polarization is such that many multicultural societies are close to tearing apart. For some this process has already begun and is probably irreversible.

Iran

The Americans were caught both unawares and unprepared by the unrest of 1978 and the subsequent Islamic Revolution of 1979. In January 1977, the US State Department's Bureau of Intelligence and Research predicted that Iran would most likely remain stable under the shah's leadership. It predicted that prospects were good and relatively clear sailing could be expected well into the 1980s. In December 1977, during a stopover in Tehran, US President Jimmy Carter described Iran under the shah as "an 'island of stability' in one of the world's more troubled areas."[1]

---

1. Crist, *The Twilight War*, 12.

"An Island of Stability"?

Determined to modernize and secularize Iran, Mohammad Reza Shah Pahlavi (commonly known as "the shah"/the king) had embarked on radical reforms. He had ordered the sale of state-owned business and launched aggressive land reforms, forcibly seizing and redistributing land, including the vast holdings of wealthy Shia clerics, which, as author David Crist notes, "struck at the heart of their wealth and power."[2]

"The shah," writes Crist, "largely dismissed Islam as a backward force that impeded the formation of a new, modern Iran."[3] His secularization policies—which included the empowerment of women and the removal of Islamic dogma from schools—earned him the ire of the very same religious establishment which had joined forces with the masses to restore him to power during the troubles of 1953.[4] Indeed, the mood on the street had changed: the youthful, modest, and popular shah had grown into a cruel totalitarian despot who didn't care whom he hurt or alienated as he drove Iran towards modernity.

Powerful religious opposition rose out of Qom, the religious heartland of Shia Islam, where Ayatollah Ruhollah Khomeini (60) was speaking publically against the shah's secularization of society. In order to vilify the shah as the puppet of an enemy US, Khomeini exploited the popular myth that the US Central Intelligence Agency (CIA) had engineered the 1953 "coup" through which Iran's elected Prime Minister Mohammad Moseddegh was overthrown.[5]

So effective was Khomeini in rousing opposition, that the shah had him arrested in 1963 and exiled the following year. Khomeini settled in the

---

2. Ibid.

3. Ibid.

4. Takeya, "What Really Happened in Iran"; see also Copley, "Zahedi Memoir Taps Archives."

5. It is indeed a myth that the US orchestrated the overthrow of Mohammad Moseddegh. After presiding over the total collapse of the economy, Moseddegh dissolved the parliament and made a grab for absolute power. Though Britain and the US did indeed foment unrest so the shah could dismiss the then-premier, the plot failed and Mosaddegh, having been forewarned, staged a counter-coup. What happened next was a totally indigenous uprising against Mosaddegh and Iran's increasingly vocal communists in support of the monarchy, particularly the young shah, for whom many Iranians held deep affection. Rather than being hapless victims of foreign meddling, Iranians had proven they could be masters of their own fate. Keen to keep the masses under their control, the clerics used the myth not only to dragnet support, but to keep Iranians paranoid, mired in victimhood, and compliant through ignorance of their own history (see Takeya, "What Really Happened in Iran" and Copley, "Zahedi Memoir Taps Archives").

Shia holy city of Najaf in southern Iraq, from where he continued to rail against the "corrupt" Pahlavi dynasty.

One of the main by-products of the shah's radical and aggressive reforms was serious social instability. Rural unemployment had soared, sending masses of religiously conservative rural poor streaming into the cities in search of work; according to Crist, the population of Tehran multiplied fivefold. With the influx of migrants came a need for social services and political representation—something the religious establishment was only too pleased to provide.

In 1975, the shah cancelled elections and abolished the opposition in favor of a single party state. Opposition swelled, with educated elites and Marxists joining the ranks of the opposition alongside the students, the unemployed, and the entire religious establishment. Iran was anything but "an island of stability."

Strategic analyst Gregory R. Copley has remarked that when he visited Tehran in the 1970s, "there were no Farsi-speakers in the U.S. Embassy in Tehran; neither in the State Dept. element, nor, apparently, in the CIA component there."[6]

Regardless, that the US was so oblivious of trends within Iran is actually quite remarkable, for the situation was clearly ripe for unrest.

The Unravelling

"The shah's power began to unravel in late 1977," writes Crist. "Khomeini's eldest son died, likely of a heart attack, but Khomeini accused the shah and his secret police of murdering him. A short time later, on January 7, 1978, an article published in a government newspaper ridiculed the ayatollah, questioning his religious credentials and even his sexual preference. Riots erupted in the religious city of Qom. In the resulting mayhem police shot several protesters."[7]

It was essentially all downhill from there. On February 18, 1978, riots erupted in every major city across Iran. A pattern emerged: riots would erupt; they would be repressed with deadly force; there would be forty days of mourning; then fresh riots would erupt and the cycle would start over. Each fresh outbreak of rioting was more violent than before, and with the US blocking sales of tear gas, the regime had only limited means of crowd control.

6. Copley, "Zahedi memoir taps archives."
7. Crist, *Twilight War*, 13.

Encouraged by the perception that the US was abandoning its ally and no longer backing the shah's regime, the opposition escalated its demonstrations, strikes, riots, and clashes with police through 1978. Venues viewed as Western or decadent were targeted for attack, and a cinema was set on fire, resulting in the deaths of more than four hundred patrons. A rumour was spread accusing the shah's regime of starting the fire to discredit the rioting religious opposition. Though false and contrary to all the evidence, the rumour sent hostility skyrocketing. Crist describes this moment as "the beginning of the end of [the shah's] quarter-century reign."[8]

The shah wasn't the only one wanting Khomeini silenced. Exceedingly anxious not to see his own restive Shi'ite majority incited, Iraqi president Saddam Hussein (a Sunni) ordered Khomeini out of Iraq. Khomeini sought refuge in Kuwait only to be turned away. Ebrahim Yazdi, Khomeini's close advisor, advised the cleric to seek refuge in a democratic country where he would have religious freedom and be able to use the free press to spread his message. In October 1978, Khomeini (by then in his mid 70s) settled in Paris, France, where he could incite Islamic revolution in Iran free of the constraints he had previously endured under the Baathist[9] regime in Iraq. In Paris, Khomeini assumed leadership of the anti-shah movement's Islamic element, labeling the shah's regime a "Satanic government" and advocating it be washed away in "torrents of blood."[10]

In Muharram (December) 1978, revolutionary elements keen to exploit the heightened religious fervor during this month[11] distributed audio-cassettes of Khomeini's sermons amongst the masses. The cassettes, which had been smuggled out of France to incite revolution, fuelled a marked escalation in protests, strikes, and street clashes.

Like many in the revolutionary movement, Daniel Shayesteh (a student at the time) was motivated not by fundamentalist Islam—something he says he did not fully understand—but by the difficult and repressive social conditions that ordinary Iranians experienced under the Shah.

"I had a problem," explains Daniel, "with the socio-political system in Iran. Why should a student who is working tirelessly for his future struggle with poverty in a rich, oil-based country be threatened with termination of

---

8. Ibid., 14

9. Ba'ath is Arabic for "Renaissance" or "Resurrection." The Baath Party is a secular, socialist, anti-Islamist and anti-imperialist political party espousing pan-Arab unity.

10. Trofimov, *The Siege of Mecca*, 55.

11. Muharram, the first month of Islamic calendar, is a period of mourning and religious fervour amongst Shi'ites. The tenth day of Muharram—the Day of Ashura—is a very important day of the Mourning of Muharram.

his studies and be forced to sleep on the streets? I turned my anger over such conditions towards the Shah. The country was rich, but only for rich people. Middle class citizens, villagers, and students suffered. It was not difficult for me to find a motivation to participate in the student's revolutionary movement against the government of Iran."[12]

According to Daniel, most of the revolutionary students did not understand how society would be changed under the rule of Islam. "We were told that if we expected to be the best nation in the entire world we must follow the Mullahs [Islamic clerics] and commit ourselves to the Ayatollah Khomeini."[13]

Khomeini convinced the revolutionaries that his intention was to rescue Iran from economic hardship and dictatorship. He spoke about restoring the equal opportunity, freedom, and democracy that the shah had stolen.

"We were misinformed and brainwashed," writes Daniel. "Without question or investigation we believed that to follow Islam was to follow our leader blindly. We believed that Islam would fill in all of the inconsistencies of our culture, all the gaps between the rich and the poor, and suddenly we would be a democracy. It [the revolution] was a blindside attack on those of us who wanted equality and peace."[14]

That Problematic Cold War Prism

Author, historian, and former marine David Crist—whose father, George Crist (a four-star marine general) was stationed in the Middle East through the 1980s—believes the reason the American government failed to recognize the religious aspect of the Khomeini-led Iranian opposition is because it viewed everything through a Cold War prism.[15] The CIA, notes Crist, was in Iran to monitor the Soviet Union and track communists; they did not have relations with Shia clerics and were not even aware that the shah was gravely ill. Some in the US administration even speculated that Khomeini supporters might serve as a natural bulwark against the communists. Many even believed Khomeini represented democracy.[16] The American ambassador in Tehran predicted optimistically that the overthrow of the shah (a

12. Shayesteh, *The House I Left Behind*, 73.
13. Ibid., 73-74.
14. Ibid., 75.
15. Crist, *Twilight War*, 63-68.
16. Ibid., 15-16.

US ally) would lead to the creation of a benign pro-Western government where Khomeini would play a "Gandhi-like" role.[17]

The US administration of President Jimmy Carter decided against supporting any crackdown on protestors; instead, it encouraged the shah to move towards greater democracy. Carter's national security adviser, Zbigniew Brzezinski, a Polish-born immigrant, lamented Carter's policy of appeasement, bewildered by US ignorance that could not see that the various parties contending for power in Iran were "not motivated by a spirit of compromise, but by homicidal hatred."[18]

By January 1979, Carter had washed his hands of Iran. Without American support, the shah knew he had no option but to flee.

Revolution!

Daniel Shayesteh writes:

> When the Shah left on January 16, 1979, the Air Force joined the revolutionaries, rendering the government incapable of controlling public demonstrations and riots . . . After the Shah had vacated his throne, the Ayatollah Khomeini quickly entered the scene . . . Khomeini's arrival on February 1, 1979, also signaled defeat for the general army, which eventually surrendered. The Shah's government collapsed, the Shah's prime minister escaped, and the revolutionaries took over. Tears of happiness flowed freely from all who supported the Revolution, making Khomeini's return a day of celebration. We had overthrown the most powerful government in the Middle East and believed that we had opened the door for all Iranians to take part in the governing of their country. What a heartbreak only months after the Revolution when we learned our zealous allegiance to the Mullahs had been abused and our plans for Iran's future had been ignored for the sake of establishing a theocratic government—Islam.[19]

While some in the Carter administration would trivialize the Iranian revolution, failing to grasp its significance, others went so far as to cheer it. The US ambassador to the United Nations, Andrew Young, praised the "vibrant

---

17. Trofimov, *Siege of Mecca*, 55.
18. Ibid., 56.
19. Shayesteh, *The House I Left Behind*, 78–80.

cultural force" of Islam and predicted that Khomeini would be "somewhat of a saint when we get over the panic."[20]

Meanwhile, shockwaves reverberated across the Arab world as the Shi'ite Revolution triggered widespread anxiety amongst Sunni Arab regimes that saw the rise of a Shi'ite theocracy in Tehran as a direct threat to their power. Not only did the Iranian revolution revive the historic enmity between the two sects of Islam (the Sunnis and the Shi'ites), it undermined the House of Saud's claim to leadership of the Muslim world and threatened its grip on its oil-rich, Shia-dominated Eastern Province on the Persian Gulf.

In exchange for security guarantees from the US, Saudi Arabia increased oil production for US benefit. The US supplied the Saudis with materiel, including sophisticated F-15 fighter jets, and hundreds of US soldiers were secretly stationed in the country. While the CIA did offer limited assistance, it did not believe Saudi Arabia faced any real threat. Furthermore, the CIA had great difficulty gathering information in what Yaroslav Trofimov describes as the "tightly knit and pathologically secretive" Saudi kingdom.[21] Despite the US "security umbrella", which included CIA assistance, no one in Saudi Arabia—not the Saudis and not the CIA—was aware that a Sunni revolution was brewing.

On November 4, 1979, Iranian revolutionary students stormed the US embassy in Tehran, seizing sixty-four hostages. Despite the fact that the US embassy had been targeted in February, and despite the fact that intelligence estimates had warned of imminent dangers, the embassy was totally unprepared. Ayatollah Khomeini endorsed the seizure and opposed any negotiations with "The Great Satan."

The fall of the US embassy coincided with the hajj of 1979, when some 100,000 Muslims from all over the Muslim world would flood into Saudi Arabia to join the locals in the pilgrimage to the Ka'ba in Mecca. It would be a time of immense anxiety for the Saudis, as regional tensions were soaring. However, although trouble was certainly brewing, it would not be Iran or any Shi'ite that would cause trouble in Mecca during the hajj of 1979.

Saudi Arabia

When American explorers tapped oil in eastern Saudi Arabia in 1938, thousands of US oil experts and construction engineers flooded into the desert kingdom, along with military personnel for security. Needless to say, conservative, fundamentalist Saudis were not impressed. The influx of

20. Trofimov, *Siege of Mecca*, 57.
21. Ibid., 59.

foreigners facilitated the emergence of "un-Islamic" recreational activities such as watching television and social mixing over drinks, and it violated the deathbed wish of the Muslim Prophet Muhammad. While dying, Muhammad had reportedly given these orders: "Expel the pagans from the Arabian Peninsula"[22] and "Two deens [faiths] shall not co-exist in the land of the Arabs."[23]

Opposition simmered, and as Trofimov notes, "One of the more virulent early protestors against American penetration was an up-and-coming scholar named Abdulaziz Bin Baz" who was highly respected by the Saudi *Ikhwan*—that is, the Muslim *Brothers*, a Wahhabi ultra-religious militia comprised of Bedouin tribesmen.[24]

Despite simmering domestic opposition and widespread chaos in the Muslim world, the House of Saud was secure in its role as the custodian of Mecca and Medina, Islam's holy places. Commencing 1955, the House of Saud furthered its Islamic credentials by massively enlarging Mecca's Grand Mosque, even if they removed whole neighborhoods in the process. Through the 1950s and 1960s, the House of Saud consolidated its role as the guardian and defender of Islam by receiving thousands of MB members fleeing persecution in secular, Arab nationalist Egypt and Syria.

In May 1962, the Saudi government sponsored a conference in Mecca aimed at countering Arab nationalism and Nasserism (the secular, socialist philosophy espoused by Egyptian president Abdel Nasser) and promoting Islamic reformation, specifically Wahhabi Islam. The Muslim World League was thus established, with its headquarters in Mecca, under full Saudi control. In the words of Dore Gold, "This new organization, dedicated to fostering pan-Islamic solidarity, would revive Saudi Wahhabism and spread it globally, for it sought not only to convert Christians to Islam but also to convince Muslims to adopt Wahhabism."[25]

The House of Saud was aided in its task by its newfound wealth as oil flowed out and cash flowed in. But while the Saudi royals were growing rich on oil profits, the Bedouin settlements remained mired in grinding poverty. To escape their mud houses, camel herding, and date growing, many young Bedouin men sought out positions in the Saudi National Guard. Trofimov explains that while the regular military was filled with ambitious young officers from cosmopolitan coastal cities, many of whom were Arab

---

22. *Sahih Bukhari*, Volume 4, Book 52, Number 288.
23. *Malik's Muwatta*, Book 45, Numbers 45.5.17 and 45.5.18.
24. Trofimov, *The Siege of Mecca*, 20.
25. Gold, *Hatred's Kingdom*, 77.

nationalists or socialists, the National Guard absorbed the *Ikhwan* and recruited amongst the religiously conservative tribes.

Following Sunni tradition, the Saudi state is ruled by a strongman whose primary job is to protect Islam. As the ruling power protects Islam, the religious clerics legitimize and protect the ruling power. This mutual pact between the ruling and religious establishments is a longstanding Sunni tradition.

When Saudi Arabia's King Faisal came to power in 1964, he knew he had to maintain the symbiotic relationship with the clerics in order to remain in power. Likewise, the clerics knew they had to maintain their relationship with the monarchy in order to reap the benefits of that power. While the ministries of foreign affairs, finance and defense would remain the exclusive province of the House of Saud, Faisal gave the clerics control over the Ministry of Pilgrimage and Awqaf (religious endowments), the Ministry of Education (from 1963), and the Ministry of Justice (from 1970).

With Wahhabi clerics controlling education, it was inevitable that Saudis would be radicalized from early childhood. When the clerics secured control of higher education in 1975, they made Wahhabi religious courses mandatory in all universities. The "Wahhabization" of Saudi society had begun.

All the while, modernization and liberalization were continuing apace, *widening the divide* between the modernizing ruling establishment and the Wahhabi religious conservatives.

Leading the anti-modernization drive was none other than Sheikh Abdulaziz Bin Baz. His *dawa* (missionary) movement, through which young men were trained in hyper-conservative Salafi ways (i.e., the ways of the prophet and his companions as practiced in the seventh century), attracted an ever-increasing number of restless, disenchanted Bedouin. Of course, the religious teaching they received from the Wahhabi clerics made them even more restless and disenchanted.

Simmering Beneath the Surface

By 1977, some young Salafi Bedouin, having been fed a diet of Wahhabism in their schools and universities, had grown deeply disenchanted with the House of Saud and the clerical establishment that tolerated its un-Islamic behavior, especially its import of American decadence.

One malcontent named Juhayman al-Uteybi, a Bedouin in the Saudi National Guard, had grown so thoroughly disillusioned with the entire religious establishment that he had started debating, writing, and agitating for change. He strongly opposed the presence of foreigners in Saudi Arabia, especially Christians, and he detested the cinemas and places of entertainment established for them. Juhayman also protested against the regime's tolerance of Shi'ites, whom he regarded as polytheists on the grounds that they venerated Ali and Husayn. As far as Juhayman was concerned, Shi'ites were heretics who should be forced to choose between Sunni Islam or the sword.

Juhayman attracted a following of disaffected young students, but his views did generate controversy, dividing the clerics and earning him the opposition of Sheik Abdulaziz Bin Baz. Yet even the clerics who opposed Juhayman agreed that his theology was faultless and merely represented the teachings of the Wahhabi clerics. Irrespective of his faultless theology, Juhayman was deemed a threat and issued with a warning.

Juhayman was convinced that the religious establishment was betraying Islam by siding with a regime (the House of Saud) that it knew was violating Islamic rules—and all for reasons of political expediency. Knowing full well that the regime would seek to kill him and then legitimize the killing by labeling him a Khawârij (i.e., an extremist/*takfiri*), Juhayman threw down the gauntlet and declared the Saudi regime illegitimate.

Ripe for Revolution

Socially and economically, Saudi Arabia was ripe for revolution. After the 1973 oil-driven economic boom, many young Bedouin had migrated to Riyadh, drawn by the bright lights and the prospect of work. Many were conservative Muslim idealists who were determined to live conservatively as Salafis (i.e., as seventh-century Muslims). For Juhayman, recruiting followers from amongst the university students in Medina and Riyadh was easy; after all, they had already been indoctrinated in Wahhabi Islam. Gradually his movement grew and gained momentum.

In early 1978, Juhayman decided to publish a collection of his teachings to extend his reach and ensure his teachings were not being distorted. Being strongly anti-regime and subversive, Juhayman's manuscript could not be presented to any Saudi publisher. Instead, it was smuggled into Kuwait, where sympathetic MB activists facilitated its publication. With Juhayman's words in print, the long-suspicious Saudi authorities had incontrovertible proof of the subversive nature of his activities. Arrest warrants were issued.

Alerted to fact that his name headed a regime hit list, Juhayman fled deep into the desert. Twenty-five of his most senior followers were not so fortunate, and they were arrested. Amongst those arrested was a young student of poetry named Mohammed Abdullah (25).

Mohammed Abdullah had been arrested once before, some years earlier, while he had been working as an administrator in a Riyadh hospital. The experience had been both traumatizing and disillusioning. Money had gone missing from the hospital safe, and Mohammed was accused simply on the grounds that he was poor and had come from one of the poorest regions of Saudi Arabia. Despite having no evidence against him, Saudi police arrested Mohammed and tortured a confession out of him. Only later, when the real thief was caught with the cash, was Mohammed released from prison—minus his fingernails.[26]

Juhayman sent an emissary to his former teacher and ideological ally, Sheik Abdulaziz Bin Baz, now a leading cleric with immense influence. Bin Baz persuaded Prince Nayef (then Minister of Interior) to let him question Mohammed Abdullah and the other imprisoned religious dissidents. After doing so, Bin Baz deemed them harmless. He saw them as zealous young promoters of true Islamic morality, defenders of pure Wahhabi Islam, their only fault being immaturity which left them a bit ignorant of how things worked politically. At Bin Baz's insistence, the dissidents were released. "Energized by this support from the ulema—and radicalized by the beatings they suffered in Prince Nayef's jails, Juhayman's militants emerged from their ordeal with a strengthened faith."[27]

Not far away, Egypt too was simmering. Egyptian president Anwar Sadat had switched his Cold War allegiance from the Soviets to the US and released from prison thousands of MB activists jailed by Nasser. But in Egypt, as in Iran and Saudi Arabia, a movement for Islamic reformation was gaining momentum—one which rejected soft, pragmatic Islam in favor of traditional, puritanical, uncompromising Islam. The Egyptian movement comprised secret cells of religious dissidents. Known as Gamaat Islamiya ("Islamic Groups"), the Egyptian movement was especially prevalent on the campus of Cairo University. In addition, a secret offshoot of Gamaat Islamiya known as "Islamic Jihad" broke away to plot the assassination of the "infidel" Anwar Sadat, whom they deemed a traitor for brokering peace with Israel. Prominent amongst this group was a graduate of Cairo University's medical school named Ayman al-Zawahiri.[28]

Though vaguely aware of events in Egypt and Iran, Juhayman was not influenced by them. Totally focused on the Saudi situation, Juhayman was determined to find solutions in the Qur'an and hadith.

26. Trofimov, *The Siege of Mecca*, 38.
27. Ibid., 42.
28. Ibid., 43. Ayman al-Zawahiri went on to become Osama bin Laden's deputy in Afghanistan. He assumed the leadership of al-Qaeda after bin Laden was assassinated in Pakistan on May 2, 2011.

The Mahdi Cometh

One day, while studying the hadith, Juhayman stumbled across a reference to the Mahdi. Never mentioned in the Qur'an, the Mahdi appears in the hadith as the Islamic Messiah who returns amidst chaos and a great falling away of Muslims to usher in the End of Days.

According to Islamic eschatology (the doctrine of the end times), the Mahdi will lead the final jihad in which all the Christian cities of the world will be captured. Jesus, too, will appear, following the Mahdi and killing all those who said that he (Jesus) had been crucified (see Q.4:156–159[29]). The hadith elaborate, saying that Jesus will kill all pigs (the food of Christians), destroy all crosses (the symbol of Christians), and abolish the *jizya* (which means there is no longer protection available for Christians).[30] According to the hadith, Jesus and the Mahdi will rejoice at the elimination of Christians. Not a single infidel will survive the final jihad to end all jihads.[31]

The hadith provide a precise description of the Mahdi's name and appearance: he will bear the same name as the prophet (Muhammad) and even look like the Prophet Muhammad: tall and fair-skinned with a broad forehead and prominent nose. Indeed, he would look like Mohammed Abdullah, who also was tall, with fair skin, hazel eyes and black hair—by all accounts a man of stunning appearance.

Furthermore, the hadith provide a precise description about the timing of the Mahdi's appearance: the Mahdi will appear in Mecca, right after the hajj at the turn of an Islamic century. As it happened, the forthcoming hajj of 1979 would be the last hajj of Islam's fourteenth century.

---

29. "And [We cursed them] for their disbelief and their saying against Mary a great slander, And [for] their saying, 'Indeed, we have killed the Messiah, Jesus, the son of Mary, the messenger of Allah.' And they did not kill him, nor did they crucify him; but [another] was made to resemble him to them. And indeed, those who differ over it are in doubt about it. They have no knowledge of it except the following of assumption. And they did not kill him, for certain. Rather, Allah raised him to Himself. And ever is Allah Exalted in Might and Wise. And there is none from the People of the Scripture but that he will surely believe in Jesus before his death. And on the Day of Resurrection he [Jesus] will be against them [the People of the Book/Christians] a witness" (Q.4:156–158).

30. "Fight those who do not believe in Allah or in the Last Day and who do not consider unlawful what Allah and His Messenger have made unlawful and who do not adopt the religion of truth from those who were given the Scripture—[fight] until they give the jizyah willingly while they are humbled" (Q.9:29). *Jizya* is protection money mandated by the Quran, which Christians are forced to pay under Sharia to secure their right to life.

31. For more on the Islamic Jesus, including reference to the Quran and Hadith, see: Durie, "Isa, the Muslim Jesus."

Convinced that the End of Days was upon them, Juhayman established a training camp in the Arabian Desert and started training his revolutionaries in military tactics. He assured his followers, many of whom were members or former members of the Saudi National Guard, that the weapons were only for defensive purposes; he was convinced that the Muslim masses would recognize Mohammed Abdullah as the Madhi when he was revealed to them.

Subsequently, Mohammed Abdullah's sister reported that she'd had a vivid dream in which she saw her brother standing by the Ka'ba inside Mecca's Grand Mosque receiving adulation as the promised Mahdi. Before long, militants and sympathizers from far and wide reported having had the same dream. Eventually the resistant Mohammed Abdullah became the reluctant Mahdi.

Juhayman sent an emissary to inform Bin Baz that they intended to reveal Mohammed Abdullah as the Mahdi very soon. As the emissary made no mention of Juhayman's stockpiles of weapons or of his military training camp in the desert, Bin Baz did not perceive the movement to be threatening. While Bin Baz did not accept that Mohammed Abdullah could possibly be the Mahdi, he saw no need to crush Juhayman's movement. He merely warned Juhayman against doing anything that could stir up *fitna* (strife, doubt), for that would be unacceptable. Neither did Bin Baz see any need to alert the authorities, whose eyes were firmly fixed on events unfolding in Tehran as Ayatollah Khomeini consolidated his power through purges and bloodspilling. The Saudis were convinced that the clerical regime of Khomeini in Tehran had designs on the whole Persian Gulf, including Saudi Arabia's oil-rich, Shi'ite-dominated Eastern Province.

In early November 1979, as the hajj season commenced and many thousands of pilgrims flooded into Mecca, all eyes were fixed on events in Tehran, where revolutionary students had seized the US Embassy and taken sixty-four hostages. While the international news media was fixated on the hostage crisis, and while Riyadh was in a virtual state of panic over revolutionary Iran's intentions in the Persian Gulf, Juhayman was setting the stage for his revolution. Weapons were being ferried into Mecca's Grand Mosque through the construction entrance—the "Bin Laden accessway"—courtesy of sympathetic insiders. As the religious students had all gone home, the mosque's vast labyrinth of underground, basement chambers, known as the Qaboo, was quiet and empty.

In the closing hours of November 19, 1979—the last day of the year 1399 on the Islamic calendar—Juhayman and Mohammed Abdullah quietly entered the city of Mecca and took up their positions.

The Siege of Mecca

At dawn the next day—the first day of Muharram 1400 on the Islamic calendar (November 20, 1979 on the Western calendar)—Juhayman's revolutionary forces seized control of Mecca's Grand Mosque, Islam's most holy site. With snipers in position, the gates were locked. Juhayman oversaw the military operation while Mohammed Abdullah's brother, Sayid, delivered an oration. The end of the world was coming, he said, and he exhorted the masses to receive the Mahdi and join with Juhayman in the fight against corruption, immorality, and unbelief.

At that point, Mohammed Abdullah was ushered into their presence. As the militants cleared a passage for him, Mohammed Abdullah, "submachine gun in hand,"[32] walked towards the Ka'ba where Juhayman was waiting for him. Worshippers gasped in awe. One by one the revolutionaries bowed before him and declared their allegiance; worshippers (now hostages) followed suit.

The mosque's imam, Sheikh Mohammed Ibn Subeil, shed his religious cloak and scurried through the crowd to his quarters above the Fatah Gate from where he phoned his superiors and alerted the authorities. It took the police more than an hour to respond; a single officer in a jeep was sent to investigate. Upon arriving at the gate, the jeep was sprayed in bullets courtesy of Juhayman's snipers, and the driver fell bleeding out of his vehicle. When the jeep did not return, the Saudi police dispatched a convoy of vehicles. Upon arrival at the mosque, they too met with a hail of gunfire; eight officers were killed instantly and thirty-six wounded. The killing had only just begun.

The details of the two-week siege and its ultimate resolution have been documented by Yaroslav Trofimov in his book *The Siege of Mecca: The 1979 Uprising at Islam's Holiest Shrine*.

"Saudi officials," writes Trofimov, "had severely misjudged the extent of resistance that Juhayman's men could offer in Mecca, and as a result Saudi troops had been mauled in a veritable massacre. The Saudi National Guard no longer wanted to fight in the Grand Mosque. The Americans had tried to help on the ground—and failed. France was the only hope left. It had become the French Republic's responsibility to rescue a monarchy that guaranteed the Free World's oil supplies."[33]

The story of how it all unfolded is truly gripping, and for that you'll need to purchase Trofimov's book. It will be enough for our purposes to

---

32. Trofimov, *The Siege of Mecca*, 69.
33. Ibid., 188.

focus on how the House of Saud managed to get American and then French troops into Mecca—a city forbidden to infidels—let alone into the Grand Mosque itself.

The Fatwa that Changed Everything

Reluctant to even point their weapons in the direction of the most venerated holy site, let alone kill fellow Muslims, Saudi security personnel were being slaughtered. Furthermore, many security personnel were wondering if maybe the Mahdi had indeed arrived.

Unless Saudi Arabia's King Khaled could get a fatwa (a religious ruling) from the kingdom's most senior clerics—one that would give Saudi security personal permission to fight *and* give the regime permission to invite non-Muslim (*kafir*/infidel) forces into Mecca and into the holy mosque— then the House of Saud would meet the same end as the shah of Iran.

King Khaled summonsed Sheikh Abdulaziz Bin Baz, along with twenty-nine other senior clerics, to the royal palace in Riyadh. Sitting down with the stressed and desperate Saudi king, Bin Baz and the clerics knew they had the House of Saud exactly where they wanted it. The fatwa would not come cheap.

After a lengthy debate about the situation inside in the mosque, the clerics agreed that Mohammed Abdullah could not possibly be the Mahdi. Despite this, the Wahhabi clerics had considerable sympathy with the revolutionaries, whom they regarded as pious, albeit hot-headed, deeply religious conservatives. Though the Americans were busy blaming Iran for the Mecca uprising, the clerics knew full well that it was a Wahhabi revolt led by those who had been trained by Bin Baz and in schools the Wahhabi clerics had themselves founded.

Fully aware that they held all the cards, the clerics set out their demands and engaged in a bit of quid pro quo. They would sign a fatwa recognizing the House of Saud's legitimacy, on the condition that from now on the ruling House of Saud would live up to its Islamic responsibilities, beholden to the clerics.

"There should be no more women on TV," writes Tofimov, "no more licentious movies, no more alcohol. The social liberalization that had begun under King Faisal should be halted and, where possible, rolled back. And billions of Saudi petro-dollars should be put to good use, spreading the rigid Wahhabi Islam around the planet . . . As some Saudi princes described it later, the ulema [clerics] essentially asked al-Saud to adopt Juhayman's agenda in exchange for their help in getting rid of Juhayman himself."[34]

The mostly young Sunni revolutionaries who perished in the Qaboo underneath the Great Mosque in late November and early December 1979, were, as Dore Gold notes, "the products of mainstream Saudi institutions."[35] Both Juhayman and Mohammed Adbullah had studied in Saudi universities, and the former had also studied under Sheikh Bin Baz, who went on to become the grand mufti of Saudi Arabia.

Concerning the fatwa issued by Bin Baz and the *ulama*, Gold comments that it essentially expanded the *ulama*'s authority in "supervising the kingdom's Wahhabi character."[36] Gold quotes a Saudi journalist at Harvard University, Sulaiman al-Hattlan, whose analysis echoes that of the Saudi princes: "Though the government killed the extremists, it then essentially adopted their ideology . . . to appease the Islamists, perhaps fearing further extremists threats."[37]

Gold describes how, after the siege of Mecca, the Saudi leadership gave the *ulama* much greater authority in the kingdom's affairs; the power of the *ulama* increased considerably, especially that of Sheik Abdulaziz Bin Baz, whose influence grew phenomenally. As Gold notes, Bin Baz was tremendously hostile to Christians and Jews, teaching that "According to the Koran, the Sunnah, and the consensus of Muslims it is a requirement of the Muslim to be hostile to the Jews and the Christian" and "it is a religious requirement to despise the infidel Jews and Christians . . . until they believe in Allah alone."[38]

Bin Baz advanced the idea that Islam must have a global reach if it is to counter Christian missionary activity. A strong advocate of jihad as the means of removing all obstacles to the spread of Islam, Bin Baz taught that jihad was the means by which the door was opened to *da'wa* (Islamic missionary activity). He also promulgated the idea of financial jihad (*jihad bi-l-maal*), leading to the rise of Islamic "charities" and other money-raising schemes, such as halal certification, from the early 1980s.

The fatwa ensured that Bin Baz and the Wahhabi *ulama* would have an unlimited flow of Saudi petro-dollars with which to spread intolerant, pro-Sharia, pro-jihad, anti-Semitic and anti-Christian, Wahhabi Islam right across the globe.

34. Ibid., 100.
35. Gold, *Hatred's Kingdom*, 107.
36. Ibid., 109.
37. Ibid., 110.
38. Ibid., 111.

Since 1979, Saudi petrodollars have been used to build thousands of large, beautiful mosques all around the world—mosques designed primarily to attract locals to Wahhabi Islam. Many of these mosques, which routinely offer free (Saudi-funded) education, are built in strategic areas where no Muslims exist.

Since 1979, Saudi petrodollars have been used to grant scholarships to poor African and Asian Muslims so that they can be educated in Wahhabi Islam in Islamic universities across the Middle East before returning home to radicalize the locals.

Since 1979, Saudi petrodollars have been used to finance international jihad in Afghanistan, the Balkans, Africa, the Caucasus, Asia, and Mesopotamia—ensuring the jihadists are kept busy far away from Saudi Arabia.

Since 1979, Saudi petrodollars have been used to establish departments and fill chairs in Islamic Studies in Western universities, through which the Wahhabis can take control of the narrative and subvert the West with regards to Islam's political mandate and intentions.

Actually, it is amazing what a band of committed, imperialistic, fundamentalist ideologues can achieve when guaranteed absolute freedom and unlimited funds.

Gaddafi Perceived What the West Did Not

The late Libyan dictator Muammar Gaddafi might have been a cruel and eccentric megalomaniac, but he was also a committed anti-Islamist, frequently railing against "the bearded ones", as he called them. After the September 11, 2001 terror attacks in New York and Washington, Gaddafi renounced Libya's weapons of mass destruction (WMD) and opened up all of Libya's facilities to international inspectors who dismantled all of Libya's chemical and nuclear weapons programs, as well as its longest-range ballistic missiles.[39] Normalization followed, and Gaddafi allied with the West in the War on Terror,[40] keeping al-Qaeda in the Islamic Maghreb (AQIM)[41] hemmed in and hamstrung for years.

Why did he do it?

---

39. Arms Control Association, "Chronology of Libya's Disarmament and Relations with the United States."

40. Norton-Taylor, "Gaddafi seen as ally in war on terrorism."

41. The Maghreb refers to northwest Africa; it stretches from Libya through Algeria, Tunisia, Morocco, and Mauritania. Al-Qaeda in the Islamic Maghreb is a predominantly Algerian terrorist organization operating in the Sahara and the Sahel.

In May 1989, while the West was fixated on events in Eastern Europe and the Soviet Union—where President Mikhail Gorbachev's policies of *glasnost* (openness) and *perestroika* (re-structuring) had paved the way for radical transformation—Gaddafi was more concerned about Muslim radicalization and the rise of militant Wahhabi Islam.

Terrorism analyst Yossef Bodansky explains:

> In late May [1989], twenty-one Arab monarchs and other heads of state, as well as dozens of senior officials and staff, gathered in Baghdad for an all-Arab summit... Qadhafi [Gaddafi] delivered an alarming and perceptive speech. Time was running out for the Arab world, he proclaimed. The Arab political system was on the verge of collapse because of the popular groundswell of Islamist radicalism. Furthermore, the new wave of radicalism was all-Islamic and thus undercut the region's Arab identity. 'We must all, virtually today,' Qadhafi warned, 'establish a joint alliance to stand strong and steadfast against the radical-extremist Islamic groups that are seeking to take over the entire Middle East. They multiply with the speed of lightening. We are likely to wake up one morning to face the masses raising slogans to the effect that 'Islam is the solution to all our economic and social woes' and demanding that we, the present rulers, vacate the arena'.[42]

To Gaddafi's dismay, the Arab leaders were not interested in combating radicalization or the rise of militant Wahhabi Islam. Led by Iraq's Saddam Hussein, the Arab leaders firmly believed they could exploit the Wahhabi militants for their own ends. As Bodansky explains, the Arab leaders believed that the militant "networks were indispensable to launching terrorist operations at the heart of the West."[43]

In response to Gaddafi's concerns, Saddam Hussein proposed that the Arab leaders promote an all-Arab, as distinct from Islamist, jihad—a jihad the Arab dictators would facilitate rather than one to which they would succumb.

As history will attest, Gaddafi was right! The enemy of my enemy is NOT necessarily my friend.

1979: A Pivotal Year

The year 1979 will go down in history as being the year in which Islamic reformation came of age and went into overdrive. It was the year that

---

42. Bodansky, *High Cost of Peace*, 31.
43. Ibid.

revolutionary, fundamentalist, and aggressive factions within *both* sects of Islam—Shi'ite and Sunni—were massively empowered. It was the year that fundamentalist Islamic clerics were catapulted out of the fringes into the halls of state power, from where they would dictate policy and gain access to state funds.

While the consequences and implications of the Islamic (Shi'ite) Revolution in Iran were obvious, the consequences and implication of the siege of Mecca's Grand Mosque and the failed Islamic (Sunni) Revolution in Saudi Arabia were not. Consequently, Saudi Arabia's Wahhabi clerics have been able to Wahhabize Sunni Muslims and fund *da'wa* and military, intellectual, and economic jihad globally—all with impunity, protected from any jihadist blowback by a US security umbrella.

Today, as modernizing Muslim dissidents are intimidated, bashed, and murdered; as Sunni versus Shi'ite sectarian conflict escalates and spreads destroying everything in its path; as Islamic intolerance soars to new heights; and as Muslim persecution of Christians reaches levels unseen in a century—we in the West need to wake up!

The time has come to end denial and confront reality, realizing that we are *decades behind the game*.

— 5 —

The Shia Crescent

The Middle East will not be defined by the Arab identity or by any particular form of national government. Ultimately the character of the region will be decided in the crucible of Shia revival and the Sunni response to it—Vali Nasr, 2006.[1]

IN DECEMBER 2004, AS Iraq's first democratic elections loomed,[2] Jordan's King Abdullah II raised a "red flag" alerting the US and her coalition partners to the threat posed by Iranian interference in Iraq. "It is in Iran's vested interest," said King Abdullah, "to have an Islamic republic of Iraq . . . and therefore the involvement you're getting by the Iranians is to achieve a government that is very pro-Iran."

Abdullah expressed his concern that if pro-Iran parties or politicians dominated the new Iraqi government, it would herald the rise of a "Shia Crescent" over the Middle East. This, he warned, would alter the traditional balance of power between the Sunnis and the Shi'ites and pose new challenges to US interests and allies. "If Iraq goes Islamic republic," warned Abdullah, "then yes, we've opened ourselves to a whole set of new problems that will not be limited to the borders of Iraq . . . Strategic planners around the world have got to be aware that is a possibility . . . Even Saudi Arabia is not immune from this. It would be a major problem," one that would "propel the possibility of a Shiite-Sunni conflict even more."[3]

In reality, however, the term Shia Crescent is a misnomer, something Abdullah himself subsequently acknowledged. On January 11, 2005, the executive director of the Washington Institute for Near East Policy, Robert Satloff, interviewed King Abdullah II at his private office in a secluded compound outside of Amman. When he asked Abdullah to explain his comment

---

1. Nasr, *The Shia Revival*, 22.
2. On January 30, 2005, Iraqis went to the polls to elect a 275-member National Assembly that would have a mandate to draft the constitution and rule until the new constitution came into force.
3. Wright and Baker, "Iraq, Jordan See Threat To Election From Iran."

about the threat posed by the emerging Shia Crescent, the king made it clear that the threat does not emanate from Shi'ism or Shi'ites per se, but from the belligerent, revolutionary regime in Tehran. Abdullah explained:

> The Hashemites [the king's tribe] are from Ahl Al Bayt [the family of the Prophet] and do not have a problem with Shi'ites. We are as close to them as we are to the Sunnis. But, there are many people in Iraq—including Shi'ites—who have their own concerns about Iran [i.e., the regime].
>
> We keep saying that the core problem in the Middle East is the Israeli-Palestinian one, but for the first time, my fear is that if things do not quickly settle in Iraq into an inclusive process that brings stability and security, then the Israeli-Palestinian issue may no longer be the core problem. In that situation, the core problem is going to be based around Iraq, and it's going to be a terrible conflict within Islam—a Shi'ite-Sunni conflict—which would be devastating for this part of the world. The so-called issue of "the crescent" was taken out of context and blown out of proportion. My concern is political, not religious, revolving around Iran, Iran's political involvement inside Iraq, its relation with Syria and Hezbollah, and the strengthening of this political-strategic alliance. This would create a scenario where you have these four [Tehran, Baghdad, Damascus and Hezbollah] who have a strategic objective that could create a major conflict. I don't have any problem with Shi'ites. I have a real problem with certain Iranian factions' political influence inside Iraq. Our argument to the United States is that a capable, independent, secure Iraq is the best way of containing Iran.[4]

Subsequently in 2007, as Iraq convulsed in sectarian war, a journalist from the London-based *Sharq al-Awsat* newspaper put it to Abdullah that Iranian officials were "looking forward to a full Shia moon, not just a Shia crescent."[5]

Abdullah responded by clarifying yet again that he had never used the term "Shia" in a sectarian sense. "Let's not delve into these labels," he said, insisting that he had been referring to "political alignments" as distinct from sectarian ones.

The point remains valid, though; for it is Iran's strategic objective to exert influence or even control over not just a "crescent"—from Tehran through Baghdad and Damascus to Hezbollah on the northern border of Israel—but over a "full moon": that is, from Tehran through Baghdad and

---

4. Satloff, "King Abdullah II: 'Iraq is the Battleground - the West against Iran.'"
5. Black, "Fear of a Shia full moon."

the entire Levant, as well as Saudi Arabia and the whole Persian Gulf. Of course, King Abdullah was fully aware of that. Indeed, that was precisely why he was so anxious. He knew that this political alignment could translate into *success* for Shi'ism, *success* for Islamic resistance, and *success* for the revolutionary clerical regime in Tehran—and that this would ultimately threaten his own survival as a US-allied Sunni modernizer in restive, radicalized, majority-Palestinian, highly volatile Jordan.

The Axis of Resistance

The other name by which this political alignment is known—the Axis of Resistance—is definitely more accurate. For starters, not all members of the Shia Crescent are Shi'ite. With a one percent Shi'ite minority, Syria is definitely not a Shi'ite state. Syrian president Bashar al-Assad is not Shia; he belongs to the Alawite sect, which has traditionally been despised, rejected, and persecuted as heretical by both Sunnis and Shi'ites.[6]

Led by the revolutionary Shi'ite clerical regime in Iran, the Axis of Resistance comprises governments and groups that are committed to *Islamic resistance* (as distinct from acquiescence). The Axis of Resistance resists the state of Israel and all Western influence and interference in the Middle East.

In resisting Israel, the Axis of Resistance also resists all Muslim governments that have signed peace treaties with Israel. Before Iran's Islamic Revolution (1979), Iran and Israel were friends—allies in the face of Sunni aggression. The states even remained aligned through the Iran-Iraq war (1980s), with Israel regarding populist Arab leader Saddam Hussein as a more imminent and existential threat than Khomeini. Today, however, while many Iranians are friends of Israel,[7] the Islamic revolutionary regime in Tehran most definitely is not.

In resisting Western interference and the US presence in the region, the Axis of Resistance also resists all Muslim governments that have allied with the "Great Satan" (America) and permit US military bases in the *dar el-Islam* (the abode of Islam). It especially resists the House of Saud in "the Land of the Two Holy Mosques", which permits this sacrilege in direct contravention of Muhammad's deathbed commands.[8]

---

6. While still revering Muhammad as the founder of Islam, the Alawi sect—like the Baha'i and Ahmadiyya sects—also reveres a subsequent prophet. This is totally unacceptable in mainstream Islam, which maintains that Muhammad gave Allah's final word.

7. Edry, "Israel and Iran: a love story?"

8. While in the process of dying, Muhammad reportedly gave these orders: "Expel the pagans from the Arabian Peninsula" (*Sahih Bukhari*, Volume 4, Book 52,

Understandably, this commitment to Islamic resistance is also deeply attractive to many radicalized Sunni Muslims. Consequently, despite being Sunni and inherently anti-Shi'ite, Egypt's MB, Gaza's Hamas, the Palestinian Liberation Organization (PLO) and even al-Qaeda will display flexibility, adopt pragmatism, and cooperate with revolutionary Shi'ite Iran to advance their shared goal of Islamic resistance.

As it rises, the Shia Crescent casts a deep, dark, and menacing shadow over Mesopotamia's Fertile Crescent, home to most of region's ethnic-religious minorities, including the indigenous Christian Assyrians. It also threatens all US-allied Sunni dictators, particularly King Abdullah in Jordan, which shares a long border with Israel, and the House of Saud, which extracts virtually all its wealth from its oil-rich but Shi'ite-dominated Eastern Province on the Persian Gulf.

Iraq: The Buffer State

After World War I, the Ottoman provinces of Basra (comprising oil-rich, mostly Shi'ite southern Iraq—which at that time included Kuwait), Baghdad (comprising mostly Sunni central Iraq), and Mosul (ethnically and religiously diverse northern Iraq, including oil-rich Kirkuk) were combined—but without Kuwait—to create the modern-day state of Iraq over which a Sunni Arab Hashemite king was installed.[9] A British protectorate since 1899, Kuwait was kept separate under the control of a local Sunni Arab Sheik.[10]

Independent since 1961, Iraq has existed as a buffer state straddling the ethnic and religious fault lines between the Sunnis and Shi'ites *and* between the Persians, Arabs, and Turks.

Iraq's strategic value increased markedly after the Iranian Revolution of 1979. As a Sunni Arab nationalist, Saddam Hussein could stand as an ideological bulwark between revolutionary Shi'ite Iran and the US-allied

---

Number 288) and "Two deens [faiths] shall not co-exist in the land of the Arabs [i.e., Arabia]" (*Malik's Muwatta*, Book 45, Numbers 45.5.17 and 45.5.18).

9. Hashemite: one who belongs to the Banu (clan) of "Hashim", an Arabian clan within the larger Quraysh tribe. As natives of the Hijaz region of western Arabia (along the Red Sea), the Banu Hashim assisted the British in their campaign to overthrow the Turks and were rewarded with kingdoms in Hijaz, Iraq, and Transjordan. In Hijaz, the dynasty ended in 1925 when the Hijaz was annexed by al-Saud of the Nejd (central Arabian highlands/plateau). In Iraq, the dynasty ended in 1958 when the Hashemite king was assassinated in a coup. At the time of writing (2015), only in Jordan did the dynasty continue, albeit with considerable and growing opposition.

10. Davidson, *After the Sheikhs*, 18–19.

Saudi Arabia. Under Saddam's rule, Iraq could exist as a geographic wedge between the revolutionary clerical regime in Tehran and its strategic ally in Damascus, Syria.

The Iran-Iraq War (1980–1988)

Once installed in Tehran, Ayatollah Khomeini moved to settle scores with Saddam Hussein, who had expelled him from Najaf in southern Iraq in 1977 at the request of the US-backed shah of Iran. Holding Saddam and his secular Baath Party in contempt, Khomeini openly incited Iraqi Shi'ites to revolt. Emphasizing Muslim unity, Khomeini rejected the Western concept of nation states and national identity. As author David Crist explains, "The *umma*, or community, was the sole basis for Islamic politics, and the concept of a united Islamic nation drove the Iranian revolutionary vision. 'We will export our revolution throughout the world . . . until calls 'There is no god but God and Muhammad is the messenger of God' are echoed all over the world,' said the Supreme leader during one of his many similar-themed Friday sermons."[11]

Khomeini was not all talk either; his revolutionary forces assassinated twenty Iraqi officials in 1980 alone.[12] Tensions escalated at the Iran-Iraq border, and skirmishes became common as the states lurched towards all-out war.

In Saddam's assessment, the Iranian Army was weak, having been decimated by the revolution and subsequent purges; it was not the Shah's army. Not only did Saddam have a low view of Iran's military capabilities, he also had a grandiose view of himself as the leader and champion of Arab resistance. Promoting himself as the new Saladin (who was actually a Kurd), Saddam lauded himself as the hero who would defeat the "Crusaders", reconquer the Levant, and "liberate" Jerusalem for the Muslims just as Saladin had done in the latter part of the twelfth century.

The Americans, meanwhile, viewing everything through a Cold War prism, assessed that Khomeini—being a religious man—would make a fine US ally and bulwark against the atheistic soviet communists. To this end, the Americans shared CIA intelligence with the new Iranian minister of foreign affairs, Ebrahim Yazdi, and warned him that Saddam Hussein was planning an invasion—a warning the Iranians dismissed as ridiculous. Crist writes: "Iran's dismissal of the CIA's warning could have proven fatal

---

11. Crist, *The Twilight War*, 86.
12. Ibid.

for the fledgling Islamic Republic— had their antagonist not been Saddam Hussein."[13]

On September 22, 1980, Saddam ordered his forces into Iran on the pretext of settling a territorial dispute over the Shatt al-Arab—a waterway formed by the confluence of the Tigris and the Euphrates Rivers that empties into the Persian Gulf and forms the boundary between Iran and Iraq.[14] It was, as Crist describes, an "anti-blitzkrieg", in which the Iraqi army moved "glacially", giving the unprepared Iranian forces all the time they needed to mount a response.[15]

War a "Godsend"

Not everyone hates war. Indeed, Saddam Hussein and Ayatollah Khomeini both saw the war as something imminently exploitable. For Saddam, this was his chance to snatch the oil fields east of the Shatt al-Arab, in Iran's Arab-dominated Khuzestan province across the water from Basra. For Khomeini's revolutionary regime, this was not merely an opportunity to overthrow the Baath regime in Baghdad, but the perfect opportunity to rally a divided nation and legitimize a state of emergency. Steven Ward, a senior Iranian analyst at the CIA, has commented that Iraq's invasion of Iran proved to be "godsend" to the new Islamic republic: "The Iraqi aggression ensured the clerical regime's survival by reviving the public's nationalism and diverting attention from the country's slide into tyranny."[16]

Bit by bit, the Iranian armed forces chipped away at Saddam's army. Eventually, on May 24, 1982, the Iranian military liberated the border city of Khorramshahr, thereby ending Iraqi occupation of Iranian territory. Saddam offered a cease-fire.

While no one in Tehran advocated accepting the cease-fire, the Iranians were divided about how to proceed. While some wanted to press on into Basra, overthrow Saddam, and establish an Islamic state inside Iraq, others argued for seeking punitive reparations, adding that Iran should not allow itself to be seen as the aggressor. The pro-war camp insisted that an invasion

13. Ibid., 87.

14. Iran claimed sovereignty over the eastern side of the river to the "thalweg" (the deep-water mark which runs roughly down the centre). Iraq, meanwhile, claimed the entire river to the low-water mark on the east bank—as was the case in Ottoman times. The Algiers Accord of 1975 fixed the border roughly along the thalweg. Iraq did not accept this, for there was a lot of money to be made from controlling shipping in the Shatt al-Arab.

15. Crist, *The Twilight War*, 88.

16. Ibid., 89.

of Iraq was necessary if Iran was to broker peace from a position of strength. Initially Khomeini had been reluctant to invade. However, Iranian intelligence operatives and the Iranian Revolutionary Guards Corp (IRGC)—an elite military unit created in 1979 to protect the Islamic revolutionary regime—convinced him that Iraqi Shi'ites were ripe for revolution and that Basra and possibly even Kuwait could be taken.

On June 21, 1982, Ayatollah Khomeini made a most significant speech in which he publically revealed his expansionist vision for a Shia Crescent stretching across the Middle East. To justify Iran's invasion of Basra and rally that nation to war, Khomeini held up not a stick, but a carrot, declaring: "The road to Jerusalem goes through Karbala."[17]

The War's Big Winners

THE IRANIAN REVOLUTIONARY GUARDS CORP

And so the war continued, much to the delight of the IRGC and Basij (Islamic revolutionary youth paramilitary) which were able to continue building up their forces, from 20,000–30,000 members in 1981 to 250,000 by 1988, while receiving the lion's share of the military budget. As Ali Alfoneh, a senior fellow at the Foundation for the Defense of Democracies notes: "The IRGC essentially sacrificed Iran's national interest and hundreds of thousands of Iranian lives for the sake of its corporate and organizational expansion."[18]

Khomeini acquiesced to the IRGC because the survival of the clerical regime depended on the IRGC's willingness to suppress internal opposition. (The same is true today, which begs the question, "Who really rules Iran?")

WESTERN ARMS MANUFACTURERS

Iran's war effort also benefited from Cold War hostilities. Through 1985 and 1986, the administration of US President Ronald Reagan covertly supplied enormous quantities of missiles and spare parts to Iran in what came to be known as the Iran-Contra Scandal.

Though designed to facilitate a détente with Iran so as to keep it from drifting into the Soviet Union's sphere of influence, the scheme ultimately degenerated into an arms-for-hostages deal though which three Americans

---

17. Ibid., 95.
18. Alfoneh, "The Twilight War," reviewed for *Middle East Quarterly*.

taken hostage in Lebanon were eventually released—although Hezbollah quickly replaced them by snatching three more.

Khomeini might have been rabidly anti-American, but he was a pragmatist when it came to acquiring weapons. Ultimately, however, his opponents got wind of it and leaked reports that the Ayatollah was doing deals with the "Great Satan." The leak embarrassed Khomeini, badly burned the Reagan administration, and absolutely infuriated America's Sunni Gulf Arab allies, who started to doubt if the US could be trusted.

In an effort to repair the damage, the US revamped Operation Staunch to stem the flow of weapons to Iran.[19] According to Crist, the operation met with immediate success: "Munitions sales by Western Europe to Iran dropped dramatically, from $1 billion in 1986 to less than $200 million in the first half of 1987, and only four NATO nations sold arms to Iran, a drop from twenty-three the year before. At the end of that year, the United Kingdom ordered Iran to close its weapons procurement office in London through which Tehran purchased an estimated 70 percent of its weapons."[20]

The US also threw itself into the Tanker War[21] being waged in the Persian Gulf, assigning US naval vessels to escort US-flagged Kuwaiti tankers through the Persian Gulf to Kuwait, shielding them from Iranian attack.

Chemical Weapons and a Passenger Jet

The decisive breakthrough in the Iran-Iraq War came in April 1988, when two major military assaults, though not coordinated, combined to deliver a near-fatal blow to Iran. On April 17, Iraqi forces armed with nerve agents and blistering mustard gas reconquered the al-Faw Peninsula.[22] The very next day, the US launched Operation Praying Mantis, which would finally break the back of Iranian dominance over the Persian Gulf.[23]

The fatal blow came on April 29, 1988, when, in the "fog of war", a US warship in Iranian waters in the Persian Gulf shot an Iranian passenger

---

19. First launched in December 1983, Operation Staunch involved American embassies in US-allied states urging their host governments to stop transfers of arms to Tehran. Riddled with loopholes, the operation was violated from its inception and largely ineffective.

20. Crist, *The Twilight War*, 205.

21. The war between Iran and Iraq for control of the Persian Gulf was known as the Tanker War. Launched by Saddam in early 1984, each side targeted oil tankers to deprive its opponents of oil trade and in the hope that foreign states might be drawn into the conflict.

22. Ibid., 338.

23. Ibid., 339–357.

jet out of the sky. Iran Air Flight 655 was carrying 290 passengers; there were no survivors. The US navy and government closed ranks behind the *Vincennes*' crew and their commanding officer Captain William Roger, even awarding him the Legion of Merit medal.[24]

Iranian leaders concluded that the West—in particular the US—would never allow them to win the war. The commander of the IRGC, Mohsen Rezaei, expressed the opinion that there would be no victory in the next five years unless almost unlimited resources were to be directed to the IRGC and the military, and unless Tehran developed a nuclear bomb that could be used as leverage to force the US out of the Persian Gulf.

Khomeini accepted a cease-fire, and on August 20, 1988, the guns fell silent.

The war should have ended after twenty-one months. Instead, it was purposefully prolonged for a further six years just so the regime in Tehran could consolidate its power and the IRGC could expand its organization. The prolongation of the war was further enabled by the West, which was happily arming both sides without regard to the escalating death toll.

The Buffer is Bled Dry

The Iran-Iraq War bled Iran dry; likewise Iraq, which found itself laden with war debt far beyond its ability to repay.

At the Baghdad Summit of May 1989, Iraqi president Saddam Hussein sought reparations from the Arab states on the grounds that they had benefited from his war against Iran. It was to no avail. He also pressed the Arab leaders for an Arab jihad against Israel and the West, but to his dismay they were only interested in oil and money matters. Further to this, Saddam demanded to be acknowledged, and even lauded, as the savior and leader of the Sunni Arabs.

When the Arab states refused Saddam both reparations and adoration, a furious, slighted, and disgusted Saddam Hussein secretly shifted his alignment, quietly taking steps towards rapprochement with the spearhead of Islamic resistance: Iran.

Determined to lead the Arabs against Israel and the West, Saddam got busy bolstering his Islamic credentials in the knowledge that jihadists were driven by religious, not nationalist aspirations.

After learning from Iraqi, PLO, and soviet East German intelligence that virtually all the jihadist organizations in Western Europe were controlled by Syria and Iran, Saddam decided to formalize his relationship with

---

24. Ibid., 365–371.

Tehran. On July 28, 1990, Baghdad and Tehran signed a formal pact wherein they agreed to cooperate in an all-Islamic jihad to expel the "Great Satan" from the Middle East, eliminate Israel, and establish an ecumenical Islamic republic—essentially a caliphate—across the whole region.[25] Saddam Hussein, the new Saladin, would show the Arab leaders who was in charge.

However, there was one thing Saddam needed to do before he could lead the Arabs against Israel and the West: he needed to reimburse and rebuild Iraq. To that end, he needed to annex oil-rich Kuwait.

Iraq invaded Kuwait on August 2, 1990. Kuwait fell after only two days of fighting and was declared the nineteenth province of Iraq.

Gulf War I (August 1990–March 1991)

- America invades the Middle East.
- Saddam Hussein is defeated and humiliated.
- The buffer (already bled dry) is shattered.
- Military victory goes to the US.
- Strategic gains go to Iran.

When the US launched Operation Desert Storm in January 1991, it did so *not* for moral or humanitarian reasons, regardless of its claims. The truth, asserts terrorism analyst Yossef Bodansky, is that the US went to war in Kuwait "to protect its access to cheap oil with no thought of the potential consequences for its allies in the region."[26]

Bodansky explains: "The West went to war for a pragmatic reason, not a principled one, particularly given that Iraq's historical claim to the territory of Kuwait is valid. Hence no one in the Muslim world—whether a supporter or enemy of Iraq—has ever accepted the declaration that the U.S.-led coalition was assembled to protect a small country from an aggressor."[27]

Further complicating matters was the fact that Saddam Hussein had long been a champion of the Arab masses, who loved and lauded him for his resistance to the US and his material support for the Palestinians. Consequently, Arab regimes were reluctant to support the US in a war against Saddam. But support the US they did, while suppressing Arab outrage through the usual means: ramping up repression and rolling out cash.

---

25. Bodansky, *The High Cost of Peace*, 31–38.
26. Ibid., 41.
27. Ibid., 41–42.

Though reluctant, Syria participated in the US-led coalition on the pretext of removing US justification for keeping their forces in the Gulf. Washington subsequently rewarded Syrian participation by accepting Syria's brutal October 1990 occupation of Beirut.[28] The US-allied Sunni Arab states also rewarded Syria by giving it the lion's share of the booty, including tanks, artillery, and combat vehicles captured from Iraq.[29]

On the other hand, despite having lost its revolutionary leader Ayatollah Rouhollah Mousavi Khomeini, who had died in June 1989, Iran maintained its stance of resistance—firmly opposing any US intervention in the Middle East. Tehran supported Saddam's invasion of US-backed Kuwait and agreed not to exploit the crisis to Iraq's detriment. On August 15, 1990, Saddam expressed his gratitude to Tehran by recognizing Iran's sovereignty over the disputed eastern portion of the Shatt al-Arab, which Iraq still occupied in violation of UN Security Council Resolution 598.[30] Subsequently, Iraqi forces withdrew from the disputed border territory over which Iraq and Iran had fought for eight long years at the cost of more than a million lives.

In Tehran, Iran's new supreme leader, Ayatollah Ali Hosseini Khamenei, declared that anyone who died resisting "American aggression, greed, plans, and policies in the Persian Gulf" would be considered a martyr. His decree had a huge impact on Shi'ites all around the Gulf.[31]

All through the 1980s—the Iran-Contra Scandal aside, the US had backed Saddam Hussein's Sunni dictatorship as a bulwark against the expansion of revolutionary Shi'ite Iran. Yet a mere two years after the end of the Iran-Iraq War, the US was preparing to strike that bulwark a devastating and humiliating blow. Fearing the consequences, the Arab regimes came up with a solution to avoid war. According to Bodansky, the Arabs proposed that Saddam be offered an honorable way out of Kuwait while being permitted to retain control of the oil fields.[32]

Moscow endorsed the Arab initiative, but the US would have none of it. Furious, Saddam responded by fanning the flames of Islamic jihad across the region. While the US was largely oblivious to these undercurrents, it couldn't help but notice that Arabs were defecting in large numbers, leaving the various Arab armies for Islamic jihadist outfits.

---

28. Ibid., 51.

29. Ibid., 75.

30. UN Security Council Resolution 598 (July 20, 1987) called for a ceasefire and for both sides to withdraw to the internationally recognized border—roughly down the middle of the river—as determined in the Algiers Accord (1975).

31. Bodansky, *The High Cost of Peace*, 43.

32. Ibid., 52.

In late February 1991, Saddam agreed to withdraw from Kuwait, but again the US would have none of it. Instead, the US launched a ground offensive: Operation Desert Storm. Scenes of massive devastation were broadcast around the Arab world, further radicalizing the Arab masses and fuelling the Islamist cause.

Despite its aggression against Saddam Hussein, the US still wanted him to remain in power. It did not want to see Iraq fragmented or Iraq's Shi'ite majority empowered— it still considered a Shi'ite ascent contrary to the interests of America and her Gulf Arab allies.

Consequently, when Iraqi Kurds and Shi'ites rose up against Saddam Hussein in March and April of 1991 with the expectation that the US would help them topple the cruel and belligerent dictator, the US stepped back and watched as Saddam ordered the protesters mercilessly crushed.

Watching from the sidelines, the Sunni Gulf Arab monarchies were greatly relieved that Saddam was being permitted to repress Iraqi Shi'ism and remain in control. The last thing the House of Saud wanted was a Shi'ite ascendency in Iraq that could energize Saudi Arabia's long-suffering Shi'ites—concentrated along the oil-rich Persian Gulf—and destabilize the Saudi state.

Also watching from the sidelines were millions of Iranians, their Shi'ite zeal boiling as Saddam's Republican Guard massacred Shi'ites and desecrated their holy shrines in Najaf and Karbala. Iraqi Shi'ite clerics issued fatwas against Saddam Hussein, further agitating Iranian Shi'ites who were chafing at the bit to assist their co-religionists in Iraq.

Despite all this, and regardless of the fact that Tehran had deployed some 20,000 to 30,000 non-Iranian Shi'ite troops (mostly Iraqi nationals /Arab Shi'ites) to the border, the regime in Tehran was reluctant to intervene. "In the end," writes Bodansky, "Tehran decided it would rather have a stable—albeit ruthless and anti-Shi'ite—government in Baghdad than chaos and fratricidal violence," that could draw in Iranian Shi'ites and spill over into Iran. And so "Tehran quietly notified Saddam that Iran was prepared to help sustain his regime if Iraq would join the Iranian-Syrian axis."[33]

Even as the conflict had raged, Iran had been making plans for a post-war Middle East. The war had pushed Saddam Hussein into the Iranian orbit, but Tehran was still reluctant to trust him completely. However, by December 1991, Saddam was negotiating with Syria's President Hafez al-Assad, "proposing cooperation against 'common enemies.'"[34] Discussions were held to propose ways and means of evading crippling US sanctions.

33. Ibid., 70–71.
34. Ibid., 80.

By April 1992, Iraq had recognized Iranian strategic leadership; goods from Syria and Lebanon were available in Iraqi markets; and Iran was facilitating the delivery of military material to Iraq from China and North Korea.[35]

Concerned that Iraq's Kurds and Shi'ites might make another attempt at revolution, Saddam spent much of the decade after Gulf War I constructing "an entire underground apparatus for counterrevolution," establishing safe houses and weapons caches that included bomb-making materials throughout the country. Intended for use against domestic enemies, they would instead be used against foreign invaders.[36]

Saddam also licensed "a grey market . . . in effect, a state-tolerated organized crime network." Intended to evade sanctions, this would instead be used to fund insurgency and terror against US and allied occupying forces.[37]

Most critically, in an effort to boost his Islamic credentials, the formerly anti-Islamist Saddam facilitated the Islamization of Iraq. However, while he flirted with Islamists in the belief that he could co-opt them or at least win their favor, he also knew they had to be watched. To that end, Saddam funneled high-level Baathist officers into the mosques. Intended as spies and subversives, these officers would later emerge as dedicated Salafists.[38] Although Saddam intended to appease Islamists and win the support of jihadists through Islamization, in effect he facilitated radicalization. And as Islamization and radicalization progressed apace, this in turn triggered a new trend: the Christian exodus. Iraq was changing, and Christians with means were emigrating.

Iran and the Art of Deterrence

> Deterrence | *noun* | de·ter·rence: the act of making someone decide not to do something; the act of preventing a particular act or behavior from happening.
>
> [In] politics: the policy of developing a lot of military power so that other countries will not attack your country.[39]

---

35. Ibid.
36. Weiss and Hassan, *ISIS*, 21.
37. Ibid., 22.
38. Ibid., 22–24.
39. Merriam Webster Dictionary, http://www.merriam-webster.com/dictionary/

After Gulf War I, Iran was more convinced than ever that the New World Order promoted by the administration of President George Bush senior was an imperialistic vision that threatened every resource-rich region of the Middle East. As far as Tehran was concerned, the only way to guarantee the survival of the Islamic republic was through deterrence. To that end, Tehran began negotiating with China, North Korea, and Pakistan for the purpose of acquiring nuclear weapons capabilities.

Through 1991, as the Soviet Union was tearing apart, Iranian intelligence operatives scoured Central Asia for weapons, technologies, and nuclear material. The Iranians struck gold in mid-1991, when Kazakhstan offered them access to soviet nuclear weapons.

"In December [1991]," writes Bodansky, "the Kazakh deal came to fruition, and Iran made its first purchase of nuclear weapons. The deal included two 40-kiloton warheads for a SCUD-type surface-to-surface ballistic missile; one aerial bomb of the type carried by a MiG-27; and one 152-mm nuclear artillery shell. These weapons reached operational status in late January 1992 and full operational status a few months later."[40]

In just a few months, Iran had taken massive strides towards fulfilling its grand strategy of establishing an Iranian arc of influence stretching from Tehran to the Mediterranean and establishing Iranian hegemony over the Gulf, and indeed, over the entire Middle East.

By early July 1992, continues Bodansky, "the strategic axis from the Mediterranean to the Indus was a reality," and Tehran was urging the Gulf States to fall in behind Iranian leadership for the purpose of evicting the US from the Near East.[41] Though the balance of power appeared to be holding—albeit only just—in reality it had already shifted; the Iran-led Shi'ite ascendancy had begun. And with the belligerent, anti-Semitic clerical regime in Tehran now in possession of nuclear weapons, it could advance its agenda across the region whilst remaining essentially untouchable. Such is the value of nuclear weapons: deterrence.

The outcome of Gulf War I might have been a military victory for the US-led coalition, but it handed Iran significant strategic gains. Through its actions, the US had undermined, if not shattered, the Iraqi buffer while pouring fuel on the fires of Islamic jihad.

Bodansky comments that "even the most pro-Western officials considered the defeat of Iraq to be the beginning of the real war."[42]

---

deterrence.

    40. Bodansky, *The High Cost of Peace*, 77.
    41. Ibid., 82.
    42. Ibid., 67.

Gulf War II

- Invasion and regime change.
- Occupation and resistance.
- The Shia Crescent becomes a reality.

On March 16, 2003, as the drums of war pounded and the US prepared to invade Iraq—ostensibly for the purpose of disarming Iraq of its WMDs, a Syrian delegation led by President Bashar al-Assad was meeting in Tehran with Iranian leaders including Ayatollah Ali Khamenei and President Mohammad Khatami. According to Bodansky, "Khamenei opined that 'changing the geopolitical situation in the region was far beyond America's capabilities and resources.' Khamenei surmised that while the United States should be expected to occupy Iraq, 'the resistance put up by various nations will ultimately inflict the greatest blow to America and result in the disintegration of that country's status as a superpower.'"[43] To hasten that end, Axis of Resistance powers Syria and Iran immediately began expediting the flow of thousands of jihadists through their territories into Iraq, to fight the US and render Iraq ungovernable so as to bog the US down in a debilitating quagmire.[44]

Operation Iraqi Freedom commenced on March 21, 2003, with the bombing of Baghdad. Having already been decimated a decade earlier, the Iraqi military had little left to offer. Opting to live rather than die fighting a losing battle, multitudes of Republican Guards simply ripped off their uniforms and melted back into the Sunni population. With US forces facing little resistance, the regime was quickly toppled.

As Iraqi security disintegrated, Damascus came to Baghdad's aid and facilitated the movement out of Iraq of weapons (hidden in secret caches along the Euphrates in western Iraq) and senior Iraqi leaders wanted by the US. America warned Damascus that if it did not stop "behaving badly", Washington would have to reassess its policy towards Syria. Damascus was unfazed until the Beirut *Daily Star* quoted CIA operative Robert Baer as saying that the Pentagon had "pretty much decided to go after Syria." Fearing a US attack, Assad appealed to Arab leaders who in turn brokered a deal with the Americans that would see war averted in exchange for the return of roughly six "big names" who were subsequently shoved back over the border into the arms of American operatives. As 2004 was an election year, the White House decided that no further action should be taken as any

---

43. Bodansky, *The Secret History of the Iraq War*, 249–250.
44. Ibid., 250.

escalation or expansion of the war would hurt President George W. Bush's chance of reelection. Instead, the focus would be on peacemaking, achievement, and the illusion of victory.[45]

On May 1, 2003, George W. Bush delivered a speech on the deck of the aircraft carrier USS *Abraham Lincoln*. With a banner behind him reading "Mission Accomplished", he declared the end of combat operations in Iraq. The US and her allies had prevailed, he said, and their efforts would now turn to reconstruction. "The tyrant has fallen and Iraq is free."[46]

In toppling the Iraqi regime, the US administration of President G. W. Bush achieved precisely the outcome the administration of President Bush senior had determined in 1991 was *not* in the interests of either the US or her Arab allies.

Feel-good scenes flooded our television screens as Iraq's long-repressed majority Shi'ites celebrated their liberation openly in the streets. Iraq's Sunnis would not be celebrating, though, for their world had just been turned upside down. Compounding their trauma, the reckless de-Baathification process saw multitudes of largely secular/nominal Sunnis lose their status and livelihoods purely on account of their links with the secular Baath Party. Unemployed, humiliated, and disenfranchised, Iraqi Sunnis lurched instead towards resistance, radicalization, and civil war.

What makes this situation particularly distressing is the knowledge that it did not have to be this way. Saddam could have been removed without upending the entire system.

In late 2002, as Washington mounted its case for a war to remove Saddam Hussein, Moscow—which had "long-term involvement in and intimate knowledge of Saddam Hussein's Iraq"—objected. President Putin advised the G. W. Bush administration that instead of going after Saddam, they should concentrate on the real sponsors of Islamic terror, specifically Pakistan and Saudi Arabia, and put an end to the Saudi funding of Wahhabi extremism.[47]

Washington would have none of it.

Bodansky explains:

> Russian experts warned that the problem in Iraq was not just Saddam and his weapons of mass destruction, but rather the prevailing radical militant trends. They urged the Americans to be ready to deal with radicalized populations, Sunni Islamist militancy, a radical Shiite population under Iranian influence,

---

45. Ibid., 259–265.
46. "Bush makes historic speech aboard warship."
47. Bodansky, *The Secret History of the Iraq War*, 80–81.

the flow of al-Qaeda operatives, and Kurdish-Turkish and Turkman-Arab hatred—all of which were likely to intensify in reaction to an American invasion of Iraq. "The insistence of the administration on connecting the war against Iraq to the war on terrorism not only endangers and undercuts the American achievements to date, and these are great, in the global war against terrorism, but actually creates and opens new venues for terrorism," opined a Russian expert, reflecting the Kremlin's position.[48]

Despite being desperate for Russian intelligence on Iraq, the US was not willing to guarantee that a post-Saddam regime would recognize either Iraq's outstanding debt to Russia or Russia's existing oil contracts in Iraq. This caused considerable alarm in Moscow.

In November 2002, the Russian National Security Council (RNSC), which maintained voluminous intelligence on Iraq, suggested that Moscow engineer a "pre-emptive coup" in Baghdad that would topple Saddam while protecting Moscow's economic interests. A detailed plan was drafted with the utmost seriousness.[49]

Then, writes Bodansky, the Russian leadership made a cardinal error. "On behalf of the Kremlin, Russian intelligence notified the CIA of its plans, to make sure that no U.S. asset was killed and no U.S. intelligence activities were thwarted as a result of the Russian-inspired coup."[50]

Washington would have none of it.

In fact, writes Bodansky, Washington went so far as to betray the Russians, leaking their plans to Egyptian intelligence with the full knowledge that Baghdad would be forewarned. When the Russians learned of the betrayal, they quickly shelved their plans, along with any obligation to share intelligence with Washington.

In early February 2003, in a last-ditch effort to avoid war, Russian former prime minister Yevgeny Primakov flew into Baghdad to try and convince Saddam Hussein to hand over all his WMD in a proper manner. In meetings over February 22–24, Primakov—who was fluent in Arabic—outlined a plan designed to remove any grounds for a US invasion. Endorsed by Russia's President Vladimir Putin, the plan mandated disarmament and a transfer of power, while also making provision for sanctuary and supervised protection of regime personnel, as well as immunity from war crimes charges. The plan impressed Turkey and the Arabs as it retained the balance

48. Ibid., 81.
49. Ibid., 82.
50. Ibid., 82–83.

of power, thereby keeping the Kurds and the Persians in check, and they were almost certain Saddam would accept it.[51]

Washington, however, would have none of it.

The decision had been made. The US would demonstrate its power and resolve by invading Iraq, overthrowing a belligerent dictatorship, and establishing a democracy in Baghdad more amenable to US interests.

And in December 2004, as US-allied King Abdullah of Jordan watched it all unfold, he gasped at the realization that Ayatollah Khomeini's dream of a Shia Crescent over the Middle East was becoming a reality.

Syria: The Weak Link

Syria's place in the Shia Crescent is far more complex. While Iraq is majority Shi'ite (around 65 percent) and Arab Shi'ites have a long history of friendly ties to Persian Shi'ites, Syria, on the other hand, is only around one percent Shi'ite and 75 percent Sunni, making its position in the Shia Crescent far more delicate.

Considering Syria had been dominated by Sunni Muslims for over a millennium, how on earth did it ever come to be part of the Shia Crescent?

The Rise of the Alawites

About seven percent of Syrians belong to the Alawite sect of Islam. Like Baha'is and Ahmadiyyas, Alawites revere Muhammad as the founder of Islam, but follow a subsequent prophet while still regarding themselves as Muslims. As far as fundamentalist Islam is concerned, anyone who holds that someone other than Muhammad is the supreme and final messenger of Allah is a heretic and an infidel, worthy of death.

When Shi'ites, Ismailis, and other non-Sunni sects, including Druze (3 percent) and Alawites (7 percent), are added together, non-Sunni Muslims comprise about 13 percent of Syria's population. Meanwhile, about 10 percent of Syrians are Christian, mostly Armenians and indigenous Assyrians.[52] Around 75 percent of Syrians are Sunnis, and while most are Arabs, a Kurdish minority (around 10 percent) exists in the northeast.[53]

---

51. Ibid.,149–150.

52. Assyrians are also known as Syriacs or Chaldeans, although the latter is more a denomination distinction than a racial one.

53. Bhalla, "Making sense of the Syrian Crisis."

The Alawites diverged from the mainstream Twelver (also known as Imami) branch of Shi'ite Islam in the ninth century under the leadership of Ibn Nusayr, which is why they were long known as Nusayris. To legitimize the slaughter of Alawites, Sunni jihadists routinely refer to them as Nusayris to emphasize their divergent and heretical nature. They are also sometimes referred to as "little Christians", for they share many things in common with Christians. While Alawites reject many Islamic practices—such as the call to prayer, attendance at mosque, observance of Sharia, making a pilgrimage to Mecca, and prohibition of alcohol—they celebrate Christmas and revere many Christian saints. Their main link to Shi'ism is their reverence of the fourth caliph, Ali—Muhammad's cousin and son-in-law, leader of the Shi'ites. In order to avoid crippling discrimination and harsh persecution, Alawites often practiced *taqqiya*, the Islamic practice of concealing one's faith through deception. Under Sunni domination, the Nusayris/Alawites existed as poor, marginalized, persecuted peasants and serfs (slaves)—something else they had in common with Christians.

In 1920, after World War I, Syria was made a French mandate. As a counterbalance to Sunni power, France moved to empower the religious minorities, specifically the Nusayris. To that end, France persuaded the Nusayris to change their name to Alawites to emphasize the sect's relationship to the Prophet Muhammad's son-in-law and its link to Shi'ism.

Under French colonial rule, the Christians were freed from their *dhimmitude* and religious minorities were able to enjoy opportunity, liberty, and equality before the law for the first time in nearly 1300 years. Most significantly, in order to dilute Sunni hegemony, the French opened up the Syrian security apparatus to allow for an influx of Alawites into military, police, and intelligence posts.

When the French mandate ended in 1946 and Syria was declared independent, the Sunni elite took their revenge and the Alawites suffered fierce Islamic resistance and purges. Middle East expert Reva Bhall elaborates:

> The Sunnis quickly reasserted their political prowess in postcolonial Syria and worked to sideline Alawites from the government, businesses and courts. However, the Sunnis also made a fateful error in overlooking the heavy Alawite presence in the armed forces. While the Sunnis occupied the top posts within the military, the lower ranks were filled by rural Alawites who either could not afford the military exemption fees paid by most of the Sunni elite or simply saw military service as a decent means of employment given limited options. The seed was thus

planted for an Alawite-led military coup while the Sunni elite were preoccupied with their own internal struggles.[54]

Another significant factor in the reversing of Sunni-Alawite fortunes in Syria was the establishment in 1947 of the secular, socialist, Arab nationalist Baath Party. Syria's minorities embraced the Baath Party, as it gave them a political vehicle around which to organize. However, it also caused huge fissures within the Sunni camp, dividing modernizing pro-secular Sunnis (mostly urban, educated, business-orientated, nominal Muslims) from the traditionalists (mostly rural, madrassa-educated, devoutly religious, conservative Islamists).

"In 1963," writes Reva Bhalla,

> Baathist power was cemented through a military coup led by President Amin al-Hafiz, a Sunni general, who discharged many ranking Sunni officers, thereby providing openings for hundreds of Alawites to fill top-tier military positions during the 1963–1965 period, on the grounds of [their] being opposed to Arab unity. This measure tipped the balance in favour of Alawite officers who staged a coup in 1966 and for the first time placed Damascus in the hands of the Alawites. The 1960s also saw the beginning of a reversal of Syria's sectarian rural-urban divide, as the Baath party encouraged Alawite migration into the cities to displace the Sunnis.[55]

But the Alawites were fractious, leading to coups and counter coups. Eventually, in 1970, Defense Minister General Hafez al-Assad seized power and united the Alawite clans. The al-Assad family stacked the security forces with loyal clansmen and built strong patronage networks amongst their allies—the Druze, the Christians, and the modernizing Sunni military and business elite. The state assumed control of religious affairs and repressed all expression of political Islam. Dissent was not permitted; stability was paramount. Syria's MB, which had been founded in 1942 as an extension of the MB in Egypt and had been active in Syrian politics since 1946, was banned in 1964.[56]

Though the Alawites held the reins of power, nationally the Sunnis were still the majority and regionally the Alawites were still regarded as heretics. Perceiving the need for regional allies, Syrian President Hafez al-Assad forged close bonds with Iranian-born Lebanese cleric Musa al-Sadr,

---

54. Ibid.
55. Ibid.
56. "Syria in Crisis: The Muslim Brotherhood in Syria."

Lebanon's most prominent Shi'ite leader. A vocal advocate of increasing Shi'ite power in Lebanon and waging war against Israel, Musa al-Sadr recognized an opportunity when he saw one. In 1973, al-Sadr issued a fatwa recognizing Lebanon's Alawites as Shi'ites, which paved the way for relations to develop between Lebanon's Shi'ites and geostrategically significant Syria.[57]

And so Syria, though less than one percent Shi'ite and with a 75 percent Sunni majority, was drawn into the Shi'ite fold. While this was a coup for the Alawites—providing them with security courtesy of regional allies—it was an even greater coup for Lebanon's Shi'ites, who gained significant strategic depth.

In 1980, Hafez al-Assad formed a strategic alliance with Iran. While Assad was willing to support Iran in its war against Iraq, he was no fan of Khomeini or his Islamic revolution. As we shall see, that did not stop the alliance from developing to a whole new level in 1982.

The Rise of Hezbollah (Hizb Allah/Party of God)

Tehran saw the Lebanese civil war (1975–1990) as an opportunity, indeed, another "godsend", to export Islamic revolution and resistance—this time into Lebanon. Wary of Iran's intentions, Hafez al-Assad initially allowed only a limited number of Iranian Revolutionary Guards to transit through Syria.

Then, in June 1982, at a critical juncture of the Lebanese Civil War with Israeli forces pursuing Palestinian militants deep inside Syrian-occupied Lebanon, Israeli Defense Minister Ariel Sharon ordered attacks on anti-Israeli Syrian air-to-air missile sites in Lebanon's Bekaa Valley. Though the Syrian air force responded, the daylong dogfight saw Israeli pilots knock eighty-two Syrian jets out of the sky without a single loss of their own.[58] In response, Syrian President Hafez al-Assad opened the floodgates for Iranian Revolutionary Guards to flow through Damascus into Lebanon. "Within three years," writes Crist, "this Iranian delegation [of 800 Revolutionary Guards] united several disparate Shia fighters into the Islamic Republic's biggest foreign policy success: Hezbollah, or Party of God."[59]

---

57. Sindawi, "The Shiite Turn in Syria." Al-Sadr's *fatwa* served to consolidate the 1972 *fatwa* from Ayatollah Hasan Mahdi al-Shirazi (1935–80), an Iranian-Iraqi Shia exiled to Lebanon who was also close to Hafez Al-Assad. Al-Shirazi had also decreed that the Alawites should be considered legitimate Twelver Shi'ite Muslims.

58. Crist, *The Twilight War*, 110.

59. Ibid., 123.

Since then, Iranian Revolutionary Guards have served alongside the all-Alawite Syrian Republican Guards to protect the Assad regime. Hafez al-Assad also opened the door to Iranian Shi'ite missionaries. Subsequently, a number of Sunni families that had originally been Shi'ite, but had converted to Sunni Islam in order to escape discrimination and persecution, reverted to Shi'ism. Most converts to Shi'ism were, however, from Alawite and Ismaili backgrounds.[60]

Relations with Iran grew even stronger after Bashar al-Assad came to power in 2000. Hundreds of thousands of Iranian and Iraqi Shi'ites have since been naturalized as Syrian citizens. Iran has also sponsored the restoration and preservation of significant Shia shrines and tombs in Syria, the most significant being the Shrine of Sayyidah Zaynab. In the subsequent decade, the number of pilgrims visiting Syria's Shia Shrines increased ten-fold.

Nothing, however, drew Syrian Sunnis to the Iran-led, Shi'ite-dominated Axis of Resistance as did Hezbollah's 2006 war against Israel. In April 2007, *The New York Times* reported that "The Middle East is abuzz with talk of 'Shiitization.' Since the war in Lebanon last summer, newspapers, TV news channels and Web sites in Egypt, Saudi Arabia and elsewhere have reported that Sunnis, taken with Hezbollah's charismatic Shiite leader Hassan Nasrallah and his group's 'resistance' to Israel, were converting to Shiite Islam." Although *The New York Times* noted that "Much of the buzz is surely propaganda from the region's Sunni governments, which are known to whip up fears of Shiite plots when it suits them,"[61] the article had picked up on a trend: radicalized, disenchanted Sunnis were gravitating towards the more fundamentalist and belligerent Axis of Resistance.

Despite Damascus' solid position within the Shia Crescent/Axis of Resistance and evidence of "Shiitization" (which is marginal at best), Syria remained a Sunni majority state where many Sunnis still dreamed of restoring Sunni hegemony. Indeed, Syria might have been the Shia Crescent's most valuable strategic asset, but as a Sunni-majority state, Syria was also its weakest link.

Iran Rises

- The Sunni response.
- Sectarian civil war in Iraq.
- Nuclear deal confirms Iranian power.

60. Sindawi, "The Shiite Turn in Syria."
61. Tabler, "Catalytic Converters."

In 2005, Iraq's first democratic elections resulted in a pro-Iran parliament and the subsequent appointment of Iranian puppet Nuri al-Maliki as president. All the pieces of the Shia Crescent were now firmly slotted into place—Tehran, Baghdad, Damascus and Hezbollah—to form an arc of Iranian influence. Ayatollah Khomeini's "road to Jerusalem" was complete.

If this generated extreme anxiety amongst the Middle East's US-allied Sunni Arab dictators, then the events of late 2007 would send them absolutely apoplectic!

The regional struggle for supremacy escalated markedly through 2005, as it became increasingly evident that the US would not achieve its goal of establishing a pro-US democracy in Iraq and Khomeini's dream of a Shia Crescent had become a reality. Sunni resistance would be fierce; sectarian tensions soared.

Full-scale sectarian civil war erupted in Iraq in February 2006 when Shi'ites retaliated after AQI bombed of one of Shia Islam's most sacred shrines, the gold-domed al-Askari Mosque in Samarra (125 km north of Baghdad). Violence quickly spun out of control as Shia death squads retaliated to every AQI attack in a spiraling cycle of violence that saw the death toll skyrocket.

Struggling in Afghanistan, bogged down in Iraq, overextended and hemorrhaging funds, the US was by mid-2007 desperate to see an end to Iraq's bloody sectarian conflict. All the US wanted was to get out of Iraq with some dignity. Cognizant of this, the Iranians resolved to exploit the situation to their benefit. They were also acutely aware that 2008 was an election year in the US—a year in which the US administration would be not only profoundly distracted, but desperately keen to present the electorate with positive images and narratives of achievement and success. What's more, a retiring US president might be considering his legacy. As far as Iran's mullahs were concerned, this was the perfect time to consolidate their strategic gains.[62]

Aware that Iran would go to any lengths to gain regional hegemony, the Saudis brokered a deal with the regime in Tehran. According to terrorism analyst Yossef Bodansky, the Saudis agreed to accept Iranian hegemony and support Iran's efforts to squeeze the US out of the region, in exchange for Iran recognizing the House of Saud and accepting Saudi Arabia's territorial integrity.[63]

In August 2007, Tehran and Baghdad developed strategies aimed at delivering the US their desired "achievement" while still maintaining

---

62. Bodansky, "Washington's Deal with Iran."
63. Ibid.

control of the overall regional dynamic. Iran agreed to reduce anti-US violence, restrict the flow of weapons, and rein in the Shi'ite militias to break the cycle of violence. That, it was agreed, would pacify Iraq enough to enable the US to withdraw with dignity and the illusion of success.

The US Accepts Tehran's Terms

In a January 2008 analysis, terrorism analyst Yossef Bodansky revealed: "In early September 2007, as official Washington was preparing for the crucial report to Congress by Ambassador Ryan Crocker and Gen. David Petraeus, commander of the Multi-National Force–Iraq (MNF-I), the White House was apprised of Tehran's 'proposal' and decided to give it a try."[64]

By mid-November 2007, violence and US losses in Iraq had dropped to pre-February 2006 levels. Though the White House attributed the success to the US troop "surge", in reality, Iran had stemmed the violence pursuant to a US withdrawal.

By this time, the US government had conceded that its original goal of establishing a pro-US administration in a democratic Iraq was no longer realistic. What's more, it knew that little to nothing could be done about it. The US could not put Iran out of action, nor could it withstand the Shi'ite retaliation that would result from any US missile strike on Iranian facilities. The truth was sinking in: the war in Iraq had already been lost, and Iran was emerging as the ascendant regional hegemonic power.

Over November 29–30, 2007, Iraqi Islamic Council Chairman Abdul-Aziz al-Hakim met with US leaders in Washington to deliver an "olive branch and veiled ultimatum." Bodansky elaborates: "According to Hakim, Tehran now dominated the course of events and was offering Washington a choice between honourable withdrawal or cataclysmic regional war on Tehran's terms."[65] United States President G. W. Bush accepted the Iranian offer. Iran would quell the violence pursuant to a US withdrawal from Iraq. The US would claim success despite Iran securing strategic gains.

When Hakim arrived back in Baghdad on December 2, 2007, he immediately notified the Iranians, who sent emissaries to Baghdad to gather information from him. Tehran accepted that while the deal with the US administration was to remain secret, the US would send a signal designed to assure the Iranians that the threat of a US missile strike was over.

Without wasting time, the Iranians forewarned the Sunni Arab regimes to expect a very big and surprising announcement out of Washington. The

64. Ibid.
65. Ibid.

Emir of Qatar responded by immediately inviting Iranian President Mahmoud Ahmadinejad to attend the Gulf Co-operation Council (GCC) summit over December 3–4, in Doha, Qatar. Arab journalist Omran Salman commented on the significance of this by noting that the GCC—which comprises Bahrain, Kuwait, Oman, Qatar, Saudi Arabia, and the United Arab Emirates—was "founded in 1981 with the fundamental goal of standing up to the danger presented by Iran to the states of the region."[66]

Iranian opposition sources told Bodansky that Iranian President Ahmadinejad met with US Secretary of Defense Robert Gates in Doha just prior to the commencement of the GCC summit, to reaffirm their understanding "that the US would recognise Tehran's hegemony over all the areas surrounding Iran in return for stable flow of oil and gas from and via these regions, as well as a 'secret non-aggression pact' between the US military and the Iran-sponsored insurgent forces that should lead to a US honourable withdrawal from Iraq."[67]

On December 3, 2007, as Ahmadinejad was glorying in his position as the first non-Arab guest to attend the GCC, the announcement from Washington came through. According to the latest National Intelligence Estimate (NIE), the US was confident that Iran had halted its nuclear weapons program.[68] This assessment, which amounted to a total reversal of the US position vis-à-vis Iran, meant that the US no longer had any legitimate grounds for considering a missile strike on Iran.

On December 5, 2007, Iranian President Ahmadinejad publically gloated that the Iranian nation had achieved a great victory.

On December 6, Gates flew to Baghdad, where he delivered new orders to the troops while General David Petraeus praised Shia leader Moqtada al-Sadr (a radical, "firebrand", vehemently anti-American cleric) for his efforts at restoring stability.

In Iran, security forces were informed of their critical role in stabilizing Iraq and stopping the fratricidal violence so as to facilitate a US withdrawal. Baghdad made it clear that the US would not be permitted to maintain military bases in Iraq. Rather, Iraq's security would be maintained through engagement with its neighbors.

On December 12, 2007, King Abdullah of Saudi Arabia formerly invited Iran's President Ahmadinejad to take part in the hajj ceremony in Mecca. This was the first time in the history of Saudi-Iranian relations that

---

66. MEMRI, "The Era of Iranian Hegemony in the Middle East Is Upon Us."
67. Bodansky, "Washington's Deal with Iran."
68. "Key Judgments From a National Intelligence Estimate on Iran's Nuclear Activity."

the Saudi king had invited the president of the Islamic Republic of Iran to make the pilgrimage to Mecca.

Arab journalist Omran Salman noted: "Saudi King 'Abdallah bin 'Abd Al-'Aziz . . . hastened to send an official invitation to Ahmadinejad to perform the *hajj* and thus become the first Iranian president to perform the *hajj* while still in office . . . It doesn't take much to see, that all this is a result of the uneasiness felt by the Gulf regimes friendly to the US at Iran's increasing power and the US's retreating power."[69]

When Ahmadinejad performed the hajj on December 17, 2007, he was afforded all the privileges of an honored guest. According to Bodansky, Ahmadinejad met on the sidelines with a host of radical and terrorist Arab organizations invited to Mecca by the Saudi regime. Having travelled to Mecca under the guise of performing the hajj, they met with Ahmadinejad and key Gulf Arab leaders to discuss the new reality in the Middle East, particularly in the Persian Gulf. In Washington, meanwhile, the Bush administration was boasting of its achievements in Iraq.

It is no wonder that observers like myself watched the Iran-US nuclear talks of 2015 with a profound sense of déjà vu.

The Post-US Greater Middle East

Yossef Bodanksy concluded his January 2008 analysis by offering a forward glance over the "post-US Greater Middle East." He predicted that US-allied Arab Sunni dictators would be irreversibly weakened, while the elite of the religious clans beholden to Iran would be empowered. He also predicted the rise of militant Shi'ism and the empowerment of jihadist forces in the Sunni heartland of Jazira (Mesopotamia). Furthermore, he warned that regional powers (neo-Ottoman Turkey,[70] Mahdivist Iran,[71] and the Arabs) were already posturing, keen to fill the power vacuum left in the wake of the US withdrawal.

"This cataclysmic struggle, which I believe will dwarf all regional wars to date, has barely begun," he said.[72]

---

69. MEMRI, "The Era of Iranian Hegemony in the Middle East Is Upon Us."

70. Neo-Ottomanism is a political ideology that aspires to empire and promotes greater political influence in and ties between Turkey and the regions formerly part of the Ottoman Empire.

71. The Mahdivists believe that the world is on the brink of the End of Days, and consequently, the return of the Islamic Messiah, the Mahdi, is imminent.

72. Bodansky, "Washington's Deal with Iran."

A Financial Crisis Seals the Deal

In August–September 2008, the US housing market collapsed, triggering the Global Financial Crisis. In the blink of eye, US economic leverage evaporated.

Already critically weakened by events in Iraq, the Middle East's US-allied Sunni Arab dictators would never be able to survive the loss of US economic aid. Without US backing, US-allied Sunni Arab dictators such as Egypt's Hosni Mubarak would struggle to maintain the supply of amenities and staples such as oil and bread to their disaffected, restive, and increasingly radical populations.

Without US support, these unpopular dictators would never survive the rising tide of anger, especially in this age of ever-increasing openness where news and rage can be shared in real time and mass responses organized in a heartbeat via social media.

With the stage set, the clock was now ticking down to the next great drama: the "Arab Spring."

— 6 —

The "Arab Spring"

According to the Western narrative, the "Arab Spring" was a historic movement in which the Arab masses rose up in popular revolutions in pursuit of liberal, Western-style democracy. Furthermore, in the subsequent struggles—described as being between totalitarian tyrants and the democratic masses—good (i.e., "democracy") was destined to prevail. Consequently, Western governments determined that in order to be on "the right side of history", they would throw their support behind the masses.

Though it sounds fantastic, this narrative is complete and utter rubbish.

Being anti-government does not necessarily equate to being pro-liberal or pro-Western-style democracy. The forces that rose against the Arab dictators were hugely diverse, comprising human rights advocates and free speech activists, right through to hardline pro-Sharia, Salafi/Wahhabi Islamic fundamentalists. The only thing uniting the protesters was their desire for change.

Considering how it all turned out, perhaps it is time to put aside the false Western narrative and take a fresh look at what really happened in the so-called Arab Spring.

Only in Tunisia, where the Arab Spring started, was the uprising spontaneous. And the cry of the protesters was not for "democracy" as much as it was for basic human dignity.

While each subsequent uprising was unique in regards to the reasons for the uprising, the makeup of the players involved, and the role of the military, they were alike in that dark forces were ready to exploit the unrest for their own personal and political gain.

Indeed, it did not take long for the Arab Spring to morph into a Sunni intifada with regional geopolitical implications.

Yearning for a brighter, more equitable, just, and secure future—even for a liberal, Western-style democracy—Middle Eastern Christians featured highly in the early protests, particularly in Egypt and Syria where they have long formed a significant minority. But as the MB moved in and hijacked the movement, Christian anticipation turned to anxiety, even antipathy. For Middle Eastern Christians knew—courtesy of their long historical memory—that any shift away from secularism back towards an Islamic order would benefit only Muslims at the expense of Christians. What's more, after a generation of Wahhabi radicalization courtesy of Saudi Arabia, a return to the Islamic order would spell not merely discrimination, subjugation, persecution, and *dhimmitude*, but also massacre, exile, and probably genocide.

Christian leaders warned the West, but to no avail. Being mostly of the opinion that Islam is inherently benign, even peaceable (a sort of oriental version of Christianity) and that humanity, which is on a path of continuous linear progress, is inherently good[1] (so that all that is required for selfless benevolence to flourish is liberty), Western leaders scoffed at their warnings and turned a deaf ear to their pleas.

Once Upon a Time in Tunisia

Mohamed Bouazizi was only three years old when his father died. Though his mother remarried, her second husband suffered health problems and was unable to find regular work. The family lived in Sidi Bouzid, an impoverished town 300 km south of the Tunisian capital, Tunis.[2]

When he was only ten years old, Mohamed started a small business selling fresh fruits and vegetables. Every day he would take his cart to the market and load it up with fresh produce before heading out with his groceries and scales to sell the produce through the streets. When Mohamed was not out working, he was at school. Life was difficult, but his produce business provided his struggling family with income they desperately needed.

Being incredibly poor, Mohamed could not afford the fee to license his cart. Consequently, he was routinely bullied and intimidated by police who, without any compassion, empathy or respect, looked down on him and saw him simply as a soft target.

---

1. The belief that humanity is inherently good is a theological error based on human arrogance. Unique amongst all world religions, the Bible is unique in teaching that while God created everything good—including human beings—humanity freely chose to reject God, and as a consequence it is corrupted. That does not mean that human beings are pure evil, it just means that we have a natural tendency or inclination towards sin (i.e., lust, hate, greed, pride, selfishness, covetousness, etc.). Though we resist being called "sinners," we still recognise that selfless benevolence is "extraordinary", and that greed and lust etc. are "only natural."

2. Ryan, "The Tragic Life of a Street Vendor"; Ryan, "How Tunisia's Revolution Began."

After completing his secondary schooling, nineteen-year-old Mohamed opted out of studies, choosing instead to work fulltime. If he could earn more, he reasoned, his five younger siblings would have the chance to stay in school. In pursuit of better wages, Mohamed applied to join the army, only to be rejected. In fact, Mohamed applied for many jobs, but with high unemployment, all he ever managed to get for his efforts was rejection. All the while, he continued to take his wooden cart to the market every morning, load it up with produce, and then walk it more than 2 km back to the local *souq* (market). It was hard work; he was saving for a pickup truck.

As if life was not difficult enough, Mohamed was bullied by police on an almost-daily basis. Occasionally they would confiscate his produce and even his scales, or they would fine him for running a produce stall without a permit. In mid-2010, police sent a fine to his house for four hundred dinars: the equivalent of two months' earnings.

On the morning of December 17, 2010, a policewoman named Fedya Hamdi confronted Mohamed (now 26) as he was on his way to the market. She started by confiscating his unlicensed cart, and when he tried to pay the ten-dinar fine (a sum equivalent to a good day's earnings), she refused to accept it. Instead, she slapped him, spat in his face, and hurled offensive and humiliating insults at him, slurs intended to hurt the honor of his dead father.

Mohamed could not afford to lose his cart, so he went to the provincial headquarters to make a complaint. They sent him away, refusing to even see him. At 11:30 a.m., the desperate and despairing young man returned to the elegant white building, poured fuel over himself, and set himself on fire.

Massively burned yet still alive, Mohamed was hospitalized in a critical state.

Dhafer Salhi, a local lawyer who witnessed Mohamed's self-immolation, petitioned the head of police, urging him to meet with the young man's family, immediately, so as to defuse the anger on the street. Salhi warned the police that if they didn't address the situation, the whole country would burn. But the chief of police was dismissive, doubtless reasoning, "Who cares if one poor street vendor tries to kill himself?"

News of Mohamed Bouazizi's self-immolation spread through his hometown of Sidi Bouzid. Mohamed's friends and admirers poured into the streets, shocked, distraught, and outraged.

Mohamed was not the first Tunisian to attempt suicide or even to self-immolate on account of despair and humiliation. What made Mohamed Bouazizi's desperate act different was the response of his friends. They knew that Tunisians would identify with Mohamed's hardship and humiliation. They knew that Tunisians would be outraged by the way the authorities had treated him. Critically, they were determined to ensure Mohamed's suffering would not be in vain.

Social Media

That afternoon (December 17, 2010), Mohamed's mother Menobia led a peaceful protest outside the municipality headquarters while two of Mohamed's relatives—Rochdi Horchani and Ali Bouazizi—filmed the event, conducted interviews, and posted the footage to Facebook. Tunisia has 3.6 million Internet users, which is 39 percent of the population, and 31 percent of these users are on Facebook, one of the highest numbers on the African continent.[3]

The footage was picked up by the pro-MB, Qatar-based *Al Jazeera*, which has a media team devoted to trawling the Internet in search of useful videos from across the Arab world. That evening, the video was aired on *Al Jazeera*'s Mubasher channel and subsequently on numerous satellite channels. As the Tunisian trend of increasing openness and connectedness converged[4] with the Tunisian trend of escalating frustration and disillusionment, outrage spread and protests erupted. Clearly, multitudes of Tunisians cared about the fate of this poor vendor, not the least because so many identified with him.

While the Internet and satellite TV channels buzzed with news of a Tunisian uprising, Tunisia's state-censored media ignored the protests. Doubtless the government was expecting the protesters would eventually run out of steam. But the protests rolled on and tensions soared.

On December 29, 2010, Tunisia's Nessema TV channel broke the silence to report that Tunisian President Zine El Abidine Ben Ali had visited Mohamed Bouazizi's bedside at the hospital in Ben Arous. But if Ben Ali thought he could diffuse tensions with a photo opportunity, he was sorely mistaken. For what Tunisians saw was not a compassionate president rising to the occasion. Instead, they saw a downtrodden young man, bandaged

---

3. "Internet World Stats: Usage and Population Statistics."

4. It is ironic that the openness and modernity that Tunisian President Ben Ali had fostered was to be so integral to his downfall. Surely Mikhail Gorbachev would sympathize, for it was it was the openness and modernization introduced by *glasnost* and *perestroika* which fatally undermined the communist regime in the Union of Soviet Socialist Republics (USSR). The lesson for all dictators has been this: you cannot permit openness and facilitate connectedness unless you are sure the people will be happy with what they are going to see and hear. While many in the West assumed openness would generate reform, the opposite is turning out to be true. For after an era of increasing openness, state censorship and repression are making a dramatic comeback.

from head to toe with a single opening around his burned black lips through which a feeding tube was inserted down his scorched throat, fighting for his life in the presence of a leader who could have made a difference but didn't.[5] Needless to say, the image did not produce the reaction Ben Ali had hope for.

When Mohamed Bouazizi finally succumbed to his injuries on January 4, 2011, the nation erupted. Fed up with high unemployment, inequality, and nepotism, tens of thousands of Tunisians poured into the streets of Tunisia's cities calling for the government's downfall. Daily they clashed with police as the country descended into a spiral of violence. From his palace, behind the barricades, Ben Ali asked the military to step in and suppress the uprising. They refused, and on January 14, 2011, Ben Ali and his family fled Tunisia for Saudi Arabia. Ben Ali's twenty-three-year reign was over. Mohamed Ghannouchi assumed control as interim president.

Dignity

According to his mother Menobia, "Mohamed did what he did for the sake of his dignity."

As victims of high unemployment and soaring inflation, most protesters were appealing for the same: dignity. "We are here because we want our dignity," two university-educated unemployed protesters told *TIME* magazine. "We don't want to have to rely on political favors or bribes to get jobs; we need to clean out the system."[6]

Dignity! That is what the masses wanted—dignity; to be treated with respect as human beings; to have justice and opportunity, and *not* to be forced to struggle against corruption and grovel for crumbs. Dignity!

The Tunisian uprising was wide and deep, spreading to all corners of the land and to all levels of society, and Tunisia's highly respected and forever-neutral military did not intervene. What's more, the revolution was over so quickly that no one had time to hijack it. (Attempts to hijack it would come later.)

Those seeking to replicate the "revolution" in other Arab states would find that their circumstances were different. For not only is each state unique, but more critically, protesters in subsequent uprisings would find that various powers and interested parties—both within (such as the MB) and without (foreign powers, both state and non-state actors)—would be prepared for the wave and determined to ride it.

5. "How a Fruit Seller Caused Revolution in Tunisia" (includes photo).
6. Abouzeid, "Bouazizi: The Man Who Set Himself and Tunisia on Fire."

The "Arab Spring" Heats Up

On Saturday January 15, 2011, just one day after the fall of the Ben Ali regime in Tunisia, Mohsen Bouterfif died in an Algerian hospital from burns he suffered in a self-immolation.[7]

Mohsen Bouterfif lived in Boukhadra, in Tebessa province some 700 km east of Algiers. He had met with the mayor of Boukhadra on the Thursday, in the hope that the mayor might be able to find him housing and a job, but to no avail. His hopes dashed, Mohsen stood in front of the town hall, doused himself in gasoline, and set himself on fire. Moshen's desperate act was one of four self-immolations to occur in Algeria within the space of four days. Only Mohsen's act was fatal.

After Mohsen died, about one hundred young men protested in Boukhadra. To pacify the masses and prevent the protests from taking hold and spreading, the governor of Tebessa province sacked the mayor, while the central government cut the price of sugar and cooking oil.

On Monday January 17, 2011, Abdu Abdel-Monaim Kamal (49), a restaurateur, set himself on fire outside the Egyptian Parliament in Cairo. A policeman who was close by managed to extinguish the flames, and Kamal was quickly taken away by ambulance with superficial burns.

In Mauritania, Yacoub Ould Dahoud (40), a father with a graduate degree from France who belonged to a wealthy family, set himself on fire protesting against alleged government mistreatment and political marginalization of his tribe.[8]

The very next day, Mohamed Farouk Hassan (40), a lawyer, set himself on fire in Cairo, protesting rising prices. Mohamed was hospitalized with non-life-threatening injuries.

In Egypt, five men self-immolated within the space of a week.

The BBC reported on January 19, 2011, that an Egyptian Facebook group had called for street protests on January 25, which the organizers were calling a "day of revolution against torture, poverty, corruption and unemployment."[9]

On January 22, 2011, thousands protested in Sana'a, Yemen, after the authorities arrested Tawakul Karman, a political dissident. Meanwhile, protesters were also mobilizing in Oman, Syria and Morocco.

On January 25, 2011, huge mass protests erupted in multiple Egyptian cities. The very next day the Egyptian military commenced its crackdown.

---

7. "Algerian Dies in Self-immolation, Echoing Tunisia."
8. "Egyptian, Mauritanian Set Themselves on Fire."
9. "Egyptian Man Dies after Setting Himself Alight."

By January 29, 2011, the protests in Sana'a, Yemen, had swelled to the tens of thousands, with protesters calling for President Ali Abdullah Saleh to step down.

In Egypt, President Hosni Mubarak pressed through some political reforms in the hope that reforms would satisfy the protesters. Not a chance!

Long a powerful political player, the Egyptian military then made its move, switching allegiances to side with the protesters.

The Egyptian Military

The Mubarak regime was little more than a military dictatorship in civilian garb. While it had democratic elements and was nominally secular, the ruling National Democratic Party (NDP) was an authoritarian party controlled ultimately by the military. The military—long regarded as the most modern and progressive element of society—was invested with sweeping powers. Egypt's presidents—Nasser, Sadat, and Mubarak—had all been senior military figures who simply removed their uniforms upon entering politics.

The Egyptian military had long expected that when Mubarak retired, he would hand power over to a senior military figure. So when Mubarak began grooming his son, Gamal, with the intention of establishing a Mubarak dynasty, the military was incensed. The popular uprising provided a perfect cover under which the military could make its move to get rid of Mubarak and hold on to power. By switching sides and backing the protesters, the military essentially staged an undercover coup.

When Hosni Mubarak resigned on February 11, 2011, a military council was named to govern in his place. The crowds in Tahrir Square celebrated what they thought was their victory, a win for people power, a triumph for democracy. The reality was, however, that had the military stayed loyal to Mubarak, the protesters alone could not have removed him. As Stratfor Global Intelligence stated at the time: "In a genuine revolution, the police and military cannot contain the crowds. In Egypt, the military chose not to confront the demonstrators, not because the military itself was split, but because it agreed with the demonstrators' core demand: getting rid of Mubarak. And since the military was the essence of the Egyptian regime, it is odd to consider this a revolution."[10]

On February 13, 2011, the Supreme Council of the Armed Forces (SCAF) abolished the constitution and dissolved parliament, promising a new constitution to be ratified by a referendum. The Supreme Council declared that it would rule Egypt for six months or until it determined that

---

10. "Egypt: The Distance Between Enthusiasm and Reality."

Egypt was ready to hold parliamentary and presidential elections. The military had massively increased its power.

The "Arab Spring" Gets Complicated

By February 14, 2011, protests had erupted at Pearl Roundabout in central Manama in Shi'ite-majority, Sunni-ruled Bahrain on the Persian Gulf. While the protesters were mostly Shi'ite, they were not primarily protesting along sectarian lines. Like those in Tunisia and Egypt, their hopes were set on dignity and reform. They were not going to get it; Shi'ites would definitely not be permitted to rise.

By February 15, protesters were mobilizing against Gaddafi in Libya, and these protests were totally different yet again. Events in Tunisia and Egypt had inspired Gaddafi's opponents, giving them grounds for hope and confidence. Maybe, they reasoned, they could ride this wave and exploit this window of opportunity to remove Gaddafi under the cover of the Arab Spring. Gaddafi's opponents were diverse—tribal, political, religious—united only by their desire to be rid of him.

After seizing power in 1969, Gaddafi—a committed socialist—abandoned the 1951 UN-backed constitution and centralized power in Tripoli. Before then, Libya had functioned as three autonomous regions—Tripolitania (west), Cyrenaica (east), and Fezzan (south)—held in balance under one flag by a constitution prepared by Libyans with assistance from the UN. Those who drafted the Libyan democratic constitution of 1951 had been very careful to address and balance Libya's complex realities—particularly the tribal, regional, and religious differences within the country. Strategic analyst Gregory R. Copley elaborates: "The 1951 Constitution put *Seyyid* Idris al-Senussi into power as King Idris I. That was done specifically because the Senussi family, leaders of the moderate and Westernist *Sanusiyyah* Muslim movement, were outside the tribal framework of Libya, and therefore gave no advantage to any single tribe . . . The 42 years of Qadhafi [Gaddafi] power in Libya were hallmarked by the removal of this neutral leadership and the imposition of the dominance of the al-Qadhadhfa tribe over the other 140 or so tribes of Libya."[11]

When protests erupted in oil-rich Benghazi, capital of the Cyrenaica region, on February 18, 2011, the protesters were flying the red, black, and green tricolor flag of the 1951 constitution. These protests were about far more than Gaddafi.

---

11. Copley, "Libya, Africa, and the Mediterranean After Qadhafi."

Gaddafi may have identified himself as a Muslim, but he was a committed anti-Islamist and allied with the West in its "War on Terror." Within this context, oil-rich Benghazi had become a hotbed of radical fundamentalist Islam. Led predominantly by anti-liberty, anti-democracy Islamists—many affiliated with al-Qaeda—as well as various mutually hostile tribal factions, the Benghazi protests were essentially about decentralization and greater autonomy for the oil-rich region. They were not going to get it; too many other powers had interests in Libya.

Despite the severe unrest and ubiquitous nature of the Western narrative, Gaddafi remained extremely confident. He was certain the West would not want to do anything to destabilize Libya, for such actions would go against the West's own security interests. "Should the situation in Libya be unstable," Gaddafi warned in a March 28, 2011, interview with Russia Today, "al-Qaeda will establish its rule and Libya will get transformed into another Afghanistan. Millions of refugees will flood Europe, which will make the whole Mediterranean region suffer."[12] Gaddafi was certain the West did not want that.

As February rolled into March, protests escalated in Bahrain, Yemen, Jordan, Morocco, and Oman. Tunisians, too, returned to the streets, demanding the resignation of interim president Mohamed Ghannouchi.

On March 5, 2011, ahead of a planned "Day of Rage", Saudi Arabia's Interior Ministry issued a statement banning public protest: "The kingdom categorically prohibits all forms of demonstrations, marches, or protests, and calls for them, because that contradicts the principles of the Islamic Sharia, the values and traditions of Saudi society, and results in disturbing public order and harming public and private interests." [13]

The decree was endorsed by the Council of Senior Religious Scholars, the highest body for interpretation of Islamic law and supported by the Sunni Wahhabi clerics. "Islam strictly prohibits protests in the kingdom because the ruler here rules by God's will," Sheikh Abdel Aziz Alasheikh told worshippers in Riyadh's central mosque. Meanwhile, King Abdullah defused tensions and pacified the masses by the usual Saudi means: he unveiled an unprecedented financial package, releasing some $37 billion to pay for unemployment benefits, education, and housing subsidies.

By March 8, 2011, the situation in Sana'a, Yemen, had come to a head: security forces opened fire on protesters, wounding one hundred.

---

12. Muammar Gaddafi, interview with Russia Today. See also Roberts, "ISIS Threatens to Send 500,000 Migrants to Europe."

13. Black, "Saudi Arabian Security Forces Quell 'Day of Rage' Protests."

Subsequently, opposition forces rejected President Saleh's offer of a new constitution and parliament.

On March 14, 2011, the situation at Bahrain's Pearl Roundabout came to a head: Crown Prince Salman bin Hamad al-Khalifa asked Saudi Arabia to send security forces into his country. An estimated one-thousand-strong contingent of the Saudi Arabian National Guard entered Bahrain, ostensibly in response to a "security threat" to supposedly protect strategic sites and infrastructure. Bahrain's main opposition bloc described the Saudi-led intervention as a "declaration of war" and urged the UN to intervene. While the US called for restraint, it refused to recognize the invasion as an invasion.[14]

Bahraini and Saudi security forces (Sunnis) crushed the protesters (mostly Shi'ites) and even the Pearl Roundabout itself, including the ninety-meter-tall monument[15]—all with the tacit approval of the US-led West. Even when Bahraini doctors were dragged before courts, tortured and jailed for sedition because they had treated the wounded,[16] the response of the democratic West was stony silence.

Subsequently, Western media would express its confusion over what it regarded as "mixed responses." What they failed to appreciate was that *who falls* was far less important than *who rises*. The West would only champion "democracy" when it was perceived to advance Western interests; so much for standing on the moral high ground.

Clearly, the Arab Spring would not be a Spring for all Arabs. Clearly, there would be no Spring for vilified, persecuted, downtrodden minority Arab Shi'ites.

Up until this point, the Islamic regime in Tehran had been backing the uprisings, seeing them as an "Islamic Awakening" akin to the Iranian Islamic Revolution of 1979—after all, the similarities were profound. As the protesters ousted their US-backed, anti-Islamist dictators, few cheered louder than Iranian President Mahmoud Ahmadinejad.

However, as events in Bahrain made clear, this movement was less of an "Arab Spring"—that is, an Arab movement to advance Arab democracy—and more of a Western-backed Sunni Islamic intifada.

---

14. Chulov, "Saudi Arabian Troops Enter Bahrain as Regime Asks for Help to Quell Uprising."

15. The ninety-meter monument in the center of the Pearl Roundabout comprised six white curved beams topped with an enormous cement pearl. It had been built as a tribute to the kingdom's history as a pearl-diving center.

16. Human Rights Watch, "Bahrain."

Syria

When Syria's MB was banned in 1964, armed MB members responded with assassinations and bombings in which several Baath Party officials were killed and government properties destroyed. In 1979, the Combatant Vanguard split from the MB to wage war against the Syrian regime. It launched an attack on the military artillery school in Aleppo in which eighty-three Alawite student officers were massacred. Subsequently, in 1980, President Hafez al-Assad issued a law making membership of the MB a capital offense. Religion would not be permitted in politics.[17]

The MB insurgency escalated until February 1982, when the Syrian government launched a military intervention to put down an uprising in Hama, killing more than 10,000 mostly MB supporters, arresting some 20,000, and blacklisting a further 600,000.[18] After that, the MB withdrew from political life; its leadership fled overseas while members and supporters went underground.

After Bashar al-Assad came to power in 2000, the Syrian MB began to organize its members for action. However, its efforts to have the ban lifted were to no avail and the MB remained a banned organization.

In February 2011, the Assad government moved quickly to crush Arab Spring protests organized on Facebook. By mid-March, opposition was emerging from the flashpoint city of Daraa in Syria's largely conservative Sunni southwest. From Daraa, the demonstrations spread to the Kurdish northeast, and, most critically, to Aleppo and the suburbs of Damascus. All the while, Syria's Christian leaders were warning that the protests were taking a sinister turn.

At the outset of Syria's Arab Spring protests, the MB cautiously refrained from participating. Its first official statement in support of the uprising was issued only at the end of April 2011, when it openly called for the regime of Bashar al-Assad to be toppled. On April 29, 2011, Syria's MB led the protests for the first time, in what it labeled a "Day of Wrath."

The Melkite Patriarch of Antioch and All the East, Gregorios III Laham, warned that while the protests were not as yet sectarian, being rooted as they were in grievances that were social (repression and inequality) and economic (unemployment plus massive fuel and food price hikes), criminals had become involved and weapons were flooding in. He also warned that fundamentalist Muslims were calling for jihad.[19]

17. "Syria in Crisis: The Muslim Brotherhood in Syria."
18. Sindawi, "The Shiite Turn in Syria."
19. Cervellera, "Syria: Melkite Patriarch on Fears of a Future of Chaos and Fundamentalism."

On May 11, 2011, Christian aid group Barnabas Fund reported that as demonstrations against the Syrian government intensified, Christians were coming under increasing pressure to join the uprising or leave. "In one Christian village outside the southern city of Deraa a home came under fire by a group of masked men on motorbikes, while Muslim residents in the village of Hala have issued an ultimatum to their Christian neighbours either to join the demonstrations against President Bashar al-Assad's regime or to leave. Their demands are making life extremely difficult for the Christians, who have closed their shops and are considering what course of action to take. Churches have also received threatening letters."[20]

In a letter to Western leaders, a senior Syrian church leader made this appeal:

> Ask the Heads of State of Arab countries to work for real development . . . But don't encourage revolutions. The situation has deteriorated into organised crime, robbery, fear, terror being spread, rumours of threats to churches . . . Fundamentalist groups are threatening citizens and wanting to create "Islamic Emirates" . . . Christians especially are very fragile in the face of crises and bloody revolutions! Christians will be the first victims of these revolutions, especially in Syria. A new wave of emigration will follow immediately.[21]

On May 13, 2011, Bloomberg News published a daunting article by diplomatic and UN correspondent Flavia Krause-Jackson titled, "Syrian Christians Say 'Arab Spring' Changes Could Hasten Extinction." [22] It is a confronting report. "As the Arab Spring protests reach Damascus," she writes, "Syrian Christians look warily at a future without a time-tested autocrat to protect them from religious intolerance."

Krause-Jackson quotes Archbishop Cyril Aphrem Karim, leader of a US branch of the Syriac Orthodox Church of Antioch, who observed: "History has proven to us that Christians [in the Middle East] have always had more secure lives, better treatment by people who may be looked on as dictators, like Saddam Hussein. [In Syria], our feeling is, if the regime falls, the Salafis and the Muslim Brotherhood will seize power and that is bad news for us." According to Archbishop Karim, protesters in the streets of Damascus could be heard chanting: "Christians to Beirut, Alawis to the grave." As

---

20. "Syrian Christians Threatened: Join Anti-government Uprising or Leave."

21. Ibid.

22. Krause-Jackson, "Syrian Christians Say 'Arab Spring' Changes Could Hasten Extinction."

to the plight facing Syria's Christians, Krause-Jackson ominously warned: "A history that predates Islam won't guarantee the communities' survival."

Archbishop Karim told Krause-Jackson that while he frequently travels to Washington and has had repeated meetings with State Department officials and lawmakers, he does not hold out much hope that the US will do anything to help Syria's Christians. "I don't feel the U.S. is really concerned by Christians in the Middle East," Karim said. "There is just not much sympathy."

And all the while, notes Krause-Jackson, "Christian communities are staring at extinction."

Raising the Stakes

On June 3, 2011, Yemeni president Ali Abdullah Saleh and numerous Yemeni government officials were worshipping in the palace mosque when a massive improvised explosive device (IED) exploded in their midst. Seven people were killed and more than eighty-seven injured. President Saleh, Prime Minister Ali Mohammed Mujawar, and several other senior figures were critically wounded. President Saleh was airlifted to Saudi Arabia, suffering multiple shrapnel wounds, broken bones, smoke inhalation, internal bleeding, and extensive burns.

Appearing on Yemeni TV on July 7, 2011, President Saleh—still at that time in Saudi Arabia receiving treatment, including multiple surgeries for his injuries—stressed that dialogue was essential to solving Yemen's problems. Saleh said he welcomed power sharing, but stressed that it should be "within the framework of the constitution and in the framework of the law."[23]

On August 3, 2011, the Arab world was transfixed by images of former Egyptian strongman-president, Hosni Mubarak (83), on a stretcher inside a cage in a Cairo courtroom, his co-accused sons by his side. Prosecutors read out the charges against him, along with descriptions of the unarmed protesters he was accused of killing.[24]

On Sunday August 21, 2011, Libya's rebels entered the capital, Tripoli, courtesy of air support from the North Atlantic Treaty Organization (NATO). Seventy-two Libyan civilians—including twenty women and twenty-four children[25]—were killed when this coalition of Western powers

23. "Yemen President Ali Abdullah Saleh appears on TV."
24. Hauslohner, "The Dictator in His Cage: Hosni Mubarak Goes on Trial in Egypt."
25. Mepham, "Nato Must Investigate the Civilian Casualties of Its Libyan Campaign."

bombed the capital city of a country that had not attacked or even threatened the West—an ally, what's more, in the "War on Terror."

By August 24, it was over: the regime had fallen. After facilitating the removal of the dictator in Tripoli, the US, United Kingdom and France simply installed another dictator in Tripoli. This time the dictator was an Islamist, an "Arab Afghan"—that is, an Arab veteran of the Afghan jihad. His name was Abdel Hakim Belhadj, but he was also known as "the sheikh."[26] After the Afghan War he returned to Libya and, with other "Arab Afghans", founded the Libyan Islamic Fighting Group (LIFG). This same group would go on to murder US Ambassador John Christopher Stevens (52) in the September 11, 2012, terror attack on the US consulate in Benghazi.[27]

Gaddafi might have been toppled, but with centralized power restored, Benghazi's wealth would continue to flow to Tripoli—meaning Libya's civil war would roll on and on and on.

What's more, in a catastrophe of monumental proportions, Libya's numerous weapons caches were raided. The raids enabled vast quantities of weapons to move into the hands of arms traders, belligerents such as Tuareg separatists, and terrorists such as AQIM. Ultimately these weapons would end up in the hands of jihadists in Somalia, Nigeria, Mali, Syria, and goodness knows where else.

Two months later, on October 20, 2011, the ousted Libyan strongman-dictator Colonel Muammar Gaddafi was found hiding in a drainpipe outside his hometown of Sirte. Dragged from the pipe by a mob of "bearded ones", Gaddafi was brutalized and sodomized with an army knife by bloodthirsty Islamic jihadists to cries of *"Allahu Akbar"* (Allah is greater). Eventually the blood-soaked former dictator was summarily lynched while euphoric jihadists captured the images on their mobile phones in much the same way other killers might collect trophies.[28]

Upon hearing the news that Gaddafi was dead, British Prime Minister David Cameron effused, "People in Libya today have an even greater chance after this news of building themselves a strong and democratic future. I'm proud of the role that Britain has played in helping them to bring that about and I pay tribute to the bravery of the Libyans who've helped to liberate their country. We will help them, we will work with them, and that is what I want to say today."

Likewise, British Labour Party leader Ed Miliband rejoiced that Gaddafi's brutal death marked the end of a period of "brutality and repression."

26. Cheterian, "Libya's Rebel Leader with a Past."
27. Cartalucci, "US-Backed Terrorists Murder US Ambassador in Libya."
28. Shelton, "The Death of Gaddafi."

"I pay tribute to the Libyan people for standing up to the former regime and seeking to define their own democratic destiny," he said. "We should be proud of the support that our armed forces have given to that cause. We should all hope that this day also marks the end of the armed conflict and the start of a period of stability where we see a transition to democratic government."[29]

"We came, we saw, he died!" declared a jovial US Secretary of State Hillary Clinton upon learning that Gaddafi had been lynched.[30]

But the Benghazi uprising never had anything to do with liberal, Western-style constitutional democracy.

Energized by Gaddafi's barbaric lynching, tens of thousands of Syrian protesters poured out onto the streets of Damascus the very next day chanting, "Your turn is coming Bashar."

According to The Associated Press, one of the protest banners read, "Ben Ali fled, Mubarak is in jail, Gadhafi is killed, Assad . . . ?"[31] And, of course, to that they could have added, "Saleh is burned."

With that declaration of war, with that threat to his life, Bashar al-Assad knew the time had come to put an end to the so-called Arab Spring once and for all.

Syria would be where the Western-backed, MB-led Sunni intifada would finally meet its match.

---

29. "Colonel Gaddafi Dead: David Cameron Says He Is 'Proud of UK's Role in Libya.'"

30. "We came, We saw, He Died: What Hillary Clinton Told News Reporter Moments after Hearing of Gaddafi's Death."

31. "Protesters in Syria, Yemen Take to Streets, Inspired by Gadhafi Death."

— 7 —

Myth Busting the Syrian Crisis

ON TUESDAY JANUARY 10, 2012, Syrian President Bashar al-Assad delivered a speech in the Damascus University Auditorium:

> Today I am addressing you ten months after the outbreak of the unfortunate events which befell the country imposing new circumstances on the Syrian arena . . .
>
> At the beginning of the crisis, it was not easy to explain what happened. Emotional reactions and the absence of rationality were surpassing the facts. But now, the fog has lifted, and it is no longer possible for the regional and international parties which wanted to destabilize Syria to forge the facts and the events.

Entitled "Syria Will Remain Free",[1] the speech covered topics such as social and political reform, noting that a new constitution would soon be put to a popular referendum and highlighting the importance of national dialogue.

Assad continued:

> Our utmost priority now, which is unparalleled by any other priority, is the restoration of the security we have enjoyed for decades, and which has characterized our country, not only in the region but throughout the world. This will only happen by striking these murderous terrorists hard. There is no compromise with terrorism, no compromise with those who use arms to cause chaos and division, no compromise with those who terrorize civilians, no compromise with those who conspire with foreigners against their country and against their people . . .
>
> [But] In as much as we need to strike the terrorists . . . we need to bring those who have gone astray back to the right path. There are those who made mistakes and those who have been misguided . . . That is why I believe that decisiveness is necessary

---

1. Al-Assad, "Syria Will Remain Free."

but continuing to show tolerance and forgiveness from time to time within the framework of clear criteria and sound mechanisms is equally important.

He then offered some astute analysis—astute, yet obvious to anyone with eyes to see:

[Our enemies] are trying to depict Syria as an isolated country, trying to stress this over and over again. But our points of strength lie in our strategic position. If they want to besiege Syria, they will end up besieging a whole region.

Indeed! The policy of the US-backed, Turkey-Arab Sunni axis—to support the "rebels" and effect regime change in Damascus so as to realign Syria from the east-west Shia Crescent to a north-south Sunni bloc—was built on two enormous *myths*. The first myth was that Assad has limited support. The second myth was that Syria is isolated.

These and other myths—formulated and disseminated by policymakers, to be parroted and amplified by mainstream media—were integral to the official narrative being peddled by those demanding regime change in Damascus. And anyone who challenged the official narrative could expect to become the target of mockery, vilification, and even threats.

Of course, there will always be those who, for ideological reasons, delight to challenge any Western narrative. I, however, have challenged the Western narrative with a heavy heart. As a conservative Christian who yearns to see revival in the West, I have challenged the Western narrative because I believe that truth matters. I believe that when Jesus said "know the truth, and the truth will set you free" (John 8:32), he was not only declaring a spiritual reality, but also affirming a principle that can be broadly applied.

Most critically, I have challenged the Western narrative because I care deeply about the imperilled and largely voiceless ethnic and religious minorities caught up in this crisis. I also care about the land, for Mesopotamia is the Assyrian homeland and the church's historic heartland. From Antioch (in Syria) through Edessa (in southern Turkey) to Nineveh and Baghdad (in Iraq), the Fertile Crescent was the engine room of the early church. Like multitudes of Christians in this world, I care deeply about my Christian co-religionists—my brothers and sisters in Christ—who are this day in an existential struggle for their very survival as a people in their own historic homeland. Their plight will not even begin to be addressed until the truth of their situation is known and understood—regardless of how unpalatable that truth might be.

Myth Busting the Syrian Crisis

Myth: Assad has limited support.

Myth: Syria is isolated.

In December 2011, Qatar—a staunch supporter of the MB—published the results of a YouGov poll commissioned by the Qatar Foundation ostensibly to demonstrate Arab support for regime change in Damascus. While the poll did indeed show that the majority of Arabs wanted Assad removed, it also showed that the majority of Syrians did not![2] As reported by conflict analyst Aisling Byrne, "A YouGov poll commissioned by the Qatar Foundation showed last week that 55% of Syrians do not want Assad to resign and 68% of Syrians disapprove of the Arab League sanctions imposed on their country."[3]

Myth Busted: The December 2011 YouGov poll proved that Assad has majority support.

Myth Busted: Those calling for regime change were clearly not motivated by "democracy."

Despite these findings, the Qatar Foundation still used the poll to advocate for regime change on the ground that that 81 percent of *Arabs*—that is, Egyptian, Jordanian, Palestinian, Saudi, Yemeni, and other regional Arabs—believed Syria's President Bashar al-Assad should go. "One is left wondering," wrote Byrne, "who exactly is Assad accountable to—the Syrian people or the Arab public?" Despite the report's damning implications, the Syrian opposition jumped on the results, announcing that they did not consider Arab intervention to be "foreign."

The YouGov poll totally debunked the false Western narrative that the Syrian crisis was a case of Assad versus the rest—a case of a hated dictator clinging to power versus a desperate people yearning for liberty. Indeed, Assad's support base was broad and strong, for Syria's ethnic and religious

---

2. "Syria's President Assad—Should He Resign?" (Polling dates: December 14–19, 2011.) The poll results referred to in the text are no longer available, for they have since been re-published in a way that hides the actual results. The original report showed results by country; as such, Syria's results were clear (and for Qatar, embarrassing). The report now available on the Doha Debates website has the results listed by region, meaning Syria's results are now diluted and hidden by their inclusion within the results for "the Levant", a region comprising Syria, Jordan, Palestine, Lebanon, and Iraq.

3. Byrne, "A Mistaken Case for Syrian Regime Change."

minorities (comprising around 25 percent of the population) plus the modernist, largely secular Sunni Muslims who comprised the pro-business urban elite were fully aware that their own and Syria's future lay in Syria remaining secular.

When the Syrian MB came out on April 29, 2011, to lead the "Day of Wrath", it should have been clear that far from being a case of Assad versus the rest, Syria's developing crisis was a case of fundamentalist Sunnis—comprised mostly of radicalized, madrassa-educated youths who had migrated from rural areas into city slums—verses the rest (that is, the majority of Syrians).

Byrne observed that "not a single mainstream major newspaper or news outlet reported the YouGov poll results," as it didn't "fit their narrative."

Another report that shattered the Western narrative and yet was still used to argue for regime change was the January 27, 2012, report by the League of Arab States Observer Mission to Syria.[4] Like the December 2011 YouGov poll, this report turned the US-backed Turkey-Arab Sunni narrative on its head, which is doubtless why the report was so decisively quashed—until it was leaked, debunking two more myths.

> *Myth:* The Syrian crisis is driven by an evil murderous regime that is "murdering its own people" and is "guilty of crimes against humanity."[5]

> *Myth:* The support given by America, Turkey, Saudi Arabia, and Qatar to those opposing Assad is driven by humanitarianism and a devotion to human rights.

After making it clear that President al-Assad had cooperated fully with its observer mission, the January 2012 League of Arab States Observer Mission to Syria report proceeded to document the extreme violence—including kidnapping, murder, terrorism, and sabotage—being perpetrated by "armed groups" against government and civilian facilities. It also noted that incident reports, such as those from the London-based Syrian Observatory of Human Rights, were routinely exaggerated or even, upon investigation, completely unfounded.

Author Pepe Escobar, an expert on the geopolitics of the Middle East, wrote a stinging critique of the Arab position: "The report is adamant. There was no organized, lethal repression by the Syrian government against

---

4. "Report of the Head of the League of Arab States Observer Mission to Syria."
5. Stenhouse, "What Is Going On in Syria?"

peaceful protesters. Instead, the report points to shady armed gangs as responsible for hundreds of deaths among Syrian civilians, and over one thousand among the Syrian army, using lethal tactics such as bombing of civilian buses, bombing of trains carrying diesel oil, bombing of police buses and bombing of bridges and pipelines."[6]

> *Myth Busted:* The Syria government was not *systematically* killing peaceful Syrian civilians.

Rather, according to the Arab League Observer Mission, "armed groups" were waging a campaign of terror against civilians and government facilities resulting in mass casualties. Despite this finding, the Arab league dismissed its own report and recommend that the UN Security Council move to adopt a resolution demanding a Syrian Arab Army (SAA) withdrawal—which the Security Council duly did. Russia vetoed the resolution on the grounds that this would merely open the way for "armed groups" to fill the vacuum and occupy the cities—which it obviously would. American Ambassador Susan Rice expressed disgust at Russia's "intransigence."

> *Myth Busted*: The US-Turkey-Saudi-Qatari support for the rebels had nothing to do with humanitarianism and human rights.

Indeed, the conflict in Syria is about a lot of things, but human rights is not one of them. While Turks and Arabs and Persians all know this, voters in Western democracies like to be able to justify their involvement or position on moral grounds; hence the need for a human rights-based narrative. The fact that the West's allies in this supposedly moral venture for democracy and human rights are Saudi Arabia, Turkey, and Qatar should leave us with a sneaking suspicion that the narrative may not be entirely honest.

Geopolitics and Vital Interests

As I wrote at the time (January 9, 2012), "The battle presently taking place *in* Syria includes a battle by foreign powers *for* Syria." It is a battle for hegemony; a battle over the regional balance of power; a battle that pits the US-backed Turkey-Arab Sunni axis against the Iran-led, Shi'ite-dominated Axis of Resistance of which Arab, mostly Sunni, Syria is integral. It is a battle over territory that is geopolitically strategic and critical to vital interests.[7]

   6. Escobar, "Exposed: The Arab Agenda in Syria."
   7. Kendal, "SYRIA: false narratives and propaganda."

As for economic interests, the issue is who will dominate the supply of energy to Europe. Russia, home of the world's largest natural gas company, Gazprom, has long delivered oil and gas to Europe both under the Baltic and Black Seas and overland via Belarus and Ukraine. Then, in May 2005, a British Petroleum (BP)-led and managed consortium (comprising eleven energy companies, three of which are American) began pumping Caspian crude oil through the Baku-Tibilisi-Ceyhan (BTC) pipeline from Azerbaijan through restive Georgia and volatile Kurdish-dominated eastern Turkey to the Mediterranean for sale to Europe. This of course necessitates that the governments in each of the transit states remain aligned with the West and that the Kurds are kept subdued. Traversing mountains and skirting war zones, the BTC pipeline cost an absolute fortune (US$4billion—$3billion in bank loans) and therefore needs to make a lot of money over a long period of time. However, in early 2005, just as the BTC pipeline was opening, Iran announced its intention to run a pipeline through the newly realized Shia Crescent which would pump Caspian crude from Iran through Iraq and Syria to the Mediterranean at a fraction of the cost.[8] Furthermore, in 2009, President Assad refused to sign an agreement with Qatar for a proposed pipeline to transport gas from the Persian Gulf through Saudi Arabia and Syria to Turkey for sale to Europe. Instead, in 2010, Assad signed an agreement with Iran for a pipeline to transport gas from the Persian Gulf through Iran, Iraq, and Syria for sale to Europe. That the Turkey-Arab Sunni Axis wants regime change in Damascus is unsurprising. The stakes are high!

It Is All About Iran

So, for a whole range of reasons, the conflict in Syria is all about US and Sunni efforts to realign Syria, taking it out of the Shia Crescent so as to counter the ascent of Iran. Conflict analyst Aisling Byrne concurs, describing the battle for Syria as essentially the first stage of a "war on Iran." She quotes Saudi Arabia's (now deceased) King Abdullah, who observed: "Other than the collapse of the Islamic Republic itself, nothing would weaken Iran more than losing Syria."[9]

Byrne noted that the US administration had also commented that regime change in Syria would constitute a massive blow to Iranian power in the region: "What we are seeing in Syria," she concluded (January 5, 2012),

---

8. Escobar, *Globalistan*, 41–52.

9. Byrne, "A mistaken case for Syrian regime change." See also the Al Mayadeen TV Interview with Aisling Byrne, "Syria: The Information War", and Byrne, "Covering Syria: The Information War."

"is a deliberate and calculated campaign to bring down the Assad government so as to replace it with a regime 'more compatible' with US interests in the region . . . Not for the first time are we seeing a close alliance between US/British neo-cons with Islamists (including, reports show, some with links to al-Qaeda) working together to bring about regime change in an 'enemy' state."[10]

Declaration of War

President Bashar al-Assad's January 10, 2012, speech in the Damascus University Auditorium was nothing less than a declaration of war against MB-led rebels, Islamic jihadists, and their foreign backers.

Located on the highway between the administrative capital of Damascus in the south and the commercial capital of Aleppo in the north, the industrial cities of Homs and Hama have long been MB strongholds. Homs, Syria's third-largest city after Aleppo and Damascus, quickly came to be known as "the capital of the revolution."

On February 3, 2012, after U.S,-backed Free Syrian Army (FSA) rebels provocatively ambushed and killed ten SAA soldiers at a checkpoint, the SAA launched a full-scale offensive into the opposition stronghold of Homs.

On February 22, 2012, former Finnish president and Nobel Peace Prize laureate Martti Ahtisaari met with the missions of the permanent five nations (US, Russia, UK, France, and China) at UN headquarters in New York. In a private meeting with Ahtisaari, Russian ambassador Vitaly Churkin laid out a three-point plan that Ahtisaari was convinced had the backing of the Kremlin. According to Ahtisaari, Churkin's plan involved refusing to arm the opposition, immediately establishing a dialogue between the opposition and the government, and finding an elegant way for Bashar al-Assad to step aside.[11]

Ahtisaari relayed the plan to the American, British, and French missions at the UN, but they would have none of it. Convinced the Assad government would fall within weeks, they saw no need to entertain the Russian plan that could see their nemesis Assad retire to a safe haven somewhere while the Iran-aligned government was still in place, albeit under a different leader. Russia pointed out that the dynamics in Syria were totally different to those of Tunisia or Egypt,[12] and the Syrian government would *not* be

---

10. Byrne, "A Mistaken Case for Syrian Regime Change."

11. Borger and Inzaurralde, "West 'ignored Russian offer in 2012 to have Syria's Assad step aside.'"

12. The governments in Tunisia and Egypt were Sunni led and allied to the US.

quickly toppled. It was, however, to no avail.[13] At this point in the conflict, the death toll was estimated to be about 7,500.[14]

In March 2012, Islamic militants from the opposition's Faruq Brigade reportedly went door to door through the Hamidiya and Bustan al-Diwan neighborhoods of Homs, expelling local Christians. A shroud of terror descended over the Christian community of Homs, triggering an exodus. In no time, virtually the entire Christian population of Homs had fled the city for government-controlled areas, neighboring countries, or a stretch of land near the Lebanese border known as Wadi al-Nasarah (Valley of Christians/followers of the Nazarene). Of the more than eighty thousand Christians who lived in Homs prior to the uprising, a mere remnant of four hundred mostly frail and elderly remained.[15] Staying to care for the remnant was Dutch Jesuit priest, Fr. Francis Van Der Lugt (75).

The war was now on in earnest.

It was, however, a totally asymmetric conflict in which bands of insurgents armed with knives, guns, and mortars faced the vastly superior, highly trained, and professional SAA complete with armoured divisions, an air force, and intelligence services. Except for foreign interference, it would all have been over pretty quickly.

Unfortunately, as terrorism analyst Yossef Bodansky observed in February 2012, "the more stable the Assad Administration becomes, the more determined Turkey, Qatar and Saudi Arabia become to involve the industrialised West—that is NATO—in the military intervention ostensibly to topple Assad, but actually to reverse the Iran-Shi'ite axis."[16]

Asymmetric Warfare

In order to understand this conflict, it is imperative that readers understand how modern asymmetric warfare is prosecuted, especially as we—the public—are integral to it.

When the US withdrew support, the governments fell. Syria, on the other hand, was ruled by minority Alawites (who were fighting for their lives) and it was allied to Iran. Syria was, and still is, integral to the Shia Crescent/Axis of Resistance, which would surely defend its strategic asset. Consequently, the government of Syria would *not* be easily toppled. President Putin was absolutely right.

13. Parasiliti, "Former UN Syria envoy says Iran plan on Syria 'worth discussing.'"
14. Ibid.
15. Brode, Farhat and Nisman, "Syria's Threatened Christians." See also Pontifex, "Charity gives urgent help after exodus of Christians from Homs."
16. Bodansky, "Syria's Multi-Layered Wars."

An asymmetric conflict is one fought between unequal forces: one weak, one strong. On the one hand, it might be a case of persecuted, repressed, or occupied peoples (weak) taking on their oppressive overlords (strong) in a struggle for liberty. On the other hand, it might be a case of separatists, usurpers or even terrorists (weak) taking on the state (strong) in a grab for power.

Examples of recent asymmetric conflicts include the Vietcong (weak) versus US-allied forces (strong); the Afghan mujahideen (weak) versus the soviet occupation (strong);[17] Bosnian Islamic secessionists (weak) versus the state of Yugoslavia (strong); Muslim ethnic-Albanian separatists in Serbia's Kosovo province (weak) versus the state of Serbia (strong); Muslim militias (weak) versus the state of Ivory Coast (strong); Benghazi Islamic secessionists (weak) versus the Libyan regime in Tripoli (strong); and the Afghan Taliban (weak) versus NATO (strong).

In all the examples listed, the weak prevailed against the strong. In fact, it seems to be becoming increasingly difficult in this technological age for a strong force to prevail against a weaker foe that has perfected the art of asymmetric warfare.

Traditionally, a weaker force would not pick a fight with a stronger force unless it believed it stood a fair chance of winning. This is because the only alternative to winning was losing, and probably dying. What it lacked in military might, the weaker force would have to make up for in brains and heart—that is, clever, creative, surprising, and unconventional tactics and deceptions, as well as a passion so great and a conviction so strong that fighters were willing to die for the cause. Included amongst these tactics were psychological operations designed to create the illusion of great strength—for example, excessive noise, war paint, and blatant barbarism—anything to strike terror into the hearts of the enemy to lessen their resolve, sow confusion in their ranks, or even convince them to retreat.

Today, however, there is an alternative to winning or losing and probably dying: political mileage. Militarily weak groups like Hamas or Hezbollah can achieve their goals precisely by picking a fight they know they cannot win and then making political mileage out of being weak and getting clobbered!

Historian Richard Landes elaborates:

> All asymmetrical wars take place primarily in the cognitive arena, with the major theatre of war the enemy's public sphere. The

---

17. The soviet position in Afghanistan was complicated by the emergence of nationalist movements in soviet-occupied central Europe and the overall weakening of the soviet empire in the lead up to its collapse.

> goal is to convince your far more powerful enemy not to fight. In defensive cases, from the Maccabees to the Vietnamese, this has meant getting imperial powers to "go home." But Islamists who want to spread *Dar al Islam* [the abode of Islam] conduct an *offensive* campaign: how to get your targets to surrender on their own home ground? In this seemingly absurd venture, they have had remarkable success.
>
> The mainstream news media—their journalists, editors, producers—constitute a central front of this cognitive war: the "weak" but aggressive side cannot have success without the witting or unwitting cooperation of the enemy's journalists.[18]

Since the dawn of time, asymmetric conflicts have played into the hands of imperialistic powers. If threatened by a stronger neighbour, the king of a weak state could seek protection from the king of an even stronger state: the regional superpower. If the king of the imperialistic regional superpower saw value in the weak state, he would agree and send in his forces. As long as the vassal (the king of the weak state) fulfilled the terms of the covenant and remained loyal to the suzerain (the king of the strong protector state), he and his kingdom would remain protected. Similarly, an imperialistic superpower state might exploit the vulnerability of a threatened weak state by offering protection (military aid) in exchange for access to resources and/or geostrategic gains. And so small, vulnerable, weak states were rarely independent; usually they existed as client states of imperialistic superpowers.[19]

Not much has changed; in fact, this paradigm is regaining prominence with the reemergence of a multipolar world. "There is nothing new under the sun" (Eccl 1:9).

One thing that has changed, however, is the political situation: democratically elected governments—as distinct from sovereign kings—require the consent of their constituents. No democratically elected leader will intervene in a foreign conflict if they fear it might cost them their political life.

If a prosperous, militarily strong democracy is going to extend militarily aid to a weak force, then a massive campaign must first be undertaken to saturate the electorate with propaganda, that is, "doctrines, ideas, arguments, facts, or allegations spread by deliberate effort . . . to further one's

---

18. Landes, "Islamism is winning the cognitive war—thanks to manipulative and gullible journalists."

19. This was the situation Judah faced in the eighth century BC, when it sat so uncomfortably between superpower Assyria and ascendant power Egypt. This is the setting for my book, *Turn Back the Battle*, which presents a biblical response to suffering, persecution, and existential threat.

cause or to damage an opposing cause."[20] In a democracy, it is imperative that an acceptable narrative be established that will legitimize and justify the provision of military aid. The weak force must be seen as worthy victims, and the stronger force must be so thoroughly demonized that anyone not voicing support for a "humanitarian intervention" is sure to be widely vilified.

Sometimes Western politicians wanting to legitimize an intervention will send out signals—wittingly or unwittingly—on what "red line" would need to be crossed before an intervention could be justified. For example, a massacre of at least five thousand (US President Bill Clinton to Bosnia's Islamist President Alija Izetbegović) or the use of chemical weapons (US President Barak Obama to the Syrian opposition). Once the red line is crossed—or at least, is believed to have been crossed (they are not the same)—then the intervention simply must proceed to avoid a national loss of face.

It should be understood that there is little that is humanitarian about these "humanitarian interventions." They are military interventions made in pursuit of economic and geostrategic gains; they are merely presented as "humanitarian" for domestic consumption. While unpalatable, this does explain why "humanitarian interventions" are so selective and why Christians facing violent ethnic cleansing and religious persecution in resource-rich or geostrategic allied states never see one. Instead, they are sacrificed on the altar of realpolitik, in pursuit of "vital interests."[21]

Discerning Psyops

Operations that target the mind—or the "cognitive arena," to quote Richard Landes—are known as psychological operations (psyops). And as Landes notes, the theatre for psyops is the enemy's "public sphere."

Terrorism is a psychological operation—a weapon of the weak used to extract concessions from the strong. As writer David Crist rightly observes, suicide bombers are merely "the poor man's smart bomb."[22] Although people die in a terror attack, they are not the actual targets of the operation; the target is the public (i.e., you and me). A terror attack is deemed successful when the public is so terrorized that it will pressure the government to appease the terrorists so they (presumably) won't do it again. Of course, they

---

20. *Merriam Webster Dictionary*, 'Propaganda.'
21. Kendal, "The Humanitarian/Moral Intervention: an exercise in duplicity."
22. Crist, *The Twilight War*, 129.

always do "do it again," escalating the terror and increasing the demands with each subsequent attack.

Language is a key element of psyops. Strategic, "politically correct" language is formulated and employed to establish an official narrative of victimhood while demonizing the enemy so as to justify an intervention. In an excellent interview under the title "Syria: The Information War" with Al Mayadeen TV[23] in February 2012, conflict analyst Aisling Byrne commented on the West's constant use of the term "regime" when describing Syria, but "government" when describing Saudi Arabia or Qatar. "It is illegal under the UN Charter," says Byrne, "to arm forces for toppling a sovereign government . . . [Consequently] The narrative is couched in humanitarian terms so that it creates this public support in the West" for an illegal regime change.[24]

We greatly underestimate the power of language—to our peril.

Propaganda is central to all psyops. Two of the most commonly used tactics for generating propaganda and establishing narratives are the use of human shields and the false flag operation. Once generated, the propaganda is disseminated, more often than not through mainstream media.

Human Shields

When a weak force provokes the enemy from behind a line of unarmed civilians, they can be said to be exploiting human shields. The strong force must then decide whether it will withhold fire (to protect the civilians) or return fire (in which case civilian casualties are all but guaranteed). If they return fire, the "massacre" will be reported, along with sensational (often staged) images, by eager, gullible journalists who accept the narrative unquestioningly in their rush for the exclusive scoop. The media disseminates the propaganda, and then, just as expected, a compassionate society with a high view of human life will have an emotional response. By the time the fog has lifted, everyone has moved on such that it can be difficult for the truth to gain traction.

This is precisely why Islamic jihadists establish bases in, and fire rockets from, hospitals (e.g., Gorazde, Bosnia),[25] schools and kindergartens (e.g.,

---

23. Al Mayadeen was founded in 2012 with the aim of reducing the influence of the pro-Muslim Brotherhood *Al Jazeera* and Saudi-owned *Al Arabiya*.

24. Byrne, "Syria: The Information War" and "Covering Syria: The Information War."

25. Bodansky and Forrest, "The Truth About Gorazde."

Gaza),[26] UN posts and safe havens (e.g., Lebanon),[27] and even from behind pro-democracy rallies (e.g., Andijan, Uzbekistan).[28]

The plan is for retaliatory fire to kill innocent civilians, thereby furthering the victimhood narrative and the demonization of the enemy. These are outrageous propaganda-making exercises in which innocent lives are sacrificed for political gain, and they should be condemned.

False Flags

A "false flag" operation is one in which the weaker force perpetrates an appalling attack that is then attributed to the enemy. Generally this means acquiring enemy uniforms and then brutally slaughtering disposable civilians while making sure there are plenty of eyewitnesses and reporters desperate to be first with exclusive stories and sensational images.

Psyops as Art

In *The High Cost of Peace*, terrorism analyst Yossef Bodansky explains how during the Cold War, specifically in the early 1970s, the Soviet Union increased its involvement in the Middle East, particularly its support for and exploitation of the Palestinian revolutionary movement.

"To further their joint aims," writes Bodansky, "Moscow advised the PLO to develop a political image that would gain support from Western elites. Taking Moscow's advice, Arafat sent a high-level PLO delegation headed by Salah Khalaf—also known as Abu Iyad—on a milestone visit to Hanoi. The Palestinians had lengthy discussions with a Politburo team led by General Vo Nguyen Giap, in which the Vietnamese told their Palestinian guests about their success in manipulating the Western media, to the point that they had a direct impact on the United States' ability to wage war against North Vietnam and the Vietcong."[29]

According to Bodansky, Abu Iyad has written extensively about how the Vietnamese helped the PLO develop a program that would enable the Palestinian movement to control the narrative, so that instead of being

---

26. McCoy, "Why Hamas Stores Its Weapons Inside Hospitals, Mosques and Schools."
27. "Why They Died, Civilian Casualties in Lebanon during the 2006 War." Specifically section 10, "Hezbollah Conduct During the War."
28. Kendal, "Why Andijan Changed Everything."
29. Bodansky, *The High Cost of Peace*, 9.

perceived of as a terrorist campaign, its fight would be lauded and supported as a freedom struggle.[30]

The Vietnamese introduced the Palestinians "to such issues as dealing with the U.S. media and with liberal political circles and institutions . . . Disinformation and psychological warfare experts assisted the Palestinians in formulating a 'moderate political program' . . ."[31]

On November 13, 1974, an utterly unprecedented event occurred in the UN General Assembly: a non-state representative and recognized terrorist dressed in military fatigues and bearing a sidearm addressed the members. "Today," said PLO leader Yasser Arafat, "I have come bearing an olive branch and a freedom fighter's gun. Do not let the olive branch fall from my hand. I repeat: do not let the olive branch fall from my hand."[32]

Since then, psyops have developed into a virtual art form, and the development of internet technologies, mobile phones, and social networking has made disseminating propaganda easier than ever.

While powers weak and strong have learned well how to play this game, it seems the masses are yet to catch on. The idealistic public—both the weak who are *exploited for* psyops (being routinely used as human shields) and the strong who are the *targets of* psyops (because they can influence policy in a democracy)—still find it hard to believe that they are being duped, manipulated, and exploited by powers prepared to sacrifice truth, integrity, and human beings in pursuit of economic and geostrategic gain.

Like the public in general, most journalists are appallingly ignorant of history, religion, and how asymmetric warfare works. This needs to change. Instead of just parroting and amplifying propaganda—be it acquired from shady "local sources" or an official press conference, journalists must be independent thinkers, discerning investigators, and truth seekers. They must double and triple check their "facts", to ensure that *they* and the public to whom they report are not being duped, manipulated, and exploited.

The Houla Massacre

On Friday May 25, 2012, amidst heavy shelling, a massacre took place in the village of Taldou, 25 km northeast of the city of Homs, in Homs governorate, in the region of Houla. More than a hundred people were killed, mostly women and children.

---

30. Ibid., 9, cites Abu Iyad's book, *Palestinian Without a Motherland*.

31. Ibid., 10.

32. Speech by Yasser Arafat, November 17, 1974. See also: Neff, "PLO Chairman Yasser Arafat's First Appearance at the United Nations."

Western media and political elites accepted unquestioningly the narrative being released by rebel forces: that the regime had perpetrated the massacre. The Syrian government, however, denied responsibility, blaming the deaths on "terrorist gangs."

From the outset, much of the testimony was confusing. Initially, the Syrian opposition claimed the deaths were caused by the regime's shelling. However, after it became clear that this could not have been the case as the dead had clearly been assassinated at close range, the opposition amended its narrative and blamed the deaths on Shabiha (pro-government militia). Anyone taking time to read the reports and examine the details through the prism of asymmetric conflict would have realized that this claim was highly dubious.

Survivor Rasha al-Sayed Ali (29) told reporters that "soldiers" in army uniforms had gone through the area shooting and breaking into homes. When these soldiers came to her home, Rasha told them that her father was a retired soldier and showed them her father's military identity card. To her shock, the soldiers grabbed her and forced her and the other women into a room. They then proceeded to savagely beat her father.

"Then they brought my father into the room and shot him in front of us," she said. "I saw my father's brains spill from his head."

According to Rasha, one of the armed men then shouted, "We took revenge for you, Imam Ali," thereby giving the impression that he was a Shia proud to be killing a Sunni.

"They were security men and Shabiha," said Rasha. "One of them then said to the other, what are we going to do with the children? The other replied shoot them before the elders." Sayed Ali was shot in the chest. She told reporters: "I fell to the floor. After a while, I looked around to see that all my brothers and my mother were sinking in blood. I started to crawl and could hear the cry of my cousin who was only one month old. The baby's mother was dead. Four of my sisters and my pregnant sister-in-law were killed. So was our neighbour. My brother's baby was two months old and sleeping upstairs. They shot her too."[33]

But if these men were SAA or even pro-government Shabiha, then why did they attack the family after learning that the father was a retired SAA soldier?

Maha Abdul Razziq (10) testified that she was inside her family home with her two-year-old cousin when "one of the security men broke into the house. He was holding a knife," she said. After removing the gold jewellery

---

33. Chulov and Mahmood, "The Houla massacre: reconstructing the events of 25 May."

from the infant's wrist, the armed man shot them both. Maha survived with bullet wounds to her arm and leg, while the infant died, shot through the chest. Maha was the only member of her extended family to survive the massacre. More than sixty of the victims belonged to this one family.[34]

If these armed men were members of the security forces, why would anyone be wielding a knife rather than a military-issue firearm? And why were they killing babies? What would be the point of killing babies? Contrary to establishing security, killing babies is unprofessional, it is a hate crime, and it only generates negative publicity and retaliatory rage.

A nurse treating wounded survivors surmised: "They were targeted because they were linked to the regime. The Shabiha wanted to create the impression that other forces were responsible."[35] According to this nurse, the victims were "linked to the regime"—that is, they were pro-Assad. Because the "soldiers" were wearing uniforms, the nurse concluded they must be Syrian military or Shabiha (i.e., also "linked to the regime") and that they must have killed their own supporters in the hope that the rebels would be blamed.

But if these killers were Syrian soldiers or Shabiha hoping to frame the rebels, why would they be wearing Syrian military uniforms?

Abu Jaffour told reporters that "The armed men came under the cover of shellfire from villages completely under regime control."[36] The fact that the killers struck during heavy regime shelling tells us nothing about whom they were. However, the fact that the area was being heavily shelled does indicate that the rebels were under extreme pressure and probably desperate for assistance.

Ali el-Sayed (11) survived by rolling in his brother's blood and then playing dead to fool the killers into thinking he had already been fatally shot. "I put my brother's blood all over me and acted like I was dead," he told reporters. Ali's brother, Nader (6) had been shot in the head and neck. According to Ali—the sole survivor, the armed men who killed his whole family had "long beards and shaved heads."[37]

United Nations investigators and Western media unquestioningly accepted the opposition narrative that the killers were Shabiha (pro-government militia), despite the fact that ever since the seventh century, the long beard and shaved head has been the defining look of the Khawârijite or *takfiri*: the anti-Shi'ite puritanical Sunni sect. Several newspapers actually

---

34. Ibid.
35. Ibid.
36. Ibid.
37. "How an 11-Year-Old Survived Houla Massacre."

published Ali el-Sayed's account alongside a picture of purported "Shabiha", all of whom were clean shaven with full heads of hair. Others, such as the UK's *Daily Mail*, simply omitted Ali's descriptive detail, as if the appearance of the killers meant nothing.[38]

Furthermore, the fact that most of the dead had their throats cut indicates Islamic ritual slaughter, *not* a military operation. That forty-nine of the 108 dead were children[39] indicates a terror attack (i.e., a psyop), *not* a security operation. That sixty of the dead were from one family indicates targeted revenge, a hate crime, *not* a security operation.

According to the report in *Eurasia Review*,[40] citing information from a German investigation, the victims most certainly belonged to a loyalist family believed to have converted from Sunni to Shia Islam. According to other sources, the family was Sunni but strongly supportive of the government.

An objective observer examining the facts through the prism of asymmetric warfare would have to suspect that this was a false flag operation.

As the UN Security Council discussed what measures should be taken against Assad as punishment for the Houla Massacre, Russia's deputy ambassador to the UN cast doubt on the guilt of the Syrian government. "We need to establish whether it was the Syrian authorities," Igor Pankin told reporters at the UN. "There are substantial grounds to believe that the majority of those who were killed were either slashed, cut by knives, or executed at point-blank distance."[41]

Not interested in evidence, Australia's then-Minister for Foreign Affairs, Senator Bob Carr, expelled the Syrian Charge d'Affairs, Jawdat Ali Syrian, saying Australians are "appalled at a regime that could connive in or organise the execution, the killing of men women and children."[42] Likewise, UN Secretary-General Ban Ki-moon decried the Houla Massacre as an "appalling and brutal crime involving indiscriminate and disproportionate use of force . . . [and] a flagrant violation of international law and of the commitments of the Syrian Government to cease the use of heavy weapons in population centres and violence in all its forms."[43]

Francois-Alexandre Roy lamented to Asia Times online (6 July 2012):

---

38. Parsons, "I Put My Brother's Blood All over Me and Acted Like I Was dead" (This article included a couple of fake photos from Iraq—i.e., *not* Houla).
39. "Houla Massacre: 108 Dead, Says UN."
40. "Reconsidering the Houla Massacre."
41. Ibid.
42. Coghlan, "In Response to Houla Massacre Australia Expels Syrian Diplomats."
43. Ibid.

The latest massacre that took place in Houla is one of the best examples of media manipulation: without any proof, as soon as news of the massacre came out, it was immediately blamed on government forces. The BBC even threw in a fake picture[44] of hundreds of dead bodies wrapped up in white sheets that was in fact a picture taken in Iraq by Marco di Lauro back in 2003.

The BBC conveniently said in small characters under the picture itself 'This image—which cannot be independently verified—is believed to show the bodies of children in Houla awaiting burial.' They broke the story all over the world as a means to show the ruthlessness of the Syrian regime and push the public into approval towards humanitarian/military intervention in Syria.

Soon after the picture was discovered as a fake, news that the real perpetrators of the massacre were in fact members of the FSA [Free Syrian Army] disguised as *shabiha* (thugs), and that those killed were pro-government Syrians did not receive the same 'airtime' as the original news did."[45]

Myth Busted: The US-backed FSA are not "moderates," they are not "good rebels."

As had been well established by July 2012, the Houla massacre was a false flag operation perpetrated by the FSA.

In July 2012, German intelligence estimated that 90 percent of all terror attacks that occurred in Syria in the first six months of that year were carried out by groups close to al-Qaeda. Longtime German war correspondent Jürgen Todenhöfer accused the rebels of "deliberately killing civilians and then presenting them as victims of the government." He described this "massacre-marketing strategy" as being "among the most disgusting things that I have ever experienced in an armed conflict."[46]

Even more disturbing was the fact that the German government admitted that it had received intelligence indicating that the Houla massacre was a false flag operation, but that the information remained classified "by reason of national interest." In other words, the German government deemed it not

---

44. Furness, "BBC News Uses 'Iraq Photo to Illustrate Syrian Massacre'"; note also the quote from "Oops, BBC: Iraq Photo to Illustrate Houla Massacre?": "Sometimes it looks that the mantra 'cannot be independently verified' serves as a disclaimer to publish information which wouldn't stand a chance of *ever* being verified."

45. Roy, "Regime change in Syria: A true story."

46. Rosenthal, "German intelligence: al-Qaeda all over Syria."

in Germany's interests to acknowledge the truth: that the Houla massacre was indeed a false flag operation.[47]

The Need for Discernment

> A lie gets halfway around the world before the truth has a chance to get its pants on.[48]

To think this well-known quote was popular well *before* the invention of satellite TV, the internet, the mobile phone, or the Twittersphere! Today we might say, "A lie envelopes the whole earth before the truth has a chance to blink. And by the time it has blinked, the world has moved on."

The Syrian opposition's brilliant use of psyops and manipulation of Western media converged with Western geopolitical interests and mass gullibility to ensure that Western leaders would receive popular support from their constituents for the illegal arming, training, and funding of rebel forces fighting for regime change in Syria.

Of course, all this did was prolong the conflict and facilitate its escalation. Consequently, what might have been a relatively short-lived uprising (not unlike short-lived uprisings that occur routinely all around the world) evolved into a civil war and ultimately into a regional conflagration with strong sectarian overtones and hundreds of thousands of casualties; a conflict thoroughly infiltrated and exploited by international jihadists; a conflict that has seen whole cities turned to rubble, and ancient, spectacular historic sites lost forever; a conflict that has created a region-wide and even transcontinental humanitarian crisis on a scale unprecedented in our lifetime; a conflict that could result in the eradication of ethnic-religious minorities, including indigenous Christian communities whose histories date back millennia. As 2012 rolled into 2013, most analysts were forecasting a stalemate and warning that the war could grind on for years. Such a scenario would have been deeply troubling to the Syrian government, which knew it was not in its interests to wage a long war of attrition against an enemy with access to a seemingly bottomless pit of international jihadists, a guaranteed flow of Saudi and Qatari petrodollars, US-made weapons, and possibly even US-NATO air support.

---

47. Ibid. See also Kendal, "The Syria Crisis: cutting through the propaganda."

48. This quote is attributed to Winston Churchill, and earlier variations to Mark Twain and others, but its actual origin is unknown (see http://quoteinvestigator.com/2014/07/13/truth/).

However, 2013 would see another *myth busted*: Syria most certainly was *not* isolated.

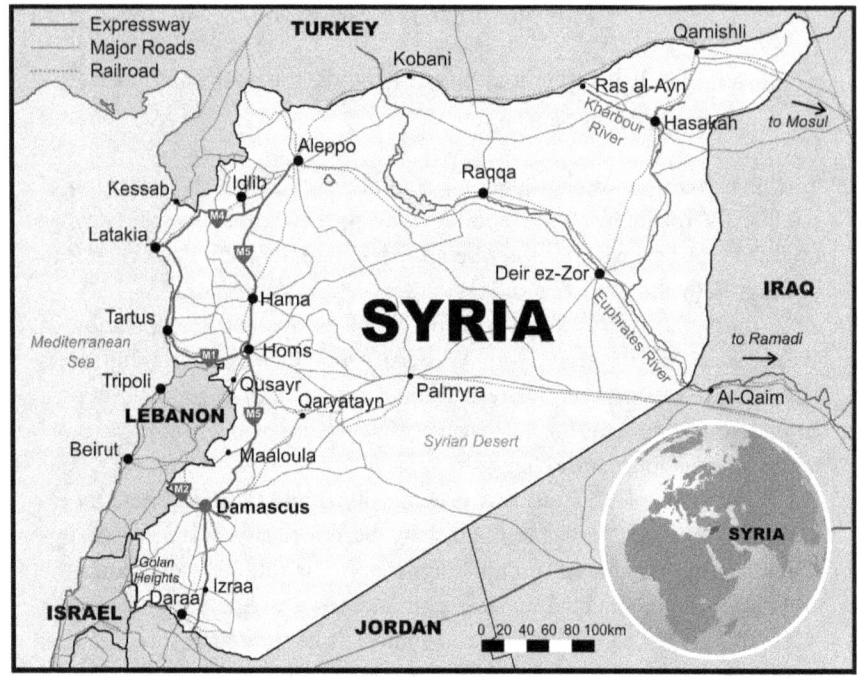

Figure 2. Map of Syria.

— 8 —

The Evolution of a War

The Fall of Qusayr

LOCATED JUST 32 KM southwest of the rebel capital Homs and only 10 km from the Lebanese border, on the main road that leads from the Damascus-Homs highway into Lebanon's Bekaa Valley is the town of Qusayr. Whoever controls Qusayr controls supply into Syria's strategic Homs-Hama industrial center, midway between Damascus (the political capital to the south) and Aleppo (the commercial capital to the north).

A battle for control of Qusayr erupted in early February 2012, and by the end of the month roughly half of the town's forty thousand residents were alleged to have fled. Prior to the exodus, around one-quarter of Qusayr's population was Christian.

As fighting intensified, it increasingly took on sectarian overtones. On June 2, 2012, local Islamic preacher-turned-brigade-leader, Abdel Salam Harb, issued an ultimatum to Qusayr's Christians: either join the MB-led opposition against President Bashar al-Assad or leave.[1] As threats rang out from mosque minarets, Qusayr's remaining Christians abandoned their homes and headed out into an uncertain future; only the most frail, infirm, and disabled remained.[2]

In early July 2012, FSA fighters seized the town hall where the local government was headquartered. As Qusayr fell to rebel forces, Islamic jihadists seized St. Elias Church, which they commandeered as their headquarters.

In a mosque sermon on October 12, 2012, Abdel Salam Harb preached a clear and unambiguous message: "There is nothing left for [Christians] in Qusayr . . . there is no return for them to Qusayr," for "Qusayr Christians are traitors"—to the evident approval of his audience.[3]

---

1. Ashkar, "The Battle for Qusayr and the fate of Saint Elias Church."

2. Brode, Farhat and Nisman, "Syria's Threatened Christians." See also Kendal, "Syria: Christians' Plight Lost Under Mountain Of Propaganda."

3. Ashkar, "The Battle for Qusayr and the Fate of Saint Elias Church."

Meanwhile, in Syria's north, the "mother of all battles" was breaking out in Aleppo.

The Battle for Aleppo

Aleppo is Syria's largest city, home to some two and half million citizens, around ten percent (i.e., 250,000) of whom are Christians. A business hub, Aleppo was Syria's commercial capital. There was little support for regime change in Aleppo.

The Battle for Aleppo commenced in July 2012, and as observers were quick to note, most of the rebels fighting in Aleppo were not Aleppons, but outsiders who could not find their way around the city without asking for directions.

From its inception, the Battle for Aleppo has highlighted the rural-urban divide in the Syrian conflict. It is the same rural versus urban, traditional versus progressive divide that characterized the 1979 Islamic uprisings in Iran and Saudi Arabia. In each case, the "revolutionaries" were mostly rural-born, madrassa-educated, radicalized youths who had migrated from the depressed countryside into the cities in search of work. Once in the cities, they were then further radicalized and organized to eventually become the foot soldiers of Islamic fundamentalist ideologues and clerics. While the rural migrants of Aleppo's poor eastern suburbs did little to resist rebel infiltration, the educated, prosperous business elite remained fiercely loyal to the Syrian government. Meanwhile, Turkey was aiding and abetting the rebels in the north while facilitating the entry into Syria of international fighters eager to join the jihad against the "infidel regime."

The Syrian government was finding it difficult to secure the north while rebels were in control of the Homs-Hama center. In order to concentrate resources into the Battle for Aleppo and the all-important western north-south Aleppo-Damascus corridor, the Syrian government withdrew SAA troops from the northeast—essentially leaving it to burn.

By the end of 2012, Aleppo was devastated, with barely a structure that had not been damaged. A burned-out shell was all that remained of the historic UNESCO World Heritage-listed *souq* (market). But the human toll was of course much worse, and Aleppons who had not fled now found themselves besieged. The question "How are we going to get out?" was quickly replaced with "How are we going to survive?", as besieged Aleppons hunkered down faced with the prospect of dying for want of food, water, infant milk formula, medicines, and heating.

With war raging on multiple fronts and a stalemate not in the government's interests, something had to give.

The Liberation of Qusayr

"With the help of thousands of fighters from Hezbollah, Iran, and Iraq, Syrian President Bashar al-Assad has achieved one of his most important military victories in the past two years by forcing the withdrawal of opposition forces from the town of al-Qusayr," wrote Elizabeth O'Bagy on June 6, 2013, in an analysis for the Institute for the Study of War.[4]

As O'Bagy explained, "Rebel control of al-Qusayr had disrupted the regime's critical ground line of supply from Lebanon's Bekaa Valley and allowed for the cross-border movement of arms to rebels. Control of al-Qusayr now secures the regime's line of communication from Damascus to the coast. Al-Qusayr now also cuts off access to cross-border weapons supplies to the rebels from Lebanon and provides an important staging ground for future efforts by the regime to retake the north and east."

O'Bagy saw the May–June 2013 Battle for Qusayr as symbolic of the conflict's transformation or *evolution* from a civil war into "a regional imbroglio that can no longer be isolated within the Syrian context." She continued:

> Although al-Qusayr may not be the decisive battle for Syria, it should be seen as an important turning point. By reasserting its military superiority in al-Qusayr, the regime has gained momentum, and through the help of Hezbollah and Iranian forces, it will likely be able to consolidate its control over the areas it now holds. This includes Syria's most populated and economically important districts. Control of these areas will facilitate their advance on areas north of Homs province and possibly allow them to reclaim important rebel-held areas in the north and the east. Moreover, the regime victory effectively cuts off an important supply route to the rebels which will leave the armed opposition in an ever more weakened position. As for now, the regime does not have the forces required to move on from al-Qusayr and advance on other areas in the north. This means that the rebels have a brief window while the regime resets its capabilities. This window may permit them to develop a counteroffensive in order to disrupt the regime's opportunity to capitalize upon its victory at al-Qusayr. However, the past performance of the armed opposition creates doubt over its ability to so. In light of the regime's regained strategic and operational

4. O'Bagy, "Syria Update: The Fall of Al-Qusayr."

initiative, it will be even more difficult for the opposition moving forward.[5]

A March on Damascus and Sarin in Ghouta.

With the SAA on the offensive, opposition forces and their foreign backers hatched plans for a march on Damascus. According to terrorism analyst Yossef Bodansky, "the U.S.-sponsored war plan was based on the Autumn [August] 2011 march on Tripoli, Libya, by a CIA-sponsored army from Tunisia which decided the Libyan war and empowered the Islamists."[6] (It is important to note here that the Islamic militant march on Tripoli in August 2011 was enabled by NATO air cover.)

Bodansky continues: "Starting Aug. 17 and 18 [2013], nominally Free Syrian Army (FSA) units—in reality a separate Syrian and Arab army trained and equipped by the CIA as well as Jordanian and other [including Saudi Arabian] intelligence services—attempted to penetrate southern Syria from northern Jordan and start a march on Damascus."[7]

After crossing into southern Syria, two units (comprising 550 soldiers in total) made haste for Daraa (in Syria's far south) with the aim of declaring Daraa the capital of a "Free Syria." Before long, however, the rebel forces found themselves up against fierce resistance from SAA-led local tribesmen determined to prevent outside elements invading their turf. By August 19-20, 2013, the rebel units were surrounded; by 21 August they were desperate, screaming for reinforcements and pleading for air cover to prevent their decimation.

"Meanwhile," writes Bodansky, "on Aug. 19, in Ghouta [on the eastern outskirts of Damascus], more than 50 local opposition fighters and their commanders laid down their arms and switched sides. A few prominent local leaders widely associated with the opposition went on Syrian TV. Denouncing the jihadists and their crimes against the local population, they stressed that the Assad administration was the real guardian of the people and their interests. More than a dozen ex-rebels joined the Syrian Government forces."[8]

Writing for Al-Monitor, Mohammed Ballout reported that by August 21, 2013, the SAA's Operation Shield of the Capital had successfully forced

5. Ibid.
6. Bodansky, "Sarajevo, 1995 and Damascus, 2013."
7. Ibid.
8. Ibid.

rebels to retreat from the strategic Jobar entrance that leads into the heart of Damascus. According to Ballout, the rebels were CIA-trained, funded by Saudi Prince Salman bin Sultan, and being led by fighters from Jabhat al-Nusra (al-Qaeda's affiliate in Syria).[9]

Ballout also revealed, "The Saudis have in Ghouta the Liwa' al-Islam armed group, which has 25,000 fighters led by Zahran Alloush. He almost certainly receives his orders directly from the Saudi intelligence chief Prince Bandar bin Sultan."[10]

Just as the SAA was closing in on the encircled, retreating, desperate rebel forces in the deep south, sarin gas was released in Ghouta with blame falling immediately on President al-Assad.

As a consequence, the Syrian government was forced to call a halt to Operation Shield of the Capital so it could facilitate the movement of UN experts—who happened to be in Damascus—and ensure their safety.

Was the Sarin Gas Attack in Ghouta a False Flag Operation?

At this point it helps to consider the facts through the prism of asymmetric warfare, understanding that the CIA-trained, Saudi-funded, al-Qaeda-led rebel forces (weak) were in a dire situation.

- On Monday August 20, 2012, US President Barack Obama publically warned the Syrian government not to use or move its chemical weapons lest it cross a "red line" and provoke a US military response (i.e., US air strikes).[11]

- By August 19–20, 2013, the rebels marching on Damascus (weak) were in a desperate situation, surrounded and facing annihilation at the hands of SAA and loyalist tribal forces (strong). By August 21 they were under extreme pressure and pleading for air cover.

- On August 21, 2013, sarin gas was released in Ghouta, where thousands of Saudi jihadists were receiving instructions from Saudi Arabia's Prince Bandar, and where Syrian nationalists had been defecting from the FSA, appalled by the infiltration of foreign jihadists who had foreign agendas and cared little for the aspirations of Syrian nationalists or the plight of Syrian civilians.

9. Ballout, "US Strike on Syria Would Help Jihadists, Not Secular Opposition."
10. Ibid.
11. "Obama Warns Syria Not to Cross 'Red Line.'"

- The SAA was advancing, with Operation Shield of the Capital successfully driving rebel forces from Jobar (north-east of Damascus and midway between Damascus and eastern Ghouta).

- The chemical attack was the *last* thing the Syrian government (strong) wanted, as it hamstrung the SAA advance. However, it was *exactly* what the rebels (weak) and their Arab and Western backers desperately needed in order to legitimize a military intervention.

As has subsequently been demonstrated by numerous investigations, the Ghouta chemical attack was most certainly a false flag operation in which predominantly Saudi jihadists killed hundreds (not thousands) of Syrian civilians deemed treacherous and expendable, at a time when the SAA was advancing, in the expectation that it would trigger much-needed US air strikes.[12]

Despite the fact that the US knew that al-Qaeda affiliate Jabhat al-Nusra was manufacturing sarin gas in quantities;[13] despite the fact that Syria's chemical weapons arsenals are monitored by America's National Reconnaissance Office and no movement had been detected (not by the Americans and not by the Israelis);[14] despite the fact that senior US mili-

---

12. Gavlak and Ababneh, "EXCLUSIVE: Witnesses Of Gas Attack Say Saudis Supplied Rebels With Chemical Weapons"; Kendal, "SYRIA: Who is Deploying Chemical Weapons?"; Shoebat and Barrack, "Evidence: Syrian Rebels used Chemical Weapons (not Assad)."

13. Hersh, "Whose Sarin?" Excerpt: "An intelligence document issued in mid-summer [July 2013] dealt extensively with Ziyaad Tariq Ahmed, a chemical weapons expert formerly of the Iraqi military, who was said to have moved into Syria and to be operating in Eastern Ghouta. The consultant told me that Tariq had been identified 'as an al-Nusra guy with a track record of making mustard gas in Iraq and someone who is implicated in making and using sarin.'" (This is a most significant report of over 5,500 words by one of the world's most seasoned and respected investigative journalists. Boycotted by mainstream media, it was eventually published in the *London Review of Books*.) See also (1) Waterman, "Syrian Rebels Used Sarin Nerve Gas, Not Assad's Regime: U.N. official" (as noted in this article, the UN Independent International Commission of Inquiry on Syria had already—as early as May 2013—concluded that the rebels were using chemical weapons in Syria. The UN and the US subsequently rejected this finding), and (2) "US Casts Doubt on Claim Syrian Rebels May Have Used Sarin Gas."

14. Hersh, "Whose Sarin?" Excerpt: "The former senior intelligence official, who had direct knowledge of the programme, told me that NRO sensors have been implanted near all known chemical warfare sites in Syria. They are designed to provide constant monitoring of the movement of chemical warheads stored by the military. But far more important, in terms of early warning, is the sensors' ability to alert US and Israeli intelligence when warheads are being loaded with sarin . . . A chemical warhead, once loaded with sarin, has a shelf life of a few days or less—the nerve agent begins eroding the rocket almost immediately: it's a use-it-or-lose-it mass killer . . . The

tary and intelligence personnel and consultants strongly disagreed with the "government assessment,"[15] US Secretary of State John Kerry insisted with shameless "newspeak" (manipulative language designed to limit free thought and restrict free speech)[16] that President al-Assad's guilt was "a judgment . . . already clear to the world."[17]

As calls for US air strikes rang out, rebel forces in Aleppo tightened the siege, cutting off the last line of supply into government-held regions of the city.[18] Rumors spread that rebel forces were preparing to surge under the cover of US air strikes.[19]

With deep angst and sadness, a Protestant pastor in Aleppo confided that the men of his church were preparing for a rebel invasion and a massacre. At church that Sunday he heard the men discussing the dire situation and wondering what could be done. He asked them if they were ready to die. A question from his young son revealed the level of stress and trauma the children were experiencing: "Dad," he asked, "when will the rebels come and kill us for being Christians?"[20]

A call to prayer rang out, and the church prayed.[21]

To Strike or Not to Strike

The rebels might have been desperate for air strikes, but for US President Obama, the call actually came at a most inopportune moment. He was in

---

sensors detected no movement in the months and days before 21 August, the former official said."

15. Ibid. Excerpt: "But in recent interviews with intelligence and military officers and consultants past and present, I found intense concern, and on occasion anger, over what was repeatedly seen as the deliberate manipulation of intelligence. One high-level intelligence officer, in an email to a colleague, called the administration's assurances of Assad's responsibility a 'ruse'. The attack 'was not the result of the current regime,' he wrote . . . The same official said there was immense frustration inside the military and intelligence bureaucracy: 'The guys are throwing their hands in the air and saying, "How can we help this guy"—Obama—"when he and his cronies in the White House make up the intelligence as they go along?"'"

16. "Newspeak": The concept comes from the George Orwell's novel *1984*. Concerning Kerry's statement, who is going to cast doubt on Assad's guilt if it truly is "already clear to the world"?

17. Hughes and Radia, "Syria's Guilt in Chemical Attack 'Clear to the World', Kerry Says."

18. Lev, "Aleppo: Syrian Rebels 'Cut Off' Regime Troops."

19. Bodansky, "Did the White House Help Plan the Syrian Chemical Attack?"

20. Correspondence between Aleppo and former missionaries in Australia.

21. Kendal, "August Update."

the process of advancing what he hoped would be his foreign policy masterstroke and legacy: a much-heralded detente with Iran, something allegedly made possible through the June 2013 "election" of a supposedly "moderate" president: Hassan Rouhani.[22] Though the demands for "retaliatory" air strikes were shrill, President Obama was acutely aware that US air strikes on Syria would totally derail any US-Iran rapprochement.

With Obama under immense pressure to carry out his threat, Russia warned that US missile strikes would most certainly destabilize the wider region, unleash a new wave of terror, and seriously undermine the system of international law—none of which would serve American interests.

On September 11, 2013, *The New York Times* published an open letter from Vladimir Putin, President of Russia, to the American people. Entitled, "A Plea for Caution from Russia," the letter provided an excellent analysis of the Syrian conflict and concluded with a respectful appeal for closer US-Russia ties built on trust. It is certainly worth a read.

Concerning the proposed US missile strike, President Putin wrote: "No one doubts that poison gas was used in Syria. But there is every reason to believe it was used not by the Syrian Army, but by opposition forces, to provoke intervention by their powerful foreign patrons, who would be siding with the fundamentalists."[23]

By September 14, 2013, President Obama had backed off, saved by a Russia-brokered deal that would allow the US to go back on its word without losing face at home. US air strikes would be withheld, and in exchange, Syria's chemical stockpiles would be destroyed. With a deep breath and a handshake, the besieged, critically weakened, and now totally demoralized rebels were abandoned to their fate.[24]

The SAA moved quickly to re-establish its ascendency and consolidate its gains. By early October 2013, the SAA had regained control over the north-south corridor and the critical M5 highway between Damascus and Aleppo. On Sunday October 5, the SAA broke through the rebel encirclement of the commercial capital (Aleppo), enabling supply to flow to

---

22. Re: "election" and "moderate": The clerics of the Guardian Council have the final say over who is eligible to stand as a candidate for president in Iran. The only moderates or reformers permitted to stand as candidates are those guaranteed not to win; they are only permitted to stand so as to give the illusion of choice. The truth is the clerics have turned the preselection process into an art form through which they can all but guarantee the outcome of the "election." The president represents the Guardian Council, which is in no way moderate.

23. Putin, "A Plea for Caution From Russia."

24. Foster, "Barack Obama's Faustian Pact with Vladimir Putin over Syrian Chemical Weapons Brings Despair to Allies."

government-held areas.[25] Though the city was still divided and the fighting far from over, Aleppons would at least have access to food, water, medicines, and fuel.[26]

In November 2013, US-Iran rapprochement proceeded—much to the horror of Israel, Saudi Arabia, and the Gulf States. The interim nuclear deal effectively formalized the nightmare scenario that Israel and the Gulf Arabs had long feared: not only would Iran get more time on the nuclear front, but it would be free to pursue its own interests across the region.

The War for the Northeast

From July 2012, as the Syrian government concentrated its war effort in the west, the Syrian Kurds exploited the opportunity afforded them by the SAA withdrawal to carve out an autonomous region in the northeast.

President al-Assad made no effort to rein in the Syrian Kurds, not simply because he was focused on securing the west, but because he knew that Kurdish empowerment would threaten and distract Syria's nemesis Turkey, which was hosting rebel bases, arming and training rebel fighters, and facilitating their entrance into Syria to fight the Syrian government. It is not without reason that the Turkish border came to be known as the "jihadi highway,"[27] or that US Vice President Joe Biden would come to lament, "our biggest problem is our allies."[28]

Fearing that a Kurdish entity in northeast Syria would embolden Turkish Kurds—specifically the Kurdistan Workers' Party (PKK), Turkey accelerated the movement of international jihadist across the Turkish border into

---

25. Mroue, "Syrian Army Reopens Key Road to Aleppo."

26. "Food and Fuel Supply to Aleppo Restored."

27. "Block the Jihadist Highway"; Cockburn, "An Obvious First Step—Close the Jihadis' Highway"; Amos, "A Smuggler Explains How He Helped Fighters Along 'Jihadi Highway.'"

28. In October 2014, US Vice President Joe Biden got himself into all sorts of trouble for telling students at Harvard University's Kennedy School of Government in Cambridge, Massachusetts: "Our biggest problem is our allies. The Turks, the Saudis, the Emirates, etc, what were they doing? They were so determined to take down [Syrian President Bashar al] Assad and essentially have a proxy Sunni-Shia war, what did they do? They poured hundreds of millions of dollars and tens, thousands of tonnes of weapons into anyone who would fight against Assad—except that the people who were being supplied were [Jabhat] Al-Nusra and al-Qaeda and the extremist elements of jihadis coming from other parts of the world" (Zen, "US VP Biden"). Despite the fact that Biden was dead right and speaking truth, he was forced to apologise to Turkey, Saudi Arabia, and the United Arab Emirates ("Joe Biden Forced to Apologise to UAE and Turkey over Syria Remarks").

northeastern Syria to fight the Kurds—specifically the PKK-aligned Kurdish People's Protection Units (the YPG). While horrendous for the residents of the northeast, it did take some pressure off Damascus.

Hasakah

Contiguous with Iraq's northern Nineveh province, Syria's northeastern province of Hasakah in the upper reaches of the Fertile Crescent is, like Nineveh, ethnically diverse and home to a sizable indigenous Assyrian community. What's more, by 2012, Hasakah was also hosting many thousands of Assyrian refugees who had fled ISI terror in Mosul and other parts of Iraq in the years prior to the outbreak of the Syrian crisis.

In November 2012, rebel fighters attacked Hasakah's city of Ras al-Ayn on the border with Turkey, storming the Christian quarter and ordering the Christians out of their homes. "More than 200 families were driven out in the night," said Sr. Agnes-Miriam de la Croix, mother superior of the Monastery of St. James the Mutilated in Qara (100 km north of Damascus). "People are afraid. Everywhere the deaths squads stop civilians, abduct them and ask for ransom, sometimes they kill them."[29]

A vocal advocate for Syrian Christians and opponent of the Islamist cause, Sr. Agnes-Miriam has been targeted by Islamists and threatened repeatedly with death. So serious were the threats that she was forced to retreat to a safe haven in Lebanon. Sister Agnes-Miriam has condemned the West for supporting the rebels despite infiltration by extremist elements and mounting evidence of gross human rights abuses including rapes, murders, and numerous kidnappings. "The free and democratic world is supporting extremists," she laments. "They want to impose Sharia Law and create an Islamic state in Syria."

Hasakah's Ras al-Ayn has considerable strategic value simply by virtue of its location on the Turkish border. On Thursday January 17, 2013, some three hundred jihadists linked to al-Qaeda-aligned Jabhat al-Nusra crossed the Turkish border with three tanks to fight the Kurds in Ras al-Ayn.[30]

As conflict spread through Hasakah and neighboring Raqqa provinces, Assyrian Christians found themselves not only caught in the crossfire, but being targeted by hard-line Islamic fundamentalists eager to sweep away everything un-Islamic. A Christian exodus ensued, which included thousands of Assyrian refugees from Iraq who had little choice other than to return across the border into volatile, insecure, ISI-occupied Nineveh.

---

29. Fagge, "Syria Rebels 'Beheaded a Christian and Fed Him to the Dogs.'"
30. "Fierce Clashes pit Syrian Kurds against Jihadists."

The withdrawal of the SAA had left the Christian community defenseless. "The Arabs had arms coming from Saudi and Qatar, the Kurds had help from Kurdistan," said Joseph. "We had no weapons at all."[31]

As hard-line Salafi/Wahhabi jihadists flowed in, the violence became increasingly religious. "It began as kidnapping for money," said one Christian refugee, "but then they started telling me I should worship Allah. I was with five others. We were tied and blindfolded and pushed down on our knees. One of the kidnappers leant so close to my face I could feel his breath. He hissed: 'Why don't you become a Muslim? Then you can be free.'"[32]

In February 2013, reporter Susanne Güsten met with refugees huddled in Mor Hanonyo, a 1,600-year-old Syriac Orthodox monastery outside Mardin in southeastern Turkey. One family of five fled Hasakah after a neighbor's child was kidnapped by rebels and held for ransom. A young man demonstrated how he was hung by his arms, robbed, and beaten by rebels, "just for being a Christian."[33]

Christians Not Safe in Camps

Father Joseph, a Syriac monk, explained why the Christian refugees head for the monasteries and not the refugee camps. "They are afraid to stay in the camps," he said. "They feel safer with their own people."

Indeed, not only are the camps full of Muslims, many of whom have been radicalized and are hostile towards Christians, but the camps have been thoroughly infiltrated by rebel fighters. Armed groups, including al-Nusra, are constantly seizing and forcibly recruiting young males from the camps. According to Evgil Turker, the president of the Federation of Syriac Associations in Turkey, al-Nusra "and other rebel groups are entrenched in the refugee camps. They round up young men in the camps, sometimes 20 or 30 a day, and send them through the border fence back into Syria." To save Christian youths from such a fate, Mr Turker's organization retrieves them from the camps. "We vouch for them and they are released to us on our recognizance," he said.[34]

In May 2013, Syriac Patriarch Ignace Joseph III Younan described the situation in his native province of Hasakah as "very critical." Christians, he said, were being pressured to leave the area. "People live in fear. They fear kidnapping and killing, and many of the Christians just want to get out in

31. Sherlock, "Syrian Christian Towns Emptied by Sectarian Violence."
32. Ibid.
33. Güsten, "Christians Squeezed Out by Violent Struggle in North Syria."
34. Ibid.

whatever way they can. It's very sad to say that there is no hope for the future for the young generations."[35]

According to the patriarch, the morale of Christians in Syria "is very, very low."

> We were warning all those involved, the countries in the region and in the West—that means the United States and some of the European Union countries, like the United Kingdom and France—that this kind of violence [Islamic violence] would lead to chaos and the chaos to a civil war. And at that time, two years ago, they chose not to believe that.
>
> Since the beginning, they just stood against the regime, calling it a dictatorship, saying the dictatorship must fall. Now the conflict is getting worse, and the ones who are paying the price are the innocent people.

Raqqa and the Al-Nusra–ISIS split

Raqqa fell to rebel forces in March 2013, becoming the first provincial capital fully under rebel control. Subsequently, however, tensions escalated within rebel ranks as a power struggle, fuelled by two competing visions, tore the rebel forces apart. By May 2013 there were two leading al-Qaeda affiliates struggling for hegemony in the north: Jabhat al-Nusra, led by Abu Muhammad al-Julani and loyal to al-Qaeda central's Ayman al-Zawahiri, and ISIS, led by Abu Bakr al-Baghdadi. Eventually, tensions spilled over into open conflict.

The dispute between al-Nusra and ISIS has its roots in a debate that commenced a decade earlier, during the Iraq war, when AQI's Abu Musab al-Zarqawi (a Jordanian, semi-literate, criminal-turned-Salafist)[36] and al-Qaeda central's Ayman al-Zawahiri (an Egyptian surgeon) diverged over the way the Iraqi jihad was being prosecuted. While both men shared the same Salafi/Wahhabi ideology and had the same goal—a caliphate in the Middle East—they diverged over tactics and strategy.

Ayman al-Zawahiri was (and is) committed to Osama bin Laden's strategic vision, which held that the Muslims' first priority must be *resistance* and driving the US out of the Middle East; then and only then could a caliphate be established and maintained. Bin Laden (a construction engineer and multimillionaire) understood that controlling territory was a

---

35. Raad, "Syrian crisis part of Western geopolitical strategy, says patriarch."
36. Weiss and Hassan, *ISIS*, 2.

dangerous trap, for as any military strategist will know, a state is a "fixed target on which the United States and its allies can focus their formidable power."[37] Consequently, bin Laden maintained that a long war should be prosecuted to exhaust and deplete the US until it was so weak that it could not overthrow any state the Muslims might establish.[38]

Most critically, bin Laden and Zawahiri were pragmatists, willing to cooperate with Iran in pursuit of shared strategic goals, such as *resistance*. Zarqawi, on the other hand, was a young, zealous, minimally educated and uncompromising, anti-Shi'ite *takfiri*[39] who believed that End Time prophecies were coming to pass and the caliphate's time had arrived.

Compounding problems was the fact that Abu Musab al-Zarqawi's *takfiri* penchant for killing Shi'ites had fueled Iraq's sectarian conflict. Not only did this have the effect of pitting Muslims against Muslims rather than US troops, it brought immense trouble to the Sunni masses who inevitably had to face blowback (i.e., unintended negative consequences) in the form of retaliation at the hands of Shi'ite death squads.

Also, while Ayman al-Zawahiri was totally focused on preparing the ground for Islamic rule and Sharia law (which would all come in good time), Zarqawi insisted that it was absolutely necessary that Sharia be enforced now and harsh Sharia penalties enacted now—without compromise and without mercy. This, he believed, was the prerequisite for *success*. This did not impress Iraq's Sunnis, most of whom were not Wahhabis. To the contrary, most had a long history of traditional tribal culture, and many were members of the secular Baath Party. While they might have despised the Americans for invading their country and turning their lives upside-down, they despised al-Qaeda even more.

Hostility towards AQI grew so strong throughout Iraq's Sunni heartland that the US was able to co-opt tribal Sunni support for the war against AQI. The Awakening, or Salvation, movement, which arose in Anbar and spread to Diyala through 2006, was a direct response by local Sunnis opposed to AQI's relentless campaign of murder and intimidation.

By June 2006, the US had located Abu Musab al-Zarqawi. On June 7, after drones confirmed Zarqawi's presence, his hideout was targeted from the air, first with "a five-hundred pound laser-guided bomb" dropped on

---

37. Stewart, "The Jihadist Trap of Here and Now."
38. Ibid.
39. *Takfiri*: a fundamentalist Sunni Muslim who deems lesser Muslims (especially Shi'ites) to be non-Muslims (i.e., *kafir*), deserving of death. The act of *takfir* is the act of calling another Muslim a *kafir*.

the location by an F-16 fighter jet, "followed by a second, satellite-guided munition."[40]

Subsequently, in October 2006, AQI—now headed by Egyptian national Abu Ayyab al-Masri— merged with several other Salafi groups to form ISI under the leadership of Iraqi national Abu Omar al-Baghdadi. While AQI had been the largest of the Salafi groups, its international nature and ties with al-Qaeda posed a problem for Iraqi nationalists. According to Iraqi nationalist and Awakening supporter, Mullah Nadhim al-Jibouri, ISI was in effect a ploy by AQI to dress up its foreign jihadism in a nationalist costume. "ISI represented al-Qaeda's attempt to hijack the political channel of the Iraqi insurgency," he said.[41]

During the "Surge" of 2007, which saw the US deploy an additional five combat brigades comprising some 30,000 soldiers, Awakening groups fought alongside US forces while receiving US training to ultimately drive al-Qaeda out of Anbar and Diyala.

While US and Iraqi forces did kill many AQI/ISI jihadists, plenty escaped and joined their "brothers" in Nineveh where they subsequently regrouped in Mosul. There they assassinated the Christian leadership and subjugated, extorted (demanded *jizya*), murdered, and terrorized Nineveh's Assyrian Christian community, triggering a Christian exodus.

Abu Bakr al-Baghdadi

In April 2010, US troops raided a safe house that was hiding AQI's al-Masri and ISI's Abu Omar al-Baghdadi; both were killed. In May 2010, Ibrahim Awwad al-Badri, better known as Abu Bakr al-Baghdadi, assumed the ISI leadership. A seasoned militant, committed *takfiri*, respected leader, and Islamic scholar with a PhD in Islamic Studies from Baghdad University, Abu Bakr al-Baghdadi set about transforming ISI from a band of terrorists into a fully fledged Islamic army. Among his recruits were scores of disenfranchised Sunnis: angry men, including military personnel and experienced administrators, who had been profoundly negatively impacted by the de-Baathification of Iraq, the reckless and disastrous policy of US Presidential Envoy Paul Bremer which saw all those associated with Iraq's secular Baath Party banned from holding positions in the new government. Also among al-Baghdadi's recruits were hundreds if not thousands of militants (nationalists and Islamists) with whom he had formed relationships between

---

40. Weiss and Hassan, *ISIS*, 61.
41. Ibid., 80.

February and December 2004 while detained in Camp Bucca, a US-run prison in southern Iraq.[42]

In August 2011, four months ahead of the US withdrawal from Iraq, al-Baghdadi sent jihadists into Syria with instructions to recruit fighters, form an organization, and establish cells. One of the first men to cross into Hasakah (northeast Syria) was Abu Mohammed al-Julani, a Syrian national from Damascus. For years Assad had facilitated the flow of jihadists into Iraq to fight the Americans; now they were coming back, to fight Assad. In December 2011, al-Julani's cell staged a series of car bombings in Damascus.

In January 2012, al-Baghdadi formally announced the formation in Syria of Jabhat an-Nuṣrah li-Ahli ash-Sham (The Support Front for the People of Sham)—also known as Jabhat al-Nusra or the al-Nusra Front. Its ranks swelled rapidly as foreign fighters flooded into Syria, mostly via Turkey, to join the jihad.

Naturally, none of this went unnoticed in Tehran where al-Baghdadi, as a committed anti-Shi'ite *takfiri*, was a person of interest.

Tehran Hedges Its Bets

Sometime between late December 2011 and early January 2012, Syrian president Bashar al-Assad quietly gave the order for an al-Qaeda figure long known to be one of the most significant and influential theorists in the international jihadist movement to be released from his prison cell in Aleppo.[43]

Commonly known as Abu Musab al-Suri, the Aleppo-born engineer had fled Syria in 1982 after the failed MB uprising in Hama. He subsequently married a Spanish convert and acquired Spanish citizenship; his wife now lives in pro-MB Qatar with their four children. Abu Musab al-Suri has written extensively on "confronting the Alawites in Syria" and on "the

---

42. Chulov, "Iraq Prison System Blamed for Big Rise in al-Qaida Violence." Chulov's extensive report exposes the role that the American-run prisons played in the formation of IS. One IS defector told Chulov that the prison system—which comprised 24 camps holding some 24,000 men—was essentially "a factory" where ideology was consolidated and networks were established. According to the defector, it was in Camp Bucca that Abu Bakr al-Baghdadi (33) established himself as a leader. What's more, his skills as a mediator earned him the respect of the Americans. "If he wanted to visit people in another camp he could," said the defector, "but we couldn't. And all the while, a new strategy, which he was leading, was rising under their [the American's] noses, and that was to build the Islamic State." See also "ISIS, the Inside Story."

43. Bodansky, "The Release of Abu-Musab al-Suri,"

failure of the jihadist experience in Syria," exploring reasons why the Syrian MB and Combatant Vanguard failed to overthrow the regime in the 1980s.[44]

Before being imprisoned in Aleppo, Abu Musab al-Suri had been active in Pakistan. On October 31, 2005, he was captured in Quetta by Pakistani Intelligence Services. A few weeks later, he was handed to the CIA and reportedly transferred to a "phantom prison" on Diego Garcia (a British island in the middle of the Indian Ocean hosting a US military base) where he was subjected to "intense interrogation." Divulging nothing, al-Suri was fast-tracked for "special rendition" and in March 2006 was "rendered" to Bashar al-Assad's Syria with the expectation that Syrian intelligence officers would extract something from him.[45]

According to terrorism analyst Yossef Bodansky (January 2012), Bashar al-Assad released Abu Musab al-Suri from prison at the request of Iran, specifically the Quds Force[46] of the IRGC, or Pasdaran. Bodansky notes that "the primary beneficiaries" of Abu Musab al-Suri's release were "the Iranians; specifically his past ally, Maj.-Gen. Qassem Soleimani", the Quds Force commander who "answers directly to Iran's Supreme Leader Ali Hoseini-Khamene'i; that is, outside the command structure of the *Pasdaran*."[47] Released along with Abu Musab al-Suri was his "life-long friend and closest companion"[48] Abu Kalid al-Suri, whom Ayman al-Zawahiri subsequently appointed as his emissary in Syria.

Tehran's plan was to have Abu Musab al-Suri (al-Qaeda's most respected master strategist) promote pragmatism—particularly cooperation with Axis of Resistance-leader Iran—and counter the rising popularity of the anti-Shi'ite *takfiri* ideology being espoused by Abu Bakr al-Baghdadi.

Bodansky noted that Quds Force commander Major General Qassem Soleimani "directly commands the Iranian and non-Iranian forces—including the *HizbAllah* and Palestinian forces—committed to supporting the Syrian forces. At the same time, Soleimani's *Quds* Forces also support various *jihadists* forces operating *against* the Assad government just to make sure that Iran was not left outside any future government in Syria. Bashar al-Assad knows this but can do nothing."

"Hence," continues Bodansky, "the objective in getting Abu Musab al-Suri released was to have him intercede with, perhaps even take over, the

---

44. Al-Shishani, "Jabhat al-Nusra's New Syria Strategy."

45. For more on US-Syria cooperation and intelligence sharing, see Hersh, "Military to Military."

46. The Quds Force of the IRGC is the special branch responsible for extraterritorial operations.

47. Bodansky, "The Release of Abu-Musab al-Suri."

48. Joscelyn, "Analysis: Zawahiri's Letter to al Qaeda Branches in Syria, Iraq."

main *jihadist* forces and particularly various vanguard movements. Tehran hopes to have them co-operate with the *Quds* Forces towards resolving the Syrian conflagration."

As Bodansky notes, whether Bashar al-Assad survives or falls is of no consequence to Tehran so long as it keeps Damascus in the Axis of Resistance. That said, when Soleimani briefed Khamenei on January 19, 2012, he was firmly of the opinion that Assad would prevail because "most of the Syrian people are loyal to the government."[49]

Al-Baghdadi Triggers a Power Struggle

On December 11, 2012, the US added al-Nusra to its list of proscribed terrorist organizations. The Department of State called the group "a new alias for AQI," noting that al-Baghdadi is "in control of both AQI and al-Nusra."[50]

The very next day, however, Ahmed Moaz al-Khatib, the head of the Syrian National Coalition (the group recognized by the US as the legitimate representative of the Syrian people) called for the terrorist designation to be dropped.[51] To bolster his demand, he presented the Friends of Syria conference meeting in Morocco with a petition signed by twenty-nine Syrian opposition groups which had pledged their allegiance to the group, promoting the slogan: "No to American intervention, for we are all Jabhat al-Nusra."[52]

Sensing al-Nusra was growing into a force in its own right, Abu Bakr al-Baghdadi moved to reassert his leadership over the group. On April 8, 2013, al-Baghdadi announced that Jabhat al-Nusra and ISI would merge to form the Islamic State of Iraq and al-Sham/the Levant (ISIS/ISIL), confirming that "al Nusrah Front is but an extension of the Islamic State of Iraq and part of it."[53]

The leader of al-Qaeda, Ayman al-Zawahiri, initially backed the move, but it did not take long for cracks to appear on the ground. Just days after al-Baghdadi's announcement, Abu Muhammad al-Julani, the emir (leader) of al-Nusra, responded with a message of his own. Al-Nusra had indeed grown into a well-connected, powerful force in its own right, and al-Julani saw no reason why he should have to submit to al-Baghdadi's leadership.

49. Bodansky, "The Release of Abu Musab al-Suri."

50. Nuland, "Terrorist Designations of the al-Nusrah Front as an Alias for al-Qa'ida in Iraq."

51. Roggio, "Syrian National Coalition Urges US to Drop Al Nusrah Terrorism Designation."

52. Sherlock, "Syrian rebels defy US and pledge allegiance to jihadi group."

53. Joscelyn, "Al Qaeda in Iraq, Al Nusrah Front emerge as rebranded single entity."

Consequently, al-Julani rejected the merge and reaffirmed his oath of allegiance to al-Zawahiri.[54]

Forced to rule on the dispute, al-Zawahiri wrote a letter dated May 23, 2013, in which he ordered that al-Baghdadi's ISIS be dissolved on the grounds that al-Baghdadi had failed to seek his advice or permission before announcing the merger. Al-Zawahiri ruled that al-Nusra, under the leadership of al-Julani, would be al-Qaeda's official force in Syria, and ISI, under the leadership of al-Baghdadi, would be al-Qaeda's official force in Iraq: two separate forces for two separate theatres. Furthermore, al-Zawahiri announced that he had appointed respected al-Qaeda figure Abu Khalid al-Suri as his emissary in Syria, with authority to rule on this matter and to make sure his orders were carried out.

But al-Zawahiri's orders were not carried out. Defying the ruling, al-Baghdadi ordered ISIS to continue the fight in Syria. Thus, ISIS and al-Nusra fighters ended up fighting side-by-side against their common enemies—be that the Syrian government or Kurdish forces. However, tensions between the two groups were high. Hostilities simmered, not primarily over loyalties but over tactics: specifically, the pragmatism of al-Qaeda central (represented by al-Zawahiri, his emissary Abu Khalid al-Suri, and strategist Abu Musab al-Suri) versus the inflexible, uncompromising, and merciless Sharia implementation and rabid anti-Shi'ite *takfirism* of Abu Bakr al-Baghdadi.

"The power struggle," explains Bodanksy, "between DI'ISH [the Arab acronym for ISIS/ISIL][55] and the various Jihadist groups affiliated with Ayman al-Zawahiri's al-Qaida (such as Jabhat al-Nusra, Ahrar al-Sham, etc) is really about the quintessential issue whether the Sunni Jihadist movement being neo-Salafi—and thus inherently anti-Shiite—can secretly cooperate with Iran and receive comprehensive assistance via the IRGC's Quds Forces (weapons, funding, guidance, shelters in Iran, etc.)."[56]

Not only were the seasoned old guard of al-Qaeda central prepared to cooperate with Shi'ite Iran—as they had done for decades in jihads all over the world (including in the Balkans), they had also heeded the lessons of Iraq, where the importance of not alienating and angering the local Muslims (whose support is essential in gathering intelligence and securing sanctuary) had been proved. While harsh treatment of Christians and other infidels was tolerated—particularly as it allowed jihadists to let off steam

---

54. Joscelyn, "Analysis: Zawahiri's letter to al Qaeda branches in Syria, Iraq."

55. DI'ISH: Al-Dawlah Al-Islamiyah fe Al-Iraq wa Al-Sham (the Islamic State of Iraq and al-Sham).

56. Bodansky, "The Khorasan Pledge."

and establish their Islamic credentials, harsh treatment of local Muslims was viewed as bad strategy and self defeating.

Abu Bakr al-Baghdadi would have none of this; he was firmly of the opinion that al-Qaeda had sold out. Furthermore, he maintained that al-Qaeda's willingness to compromise was precisely the reason why the jihad was not meeting with *success*. In order to have success, al-Baghdadi maintained, Muslims must observe reformed, puritanical, Salafi/Wahhabi Islam, and follow Allah's *guidance* as revealed in the Qur'an and the example of Muhammad. Muslims must *submit* to Allah's law (Sharia) without compromise, without mercy. If that necessitates that non-Islamic cultural heritage be erased, and that there be amputations, stonings, beheadings, crucifixions, extortion (*jizya*), the mass killings of men, and the mass enslavement of women and children—well, so be it. In particular, al-Baghdadi maintained, there should definitely be no cooperation with Shi'ites: those treacherous, heretical, apostates—those *rwafida* (rejectionists)—had to die.

ISIS Hastens to *Success*

In January 2014, ISIS ousted al-Nusra fighters from the Syrian city of Raqqa to assume full control of the city. Though analysts were alarmed, US President Obama was dismissive. When asked about the rise of ISIS, Obama scoffed and uttered his now famous understatement: "The analogy we use around here sometimes, and I think is accurate, is if a jayvee [JV, junior varsity] team puts on Lakers uniforms that doesn't make them Kobe Bryant."[57] In other words, just because amateurs dress up as professionals, it doesn't mean they are.

Then, in late February 2014, ISIS jihadists in Aleppo assassinated Abu Khaled al-Suri—strategist Abu Musab al-Suri's closest companion and al-Zawahiri's personal emissary in Syria. He was killed by the "*Kharijites* of this age," reported Hassan Abboud, leader of the Syrian Salafi group Ahrar al-Sham, referring to the ancient *takfiri* sect responsible for the assassination of the fourth Caliph, Ali.[58]

Al-Nusra responded with fury, ordering ISIS out of Aleppo. The split was now official. Opting not to fight, ISIS withdrew to consolidate in Raqqa, which is, as one ISIS jihadist boasted, "a larger area than the state of Kuwait."[59]

57. Remnick, "Going the Distance: On and Off the Road with Barack Obama."
58. Lund, "Who and What Was Abu Khalid al-Suri?"
59. Al-Ali, "ISIS Rules in Raqqa."

Video footage smuggled out of Raqqa in February 2014 revealed that ISIS was enforcing Sharia law without compromise or mercy.[60] All women, including remnant Christians, were being forced to wear the *niqab* (a full black covering, with just a slit open for eyes); the penalty for non-compliance was lashing and even death. Music was forbidden. Men and women were not permitted to mingle, and separate bakeries had been established for males and females.

To police women and supervise female prisoners, ISIS established the al-Khansa and Um Riyan brigades, comprised of single women aged 18–25 years. In September 2014, researcher Soeren Kern reported that at least half a dozen of the sixty British women who had traveled to Syria to join the jihad and/or marry a jihadist were working in Raqqa's al-Khansa brigade. In addition to zealously enforcing strict Sharia codes on all females, these women were also guarding the more than three thousand non-Muslim women being held captive as sex slaves. "It is the British women who have risen to the top of the Islamic State's Sharia police and now they are in charge of this operation," one analyst told the *Daily Mirror*. "It is as bizarre as it is perverse." One older British woman named Sally Jones (45) changed her name to Umm Hussain al-Britani and tweeted of her desire to behead Christians. "You Christians all need beheading with a nice blunt knife and stuck on the railings at Raqqa . . . Come here I'll do it for you!" [61]

In late February 2014, ISIS abducted twenty of Raqqa's Christian leaders and presented them with three options: convert to Islam, submit to Islam as *dhimmis* paying the *jizya*, or "face the sword." Faced with this choice, Raqqa's Christian leaders signed an agreement committing the Christian community to *dhimmitude*: a state of abject humiliation and subjugation, without rights, under Islam.[62]

According to the agreement, though the Christians of Raqqa would not be forced to convert, they would however be required to demonstrate respect for Islam and Muslims and abstain from all public expressions of Christianity. They would not be permitted to renovate their churches or monasteries, for these, like the Christians themselves, must be seen to be depressed and in decline. Christians would be subjugated and not be permitted to flourish or have *success* as that could generate *fitna* (i.e., strife triggered by doubt). For its headquarters, ISIS commandeered Raqqa's impressive

---

60. Beaumont, "Smuggled Video Testimony Documents Harsh Rule of Syrian Islamist Group."
61. Kern, "Britain's Female Jihadists."
62. Miller, "Syrian Christians sign treaty of submission to Islamists."

Armenian Church. The bell and cross were removed and replaced with the black ISIS flag.⁶³

In line with the agreement, ISIS imposed a crippling *jizya* (tribute/protection money) on the Christian remnant, to be collected from every Christian adult twice annually. Christians deemed wealthy would have to pay four golden dinars (worth at that time about $US730), those of average wealth would have to pay two, and the poor, one. Handing over such funds would be difficult at any time, but positively excruciating in a time of war, economic downturn, and soaring unemployment.

In the blink of an eye, Raqqa's Christian remnant had been plunged back into the pre-World War I era of classic Islamic rule in which Christians must tiptoe through the minefield of *dhimmitude*, aware that one offense, one slip of the tongue, one lapse in protocol, one objection, one act of resistance in pursuit of dignity or justice, would see "protection" withdrawn and jihad resumed. ISIS celebrated the *dhimma* pact with a statement on its Twitter account: "Today in Raqqa and tomorrow in Rome."⁶⁴

The Khorasan Pledge

In April 2014, al-Baghdadi further escalated the ideological/theological dispute. Insisting there would be no reconciliation with the wayward Ayman al-Zawahiri, al-Baghdadi threw down the gauntlet and demanded Muslims recognize his authority. Nine prominent al-Qaeda emirs from Afghanistan, Turkmenistan, and Iran—that is, from the region historically known as Greater Khorasan—immediately declared their allegiance to the new emir of the faithful, ISIS head Abu Bakr al-Baghdadi.⁶⁵ The "Khorasan pledge", as it came to be known, split al-Qaeda, not only in Syria, but internationally.⁶⁶

According to Yossef Bodansky, the defecting emirs refused to accept the excuses of al-Qaeda leaders who maintained that the only reason they were not enforcing strict Sharia was because they were trying to avoid clashes with the people. The emirs insisted they enforced more in secret than in public.⁶⁷

---

63. "ISIS seizes Armenian church in Raqqa." Kendal, "Raqqa, Syria: Christians in the lions' den." (Includes a confronting photo from Fars media (Iran) showing armed and hooded ISIS jihadis collecting *jizya* from a line of Christian men in Raqqa.)

64. Spencer, "Militant Islamist Group in Syria Orders Christians to Pay Tax for Their protection."

65. Kendal, "ISIS Takes the War Back to Iraq."

66. Mortada, "Khorasan Pledge Splits Al-Qaeda."

67. Bodansky, "The Khorasan Pledge."

"On the contrary," wrote Bodansky,

> the nine emirs stressed, the *tacit and expedient cooperation with Shi'ite Iran was not limited to the jihadists under duress in Syria but was rather a new trend in the Islamist movement.* The most glaring example of the theological corruption of the Islamist-jihadist creed was [according to the emirs] "former Egyptian President Mohammed Morsi, who was proven to be an apostate, even for those who had a semblance of comprehension. Or was it an indication of a new kind of jihad?" The emirs emphasize that Morsi's rapprochement with Iran and other apostate states, as well as his refusal to launch jihad against Israel . . . was a conscientious betrayal of the Islamist creed.[68]

"It was, the emirs believed, because of this deviation from the right and righteous path that the Islamists lost power in Egypt," says Bodansky. In other words, the emirs were of the view that al-Qaeda's lack of *success* was a direct result of theological corruption and refusal to *submit* to right *guidance*—that is, the enforcement of Sharia and killing of apostates.

Lamentations of a Patriarch

In April 2014, ISIS actually started crucifying people in central Raqqa. In what was a hugely risky and desperate cry for help, a group of courageous local youths created a Facebook page called "Raqqa is Being Slaughtered Silently" to which they posted their horrific images.[69]

The horror of what had been unleashed could no longer be denied.

As far as Syriac Patriarch Ignace Joseph III Younan is concerned, the West bears much of the responsibility, having fueled, escalated, and prolonged the crisis through its support for the fundamentalist Muslim opposition "in the name of the so-called awakening of people, of democracy." The result, he says, is the escalation of a conflict that is "very much harming our very existence."

"For us Middle Eastern Christians, the faith means a lot," stressed the Patriarch in May 2013. "For us, religious liberties come first, otherwise we would not have been surviving for centuries in this area. Western leaders don't want to understand this. Christians in the Middle East have been not only abandoned, but we have been lied to and betrayed by Western nations, like the United States and the European Union. And I believe there will be a

---

68. Emphasis added.
69. Sherlock and Malouf, "Inside an ISIL Town"; "Syrian Rebels Crucified."

time coming when the Christians of the Middle East will no longer look to the West for support." Rather, he said, Christians will do better "to look to the East, to Russia, to India, to China."[70]

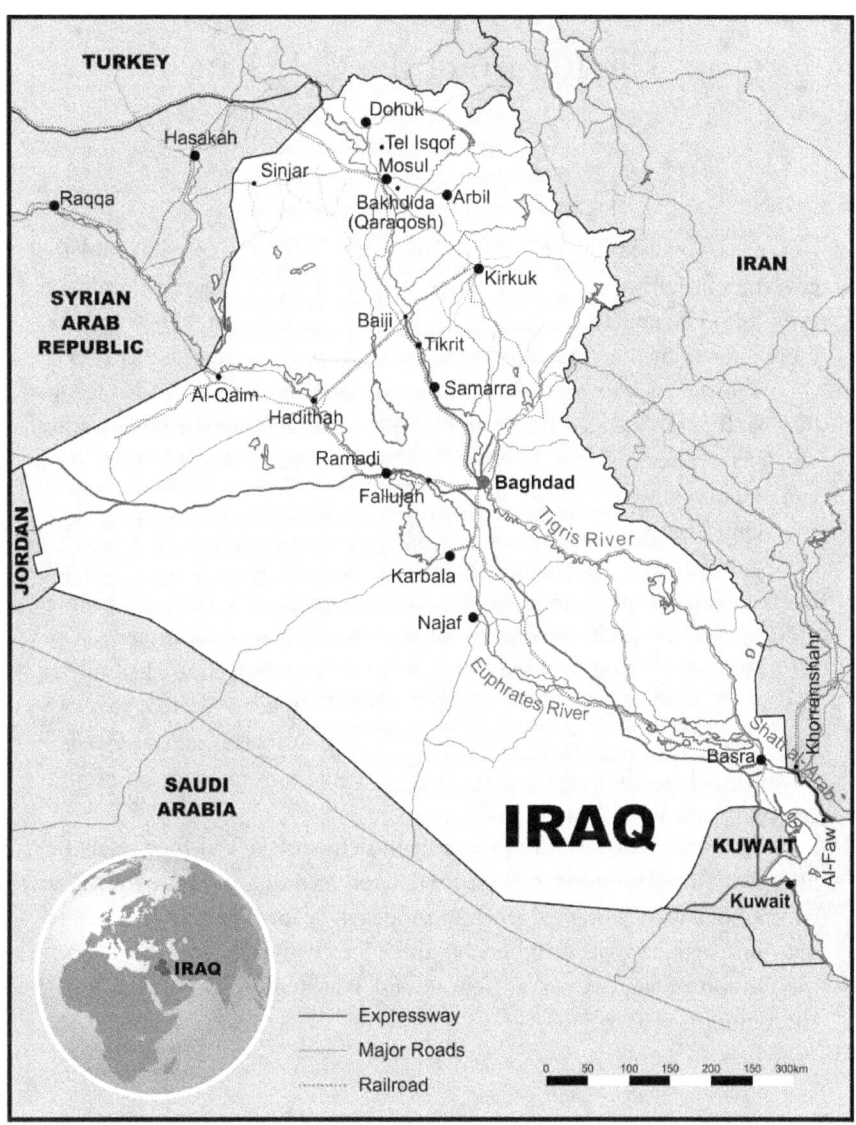

Figure 3. Map of Iraq.

70. Raad, "Syrian Crisis Part of Western Geopolitical Strategy, Says Patriarch."

— 9 —

The Return of the Caliphate

ALL EYES WERE FIXED on Syria throughout 2012 and 2013. Would the government fall? Would the West intervene? Would al-Qaeda dominate? Would ISIS be able to consolidate? It was gripping, sensational drama, far more interesting than events in Iraq, where the war was supposedly over.

The war in Iraq might have been over for the US and NATO troops that had happily headed home, but for the locals left behind the situation was far from secure. Propagandists might have been trumpeting the war's end, but in reality, a new war was already unfolding.

On Monday December 12, 2011, as the last US troops were preparing to withdraw, Iraqi Prime Minister Nuri al-Maliki met with US President Barak Obama at the White House in Washington D.C. to close the chapter of history entitled "US Occupation of Iraq (March 2003–December 2011)." The two men had nothing but praise for how the Iraq adventure had turned out. "We have proven success," boasted Prime Minister al-Maliki. "Nobody imagined that we would succeed in defeating terrorism and al-Qaeda."[1] President Obama likewise effused that Iraq could now be "a model for others aspiring to build democracy."[2]

Al-Qaeda defeated? Iraq a model of democracy? Did they really believe that?—Probably not. It is far more likely that this was pure theatre by two politicians needing to generate propaganda for amplification by media—propaganda that would enable the US to withdraw with dignity and the illusion of success just as Tehran and Washington had agreed in the latter months of 2007.[3]

---

1. Kendal, "Iraq: Propaganda versus Reality," cites "Obama, Maliki meet over Iraq future" and "Obama and Maliki Back Iraq Post-war Future."
2. Robinson, "Obama, Maliki Hail 'New Chapter' for Iraq Without US Troops."
3. See chapter 5: The Shia Crescent.

Genocide Foretold

In December 2011, as US and NATO forces prepared to depart, Iraq's Christian leaders warned that Christians in Baghdad and in the northern province of Nineveh were being left in a diabolical situation.

Latin Archbishop of Baghdad, Mgr. Jean Benjamin Sleiman, told the Catholic charity Aid to the Church in Need that Iraq's Christians were preparing for a "Christmas under siege." Christmas 2011 would be, he said, "a Christmas, between fear and sturdy faith." The war might have been over, but as the archbishop lamented, Iraq's Christians were being abandoned to a life of *dhimmitude* in which they would be repressed and persecuted, forced to pay *jizya*, subject to the Muslim majority, "helplessly witnessing crime, mafia or militia."[4]

On December 2, 2011, just ten days before al-Maliki and Obama's White House meeting, thousands of Muslims emerged from Friday prayers across Nineveh to launch attacks on Christian communities. The pogrom in the predominantly Assyrian northern town of Zakho was massive, well organized, and extremely violent, overwhelming the security forces. Businesses deemed *haram* (forbidden in Islam—e.g., licensed grocery stores) were attacked, looted, and torched. The Christian community was left traumatized and devastated.

Commenting on the violence, David William Lazar of the American Mesopotamian Organization told Fox News that he expected the sectarian situation to deteriorate in the wake of the US withdrawal. "It's a big mess," he said. When asked who would be there to ensure the safety of Christians he answered, "Basically, no one."[5]

"The Iraqi Christians . . . are living in fear," observed longtime religious liberty advocate US Congressman Frank Wolf (Republican, Virginia). "Now with the forces leaving . . . I think the Iraqi Christians are going to go through a very, very difficult time."[6]

Patriarch Louis Sako of the Chaldean Catholic Church in the northern provinces of Kirkuk and Sulaymaniyah gave voice to the pervasive fear that if the persecution continues with such intensity, "Iraq could be emptied of Christians."

In Australia, the Assyrian Universal Alliance (AUA) published an open letter to the prime minister, appealing for help from the Australian government. Dated December 12, 2011 (the day of the Obama–al-Maliki meeting),

---

4. "Iraq: Christians Prepare for Christmas under Siege."
5. Berger, "Mob Attacks on Iraqi Christian Businesses Raise Security Concerns."
6. Ibid.

the letter by Hermiz Shahen, Deputy Secretary General of the AUA, included this grave warning: "The slow genocide of the indigenous Assyrians, also known as Chaldeans and Syriacs, in Iraq now sits at the tipping point of a relentless and inexorable genocide, leading to ethnic extinction."[7]

After detailing the destruction of churches, the targeted violent persecution of Christians, and the desperate flight of more than six hundred thousand Assyrians since 2003, the AUA letter highlighted the saddest and most shameful aspect of all: "Despite the scale of this human tragedy and the drastic displacement of the Assyrians, the International Community's response has been almost non-existent and the displaced Assyrians have been left to their demise."

The letter concluded with this appeal:

> The Assyrian Universal Alliance seeks your intervention, and support for the Nineveh Plain Province Solution which entails the development of a self-governed Assyrian province in the Nineveh Plain under the jurisdiction of the central government of the Federal Republic of Iraq. We urge the Australian government to offer political support in favour of this policy in its dealings with the government of Iraq and to provide direct financial assistance for security and infrastructure development in the Nineveh Plain.
>
> Without aggressive Australian & United Nation's intervention, the Christian Assyrian community is on the verge of overt genocide or exodus on a scale unknown in modern times; potentially, 1.2 million refugees in the span of a decade. Once uprooted from Iraq, Assyrians will never be able to return. The fabric, culture and politics of Iraq and the Middle East will forever be transformed, and as Assyrians slowly assimilate into new cultures in the Diaspora, the world loses an enduring Biblical people and culture.

By December 31, 2011, all NATO and US troops had departed. Iraq's Christians had been "left to their demise."

Al-Baghdadi Launches "New Phase of Jihad"

Having established a proxy in Syria (i.e., Jabhat al-Nusra), Abu Bakr al-Baghdadi was ready to up the ante in Iraq. On July 21, 2012, al-Baghdadi used his first online statement since taking control of ISI to announce the launch of Operation Destroying the Walls: a military campaign to free

---

7. Shahen, "Assyria."

Sunnis from prison so as to "refuel" the battle ahead of a "new phase of jihad."[8]

Two days later, ISI launched a massive wave attack, targeting prisons in over twenty Iraqi cities; more than 115 people were killed. Further wave attacks on prisons took place in August and September, growing in sophistication each time. The synchronized attacks of September 9 targeted prisons in eighteen cities and killed over a hundred people. Significantly, these attacks ranged from Basra in the south to Kirkuk and Mosul in the north, proving that ISI had developed nationwide command and control capabilities. On September 27, ISI staged a complex assault on the Tasfirat prison in Tikrit, freeing more than a hundred prisoners, including dozens of terrorists.[9]

It was during these months that ISI released the first two installments of its video series, *The Clanging of the Swords*: part one was released in June 2012 and part two in August. Numerous differences set these videos apart from those of al-Qaeda central, the most salient being ISI's presentation of itself and its task.[10]

The al-Qaeda message has always been one of victimhood, feeding on the sense that Muslims are under attack and are being repressed and persecuted by the imperialist "crusader" West. Al-Qaeda has recruited fighters to their cause by adopting the position of the weak victim forced to defend its honor and fight for its rights and lands in an asymmetric conflict against a strong, controlling, occupying, infidel bully. What ISI was doing was thoroughly new, for it presented itself as strong and victorious. It was reaching out and grasping what Allah had promised—*success*—and inviting Muslims to join them.

By October 2012, analysts were warning that ISI had doubled in strength since the December 2011 US-NATO withdrawal and was now estimated at some 2,500 fighters. What's more, ISI had established training camps, allowing it to double its capacity to stage complex attacks.

In January 2013, ISI released part three of *The Clanging of the Swords*: a high-definition professionally produced documentary on Operation Destroying the Walls.[11]

---

8. Wyer, "The Islamic State of Iraq and the 'Destroying the Walls' Campaign."
9. Roggio, "Al Qaeda in Iraq Claims Credit for Tikrit Jailbreak."
10. Stern and Berger, *ISIS*, 106–110.
11. Ibid.

Sunnis Rise Up against Al-Maliki Government

In December 2012, anti-government protests erupted in Fallujah, a Sunni stronghold 70 km west of Baghdad on the Euphrates River in restive Anbar province. The Sunnis were protesting marginalization and systematic discrimination at the hands of the Shi'ite-dominated al-Maliki government in Baghdad. The regime responded with mass arrests.

On Friday January 25, 2013, coordinated Arab Spring-style protests dubbed "The Friday of no return" were held in Anbar, Diyala, and Nineveh provinces. In Fallujah, Anbar, Sunnis found their march route blocked by a cordon of predominantly Shi'ite Iraqi Security Forces (ISF). Furious at being impeded, the unarmed Sunni protesters on the front line threw rocks and water bottles at the police. A clash ensued; vehicles were torched. Ultimately, the police put down the protest using live ammunition. At least seven Sunnis were killed and more than sixty wounded. The police insist they were fired on, and probably were, as it is highly probable that armed militants had strategically fired on police from behind a row of hapless human shields.

The next day, thousands gathered in Fallujah to bury their dead. As pro-Baathists waved Saddam-era flags, others ominously waved the black flag of Islam.

Pro- and anti-government protests spread across the nation, and analysts warned that Iraq was tilting towards civil war.

At 5 a.m. on April 23, 2013, Iraqi government forces launched a surprise pre-dawn raid on a Sunni protest camp in the northern city of Hawijah in Kirkuk province. Around fifty Sunni protesters were killed, dozens were wounded, and some four hundred arrested. Tensions soared.

In Fallujah, some one thousand Sunnis took to the streets after calls for "War!" were broadcast from mosques. West of Fallujah, in Anbar's provincial capital, Ramadi, Sunnis rioted, attacking Iraqi military vehicles and personnel. Government forces responded with extreme military violence, including the use of attack helicopters. By Friday April 26, 2013, at least 215 Sunnis were dead and hundreds more were wounded.[12]

Enraged by the massacre, Anbar's Sunni tribes joined forces to fight the Shi'ite-dominated government in Baghdad. To that end, it was agreed that a Sunni defense force should be established. "In order to keep Anbar a safe place for the Sunnis, we decided to form an army called the Army

---

12. "125 Killed in Bloody Two Days for Iraq."

of Pride and Dignity with 100 volunteers from each tribe to protect our province," said Sheikh Saeed al-Lafi, a spokesman for the protesters.[13]

"Everybody has the feeling that Iraq is becoming a new Syria," Mosul businessman Talal Younis (55) told reporters. "We are heading into the unknown . . . I think that civil war is making a comeback."[14]

On December 30, 2013, the Iraqi government moved against the tribal Sunnis leading the resistance in Anbar. After just a couple of days, the ISF collapsed in the face of determined Sunni resistance. Forced onto the back foot, the Iraqi army agreed to withdraw from Anbar—a pledge it reneged on the very next day, opting instead to leave Ramadi city but remain in Anbar province.

It was into this sectarian quagmire that al-Baghdadi's ISIS/ISIL—headquartered at this time in Raqqa, Syria—was able to inject itself as the defender of Sunni interests.

ISIS to the Rescue

Fighters from ISIS/ISIL swarmed into Anbar in large numbers in January 2014; by the end of the month, they were in full control of Fallujah. While it might seem ironic that ISIS was now fighting alongside the very same Sunnis who less than a decade earlier had driven ISI out of Anbar, the marginalization and crippling discrimination that Sunnis were experiencing at the hands of the al-Maliki government had made this alliance entirely predictable.[15]

Ahmed al-Jumaili, a tribal leader in the city of Fallujah, explained the dynamic: "The people of Fallujah sympathize with ISIS militants because of their anger toward the Iraqi army, which is known as 'Maliki's forces.'"[16]

The Jihad Comes Full Circle: ISIS Returns to the Place of its Conception—Mosul

On June 9, 2014, an estimated four hundred ISIS jihadists in technical vehicles (pickup trucks mounted with machine guns) flooded into Iraq's

---

13. Naama, "Militants Kill Five Iraqi Soldiers, Sunni Protesters Form 'Army.'"
14. Ibid.
15. So predictable in fact, that I predicted it in May 2013: "Iraq: Danger as Sectarian War Looms."
16. Sadah, "Anbar Province Headed Toward Isolation."

northern Nineveh province.[17] That such an advance could have gone unnoticed, or at least unreported, by intelligence agencies monitoring drone and satellite images, is unfathomable. Yet Mosul, Iraq's second-largest city, was indeed taken by surprise.

Standing in between a few hundred rabidly anti-Shi'ite *takfiri* ISIS jihadists and Mosul's 1.8 million mostly Sunni Muslim and Assyrian Christian citizens were 25,000 mostly Shi'ite members of the ISF. The odds would have been against ISIS—which was outnumbered at least 50:1—except for the fact that Iraq's security forces now (post-Saddam) comprised predominantly young inexperienced Shi'ites, most of whom had only joined the army because they desperately needed the money. Compounding their misfortune, these soldiers were led by commanders appointed not on merit, but on loyalty to Iraqi Prime Minister Nuri al-Maliki.

What's more, ISIS had prepared the theatre brilliantly with the release of part four of *The Clanging of the Swords* just weeks ahead of the invasion. Concerning the production, authors Stern and Berger comment: "The members of ISIS's media team could no longer be considered students; they were now fully professional." And as for the content: after opening with aerial footage of Fallujah (filmed using a drone), what follows can only be described as "an untrammeled show of strength."[18] As a psyop, this video was an absolute masterpiece.

As ISIS fighters entered Mosul, Iraqi security simply collapsed as soldiers dropped their weapons, tore off their uniforms, abandoned their posts, and fled for their lives. ISIS did, however, manage to capture some 1,700 hapless Shi'ites who were then forced to march in columns into mass graves, where they were executed en masse.[19]

So ISIS captured Mosul, Iraq's second-largest city and the provincial capital of Nineveh province, in a blitzkrieg, along with its airport, banks holding an estimated US$500 million, armories stocked with US-made materiel (e.g., rockets, Humvees, tanks) and much more. They also freed up to three thousand prisoners, many of them Sunni jihadists salivating at the prospect of joining the jihad against the Shi'ite regime in Baghdad.

The ISIS invasion triggered a humanitarian catastrophe as an estimated half a million people fled Mosul to seek refuge in churches, schools, and

---

17. Roggio, "ISIS Takes Control of Mosul, Iraq's Second Largest City."
18. Stern and Berger, *ISIS*, 110.
19. Nordland and Rubin, "Massacre Claim Shakes Iraq"; Pollard, "ISIL Twitter Terror."

monasteries scattered across Nineveh, and in Iraqi Kurdistan. Among the dispossessed were an estimated one thousand Christian families.[20]

Amongst those who headed straight for Iraqi Kurdistan was a Christian couple from Mosul, who found refuge for themselves and their young children in a church in Arbil (the capital of Iraqi Kurdistan). Having already made plans to leave, they were at home eating dinner when houses on either side of them burst into flames after being hit by rocket fire. The family dropped their forks and fled, carrying nothing but their papers.[21]

An evangelical pastor subsequently told Morning Star News that the day he fled Mosul was the most terrifying day of his life. After gathering his family into the car, the pastor had set off in the stream of traffic heading out of the city. He describes the scene as one of total chaos: mortar rounds exploding as they hit their targets, displaced people streaming past the cars with whatever they could carry, terrified Iraqi soldiers peeling off their uniforms and heading for the hills.

Inside the car, the pastor's two sons lay flat on the backseat to avoid being shot. Fighting back waves of anger, fear, and grief, and blinking through the tears streaming down his face, the pastor could do little more than clutch the steering wheel of his car and just drive.

"That night was the most afraid I have ever been in my life," he said. "Even now when I remember it, I think, 'How did I do it?' Only with the Lord, with His help."[22]

Having captured Mosul, ISIS then set its sights on Baghdad. In an online statement, ISIS spokesman Abu Muhammad al-Adnani vowed to "settle the score" and expel the "safavids" (i.e., Persians, by which was meant Iran-backed Shi'ites).[23]

After seizing Tikrit and its surrounding oil fields, ISIS found its advance halted on the outskirts of Samarra, just 125 km north of Baghdad. Samarra is the site of one of Shia Islam's holiest shrines: the spectacular gold-domed al-Askari Mosque the resting place of Twelver Shi'ism's tenth and eleventh imams. The al-Askari Mosque had been targeted before, in February 2006, when a massive bomb planted by al-Zarqawi's AQI blew out the gold dome in an act of terror specifically designed to trigger sectarian conflict.

In June 2014, as ISIS advanced on Samarra, Shi'ites responded to calls from Shia leaders and fatwas from Shia clerics and flocked to defend their

20. "Up to 1000 Christian Families Flee Iraq's Second City."
21. "Mosul Christians Tell of ISIS Force' Iraqi Takeover."
22. "Displaced Iraqi Christians Ponder an Iraq without Christians."
23. "ISIS Urges Militants to March to Baghdad."

sacred site. Aware of its limitations and satisfied with its gains, ISIS made a strategic retreat, opting to consolidate in Mosul.

Just as it had done in Raqqa, Syria, ISIS imposed strict Sharia law on all Mosul's residents, publishing a set of Islamic rules to be strictly enforced across Nineveh province, without compromise and without mercy.[24]

The Return of the Caliphate—and the End of Sykes-Picot

On Friday June 20, 2014, ISIS militants seized control of the Al Qaim border crossing into Syria.[25] For the line in the sand that was the Iraq-Syria border, judgment day had arrived. As a division imposed on the Arabs against their wishes in the wake of World War I, the border represented Arab and Muslim weakness in the face of Western and infidel meddling and betrayal. It was a border no self-respecting jihadist could accept.

In March 1918 (towards the end of World War I), the British General Stanley Maude read aloud a proclamation in British-occupied Baghdad. Having liberated the Arabs from the Turks and Germans, he assured them that Great Britain and her allies were only interested in seeing the Arabs attain freedom and independence so that "the Arab race may rise once more to greatness and renown among the peoples of the Earth and that it shall bind itself together to this end in unity and concord."[26]

The promise of Arab unity and independence had been made repeatedly through 1914 and 1915 by the British high commissioner in Egypt, Sir Henry McMahon, to Hussein ibn Ali, the Hashemite Sharif of Mecca. Lord Kitchener, Britain's consul general in Cairo even suggested to Hussein that a Hashemite Arab caliphate might be established in Mecca or Medina. The "Damascus Protocol" was drafted, creating a map for the envisioned Arab superstate.

Yet even before the war had ended, those with "interests" had already exploited the chaos to make all manner of contrary agreements. "Among the most salient," writes historian Edwin Black, "was the Sykes-Picot Agreement hammered out between senior diplomats Mark Sykes of Britain, George Picot of France, and Russian foreign minister Sergei Sazonov . . . [The Ottoman *villayets*/provinces of] Baghdad and Basra were decreed British spheres of influence, while oil-rich Mosul [*villayet*, which included

---

24. Pollard, "ISIL's New Rules for Captured City of Mosul"; McElroy, "Repent or Die."
25. Roggio "ISIS Seizes Border Crossing in Western Anbar."
26. Black, *Banking on Baghdad*, 191–193.

Kirkuk] and Syria would be French, with Russia exercising a privilege over its frontier with Persia."[27]

And so it was that on May 15, 1916, the Sykes-Picot Agreement was formalized. The British, however, immediately regretted the agreement, deeming oil-rich Mosul *villayet* too valuable to cede to French interests. France conceded, and by May 17, 1916, the border that would eventually come to divide Syria and Iraq had been decided—without the Arabs ever being consulted.

Edwin Black explains that under Sykes-Picot, the promised Arab superstate would be nothing more than a confederation under French and British economic and administrative control. "What we want," wrote Charles Harding, the British viceroy of India, "is not a United Arabia: but a weak and disunited Arabia, split up into little principalities so far as possible under our suzerainty—but incapable of coordinated action against us, forming a buffer against the Powers in the West."[28]

By establishing two states both of which were to be ruled by minorities, the Western powers established a highly effective balance of power in Mesopotamia. Minority (Sunni) rule in Iraq kept the Shi'ites in check and prevented Iraq from falling under the domination of Iran. Meanwhile, minority (Alawite) rule in Syria kept the Sunnis in check.

That balance of power held until America's 2003 invasion and subsequent "democratization" of Iraq sent it all unraveling and put Mesopotamia back "in play." The consequences, particularly for the minorities, would be catastrophic. As analyst David Goldman has pointed out, "Tyranny of a minority may be brutal, but a minority cannot exterminate a majority."[29]

After seizing the Al Qaim border crossing on June 20, 2014, ISIS fighters bulldozed a road through the earthen barrier that had formed the border between Syria and Iraq. Fully cognizant of the significance of their act, the jihadists rejoiced not simply at a new era of unrestricted movement, but at "the end of Sykes-Picot"[30] — that is, the end of Western meddling in the Middle East.

On June 29, 2014, the first day of Ramadan 2014, Abu Bakr al-Baghdadi announced the formation of a caliphate with himself as caliph (ruler of Muslims). To reflect the reality on the ground, Caliph Ibrahim (i.e., al-Baghdadi) changed ISIS's name to Islamic State (IS).[31]

27. Black, *Banking on Baghdad*, 196.
28. Ibid., 197.
29. Goldman, "World Bows to Iran's Hegemony."
30. "The End of Sykes-Picot."
31. Roggio, "ISIS Announces Formation of Caliphate, Rebrands as 'Islamic State.'"

This was more than an act of defiance reversing Western meddling in and hegemony over the Middle East. It was also a direct challenge to the House of Saud. After all, the King of Saudi Arabia rules over "the land of the two holy mosques" and is the "custodian of the holy places" (in Mecca and Medina). After all, the House of Saud is the fountain from which never-ending rivers of petrodollars flow—funds that have enabled the globalization of intolerant, puritanical Wahhabi Sunni Islam and the funding of global jihad. The profligate, US-allied House of Saud is the leader of Muslims—isn't it?

Mosul Emptied of Christians

On Friday July 18, 2014, Abu Bakr al-Baghdadi (Caliph Ibrahim) issued an ultimatum to Mosul's remnant Christians: they could have until Saturday July 19 to "leave the borders of the Islamic Caliphate," otherwise, "We offer them three choices: Islam; the *dhimma* contract—involving payment of *jizya*; if they refuse this they will have nothing but the sword."[32]

To guarantee compliance, IS marked the homes of Christians with a red ن (an Arabic letter "n", pronounced "noon") for Nasara/Nazarene (followers of Jesus the Nazarene). Alongside the red ن was a message in black Arabic text which read: "Property of the Islamic State." Shi'ite homes were also marked, but with an ر (an Arabic letter "r", pronounced "rā") for *rwafidh* (rejecters).[33] And so Mosul's religious minorities, including some three thousand remnant Christians, limped into exile with little more than the clothes on their backs.[34]

Chaldean Catholic Patriarch Louis Sako could only lament: "For the first time in the history of Iraq, Mosul is now empty of Christians."[35]

Kirkuk

When the armistice that ended World War I was signed at Mudros on October 31, 1918, the Turks still held Mosul *villayet*, which at the time extended so far south as to include Kirkuk. Acutely aware of the value of Mosul *villayet*, British Mesopotamian commander in chief, William Marshall, ordered his troops to advance and take Mosul, cease-fire or no cease-fire.

32. "Iraqi Christians Flee after Isis Issue Mosul Ultimatum."
33 "ISIS in Mosul Marks Christian Homes."
34. Sisto, "A Christian Genocide Symbolized by One Letter."
35. Loveluck, "Christians Flee Iraq's Mosul after Islamists Tell Them: Convert, Pay or Die."

Over subsequent years, particularly as Turkish nationalism rose, Turkey petitioned the League of Nations in Geneva to recognize Turkey's sovereignty over the oil-rich province. Eventually, on March 11, 1926, the League of Nations Council handed down its final ruling. After considering Turkey's record of genocide, mass rape, and neglect of Mosul *villayet*, the Council decided that it should remain within the British mandate. On October 14, 1927, oil started flowing out of Kirkuk at the rate of ninety thousand barrels per day.[36]

Kirkuk's status has long been contested by Arabs, Kurds, and Turkmen.[37] Whilst in power, Saddam Hussein worked to Arabize Kirkuk, driving out Assyrians and Kurds and replacing them with Arabs, most of whom were paid to relocate. After gaining greater autonomy in 2003, the Kurdish authorities began working to reverse the process, paying Arabs to return to their regions so Kurds (at least) could return to their homes. The campaign has had only limited success, especially as Kirkuk has remained under the control of Baghdad which has interests in keeping it as Arab as possible.

In July 2014, as ISIS advanced on Baghdad, the Kurds exploited the chaos and insecurity to seize control of oil-rich Kirkuk—territory they have long claimed as their own. A major oil-production site, Kirkuk's oil reserves are believed to be almost as extensive as those in the south of Iraq.

That IS would covet Kirkuk was entirely predictable.

Qaraqosh emptied of Christians

On Wednesday August 6, 2014, as IS advanced towards Kirkuk, it overran the Assyrian town of Qaraqosh. Just 32 km southeast of Mosul, Qaraqosh—also known as Bakhdida or Hamdaniya—was the largest and oldest Assyrian town in Iraq. As in Mosul, the attack on Qaraqosh commenced with mortar fire and ended with the expulsion of the entire Christian population.

Kurdish armed forces known as *peshmerga* had been defending Qaraqosh until August 7, 2014, when they withdrew to defend Iraqi Kurdistan's long, arching, difficult-to-defend border. (Iraq's Kurdistan Autonomous Region comprises the provinces of Sulaymaniyah, Arbil and Dohuk in Iraq's

---

36. Black, *Banking on Baghdad*, 287.

37. Comprising around 2.5 percent of the Iraqi population, Turkmen are the third largest ethnic group in Iraq, behind Arabs (74 percent) and Kurds (21 percent). They are related to the Turks, speak Turkish, and are found mostly north of Baghdad, especially around Kirkuk (map: http://www.al-bab.com/arab/background/turkoman.htm). Of an estimated two million Turkmen in Iraq, some 30,000 are Christian.

mountainous northeast.) Withdrawing with the *peshmerga* were some fifty thousand Assyrian Christians.

Richard Spencer reported from Ankawa, an Assyrian district on the northern outskirts of Arbil (the capital of Iraqi Kurdistan):

> The last day of Qaraqosh's time as a Christian town, a time almost as old as Christianity itself, began with a mortar shell at nine in the morning. It came through the roof of Melad and Marven Abdullah's house on Wednesday [Aug 6, 2014], killing them instantly. Melad was nine; his cousin, Marven, four ... The family's next-door neighbour, Enam Eshoo, had popped in to deliver some fresh drinking water; she too died where she fell. The day ended with an order to evacuate. Within a couple of hours, the city's tens of thousands of inhabitants were crowding the road to Kurdistan.[38]

The Ebada Family

The Ebada family was one of a handful of Assyrian families that had not evacuated from Qaraqosh with the Kurdish *peshmerga* on August 7. For the Ebada family, flight was difficult as Mr Ebada is blind.

As IS fighters advanced through the town, a family friend came and convinced the couple to gather up their son Yas (8) and their daughter Christina (3) and flee with them to Arbil. The family was preparing to leave when men came and ordered them into a minibus on the pretext of taking them for a medical check. "I knew they were ISIS," says Mrs Ebada.

The minibus took the family to a clinic where they, along with the others who were there, were robbed of everything they had of value, including cash, jewelry, luggage, and passports. After about an hour and a half they were ordered onto another bus. Mrs Ebada tells what happened:

> We went and sat in the big bus, and then one man came aboard. I was carrying my child in my arms, I sat in the bus and he came and took her from me, snatched her from me, and left the bus. I followed him—and my little girl was crying. An old man, one of those ISIS people, who was apparently their leader, then took her.
>
> He said [in Arabic] "is this your daughter?" I said yes. He said "she is crying for you." I told him, "Give her back to me, poor girl, what is she guilty of? She is breast feeding from me.

---

38. Kendal, "IRAQ: Christians Flee the Killing Fields," cites Spencer, "Iraq Crisis."

For the sake of Allah, for the sake of Muhammad, what do you worship? Give me this little one, she is breast feeding from me. She will die if she does not see me. I am her mother."

He said to me, "Shut up. If you speak another word I will let them slaughter you. I will call them now to slaughter you." He drew his machine gun and said, "Go quickly to the bus. If you come close to this little girl you will be slaughtered, we shall slaughter you all. Come now, go!"

So I got on the bus and it left.[39]

In Arbil, Mrs Ebada told an Assyrian journalist that her last memory of her little girl is that of her crying and sobbing as a heavily bearded man carried her away.[40]

Christian Leaders Lament Unheeded Warnings

Archbishop Athanasius Toma Dawod of the Syriac Orthodox Church in the UK said that IS's capture of Qaraqosh had marked a turning point for Christians in the country. "Now we consider it genocide—ethnic cleansing," he said. "They are killing our people in the name of Allah and telling people that anyone who kills a Christian will go straight to heaven: that is their message." He said that IS had burnt churches along with invaluable ancient books and manuscripts, and that some churches had been converted into mosques.[41] A subsequent report even told of churches being used as prisons.[42]

On August 10, 2014, Patriarch Louis Sako, the Iraq-based leader of the Chaldean Catholic Church, issued a statement through the Catholic charity Aid to the Church in Need. He warned that Assyrian (also known as Chaldean and Syriac) Christians "are facing a human catastrophe and risk a real genocide."[43]

---

39. "Mother of 3 Year-old Assyrian Girl Kidnapped By ISIS."

40. According to a subsequent UN report dated October 2, 2014, IS took some five hundred women and girls captive during its rampage through Nineveh in August 2014. While most belonged to the Yazidi sect, some were Christian. The captive women were held in the Tal Afar citadel, although some 150 virgin girls were immediately transported to Raqqa, Syria, to be given as rewards to jihadists or sold into sexual slavery. See UN report: "Report on the Protection of Civilians in Armed Conflict in Iraq: 6 July–10 September."

41. "Religious Leaders Say Isis Persecution of Iraqi Christians Has Become Genocide."

42. "Churches in Mosul Are Used as Prisons by Jihadist of the Caliphate."

43. "Christians in Iraq on the Run."

According to the Archbishop, some seventy thousand displaced Christians had arrived in Ankawa, an Assyrian district on the northern outskirts of Arbil. Some were with relatives, others had crowded into churches and monasteries, and still more were sleeping in the streets and open fields in the scorching summer heat; their situation was dire. A further sixty thousand Christians had arrived in Dohuk, 80 km north of Mosul, "and their situation," he said, "is even worse than those in Arbil." Other Christians had travelled to Kirkuk, Sulaymaniyah, and Baghdad. "The churches," he said "are offering everything within their capacity."

As it turned out, IS would not be permitted to threaten the oil fields of Kirkuk. A US-led coalition provided air cover to the Kurdish *peshmerga*, assisting them just enough to keep IS at bay, while not enough to fuel a future push for Kurdish independence or even to cause any real damage to IS itself.

By mid August 2014, the genocide of Christians that Assyrian Christian leaders had warned of in December 2011 had come to pass.

The Caliphate Hastens to Success

The Bible might teach that sin is sin, but in Islam, the end justifies the means and anything is permissible if it advances Islamic success. As Islam expert Daniel Scot notes, every one of the Ten Commandments is both affirmed and contradicted in the Qur'an, which forbids and permits killing, lying, rape, theft (looting), and so on, depending on the circumstances.[44] And so it is that through murder, trafficking, pillage, smuggling, theft, and all manner of criminality, IS has managed to become the richest terrorist group in the world.

Of course, nothing has contributed to IS wealth as much as the fact that it has seized some the world's most profitable oil fields. As terror expert Professor Louis Shelley explains, "Even selling the oil at a discount via pre-invasion smuggling routes out of Iraq, ISIS can still expect over a million dollars in revenue each day."[45]

Yet, adds Shelley, while IS does make most of its money from smuggling oil, it is "a diverse criminal operation" that also engages in kidnapping

---

44. Scot, "Windows into the Qur'an." This issue of Islamic morality or ethics, and how the Ten Commandments are both affirmed and contradicted in the Qur'an, is covered in detail in Daniel Scot's *Critique of Learning From One Another*, 74–103. This handbook for parents, teachers, principals, and all interested parties is available from Ibrahim Ministries International: office@imi.org.au. It was written as a response to the Islamic propaganda being promoted in Australian schools through the government-funded "Learning from One Another" program.

45. Ibid.

for ransom and trades in cigarettes, pornography, pharmaceuticals, antiquities, looted art, passports, mobile phones, counterfeit goods, pirated CDs and DVDs, forged documents, wildlife, and drugs.[46] Shelley notes that trafficking of these commodities into Turkey from Syria has risen dramatically: for example, fuel smuggling has tripled and cell phone smuggling has risen five-fold.[47]

According to Shelley, some criminals have been lured to IS by the promise that if they advance the cause of Islam, they will be cleansed of all their sins. Among the criminals being drawn to IS are serious arms dealers, traffickers, and killers. While many are foreigners, many are not: many are angry criminal Baathists recruited by Islamists in the prison camps set up throughout Iraq by the Americans during the occupation. They include seasoned sanction-busting smugglers and corrupt administrators.

In November 2014, after securing permission and a signed guarantee of safety from none other than Abu Bakr al-Baghdadi himself, seasoned German journalist and IS-critic Jürgen Todenhöfer travelled to IS-controlled Syria and Iraq to see at firsthand how the caliphate operates.

"Life [in Mosul] seems to be normal," he told CNN.

> I say "seems" normal like life in totalitarian countries, under dictatorships . . . You have to know that 130,000 Christians have been forced to leave; that an incredible number of Shias have been forced to leave and have been killed and the Yezidis have been killed and that only the Sunnis are still in this city . . . I've been in Mosul 11 yrs ago, but I must say, because I must tell you the truth, it looked like 11 yrs ago, [but] without this plurality with Christians and Shias which was also the charm of this city.[48]

Todenhöfer observed huge numbers of fighters arriving every day from all over the world, many of them professionals—including doctors, lawyers, accountants, engineers, and computer technicians.

Todenhöfer asked one of the arrivals—a very articulate German jihadist, fluent in Islamic ideology and history—what he thought about the beheadings and the enslavement, and if he considered these things progressive. The jihadist responded without hesitation or shame, telling Todenhöfer: "It is part of our religion to instill fear into the disbelievers, and we are going to continue to behead people. It doesn't matter whether they

---

46. Dettmer and Schindler, interviewing Louise Shelley, "Islamic State is a Diversified Criminal Operation."
47. Shelley, "Blood Money."
48. Pleitgen, "Author's Journey Inside ISIS."

are Shi'ite, Christian or Jews. We are going to continue to practice this."[49] Todenhöfer notes that the jihadists are extremely confident. "We are certain," said one, "that God will bring us victory [*success*], that all countries will be conquered. We will get to Rome, Istanbul, and even to the United States; we are certain of that."

As for the US-backed FSA, one jihadist said that while IS doesn't take the FSA seriously, they do purchase arms from them. "If they get a good weapon they sell it to us."

Todenhöfer was amazed by IS's success, saying, "Al-Qaeda, in comparison for example with IS, is an empty shell—it's nothing, in comparison with IS. It comes from their success, it comes from their simple ideology, it comes from their enthusiasm that nobody can explain. I spent two days in a registration house," said Todenhöfer, "where 50 people arrived every day. And when I saw these brilliant eyes, these heavy guys—not losers who may have lost or missed their lives in their home countries—winners, people who you cannot imagine. In the city of Mosul I met people from Belgium, people from France, Britain and Sweden . . . Why? It is like a tsunami."

While definitely inspired by IS's *success*, the enthusiasm evident amongst IS followers comes largely from their firm belief that they are living in the last days—the "final hour"—and that Islamic prophecy and eschatology (i.e., theology of the End Times) is being fulfilled before their eyes and that IS is central to that fulfillment. Writer Graeme Wood highlighted this in his groundbreaking piece for *The Atlantic*, entitled, "What IS Really Wants."[50]

"The reality," writes Wood,

> is that the Islamic State is Islamic. *Very* Islamic. Yes, it has attracted psychopaths and adventure seekers, drawn largely from the disaffected populations of the Middle East and Europe. But the religion preached by its most ardent followers derives from coherent and even learned interpretations of Islam.
>
> Virtually every major decision and law promulgated by the Islamic State adheres to what it calls, in its press and pronouncements, and on its billboards, license plates, stationery, and coins, "the Prophetic methodology," which means following the prophecy and example of Muhammad, in punctilious detail . . .
>
> The Islamic State differs from nearly every other current jihadist movement in believing that it is written into God's script

---

49. See Q.8:12: "I will cast terror into the hearts of those who disbelieved, so strike [them] upon the necks and strike from them every fingertip."

50. Wood, "What IS Really Wants." See also Mauro, "The Islamic State Seeks the Battle of the Apocalypse."

as a central character. It is in this casting that the Islamic State is most boldly distinctive from its predecessors, and clearest in the religious nature of its mission . . . the End of Days is a leitmotif of its propaganda.

Todenhöfer notes that many Westerners would regard IS's plan to attack the West as fantasy and think it ridiculous. "But if someone had said six months ago [i.e. May 2014] that at the end of the year 2014, IS would run a country bigger than UK, everybody would have said, 'that's crazy.'"

Not all analysts would agree with Todenhöfer's assessment that al-Qaeda is, in comparison to IS, "an empty shell" (e.g., I would not agree. I consider al-Qaeda extremely dangerous).[51] Still, his insights into IS are incredibly significant. For as Graeme Wood so rightly notes, we need to understand IS's theology and not underestimate the group so we might "react in a way that will not strengthen it, but instead help it self-immolate in its own excessive zeal."

Turkey and the Battle for Kobani

By October 2014, IS was fighting for control of Kobani (known to Arabs as Ayn al-Arab), a Kurdish town on the eastern edge of Aleppo province in Syria's far north close to the Turkish border.

As 150,000 Syrian Kurds fled from Kobani into Turkey, a coalition of Western and allied air forces launched air strikes designed to at least hamper the IS campaign. In this, Turkey was no ally. Not only did Turkey deny the US air force access to Turkish bases, it declined to join the coalition defending Kobani. Instead, the Turks simply parked their tanks, picked up their binoculars, and watched Kobani burn. Furthermore, Kurds in Turkey were prevented from crossing the Turkish border into Syria; even the men of Kobani who had brought their families to safety were not permitted to return to help defend their city.

---

51. I would maintain that IS's inflexible brutality makes it vulnerable to a grassroots backlash and betrayal, similar to what occurred in Anbar in 2005. Furthermore, IS's status as a state—i.e., as a "fixed target"—also makes it vulnerable. Most critically, having established a narrative of strength, victory, and *success*, as distinct from victimhood and resistance, IS needs to remain successful if it is to remain legitimate. As a weak entity, IS will not be able to survive without a "suzerain"/overlord—preferably one with an air force. On the other hand, al-Qaeda's superior strategic vision, patience, and pragmatism, particularly its willingness to soften its application of Sharia so as to secure local support, along with its willingness to cooperate with ascendant Iran (the leader of the *Resistance*), makes it more dangerous in the long run.

That Kobani was ultimately liberated in January 2015, with the aid of Kurdish *peshmerga* forces from Iraq, is "a remarkable testimony to the tenacity and courage of the Kurdish resistance on the ground," wrote researcher Jonathan Spyer. "It also showcases the awesome efficacy of US air power, when given a clear mission and properly directed." Nevertheless, Spyer warned that the victory would be difficult to replicate as the Kurds are unique amongst the fighting groups—they are pro-Western, committed, and efficient, and no other group has all three qualities.[52]

Actually, the Assyrians are just as pro-Western and would be equally as committed and efficient if they were given the opportunity. As longtime allies of the West, the Christian Assyrians have already proven as much.[53]

Turkey Exposed

Nothing has exposed Turkey's regional ambitions and role in the conflict more than the Battle for Kobani. While IS jihadists may owe their zeal to Saudi Arabian-sponsored *takfiri* Wahhabi ideology, the reality on the ground is that no state is more responsible for the creation of the IS caliphate than Turkey.

It is common knowledge that IS jihadists move freely through and recruit fighters in some of Turkey's biggest cities with the tacit approval of members of Turkey's security services, local governors, and officials in Ankara.[54]

"The Islamic Caliphate was nurtured by Turkey from its very beginning," writes strategic analyst Gregory Copley, editor in chief of *Defense & Foreign Affairs Strategic Policy*. After listing a string of jihadist entities that had grown, evolved, and eventually culminated in the formation of IS, Copely states: "Massive semi-clandestine support to these groups from Turkey and Qatar—and supported at the beginning by the US and Saudi Arabia—had been designed to break Iran's hold of Syria and Iraq. But for [pro-MB] Turkey and Qatar, it was also a tool to threaten or cower [anti-MB] Saudi Arabia and isolate [Shi'ite] Iran."[55]

"Who controls al-Baghdadi?" asks Copley.

---

52. Spyer, "Islamic State Defeat in Kobani Will Be Hard to Replicate."

53. For an account of the Assyrian nation's contribution to the Allied campaign in World War I, see Wigram, *Our Smallest Ally*.

54. Bekdil, "How Turkey Fights the Islamic State."

55. Copley, "Why the Islamic Caliphate May Presage Change."

As far as al-Baghdadi is concerned, he is controlled by no-one, but in reality he cannot survive without Turkey's support, both from the initial financial and weapons support, to the long-term logistical support. Some 10 percent of his fighters are reportedly Turkish, and most of his fighters are "foreign" and need to enter his region via Turkey. By late August 2014, al-Baghdadi was working to broaden his land "border" with Turkey in order to facilitate better contact. The "caliphate" needs to export 800,000 barrels per day of oil production from the wells it captured in Syria and Iraq, and although it must do this through trucks, rather than pipelines, it is hoping for a stable traffic through Turkey, despite UN sanctions against the trade.[56]

The Return of the Caliphate—A "Godsend" for Some

Turkey's enthusiasm for the caliphate is evidenced in part by its willingness to do business with it. In July 2014, Turkey's Minister of Economy, Nihat Zeybekci, told Al-Monitor that IS was contacting individual Turkish businessmen and telling them, "Come back, we won't interfere." The response was such that Zeybekci could confidently declare: "When in the future Iraq is rebuilt, it will be Turkey doing it."[57]

Iran, meanwhile, is also exploiting the crisis. In the 1980s, Tehran prolonged the Iran-Iraq War so that it could build up the IRGC, and exploited the Lebanese Civil War so that it could establish Hezbollah. Similarly, Iran today has been exploiting the crisis caused by IS in Syria to stock Hezbollah's weapons caches near Syria's border with Israel—weapons that could be used against Israel in the Golan Heights[58]—and to establish a network

---

56. Ibid.

57. Cetingulec, "Islamic State Urges Turkish Businessmen to Return to Iraq."

58. In September 2015, Russia and Israel met on several occasions to discuss the implications of Russian involvement in Syrian in support of the Syrian government and what this might mean for Israeli security. Reporting for Al-Monitor, Saheb Sadeghi commented that despite the fact that Russia and Iran-Hezbollah are all supporting the Syrian government, Russia and Iran-Hezbollah have opposing views as to the future direction of the Syrian state and the security of Israel. "Moscow has even committed itself to preventing Hezbollah from obtaining Russian arms," writes Sadeghi. "It has also pledged to impede actions against Israel by pro-government militias and Hezbollah forces in the Golan Heights. Of note, Israel—unlike its Western allies—has not adopted or expressed a negative stance toward the Russian military presence in Syria, signaling that Moscow does not want Syria's future political system to maintain an anti-Israeli posture. In this vein, it should be borne in mind that Israel and Russia have also recently been building good relations and even signed contracts related to trade in advanced weaponry in addition to bilateral military exchanges" (Sadeghi, "Why Iran and Russia

of Shi'ite militias in Iraq and Syria that will ultimately eclipse both governments and be beholden to Tehran.[59]

Indeed, the threat of IS has afforded Iran a perfect opportunity to put "boots on the ground" in Iraq and Syria. And with boots on the ground, Iran is more likely to get the outcome it desires.

An Iraqi Sunni General told Ambassador Dore Gold that during the Ashura festival of 2015, over a million Iranians crossed the border, from Iran into Iraq, without passports or visas, to attend the Ashura festivals in Najaf and Karbala. "And," he said, "I don't know if they've left."[60]

Gold comments: "In other words, we talk about the Sykes-Picot border being dissolved, well, here's another border that seems to be dissolving and an unease [expressed by] an Iraqi Sunni who felt that Iran was taking over large parts of his country. The way he described it, ISIS was a blessing for Iran, because ISIS allows Iran to move into Iraq as the savior of Western interests against ISIS and legitimizes the eventual takeover of most of that country by Iran."[61]

Syrians are disturbed to see the same process occurring in Syria. According to a Russian official who long worked in his country's embassy in Damascus, "Assad and those around him are afraid of the Iranians," who he said arrogantly treat Syria like a colony. Most Syrians, he said, "mistrust Tehran's goals, for which Assad's position of power may no longer be decisive."[62] Author and Spiegel Online investigative journalist, Christoph Reuter reports that along with establishing militias beholden to Tehran, the Iranians are busy building Shi'ite religious centers tasked with teaching and establishing "correct" Islam and converting Syrians to Shi'ism. "All of this is taking place," writes Reuter, "to the consternation of the Alawites, who have begun to voice their displeasure [saying] 'They are throwing us back a thousand years. We don't even wear headscarves and we aren't Shiites.'"[63]

Furthermore, notes Reuter, "Iranian emissaries, either directly or via middlemen, have been buying land and buildings in Damascus, including almost the entire former Jewish quarter, and trying to settle Shiites from other countries there."

Reuter assesses the "Iranian Project" to be so far advanced that it cannot be reversed, noting that in many cases, Iran is calling the shots, contrary

---

Aren't As Closely Aligned on Syria As You Might Think").

59. Spyer and Al-Tamimi, "Iran and the Shia Militias Advance in Iraq."
60. Gold, "The Iranian Nuclear Program and Regional Instability."
61. Ibid.
62. Reuter, "The Iranian Project."
63. Ibid.

to Assad's wishes. And this, says Reuter, is why "Assad has now decided to place his fate in the hands of the religiously unproblematic Russia."

Meanwhile, the fight against IS has turned Major General Qassem Soleimani, commander of the Quds force of the IRGC, into a celebrity and cult hero in Iran. It is not beyond the realm of possibility that the crisis could be exploited by those keen to see an IRGC-led Iranian nationalist coup in Tehran.

As for IS's ideological parent, although it is existentially threatened by IS, Saudi Arabia is not going to stop its spawn crushing Shi'ites and menacing its ascendant nemesis Iran.

A North-South Sunni Wedge Splits the East-West Shia Crescent

In February 2012, terrorism analyst Yossef Bodanksy warned:

> The vast Syrian interior and western Iraq are jointly the theatre in which the fateful struggle over the Greater Middle East is being waged between neo-Ottoman Turkey, Mahdivist Iran and a Sunni Arab camp led by Saudi Arabia and Qatar. None can accept the pacification of Syria [or Iraq] before their own grand strategic and historic struggles have been decided. While Iran can live with the denial of the predominantly Sunni-tribal Syrian interior and western Iraq to non-Shi'ite forces in order to sustain the east-west Shi'ite axis [i.e., Iran will concede the Sunni interior to retain the capitals and access to Syria's Mediterranean ports], both Turkey and the Arab *bloc* must control these Sunni tribal lands in order to sustain the north-south Sunni *bloc* they aspire for. Only such a Sunni *bloc* would be able to withstand and contain the Iranian-Shi'ite ascent over the Persian Gulf and Arabian Peninsula."[64]

By mid 2014, the caliphate had materialized to form a north-south Sunni wedge through the east-west Shia Crescent. While it was not what the regime-change coalition had envisaged—i.e., a US-allied and protected Sunni bloc stretching from Yemen through Saudi Arabia, the Levant and Turkey, safe for US-Turkey-Arab oil and gas pipelines, and so on—it would do. For though Damascus remained in the hands of Iran, at least the Islamic State (IS), hammered into place by Turkey, would form a *takfiri* Sunni wedge which would split the Shi'ite bloc, hamstring Iranian ambitions, and keep Tehran in check. To that end, the caliphate has its uses and is indeed a

---

64. Bodansky, "Syria's Multi-Layered Wars."

godsend to some; which is no doubt partly the reason why the US-Turkey-Arab axis efforts to destroy IS have proved so ineffectual.

Crushing the "Fertile Crescent of Minorities"

By the end of August 2014, Nineveh had been essentially emptied of Christians. Courtesy of the forces of the caliphate, hundreds of thousands of Christians were now refugees—families, youths, and the old, frail, and lame. Forced to flee, many would perish en route. Homeless and destitute, many more would not survive the winter.

With no Assyrians left to persecute in Nineveh, IS got to work erasing Assyrian cultural heritage. In February 2015, IS released a propaganda video showing militants using sledgehammers and drills to rid Mosul and its museum of all things "un-Islamic." Incapable of seeing ancient works of art as anything other than "idols," IS destroyed irreplaceable antiquities dating back to the ninth century BC and earlier. In what UNESCO has described as "cultural cleansing," IS bulldozed ancient archaeological sites dating back to the thirteenth century BC, including Nimrud and Hatra.[65]

Cultural destruction in Syria has been no less severe. In rebel-held Deir ez-Zor, Hasakah, and Raqqa provinces, more than a hundred archaeological sites had been raided and destroyed by Easter 2015. In Syria's northern Aleppo and Idlib provinces, where al-Nusra dominates, around forty sites were raided and antiquities smuggled out via Turkey. In Homs and Daraa, numerous archaeological sites have been totally plundered and then destroyed. Amongst the looted and damaged sites—most of which are World Heritage-listed—are ancient monasteries and Byzantine cemeteries. Syria's Directorate-General of Antiquities and Museums has described the archaeological sites as "cultural disaster areas."[66]

According to an expert on Syrian cultural heritage, various armed groups (not just IS) are communicating with antiquities smugglers outside the country and selling antiquities to fund their jihad. And apparently there is no shortage of Western museums keen to acquire these objects and add them to their collections.[67]

However, he adds, the destruction is not just opportunistic; it is also strategic, employing clear methodology aimed at erasing the past and tearing down a civilisation. "The destruction of shrines is justified from a religious perspective," he explains.

65. "Islamic State Destroying Another Ancient Archaeological Site in Iraq."
66. Abdallah, "Syria's Ancient Sites Under Attack."
67. Ibid.

The looting and selling of antiquities [is justified] to buy weapons ... We certainly cannot overlook the fundamental idea of targeting the Syrian identity. Heritage is one of the basic rules that can be built upon onto have a unified identity, upon which the idea of citizenship is built. By destroying antiquities, this basis is undermined, and fear is sowed.

The destruction and looting of the monasteries and churches, along with the Mosul museum destruction, is a message stating that they [Assyrians, Christians,] no longer have a place there, be it in history or in the future.[68]

---

68. Ibid. The same extensive cultural destruction occurred in UN-administered Kosovo where over 150 ancient Orthodox churches and monasteries, some dating back to the fourteenth century, have been either partially or completely destroyed by Albanian Muslims under the watch of NATO peacekeepers [see Serbian Orthodox Diocese of Raska-Prizren, *Crucified Kosovo*]. Cultural destruction has also occurred in Timbuktu, Mali, at the hands of jihadists linked to al-Qaeda in the Islamic Maghreb (AQIM); and in Bamiyan, Afghanistan, at the hands of the Taliban; but at nowhere near the scale of that in the two historic Christian heartlands of Kosovo and Mesopotamia.

— 10 —

"A Message Signed in Blood to the Nation of the Cross"

ON SUNDAY FEBRUARY 15, 2015, IS released "A Message Signed in Blood to the Nation of the Cross." The thoroughly choreographed and professionally produced video was posted online by al-Hayat Media—the media arm of IS.

The scene is that of a quiet Mediterranean beach on the Libyan coast, onto which is marched twenty-one prisoners: twenty Copts (indigenous Egyptians) and one Ghanaian. Dressed in orange jumpsuits with their hands tied behind their backs, each prisoner is accompanied by a black-clad jihadist executioner bearing a sheathed blade. The executioners are all soldiers of IS's *wilayat* Tarabulus (a *villayet*/province of Tripoli, Libya). The prisoners are all Christians.

Once lined up along the Mediterranean shore, the prisoners, all facing the camera, are forced to their knees.

Dressed not in black, but in military fatigues, is the IS spokesman. Positioned center stage, he would have the privilege of executing the dark-skinned Ghanaian migrant, who had allegedly embraced Christ in captivity upon witnessing the faith of the imprisoned Copts.[1]

Blade in hand, the IS spokesman looks directly into the camera and delivers the message: "All praise is due to Allah, the strong and mighty, and may blessings and peace be upon the one sent by the sword as a mercy for all the world." This opening statement refers to Muhammad and is based on the following Islamic texts: "I [Muhammad] have been sent with a sword in my hand to command people to worship Allah and associate no partners with him. I command you to believe and subjugate those who disobey me" and "We [Allah] have sent you [Muhammad] as a mercy for the worlds" (Q.21:107).[2]

---

1. Ahram-Canada, http://www.ahram-canada.com/?p=51329 (Arabic), cited by Philipose, "What Made a Non Believer Chadian [sic] Citizen Die for Christ."

2. From the hadith: Subhi al-Salih, *Ahkam Ahl al-Dhimmah*, vol. 2, 736, and

The IS spokesman continues: "Oh people, recently you have seen us on the hills of as-Sham [greater Syria] and on Dabiq's plain, chopping off the heads that have been carrying the cross delusion for a long time, filled with spite against Islam and Muslims."

The reference to Dabiq is significant, for this Syrian town—which is located 48 km north of Aleppo and 14 km south of the Turkish border—is named in Islamic eschatology as the site of an apocalyptic clash between Christians and Muslims. Abu Musab al-Zarqawi (founder of AQI) identified the 2003 US invasion of Iraq as the prelude to that apocalyptic battle. The official magazine of IS—*Dabiq*—takes its name from this prophecy and opens each edition with Zarqawi's now-famous line: "The spark has been lit here in Iraq, and its heat will continue to intensify—by Allah's permission—until it burns the crusader armies in Dabiq."[3]

The reference to "heads that have been carrying the cross delusion" is, of course, a reference to Christian heads. According to Islam, Jesus was not crucified, and to claim that he was is delusional and a "great slander" or "intolerable blasphemy"—one Jesus himself will avenge when he returns.[4]

The idea that Christians are "filled with spite against Islam and Muslims," and are therefore not to be trusted or befriended, also comes straight from the Qur'an: "enmity and hatred have appeared between us and you forever until you believe in Allah alone" (Q.60:4), "Surely, the disbelievers are your ardent enemies" (Q.86:15), and "O ye who believe! Take not others than your own people as intimate friends; they will spare no pains to ruin you. They love to see you in trouble. Hatred has already shown itself through the utterances of their mouths and what their breasts hide is greater still" (Q.3:119).

This is why so many Muslims are reluctant to assimilate into Western society.

---

also cited by Ibn Taymiyyah in *Majmu' Al-Fatawa*, vol. 28, 270. See Durie, "A Message Signed with Blood to the Nation of the Cross."

3. *DABIQ* can be accessed through The Clarion Project: http://www.clarionproject.org/news/islamic-state-isis-isil-propaganda-magazine-dabiq.

4. (Q.4:156–159): "And [We (Allah)] cursed them (Christians)] for their disbelief and their saying against Mary a great slander, And [for] their saying, 'Indeed, we have killed the Messiah, Jesus, the son of Mary, the messenger of Allah.' And they did not kill him, nor did they crucify him; but [another] was made to resemble him to them. And indeed, those who differ over it are in doubt about it. They have no knowledge of it except the following of assumption. And they did not kill him, for certain. Rather, Allah raised him to Himself. And ever is Allah Exalted in Might and Wise. And there is none from the People of the Scripture but that he will surely believe in Jesus before his death. And on the Day of Resurrection he will be against them a witness.'"

> ***Grace*** (unmerited favour/love) might be the Bible's central theme, but it has no place in Islam and Muslims have no real concept of it, viewing it mostly as either weakness or deception. Consequently, when Christians claim that they hate Islam (the ideology) yet love Muslims (the people), Muslims will reject it outright as incomprehensible and nonsensical, and generally refuse to believe it, suspecting it is a lie and a deception. It is precisely because Christians are people of *grace* that they can and do hate the teachings of Islam while maintaining a deep and sincere love for Muslims.

The IS spokesman continues:

> And today, we are on the south of Rome, on the land of Islam, Libya, sending another message. All crusaders [i.e. Christians (in the broadest sense imaginable)], safety for you will be only wishes, especially if you are fighting us all together. Therefore we will fight you all together until the world lays down its burdens and Jesus, peace be upon him, will descend, breaking the cross, killing the swine and abolishing *jizya*. The sea you have hidden Sheikh Osama Bin Laden's body in, we swear to Allah we will mix it with your blood.

These lines, too, are packed with Islamic references, the salient of which is the reference to the hadith (sayings of Muhammad): "Allah's Apostle said, 'The Hour will not be established until the son of Mary [Jesus] descends amongst you as a just ruler, he will break the cross [the symbol of Christianity], kill the pigs [the food of Christians], and abolish the Jizya tax [tribute/protection money]. Money [loot] will be in abundance so that nobody will accept it (as charitable gifts).'"[5]

Far from being an act of mercy, Jesus' abolition of the *jizya* will effectively deprive Christians of the option of paying for protection, leaving them with only two choices: convert (to Islam) or die. And so will begin the mother of all jihads, through which Christianity will be eliminated and in which Jesus himself will bear witness against all those who have ever uttered the monstrous falsehood that he was crucified.[6]

The filming continues, and the twenty-one Christian prisoners—whose dignity and serenity are extraordinary—are forced down on their

---

5. *Sahih Bukhari Volume 3, Book 43, Number 656*: Narrated Abu Huraira.

6. Q.4:156–159 (see footnote 5). Muslims do not accept that Allah would allow a prophet of God to suffer such a humiliating death. As such, the suggestion that Allah would permit the persecution of a prophet is considered a blasphemy against Allah.

bellies on the sand in preparation for their simultaneous beheading. As the executioners mount their backs, pull back their heads and even as they set their blades to work, the martyrs can be heard declaring: "*Ya Rab ya Yasoo,*" which literally translates as "My Lord, Jesus Christ."

When severed, each head is placed atop its corpse, resting in the small of the back. At that point, the IS spokesman points northward across the Mediterranean Sea towards Europe and declares: "We will conquer Rome, by Allah's permission."

The camera then zooms in to show the waters of the Mediterranean red with the blood of the martyrs, while a scrolling caption spits out the final threat: "The filthy blood is just some of what awaits you, in revenge for Camilia and her sisters."

The reference to "Camilia and her sisters" alludes to a lie being propagated by Islamic fundamentalists who falsely assert that the Coptic Church had kidnapped and forcibly converted Muslim women to Christianity.[7] While there is no evidence that any such crime has ever occurred, Muslims understand the principle well, for, as an abundance of documented evidence attests, Muslims are kidnapping and forcibly converting Christian women to Islam on an industrial scale.[8]

---

7. When Camilia Shehata (a Coptic Christian) went missing in July 2010, her frantic husband (a Coptic priest) reported her disappearance to the police, anxious that she might have been kidnapped by Islamic fundamentalists for forcible conversion. His fear, shared by the whole Christian community, was reasonable, as this is a well-documented common occurrence in Egypt, practised by Islamists in cooperation with corrupt and fundamentalist Muslims in the security forces and local government (see footnote 8). As it turned out, Camilia had simply gone to stay with relatives in Cairo after she and her husband had argued. When an embarrassed Camilia returned home with police, Islamists propagated the lie that Camilia had run away and converted to Islam only to be forcibly returned and re-converted by the Coptic Church, which was holding her against her will. To quell the rumours, Camilia appeared on national TV declaring that she had never converted to Islam, but to no avail.

8. The kidnapping and forced conversion of Christian girls by Islamic fundamentalists is carried out with the collusion of corrupt police and local officials. The girls are usually raped and threats are made against their families. By these means they are forced to convert to Islam and married to Muslim men (usually to the rapist). Their children will automatically be deemed Muslim. This is nothing less than sexual slavery and human trafficking across religious lines. Though distraught Christian families seek help from the police and redress through the courts, their efforts are mostly in vain (see report by Christian Solidarity International, "The Disappearance, Forced Conversions, and Forced Marriages of Coptic Christian Women in Egypt"; also Smith, "Plight of Coptic Christians in Egypt," in particular the expert testimony of Michelle A. Clarke). The trafficking of non-Muslim girls across religious lines is also a serious problem in Pakistan, where investigators have determined that up to seven hundred Christian girls and at least three hundred Hindu girls are kidnapped, forcibly converted to Islam and married to Muslim men each year (Iqbal, "1,000 Minority Girls Forced in Marriage

Just as the blood libel lie—which claims that Jews use the blood of Christian children in their rituals—is used to incite hatred, violence, and collective punishment against Jews, the Camilia lie is used to incite hatred, violence, and collective punishment against Copts. As an example, ISI cited the Camilia lie as its motivation for its deadly October 31, 2010 siege and bombing of Our Lady of Salvation Chaldean Catholic church in the inner-city suburb of Karrada, Baghdad, Iraq, in which fifty-eight Chaldean Christians were killed and more than seventy seriously wounded.[9]

§

Still photographs of the Copts being marched onto the beach first appeared on Thursday February 12, 2015, when issue 7 of Islamic State's *DABIQ* magazine was published online. The Copts had been kidnapped in two raids, on December 29, 2014 and January 3, 2015.[10] On January 12, 2015, IS claimed responsibility, boasting they had captured Coptic crusaders. While the photos in *DABIQ* were deeply shocking, the fate of the Copts was unclear as the article did not say they had been executed.

On January 19, 2015, families of the captured Copts gathered in Cairo, where they wept and petitioned the authorities for help. Among them was Beshir Estefanos Kamel, a farmer from Minya in Upper Egypt whose brothers, Bishoy (25) and Samuel (23), were among the captives. "All we can do is pray to God for help," he said.[11]

As is generally the case, the IS "message" had two target audiences. The video was intended to "instil terror into the hearts of the Unbelievers" (Q.8:12), to extract concessions from them, and rally the believers (i.e., Muslims), spurring them into action (jihad) and drawing them into the IS camp (as distinct from the al-Qaeda camp).

To that end, the *DABIQ* article included an unambiguous call for Muslims to kill Copts, and if Copts could not be found, then any Christians would suffice. For, notes *DABIQ*, "despite the worldly and sectarian animosity of the kuffār [unbelievers/Christians]—as groups and individuals—towards each" (a sad indictment on the church), they "have allegiance

---

Every Year"; "Forced Marriages and Forced Conversions in the Christian Community of Pakistan").

9. Kendal, "Iraq and Egypt: Al-Qaeda Declares War on Christians." This attack on Our Lady of Salvation Chaldean Catholic church in Karrada, Baghdad, is detailed in chapter 1 of this book.

10. Kendal, "Libya-Egypt: A Call to Jihad against Copts."

11. Loveluck and Samaan, "Egyptian Christians Wait for News of Loved Ones Kidnapped by Isil."

to each other in the face of Islam." Consequently, IS concluded, revenge may be taken on any Christian "anywhere in the world."[12] The Islamic State also berated the "strange attitude" of al-Qaeda head Ayman al-Zawahir (an Egyptian), who, *DABIQ* claimed, had previously ruled that Copts should not be targeted as the battle was against America and the Copts were "our partners in this nation [Egypt], partners whom we wish to live with in peace and stability."[13] The article concluded: "Finally, it is important for Muslims everywhere to know that there is no doubt in the great reward to be found on Judgment Day for those who spill the blood of these Coptic crusaders wherever they may be found."[14]

But if the *DABIQ* article was supposed to incite communal pogroms against Copts in Egypt (as it most surely was), then it failed in its objective, not the least because prayers rose up across the world that there "be no jihad against the Copts."[15]

Likewise, if the video was supposed to terrorize Christians (as it most surely was), particularly the Copts, then it failed in that objective also. After two thousand years of persecution—first under the Romans and then under Islam, the Copts know how to carry the cross.

The Copts Respond with a Lesson in Grace

Sam Solomon, a convert from Islam, serves as the Islamic affairs adviser for Christian Concern (UK). Reflecting on the beheadings, he noted that IS was exceeding careful

> to dot every 'i' and cross every 't' to demonstrate at each step closer to the disfigurement and final slitting of the throats of these brave Christians that they were proceeding in accordance with the letter of the Sunnah of Mohammad and the Islamic eschatological doctrine . . .
>
> The intended 'victory' proclaimed by [the] executioners was instantly and permanently nullified by the steadfast voices of the 21—putting their trust in Christ to sustain them, not in whispers but in shouts, 'Yasouh, Yasouh, Jesus, Jesus', even as the deed was being done—literally for the world to see and hear!! And we

---

12. "Revenge for the Muslimat Persecuted by the Coptic Crusaders of Egypt," *DABIQ*, issue 7, 31. (WARNING: this magazine includes graphic images of extreme violence; images any sane person would find deeply distressing.)

13. Ibid., 32.

14. Ibid.

15. Kendal, "Libya-Egypt: A Call to Jihad against Copts."

know this was not the end of the story, according to the promise of our Lord in Rev. 2:10, '. . . Be faithful, even to the point of death, and I will give you life as your victor's crown' [NIV].[16]

On the evening of Sunday January 15, 2015, as soon as he heard that the twenty-one captives had been martyred, Ramez Atallah, the General Director of the Bible Society of Egypt, telephoned the Bible Society's publishing manager: "We must have a scripture tract ready to distribute to the nation as soon as possible," said Ramez.

When Ramez arrived at work at the Bible Society office the next morning, he was (in his own words) "sad and depressed." When a young coworker said that she was actually feeling greatly encouraged, Ramez queried her, asking what on earth was there to feel encouraged about?

"I am encouraged" she said, "because now I know that what we have been taught in history books about Egyptian Christians being martyred for their faith is not just history but that there are Christians today who are brave enough to face death rather than deny their Lord! When I saw these young men praying as they were being prepared for execution and then many of them shouting 'O Lord Jesus' as their throats were being slit, I realized that the Gospel message can still help us to hold on to the promises of God even when facing death!"[17]

That Monday (the day after the video's release), Bible Society workers got busy preparing the tract. By Tuesday afternoon it was complete. By Thursday evening, well over a million tracts entitled "Two Rows by the Sea" were ready for distribution.[18] One week after the killings, 1.65 million tracts had been distributed in what has been the Bible Society's largest campaign ever.

"Egyptians have been shocked by this news," said Ramez, "and it is the most talked about event in our country at this time . . . But the loving and caring response of Muslims all over the nation softened the blow which many Christians felt."[19] Indeed, Andrea Zaki, the president of the Protestant Churches of Egypt noted the same: "There has been a very strong response of unity and sympathy," she said. "People are describing Copts as Egyptians, first and foremost, and with their blood they are unifying Egypt."[20]

While indicative of the hope of Egypt's Copts, this was of course an exaggeration—possibly even a bit of wishful thinking. For while many of

16. "Victory over ISIS Found in the Last Words Uttered by Christians."
17. *Bible Society of Egypt Newsletter*, 1.
18. Ibid., 2 (this page includes links to the Arabic and English tracts).
19. Ibid., 1.
20. Casper, "Libya's 21 Christian Martyrs."

Egypt's more secularized urban elites were indeed sympathetic, most radicalized Muslims were not, especially those living in MB strongholds. Indeed, it was not long before Egypt's Copts—even the families of the martyrs themselves—were suffering persecution yet again.[21]

From the outset, Egyptian Christians would redeem the evil as a platform for gospel witness. Isaaf Evangelical Church, located on one of downtown Cairo's busiest streets, hung a poster on its front wall at eye level with pedestrians. It was a poster of the Egyptian flag, on which was printed: "We learn from what the Messiah has said. Love your enemies, do good to those who hate you."[22]

On the evening of Tuesday February 17, 2015, just two days after the release of the IS video, the widely respected and popular Egyptian musician Maher Fayez hosted his weekly worship program *We Will Sing* on Christian satellite channel SAT 7-Arabic. As usual, listeners phoned in—only this time there was only one subject being talked about: the twenty-one martyrs of Libya. Of all the calls that came in that evening, one left a lasting impression—it was a phone call from Beshir Estefanos Kamel.

As Beshir explained to Fayez, his two brothers were amongst those martyred by IS on the Libyan beach for their faith in Jesus. "I am proud of them," said Beshir. "They are my pride . . . They make me walk rising my head up in pride."

IS gave us more than we asked," he said. "when they didn't edit out the part where [the martyrs] declared their faith and called 'Jesus Christ' . . . IS has helped us strengthen our faith."[23]

---

21. Of the twenty Copts martyred on the Libyan beach, thirteen came from the village of al-Our in Minya, Upper Egypt. Consequently, when the Copts of al-Our sought permission to build a church in the village in honour of their martyrs, their request won the approval of none other than President al-Sisi himself. Absolutely incensed, local Muslims rioted on March 27, 2015, hurling rocks and Molotov cocktails at Coptic homes and businesses. In true Egyptian fashion, the police and local officials organised a "reconciliation session." Unable to overrule their president—who had granted permission for the church—the Muslims insisted it not be built inside the village. If the Christians wanted "peace," they would have to agree to the church being built outside the village limits. On April 29, 2015, the home of one the martyrs was attacked (see "Testimony of Samuel Tadros").

Further to this, in early April, four Coptic youths (teenagers) and a teacher were arrested in Al-Nasriyah village, Upper Egypt, and charged with "contempt of religion" (i.e., blasphemy) for mocking the actions of IS (see "Video Mocking IS Causes Riots in Egypt").

22. Casper, "How Libya's Martyrs Are Witnessing to Egypt."

23 "Brother of Two Christian Victims of ISIS Calls In to SAT-7 Live Programme 'We Will Sing.'"

Beshir continued, "Since the Roman era, Christians have been targeted to be martyred and so we have learned to handle everything that comes our way. This only makes us stronger in our faith because the Bible told us to love our enemies and bless those who curse us."[24]

Maher Fayez asked Beshir if he, or someone from his family, would get upset if he was asked to forgive his brothers' killers. Without hesitation Beshir responded by sharing what his mother said as they had discussed that very scenario. "Believe me," he said, "these were my mother's words . . . she is an uneducated woman over 60 years old. I asked her 'What will you do if you see those ISIS members passing on the street and I told you that's the man who slayed your son?' She said 'I will ask for God to open his eyes and ask him in our house because he helped us enter the kingdom of God.'"[25]

Fayez then invited Beshir to pray for his brothers' killers, and without a moment's hesitation, Beshir erupted into passionate prayer: "Dear God," he prayed, "please open their eyes to be saved and to quit their ignorance and the wrong teachings they were taught."[26]

Not only was Sat 7-Arabic flooded with calls, but within hours of the clip being posted on Facebook, it had already been viewed over 96,000 times.[27]

Young Coptic artist Tony Rezk honoured the martyrs with a truly beautiful work of art (see Figure 4).[28] Rezk confesses on his blog that waves of anger, pain, anguish, and utter contempt flooded him as he watched the IS video message.[29] But as he and a friend discussed how easy it would be to hate the killers, they knew that such a response would dishonor Christ, "who taught us to love our enemies, to bless and not curse, and to pray for those who persecute us."

---

24. Ibid. In this quote, Beshir refers to Jesus' words in the Sermon on the Mount: "You have heard that it was said, 'You shall love your neighbor and hate your enemy.' But I say to you, Love your enemies and pray for those who persecute you, so that you may be sons of your Father who is in heaven. For he makes his sun rise on the evil and on the good, and sends rain on the just and on the unjust. For if you love those who love you, what reward do you have? Do not even the tax collectors do the same? And if you greet only your brothers, what more are you doing than others? Do not even the Gentiles do the same? You therefore must be perfect, as your heavenly Father is perfect" (Matt 5:43–48, ESV).

25. "Brother of Two Christian Victims of ISIS Calls In to SAT-7 Live Programme 'We Will Sing.'"

26. Ibid.

27. "Brother of Egyptian Christians Murdered by Islamic State Prays for Killers Live on SAT-7."

28. See "21 New Martyrs of Libya Icon."

29. Rezk, "Loving Your Enemies."

"Hatred is poison," writes Rezk. "Once you allow it into your heart, it slowly begins to destroy your senses, your emotions, your humanity, and in the end it will take your life. This is why the Lord taught us to love our enemies, for our sakes, so that we would learn to be pure and holy, and full of love like our Father in heaven."

Rezk admits that "Loving your enemies is no easy task," so he leaves his readers with words from "our Orthodox Church fathers", words he says have given him great comfort:

> "But I say to you," the Lord says, "love your enemies, do good to those who hate you, pray for those who persecute you." Why did he command these things? So that he might free you from hatred, sadness, anger and grudges, and might grant you the greatest possession of all, perfect love, which is impossible to possess except by the one who loves all equally in imitation of God"—St. Maximus the Confessor.
>
> "The Truth in person says, 'Love your enemies, do good to those who hate you and pray for them who persecute you and say evil of you falsely' (Lk. 6:27). It is virtue therefore before men to bear with adversaries; but it is virtue before God to love them; because the only sacrifice which God accepts is that which, before His eyes, on the altar of good work, the flame of charity kindles" —St. Gregory the Great.

"May [these words]," writes Rezk, "bring peace into our hearts and may we learn to pray for our enemies and truly love them like Christ taught us."[30]

Sophia Jones, a young journalist with Huffington Post (US), travelled to Upper Egypt in the wake of the killings to interview the families of the martyred men. Subsequently she remarked that she did not find what she had expected.

"What I found was actually really striking when I went to al-Our," says Jones in a four-minute video interview. "I had expected people to be enraged and bitter and to want revenge. But actually there was an overwhelming feeling of love—there is this outpouring of love. Everyone talks about how cherished these men were, and how they are remembered as beloved sons and husbands and cousins and friends, and they not remembered as people who were brutally killed; they are remembered as heroes."[31]

Though the church in al-Our grieves, it is not as those who have no hope (1 Thess 4:13–18).[32] Indeed, it has not gone unnoticed that the Egyp-

---

30. Ibid.
31. Jones, "ISIS Boasted Of These Christians' Deaths."
32. *"But we do not want you to be uninformed, brothers, about those who are asleep*

tian church, in particular the families of the martyrs, has responded to this unmitigated evil not only with strength and endurance, but with amazing grace.

What a truly radical testimony these humble, faithful, broken-hearted families have given to the world.

Figure 4. '21 Martyrs of Libya', an icon painted by Tony Rezk in the Neo-Coptic iconographic style. © Antoun Rezk. Used with permission.

[i.e. those who have died], *that you may not grieve as others do who have no hope. For since we believe that Jesus died and rose again, even so, through Jesus, God will bring with him those who have fallen asleep. For this we declare to you by a word from the Lord, that we who are alive, who are left until the coming of the Lord, will not precede those who have fallen asleep. For the Lord himself will descend from heaven with a cry of command, with the voice of an archangel, and with the sound of the trumpet of God. And the dead in Christ will rise first. Then we who are alive, who are left, will be caught up together with them in the clouds to meet the Lord in the air, and so we will always be with the Lord. Therefore encourage one another with these words."* (1 Thessalonians 4:13–18) See also: 1 Corinthians 15.

— 11 —

A House Divided

DISAPPOINTED MAYBE, BUT SURPRISED? No! Middle Eastern Christians have not been surprised by Turkish, Arab, Persian, Sunni, Shi'ite, and general Muslim aggression against them. After all, their history is replete with martyrs and massacres; it is not as if these events are unprecedented.

What has surprised Middle Eastern Christians, leaving them shocked and devastated, has been the West's attitude towards them. After all, the US-led West is Christian, isn't it? Surely the "Christian West" would not arm and support those who persecute Christians and threaten the West, would it?

Like most Christians the world over, the Christians of the Middle East have been slow to realize how ideological and "post-Christian" the West has become. In general, Christians have drifted along, comfortably clueless, as Western cultural Marxists[1] have advanced their subversive, strategic "long

---

1. Renowned legal theorist and law professor Augusto Zimmermann describes Marxism as "primarily a social, political and economic theory that interprets history through a progressive prism." (The term, "the right side of history", expresses this Marxist concept.) Zimmermann adds, "In order better understand Marxism it is necessary first to explore its religious dimensions. Marxism is not just a scheme of social, economic and political transformation but also a form of secular theology . . . [containing] within itself a complete worldview that includes an explanation of the origin of the universe as well as in eschatological theory regarding the final destination of humankind . . . If the 'god' of Marxism can be described as a dialectical historical process toward communism, its 'devil' is the 'reactionary forces' that either deny or hinder the eschatological consummation of the communist paradise." Zimmermann, *Western Legal Theory,* Chapter 7, "Marxist Legal Theory."

Neo or Cultural Marxists are primarily interested in the cultural aspects of Marxism: morality, marriage, family, religion, and national identity—cultural traits Marx believed should be abolished (see Marx and Engels, *Communist Manifesto*, specifically Part II, or just do a word search).

march through the institutions"[2] in pursuit of *culture change*.[3] As is becoming clear, the demolition of Western civilization's foundations is not going to result in freedom in a godless utopia, but in authoritarianism amidst cultural collapse.

No longer guided by the Bible, Western values are now guided by "equality," by which is meant moral and cultural relativism. Today, most Western elites believe God does not exist, humanity is inherently good, and the problems of the world are caused not by "sin" (an outdated, offensive, and politically incorrect concept) but by economic hardship resulting from, more often than not, Western imperialism and other supposedly "Christian" crimes. These elites—who control the narrative through their domination of academia, media, politics, and entertainment—arrogantly insist that Christians should evolve or perish, much like the dinosaurs to which they derisively liken them. No wonder existentially imperiled Christians attract little sympathy.

"We see ourselves abandoned, even betrayed, by the so-called civilized countries of the West," lamented Syrian Patriarch Ignace Joseph III Younan in June 2014, in the wake of the ISIS conquest of Mosul. "The politicians over there have adopted confusing responses to the rise of Islamic fundamentalism, and for opportunistic reasons, have forgotten their principles of democracy, separation of state and religion and the respect of civil liberties for all minorities, women and the most vulnerable ones."

Christians, he said, "are facing the biggest challenge for their survival on the lands of their forefathers in Iraq and Syria. We are very anxious, even devastated . . . For years, Christian leaders had in vain warned the Western politicians not to foster violent uprisings based principally on sectarian religious grounds, as it was expected of the so-called Arab Spring,"

---

2. Rejecting confrontation as counterproductive, neo or cultural Marxists embarked on a patient, Mao-like "long march" to subvert and radically change Western culture. "In the Sixties and Seventies, after fantasies of overt political revolution faded, many student radicals urged their followers to undertake the 'long march through the institutions.' The phrase, popularized by German New Leftist Rudi Dutschke, is often attributed to the Italian Marxist philosopher Antonio Gramsci . . . In the context of Western societies, the 'long march through the institutions' signified—in the words of Herbert Marcuse—'working against established institutions while working in them'" (Kimball, *The Long March*, 14–15).

3. The *culture change* sought by cultural Marxists—something they define as "progress"—involves society's evolution from a Judeo-Christian to a post-Christian culture, meaning a non-Christian culture, in which Christianity is rejected as a relic of the past. It is essentially a gradual form of cultural revolution, where Christianity is rejected as counter-revolutionary.

the patriarch said. "Now we harvest the horrendous results of that macabre Machiavellian strategy." [4]

Forced to abandon ancient monasteries and church properties rich in historic and cultural memory, the church leadership has then had to watch—powerless and helplessly—as their people—their flock—endure great suffering, perish for lack of basic necessities, and flee in search of security and a more dignified existence. All across the Middle East, church leaders and religious workers—men and women, priests, nuns, pastors and lay workers—are struggling against despair, a struggle exacerbated and a despair compounded by the shock and pain of being rejected and ignored, betrayed and abandoned, by the US-led West.

A Church in Pain

From Southern Syria . . .

In November 2014, journalist Ruth Sherlock visited Izraa, a village in Daraa in Syria's deep southwest. There she found a Christian community in decline and under threat on account of Islamic rebels—many armed, trained, and funded by the West.

> Outgoing artillery shook St Elias church as the priest reached the end of the Lord's Prayer.
>
> The small congregation kept their eyes on the pulpit, kneeling when required and trying to ignore the regular thuds that rattled the stained glass windows above them . . .
>
> "I have been coming to this church since I was born," said [Mrs] Afaf Azam, 52. "But now the situation is very bad. Everyone is afraid. Jihadists control villages around us. People from here are leaving. Many are applying to emigrate."
>
> Exactly how many Christians have left Syria is difficult to say, but according to the Christian charity Open Doors, some 700,000 have left the country, which equates to some 40 per cent of Syria's pre-war Christian population.
>
> Christian leaders in the country warn of an exodus on the scale of Iraq, where the 1.5 million-strong community that lived there prior to the first Gulf War is now down to as little as a tenth of its former size.

In an accompanying video, Sherlock reports over scenes of worship inside the 1,500-year-old St. Elias Church. "Izraa's residents are starting to leave,"

---

4. "Syrian Patriarch Says Middle East Christians Feel Abandoned by West."

she says. "Christian leaders warn that the Middle East is being drained of a community that has lived here for more than 2,000 years."

Then, speaking over an image of a bearded Islamic militant firing what looks like a US-TOW[5] anti-tank guided rocket, she comments: "Only a small portion of the rebels fighting near Izraa are aligned to al-Qaeda; many are 'moderates' who have been armed and trained by the West. But still Izraa's residents don't want to take the risk. So they back the Syrian government. Painted flags on shop fronts show nationalist fervour, and as the shelling gets closer, they put their hopes in the Syrian military whose troops surround the town."

As Sherlock acknowledges in her article, local Christians do not distinguish between good and bad, or moderate and radical, Islamic jihadists. "Past experience," she writes, "has rendered such distinctions irrelevant to Izraa's Christians. After all, in Syria—and on this frontline—the 'moderates' continue to work in alliance with Nusra. And the conquest of other Christian villages by the opposition has shown that more moderate factions frequently do little to stop the jihadists imposing their will."

Sherlock's concession that "more moderate factions frequently do little to stop the jihadists imposing their will," is unduly generous considering how US-armed and trained "moderate" rebels have terrorized, looted, and executed Christians in towns and villages all across Syria, cheered on by radicalized local Muslims excited by the prospect of Islamic *success*.[6]

No—rather than risk being persecuted or killed, Izraa's Christians are leaving.

What is the solution?

> "It's simple," said Father Elias Hanout, 38, who led the prayers at Sunday's service.
>
> "If the West wants Syria to remain a country for Christian people, then help us to stay here; stop arming terrorists."
>
> . . .
>
> In Izraa . . . the sense is of having been abandoned by other "Christian nations" such as America and Britain, no matter what the promises of their leaders are.
>
> As another priest in Izraa, who asked not to be named, put it: "Please tell Mr Cameron, we don't want any help or donations—but please, equally, stop arming terrorists."[7]

---

5. TOW: tube-launched, optically tracked, wire-guided.
6. Sherlock, "Syrian Christians."
7. Ibid.

. . . To Northern Iraq

In December 2014, Morning Star News (MSN) spoke with an evangelical pastor in Ankawa, on the northern outskirts of Arbil, the capital of Iraqi Kurdistan. The pastor had fled Mosul after ISIS invaded in June 2014.

"You have your life, you have your house, you have your memories, you have your country or city, you have your friends—everything," he told MSN, "and then in one hour, you lose everything. You have to start from zero. But I can say for myself, my church and my friends—Jesus in our lives has made it able for us to continue. But it is not easy."[8]

At the refugee center in Ankawa's Mar Elia Catholic Church, MSN spoke with Fr. Douglas Bazi, a Chaldean priest who survived nine days in captivity in November 2006 after being kidnapped by Islamic militants aligned with al-Qaeda. Snatched off the street as he was walking home after Mass in Baghdad, Bazi was kept blindfolded and dehydrated. He was beaten and tortured, his face and knees were smashed with a hammer, and his back was badly damaged. Eventually the militants gave up on him, dressed him in women's robes, and dumped him on the side of a highway. Thankfully, a passerby picked him up and took him to a nearby church. Safe at last, Bazi broke down in tears of relief before the believers took him to hospital. Today, Fr. Bazi looks after twenty-six refugee centers and cares for some 1,200 "relatives."[9]

Bazi is fed up with Western elites who insist that all the Middle East needs is political and economic liberalization. He is furious that despite having no understanding or practical experience of Islam, they will insist that Islam is inherently peaceful, arrogantly believing they know Islam better than he does.

"We are in pain," says Bazi. "I am angry because I know Islam very well. In Baghdad they blew up my church. I drove by three bombings, and twice my car was destroyed. I got shot in my leg by an AK-47—by Islam, and they kidnapped me for nine days."[10]

Like the Christians of Izraa, Bazi does not distinguish between "radical Islamists" and what the West calls "moderate rebels," insisting much of what they believe, including their desire to harm Christians, is the same.

"You know who represents Islam very well?" he asks. "ISIS. They are the true Islam. So if someone says, 'No, they do not represent Islam, Hamas

---

8. "Displaced Iraqi Christians Ponder an Iraq without Christians."
9. "Tortured by Extremists—Now Caring for Refugees."
10. "Displaced Iraqi Christians Ponder an Iraq without Christians."

does not represent Islam, Hezbollah does not represent Islam.' Who's left then? Come on guys. Come on. Wake up."

Leave or Stay?

Understandably, many Christians, especially those raising children, desperately want to leave the Middle East. Equally understandably, local church leaders desperately want them to stay. Most church leaders reject the idea that they should in any way encourage or facilitate a Christian exodus, pointing out that this would only advance the Islamic agenda of ethnic-religious cleansing.

According to a pastor in Ankawa, who didn't want to be named,

> "You can't leave your heritage just because you got hurt or a disaster happened. And plus, we're talking about hundreds of thousands of people . . . How are you going to get all of them out of the country? Jesus said, 'You are the light of the world.' If you take that light from the world, what do you think is going to happen here? Where does that put us, where is the message? . . .
>
> All these years, it doesn't seem like there is hope . . . And that's why these people are suffering. They don't have good education. They don't have good jobs. And every day it's like you're sitting here and there's a thief every day, and he's calling you and saying, 'Hey I'm going to kill you, I'm gonna come and take your money, I'm going to come and take your wife, take your kids,' and threatening you every day and you're sitting and can do nothing. But as I said, they are the light of the world. If you have a true Christian here and you take him away, who is going to witness?"[11]

For his part, Fr. Bazi will not pressure Christians to stay. "I care about my people," Bazi said. "I don't care about the 'Middle East.' The Middle East for almost 2,000 years has been the same. It's the same war, the same conflict. So, why do I have to put my people inside that war? Why?"[12]

All Christians agree, however, that if Christians are to stay, then they will need not just security, but massive amounts of ongoing aid and assistance to provide services such as health and education to what is now a predominantly displaced and destitute remnant population in a devastated land.

---

11. Ibid.
12. Ibid.

The wall behind Fr. Bazi's desk is covered with scores of business cards from people representing aid organizations and other groups from around the world. According to MSN, the cards are arranged into two groups, with about 30 cards on the right and three times that many on the left.

"On the right are the people that really help us," Fr. Bazi told MSN. "On the left are people who just show up, say 'Hello,' ask if you need something, and then say goodbye. This is a time of work, not words."[13]

Future Hope

Australian author Denis Dragovic is an expert on refugees, internally displaced persons (IDPs), and post-conflict state-building. "In countries like Syria" writes Dragovic,

> when wars break out the wealthiest flee at the outbreak, saving themselves and their relatives, transferring cash, selling assets and dusting off their dual nationalities. As the war continues the middle class follow, selling what little they have remaining, first moving to neighbouring countries, planning only a temporary stay while hoping for peace. As the years go by they seek out alternative solutions, including people-smugglers to help them start new lives in the West. The poorest, lacking the resources to travel, stay behind.
>
> In the case of Syria and Libya . . . we are now [Sept 2015] in that last phase. Not only have the middle class fled, but they have decided that a peaceful resolution isn't at hand, so they seek stability for themselves and their families by migrating to Europe. While for individuals this choice is understandable, for those left behind in Syria and Libya the consequences of the loss of a middle class will be just as predictable.
>
> When the cease-fire comes and the efforts to build a lasting peace begin those who fought are always first to be rewarded with jobs, yet inevitably they struggle to transition to their new roles as bureaucrats and administrators, opening the door for corruption and incompetence. Of the others who remained, children who had grown into adulthood without a stable education, or the poor and displaced scarred by the war, they can offer little of what the country really needs.
>
> Instead the engineers and doctors, administrators and planners, those with the skills and training so desperately needed to stabilise and rebuild, will instead be establishing new lives

13. Ibid.

in France, Germany, the US or Australia with little incentive to return. The business owners whose capital is critical to restarting the economy will have invested in their new countries.[14]

Dragovic maintains that a sustainable solution must involve helping people stay, if not in their country, then at least in their region so they can eventually return. This is precisely what Middle Eastern church leaders are appealing for: security and aid that will help people stay. Since Western governments have betrayed and abandoned them, and because the burden of care is being born mostly by the local church, Middle Eastern church leaders are now making their appeals directly to the global church in the hope that the church might rise up to help them.

In August 2015, Chaldean Catholic Archbishop Bashar Warda of Arbil visited the US to raise awareness of the plight of some 100,000 Christian refugees who had flooded into Arbil following the ISIS conquest of Mosul and the Nineveh Plain in June–August 2014. Sean Gallagher of the Catholic News Service spoke to him at the Peter and Paul Cathedral in Indianapolis. When asked how his faith had been challenged and changed by the crisis, Archbishop Warda put his head in his hands and confessed that while the Christians he serves are a constant source of encouragement, he just can't understand what God is doing. "I quarrel with him every day," he confessed. "Before going to sleep, I usually hand all my crises, wishes, thoughts and sadness to him, so I can at least have some rest. The next day, I usually wake up with his providence that I would never dream about."[15]

Archbishop Warda said he sees the caring, loving hand of God helping suffering believers more effectively than he could have ever devised himself, in part through the sacrificial ministry of local churches and religious organizations.

With some 100,000 displaced people needing shelter, food, medical care, and educational services, the task could be overwhelming. But according to the archbishop, while the state could not manage it, God has managed it. "He did it through the church," he said, "and through the generosity of so many people." This, he said, has bolstered his faith, as has the undaunted hope, faith, and endurance of the displaced believers. "People come and tell their stories of persecution, and how they were really terrified, having to walk eight to 10 hours during the night. In the end, they would tell you,

---

14. Dragovic, "Migrant crisis." See also Kendal, "Christian Crisis in the Middle East."

15. Sean Gallagher, "Iraqi archbishop: Plight of fleeing Christians has challenged his faith."

'Thank God we are alive. Nushkur Allah. We thank God for everything.' That's the phrase they end with. That's strengthening, in a way."

On August 31, 2015, Melkite Greek Catholic Patriarch Gregorios III Laham published a deeply moving open letter to Syrian Christian youths, lamenting the "tsunami" of youth emigration.

> Dear young people,
>
> I am sending you affectionate, hearty greetings by way of this brotherly and fatherly letter addressed to you, which is rather a conversation with you . . .
>
> The almost communal wave of youth emigration, especially in Syria, but also in Lebanon and Iraq breaks my heart, wounding me deeply and dealing me a deadly blow.
>
> Given this tsunami of emigration . . . what future is left for the Church? What will become of our homeland? What will become of our parishes and institutions?
>
> Of course, I understand the many reasons that incite you young people to emigrate. Despite all that, I implore you to remain, arming yourselves with resolution, patience, endurance, strength and good courage.
>
> Our fathers and mothers suffered much. Many died in the frequent turmoil in our countries, especially Syria. We all know about the revolution of 1860,[16] when thousands of Christians were killed, and the churches of Damascus Old City were burnt down, from Bab Tuma to Bab Sharki. Our Cathedral of the Dormition, which had been built in 1835 by Patriarch Maximos III (Mazlum), was destroyed. My predecessor Patriarch Gregorios II (Sayyur) had it rebuilt and enlarged in 1865, and we have just celebrated the 150th anniversary of its reconstruction. Then, in 1860 there was just the cathedral, but now we have nine churches in Damascus.
>
> My dear young people,
>
> Our forebears underwent great difficulties, but they exercised patience and so the Church remained, Christianity remained and the number of Christians even grew after 1860.
>
> That is why I say again, despite all your suffering, stay! Be patient! Don't emigrate! Stay for the Church, your homeland, for Syria and its future! Stay! Do stay!
>
> I conclude this brotherly and fatherly letter by reminding you again of my love and esteem.

16. An account of the Damascus pogroms is given in chapter 3, under the heading, "Islamic Resistance", subheading, "Syria 1860."

> You are the future of the Church and your country. I shall go on praying for you every day, for Jesus, the Saviour to keep you and give you the grace of patience in the current, tragic circumstances.
>
> Be sure that the Church, with all its capabilities, is accompanying you. Our Lord Jesus, friend of young people, speaks to you, telling you, as he often did his disciples according to the Gospel, "Be not afraid. I am with you always, even unto the end of the age. Ye will be my witnesses."
>
> My dear young people, I love you,
>
> + Gregorios III
>
> Patriarch of Antioch and All the East,
>
> Of Alexandria and of Jerusalem.[17]

Of course, the Christians who stayed in Damascus after the 1860 pogroms had few options, for after centuries of *dhimmitude* they were the poorest of the poor. Today however, after decades of secularism, the Christians of Damascus (and Mesopotamia in general) are largely middle class—most are well-educated, successful business people and professionals—and consequently, they do have options.

On September 16, 2015, Metropolitan Jean-Clément Jeanbart put pen to paper as he quietly celebrated the twenty-year anniversary of his appointment as Aleppo's Melkite archbishop.

> Today, as I am writing these lines, bombs are raining down on the residential neighborhoods of the city [Aleppo]. There may be as many as 60 dead and 300 wounded. The people are bewildered; they don't know where to find shelter. Three months ago I had to move out of the archdiocesan residence, after it was heavily damaged in a bombing raid.
>
> The residents of this hardworking city, who were pretty well off now find themselves in a miserable state, after four years of this unjust, barbaric and destructive war. They are without work, without resources, without security, without water, without electricity, deprived of all hoped-for pity . . .
>
> The latest scourge that is beating us down today is the exodus of Christians, which is a form of deportation, condemning our faithful to a humiliating exile and our 2000 year-old Church to a deadly desiccation. Our attackers have done everything to bring this about. Firstly, they have terrorized the people in the

---

17. Gregorios III, "Appeal to Syria's Young People."

city; next they destroyed factories, all commerce, institutions and homes, forcing people to leave and try to make a living elsewhere. They finally made this desertion possible by allowing smugglers to organize massive convoys heading for the West. What a tragedy!

The phenomenon is very disconcerting . . . But I, like many pastors of the people of God in Syria, remain confident because we believe in Him who has promised to remain with those who are His.

On this anniversary of my episcopate, I fervently wish that you join me in asking the Lord to protect the faithful He is given into my care, so that this Church that is two millennia old, of which I am in charge, can continue its prophetic presence in this beloved country. They are waging war on us, but we want to make peace. They seek to destroy; we seek to build. They are trying to exile us; we are fighting to stay put. In brief, all that we await is peace and we want to Build to Stay.

Aleppo, Syria *Sept. 16, 2015*

Metropolitan Jean-Clément Jeanbart is Aleppo's Melkite Archbishop.[18]

Syriac Catholic Patriarch Ignace Joseph III Younan, was in Canada in September 2015 when the Western world dissolved into tears over the sight of little Alan Kurdi's body, washed up on a Turkish beach.[19]

While acknowledging that the death of any child is tragic, and while grateful to see Westerners expressing a desire a help, the archbishop lamented the total indifference he has met with over the past four years as he has tried to raise awareness of the dangers, threats, kidnappings, enslavement, beheadings, tortures, rapes, and all manner of terror being suffered by the Christian community on a daily basis.

Regarding the plight of Christians, he commented that "The Western world is not only indifferent it is [sic] an accomplice," and he singled out the US, UK, and France for "fomenting the violence under the pretext of a kind of Arab Spring." Lampooning Western policy as "naive", the patriarch derided as pure "fantasy" the West's belief that it can modernize and civilize Islamic militants involved in armed insurrection against the government. "The conflict here became bloody because of the intervention of Western

---

18. "Letter from Aleppo: 20 years a bishop—fighting for his faithful to stay in Syria."

19. Joel Gunter, "Alan Kurdi death: A Syrian Kurdish family forced to flee."
Adrian Lee, "Migrant crisis: The truth about the boy on the beach Aylan Kurdi."

countries," he said, adding that the West should have helped "find a way for reconciliation." Instead, conditions for Christians in the region have deteriorated to the point of "catastrophe," he noted, pointing out that everywhere regimes are aligned with radical Islam, and where there is no separation of church and state, you have "the most retrograde" societies, like something "out of the Middle Ages."[20]

Rather than risk a life of insecurity and *dhimmitude* in a retrograde society resembling something from the Middle Ages, Christians are leaving en masse. Their pastors, priests, nuns, and multitudes of lay workers, however, are staying, refusing to abandon the remnant. The courage of these men and women is extraordinary; their faithfulness, phenomenal; and their pain, palpable. The world has abandoned them; the church must not.

On the night before his crucifixion, our Lord prayed: "I do not ask for these [my disciples] only, but also for those who will believe in me through their word, *that they may all be one*, just as you, Father, are in me, and I in you, that they also may be in us, so *that the world may believe* that you have sent me. The glory that you have given me I have given to them, *that they may be one* even as we are one, I in them and you in me, *that they may become perfectly one*, so *that the world may know that you sent me* and loved them even as you loved me."[21]

> "Every kingdom divided against itself is laid waste, and no city or house divided against itself will stand" (Jesus, Matthew 12:25). If ever there was a time for Christian solidarity, it is now. For more on this subject of Christian solidarity, see Appendix 1, "Christian Solidarity: The Sound of Silence" and Appendix 2, "God's Human Instruments: Just Do It!"

The Christian Crisis in the Middle East

As strategic analyst and terrorism expert Yossef Bodansky explained at the outset, the first "layer" of this "multi-layered conflict" will entail "the crushing of the Fertile Crescent of Minorities by neo-Ottoman Turkey, Mahdivist

---

20. Gyapong, "Leader Says West Must Stop Syrian and Iraq Wars So Refugees Can Stay Home."

21. John 17:20–23, italics added.

Iran, and a Sunni Arab camp led by Saudi Arabia in order to enable the leading *blocs* to juggle for power."[22]

While this "crushing" of the minorities Bodansky speaks of is clearly evident, what Western policymakers have failed to understand is that it is not accidental. The Christian crisis in the Middle East cannot be explained by the African proverb—"When elephants fight, it's the grass that suffers."[23] For the Middle East's Christians are not simply the collateral damage of Turkish *versus* Arab *versus* Persian and Sunni *versus* Shi'ite rivalry. Rather, Christians are being targeted, and not merely for persecution, subjugation, and exploitation—but for elimination!

By the end of 2014, the genocide of Iraq's indigenous Assyrian Christian community was all but complete. Having been crushed and decimated, the remnant Christians were now being swept out of the arena, along with all evidence that they ever existed. Would Syria's Christians suffer the same fate? Though existentially threatened by jihadists just as intent on genocide as those in Iraq, Syria's Christians at least had the protection of their government. As far as Syria's Christians were concerned, their fate was linked to the fate of the government.

Impact of the Iran Nuclear Deal

As 2014 rolled into 2015 and negotiations on the Joint Comprehensive Plan of Action[24] on Iran's nuclear program progressed, it was becoming increasingly clear that the agreement would proceed, and it would massively empower Iran.

Clearly, if the Turkey-Arab Sunni Axis was going to remove Assad, it would have to be sooner rather than later—before Iranian funds were unfrozen and sanctions lifted giving Tehran the means to impose its will across the region. Cognizant of this, regime-changers Turkey, Qatar, and Saudi Arabia upped the ante, independent of the US.

In January 2015, Saudi Arabia's King Abdullah died and his replacement, King Salman (79), moved quickly to advance a more aggressive foreign policy. After controversially appointing his favorite son as Deputy

---

22. Bodansky, "Syria's Multi-Layered Wars."

23. "Ndovu wawili wakisongana, ziumiazo ni nyika" (Swahili).

24. The Joint Comprehensive Plan of Action (JCPOA) is an agreement signed by China, France, Germany, Russia, UK, US, the High Representative of the European Union, and Iran that will supposedly ensure that Iran's nuclear program will be exclusively peaceful. See "Joint Comprehensive Plan of Action."

Crown Prince and Defense Minister,[25] he threw Saudi forces into a proxy war in Yemen and set about mending ties between Sunni Islam's pro- and anti-MB factions.[26]

On March 2, 2015, Turkey's President Recep Tayyip Erdogan flew into Riyadh at King Salman's invitation to discuss (amongst other things) "how to increase support to the Syrian opposition in a way that aims at yielding results."[27]

Idlib Falls to Al-Qaeda

Syria's northern Idlib province extends south from the Turkish border (also known as the *jihadi highway*) to form a wedge between the commercial capital of Aleppo (to the east) and the Alawite heartland of Latakia and northwest Hama (to the west). Thus Idlib is highly strategic territory.

In mid March 2015, al-Qaeda's Jabhat al-Nusra, along with Ahrar al-Sham and five smaller jihadist groups—including some US-armed and trained rebel groups aligned with the FSA—announced they had formed an alliance and joint operations room under the banner Jaysh al Fateh (Army of Conquest) for the purpose of seizing Idlib city.[28]

On Saturday March 28, Idlib city fell to some fifteen hundred Turkey-Arab funded, al-Qaeda-linked, al-Nusra-led Jaysh al Fateh fighters to become the second Syrian provincial capital under the rebel control. The operation's success was due in no small part to the fact that the rebels had acquired American TOW anti-tank guided missiles, which they deployed against the Syrian army to devastating effect.[29]

Described by Stratfor Global Intelligence as "one of the largest and most ambitious operations of the Syrian civil war," the conquest of Idlib was a huge and potentially pivotal win for al-Qaeda, whose fighters celebrated by burning the Syrian flag.[30]

Having fled for their lives, most of Idlib's Christians were headed for the port city of Latakia. Back in Idlib city, the mostly elderly, frail, and

---

25. Miles, "Saudi Arabia."

26. Turkey and Qatar are pro-MB; Saudi Arabia, United Arab Emirates, and Egypt's President Sisi are anti-MB.

27. Lund, "Are Saudi Arabia and Turkey About to Intervene in Syria?"

28. Joscelyn, "Al Qaeda and Allies Form Coalition." See also van Wilgenburg, "The Rise of Jaysh al-Fateh."

29. Joscelyn, "Jihadist Coalition Claims Control of Idlib"; Banco, "Syrian Rebel Group Jaysh al Fatah Captures Ariha."; Hassan, "Syria's Revitalized Rebels."

30. "Qaeda, Allies Advance on Syrian Regime Bastion."

infirm remnant were being told by the rebels that if they wanted to live, they would have to either convert to Islam or submit as *dhimmis* and pay the *jizya*. Anyone not happy with that, said the rebels, should get out fast. Father Ibrahim Farah (57), of the Antiochian Orthodox Church of Idlib city, refused to abandon the remnant and was subsequently kidnapped along with several of his parishioners.[31]

According to aid workers with International Orthodox Christian Charities (IOCC), at least three hundred of the five thousand displaced persons who made it to Latakia arrived with injuries, mostly shrapnel wounds. Traumatized survivors told of seeing cars, packed with extended families, spinning out of control and crashing after their driver was shot and killed by Jaysh al Fateh snipers.[32]

Rami told IOCC that he and his nine-year-old daughter made it out by crawling through the city's sewage channels to avoid snipers. Once out of the city, the pair walked all night to reach safety. "My daughter is in complete shock from what she witnessed," said Rami, "and I can't stop thinking about my parents who are still trapped in Idlib."[33]

As the SAA battled to keep al-Qaeda affiliate Jaysh al Fateh from advancing into the Alawite heartland, IS grasped the opportunity afforded it and advanced towards Damascus.

Palmyra Falls to Islamic State

A central oasis on an ancient trade route, historic UNESCO World Heritage-listed Palmyra sits midway between the Syria-Iraq border and the Damascus-Homs-Hama core. Its central location, in a region flush with natural and military resources,[34] makes Palmyra highly strategic territory.

Islamic State forces moved into Palmyra on May 12, 2015, and by May 15 were in full control of the city. What better site for mass executions of captured government soldiers and supporters could there be than Palmyra's spectacular Roman amphitheater? In video footage subsequently released, more than twenty-five Syrian army soldiers were marched in, lined up, and forced to their knees across the stage of Palmyra's amphitheater. Behind each soldier stood a child—some of the caliphate's "lion cubs"—dressed in

---

31. See Kendal, "Syria: Situation Critical"; also "Syria: Murder and Abduction of Christians, Idlib."

32. "IOCC Assists Syrian Families Escaping Bloodshed In Idlib."

33. Ibid.

34. Williams, "IS Makes Gains in Palmyra."

full military camouflage, armed with handguns. As the crowds in the stands bayed for blood, the "cubs" simultaneously pulled their triggers.[35]

In assessing the fall of Palmyra, analysts described the city as a "strategic gateway to the west of the country"[36] and "a key transportation node that gives the Islamic State access to several Syrian provinces."[37]

Midway between Palmyra and Damascus lies the oasis of Qaryatayn. While most of Qaryatayn's Christians fled when IS invaded Palmyra, the priests remained, caring for refugees in Qaryatayn's fifth-century Mar Elian monastery. On May 21, IS fighters made a brief incursion into Qaryatayn, ambushing the car of Jesuit priest Fr. Jacques Mourad who they kidnapped along with his companion, a deacon named Boutros.[38]

On August 6, IS suicide bombers breached Qaryatayn's defenses, opening the way for IS forces to flood into the town. These forces abducted at least 230 citizens—amongst them, some one hundred and fifty Christians from six families whose names had been on a "wanted list" for allegedly "collaborating with the regime." Other residents paid large sums of money for the right to flee.[39]

These were not the first Christians to be taken captive by IS. On Monday February 23, 2015, only days after IS released its grizzly "Message Signed in Blood to the Nation of the Cross,"[40] its fighters conducted a pre-dawn raid on a string of thirty-five Assyrian villages along a 40 km stretch of the Khabour River in Syria's northeastern province of Hasakah. As some three thousand Assyrian Christians fled into the darkness, 253 were taken captive.

Then, in April 2015, IS released another "Message" to the "Nation of the Cross," this time showing the execution of 28 captive Ethiopian migrants whom IS described as "worshippers of the cross, followers of the hostile Ethiopian Church." Sixteen of the Ethiopians were lined up in the desert in *Wilayet* Fezzan (southwestern Libya), forced to their knees, and then simultaneously shot through the back of the head. The other twelve were marched onto a beach in *Wilayet* Barqa (eastern Libya), lined up along the

---

35. Calderwood, "Slaughter in the Roman amphitheatre."
36. Williams, "Why Palmyra Matters for ISIS."
37. Abi Ali, "Capture of Palmyra."
38. "Jesuit Priest Abducted in Syria."
39. Halabi, "Syria's Ever-shifting Battle Lines."
40. The video showed the simultaneous beheading of one Ghanaian and twenty Coptic Christians on a Libyan beach. (Full account in chapter 10.)

shore, forced onto the sand, and then simultaneously beheaded. Needless to say, grave fears were held for the captive Assyrians.[41]

On August 6, 2015, as IS attacked Qaryatayn, it simultaneously attacked the Assyrian village of Hawwarin, 15 km further west, forcing some two thousand mostly Assyrian Christians to flee for their lives. Fifteen kilometers west of Hawwarin, residents in the mostly Assyrian town of Sadad were taking no chances. At least forty-five residents were killed in November 2013, when rebels invaded and held some 1,500 mostly Christian families hostage for a week—looting homes, desecrating churches, and fighting the SAA while using civilians as human shields. Not waiting around for IS, Sadad's last five thousand residents took to the road, headed either for Damascus (100 km to the south) or Homs (60 km to the north).

Now amassed on both sides of the M5 Damascus-Homs Highway, IS was poised to cut the nation in two,[42] severing Damascus (the political capital) from the rest of Syria: Homs and Hama (the industrial core), Aleppo (the commercial capital), and the coastal provinces of Tartus (home to a Russian naval base) and Latakia (the Alawite heartland).

The Tide Turns

On July 26, 2015, Syrian President Bashar al-Assad delivered a somber speech defending the government's withdrawal from Palmyra. After condemning the West for its double standards on terrorism and armed opposition, Assad explained that the government was withdrawing from some areas (i.e., the vast east) in order to hold others (i.e., the main population centers in the west). Acknowledging that the army was under severe strain, he offered amnesty to all draft-dodgers and appealed for able-bodied men to present themselves for service.[43]

The tide had turned. Increased Turkey-Arab support was indeed "yielding results." All that remained to be seen was which group would strike the fatal blow that would bring down the government. Would it be the Turkey-Arab backed, al-Qaeda affiliated, al-Nusra-led Jaysh al Fateh, which

---

41. In October 2015, IS released two videos featuring captured Assyrian Christians. The first showed three Assyrian captives from Hasakah being executed before three more took their place, warning that if a ransom (estimated at $10 million) was not paid, then they too would be executed, "and there are dozens of us." The second video showed Christian captives in Qaryatayn signing *dhimma* contracts. See Kendal, "Plight of Assyrian Captives."

42. Spencer, "Assad's Forces Defeated on Roads North and South."

43. "President al-Assad's July 26, 2015, Speech"; "Syria: President Assad admits army strained by war."

was pressing into the Alawite heartland, capturing towns and military bases in northwest Hama and launching rockets deep into Latakia—the Alawite heart? Or would it be IS, which was poised to sever the M5 Damascus-Homs Highway, effectively decapitating the government? Be it a pierced heart or a severed head—either scenario would be fatal.

With shorter supply lines, more advanced weapons, and international backing, Jaysh al Fateh doubtless posed the greatest threat. Regardless of which group delivered the fatal blow, one thing was clear: IS was poised and ready to fill any power vacuum created in Damascus.

Not prepared to stand idly by as Damascus fell to IS, or as its naval base in Tartus fell to al-Qaeda-linked Jaysh al Fateh, or to watch as the inevitable and promised genocide of Alawites and Christians ensued, Russia escalated its activity on the diplomatic front, pressing for an all-inclusive anti-IS coalition that would cooperate with the Syrian government in a war against terror. Unsurprisingly, the Turkey-Arab axis declined, insisting "Assad must go!" Echoing the Turkey-Arab mantra—"Assad must go!"—the US also declined, despite its growing anxiety over the prospect of IS seizing power in Damascus. A call to prayer was issued.[44]

Enter Russia

On September 10, 2015, Stratfor Global Intelligence published satellite images of a Russian military buildup at the Bassel al Assad International Airport in Latakia.[45]

Russia has legitimate interests in Syria that require defense, in particular a small naval base in Tartus, the last Russian base outside the former Soviet Union. What's more, during the Soviet era, many Syrian elite received their higher education in Russian universities. "The goal was to forge a global, pro-Soviet intellectual elite," writes reporter Ellen Barry; "the immediate result was weddings."[46] In 2012, some thirty thousand Russian citizens were residing in Syria as it descended into civil war.

Most critically, by September 2015, at least two thousand "Chechens" (shorthand for fighters from Russia's north Caucasus region) were fighting with IS and al-Qaeda in Syria.[47] Not only are Chechens recognized as fierce

44. Kendal, "SYRIA: Appealing for the Lord's Intervention."
45. "Confirming Russia's Expanded Presence in Syria."
46. Barry, "Russians and Syrians."
47. Talbi and Ketz, "In Syria, Russia Chasing Chechens Once Again." At a research event hosted by Chatham House on September 23, 2015, delegates were told that the number of Russian fighters in Syria was estimated to be around 2,500 (see "Exporting

jihadists, they are also highly skilled. Unsurprisingly, many Chechens hold high-ranking positions as senior administrators, military commanders, and brigade leaders. "Among the legions of foreign fighters who have turned the Islamic State into the world's most dangerous terrorist organization, the Chechens stand out," writes Mike Eckel. "The Chechens aren't the largest group among the thousands of foreigners in Syria, but they may be playing an outsized role, as many, battle-hardened by years fighting Russian forces, help spearhead the Islamic State's sweeping successes through Syria and Iraq."[48] There is widespread consensus in Russia—on the street and amongst the governors—that it is better to fight these terrorist abroad than risk them returning home.[49]

On September 15, 2015, Russian President Vladimir Putin told a summit of the Russian-led Collective Security Treaty Organization that while Assad is willing to make political changes and "engage a healthy part of the opposition," the immediate priority is focused on "pooling forces in the fight against terror."[50]

"Without an active participation of the Syrian authorities and the military," he said, "it would be impossible to expel the terrorists from that country and the region as a whole, and to protect the multi-ethnic and multi-confessional Syrian people from destruction."

He reiterated his call for the international community to set aside "geopolitical ambitions" and "double standards" and join an anti-IS coalition which must, of necessity, include the Syrian government. And as the Institute for the Study of War (ISW) pointed out, "Putin backed these words with the delivery of fighter jets, main battle tanks, armored personnel carriers, and attack helicopters to an airport on the Syrian Coast reportedly being prepared for use as a forward operations base."[51]

Alexander Aksenyonok, Russia's most senior diplomat specializing in Syrian affairs, confirmed that Russian advisers were in Syria to help prevent the country's breakup, protect minority groups, and preserve Russian presence at the Syrian ports. "The primary objective," he said, "is to prevent the collapse of state institutions in Syria. Otherwise a 'Somalisation of Syria' may take place if militant forces either from Daesh [ISIS/IS] or other organisations take power."[52]

Jihad", Meeting Summary).

48. Eckel, "Battle-Tested Chechens Drive Islamic State Gains."
49. "Like Russia, Chechnya Is Being Increasingly Drawn Into Syrian Conflict."
50. Wagner, "Putin Defends Russian Military Support for Syrian Regime."
51. Kozak, "Russian Deployment to Syria."
52. Shaikh and Rosenbaum, "Russia Increases Weapon Provisions to Syria."

"The Russian deployment to Syria is game-changing," asserted the ISW. "The U.S. and its partners must fundamentally reassess their approach to the Syrian conflict in light of this critical inflection."[53]

As for the US's "partners"—specifically would-be regime-changers Turkey and Saudi Arabia, they would indeed need to reassess their approach especially as both were now facing crises of their own. Political opposition was rising in Turkey, which was essentially at war with the Kurds, while rumors of an impending palace coup were circulating in Saudi Arabia, which was stuck in a quagmire in Yemen.

"This provides a window of opportunity," wrote Indian diplomat and analyst M. K. Bhadrakumar, "to push ahead the peace process in Syria while mounting on a parallel track a concerted assault on the IS by an international coalition that draws on the Syrian army's capabilities directly or indirectly."[54]

Duelling Presidents

On Monday September 28, 2015, US President Barak Obama and Russian President Vladimir Putin put on their best suits, straightened their ties, armed themselves with loaded speech notes, and headed to the UN General Assembly in New York for a thoroughly modern duel.

Speaking first, President Obama launched a preemptive strike against Russian positions. Rejecting any suggestion that the Syrian government could be part of the solution, Obama sang the Turkey-Arab song, insisting the Syrian government was entirely the problem. "Let's remember how this started," he said. "Assad reacted to peaceful protests by escalating repression and killing that, in turn, created the environment for the current strife. And so Assad and his allies cannot simply pacify the broad majority of a population who have been brutalized by chemical weapons and indiscriminate bombing."[55]

Quiet apart from the fact that the official Western-Turkey-Arab narrative is nothing but propaganda designed to hide geopolitical ambitions behind a veneer of humanitarianism, President Obama must be condemned for his selective indignation. After all, his partners include Saudi Arabia and Turkey, both of which detain and brutalize dissidents and routinely use military force to crush protests. NATO-member Turkey—which has facilitated the rise of al-Nusra and IS—has a penchant for jailing its critics, be

---

53. "Russian Deployment to Syria."
54. Bhadrakumar, "Hopeful Signs of a Course Correction on Syria."
55. "Remarks by President Obama to the United Nations General Assembly."

they politicians, generals, judges, teachers, journalists, artists, or comedians, on the pretext of protecting Turkey from deep state conspiracies.[56] With zero religious freedom, US-allied Saudi Arabia is amongst the world's worst human rights abusers, beheading dozen of poor, mostly scapegoats every year. President Putin's response was a superb and rational rebuttal. I totally agree with analyst David Goldman who commented that it was "the most lucid account of the state of the world I have heard from any national leader in decades."[57]

Concerning the crisis in the Middle East, President Putin said:

> We are all different, and we should respect that. No one has to conform to a single development model that someone has once and for all recognized as the only right one. We should all remember what our past has taught us.
>
> We also remember certain episodes from the history of the Soviet Union. Social experiments for export, attempts to push for changes within other countries based on ideological preferences, often led to tragic consequences and to degradation rather than progress.
>
> It seemed, however, that far from learning from others' mistakes, everyone just keeps repeating them, and so the export of revolutions, this time of so-called democratic ones, continues. It would suffice to look at the situation in the Middle East and North Africa, as has been mentioned by previous speakers. Certainly political and social problems in this region have been piling up for a long time, and people there wish for changes naturally.
>
> But how did it actually turn out? Rather than bringing about reforms, an aggressive foreign interference has resulted in a brazen destruction of national institutions and the lifestyle itself. Instead of the triumph of democracy and progress, we got violence, poverty and social disaster. Nobody cares a bit about human rights, including the right to life.
>
> I cannot help asking those who have caused the situation, do you realize now what you've done? But I am afraid no one is going to answer that. Indeed, policies based on self-conceit and belief in one's exceptionality and impunity have never been abandoned.
>
> It is now obvious that the power vacuum created in some countries of the Middle East and North Africa, through the

---

56. Kendal, "Erodgan, Ergenekon, Europe and the Islamisation of Turkey."
57. Goldman, "Take Putin at His Word."

emergence of anarchy areas, immediately started to be filled with extremists and terrorists.

Tens of thousands of militants are fighting under the banners of the so-called Islamic State. Its ranks include former Iraqi servicemen who were thrown out into the street after the invasion of Iraq in 2003. Many recruits also come from Libya, a country whose statehood was destroyed as a result of a gross violation of the UN Security Council Resolution 1973.

And now, the ranks of radicals are being joined by the members of the so-called moderate Syrian opposition supported by the Western countries. First, they are armed and trained and then they defect to the so-called Islamic State. Besides, the Islamic State itself did not just come from nowhere. It was also initially forged as a tool against undesirable secular regimes.

Having established a foothold in Iraq and Syria, the Islamic State has begun actively expanding to other regions. It is seeking dominance in the Islamic world. And not only there, and its plans go further than that. The situation is more than dangerous.

In these circumstances, it is hypocritical and irresponsible to make loud declarations about the threat of international terrorism while turning a blind eye to the channels of financing and supporting terrorists, including the process of trafficking and illicit trade in oil and arms. It would be equally irresponsible to try to manipulate extremist groups and place them at one's service in order to achieve one's own political goals in the hope of later dealing with them or, in other words, liquidating them.

To those who do so, I would like to say—dear sirs, no doubt you are dealing with rough and cruel people, but they're in no way primitive or silly. They are just as clever as you are, and you never know who is manipulating whom. And the recent data on arms transferred to this most moderate opposition is the best proof of it.

We believe that any attempts to play games with terrorists, let alone to arm them, are not just short-sighted, but fire hazardous (ph).[58] This may result in the global terrorist threat increasing dramatically and engulfing new regions, especially given that Islamic State camps train militants from many countries, including the European countries.

Unfortunately, dear colleagues, I have to put it frankly: Russia is not an exception. We cannot allow these criminals who already tasted blood to return back home and continue their evil doings. No one wants this to happen, does he?

---

58. 'ph': an abbreviation for 'phonetic'—i.e. 'sounded like'.

> Russia has always been consistently fighting against terrorism in all its forms. Today, we provide military and technical assistance both to Iraq and Syria and many other countries of the region who are fighting terrorist groups.
>
> We think it is an enormous mistake to refuse to cooperate with the Syrian government and its armed forces, who are valiantly fighting terrorism face to face. We should finally acknowledge that no one but President Assad's armed forces and Kurds (ph) militias are truly fighting the Islamic State and other terrorist organizations in Syria.
>
> Dear colleagues, I must note that such an honest and frank approach of Russia has been recently used as a pretext to accuse it of its growing ambitions, as if those who say it have no ambitions at all.
>
> However, it's not about Russia's ambitions, dear colleagues, but about the recognition of the fact that we can no longer tolerate the current state of affairs in the world. What we actually propose is to be guided by common values and common interests, rather than ambitions.
>
> On the basis of international law, we must join efforts to address the problems that all of us are facing and create a genuinely broad international coalition against terrorism.[59]

To that end, President Putin proposed that the UN Security Council carry out "a comprehensive analysis of threats in the Middle East," and seek a resolution aimed at "coordinating the action of all the forces that confront the Islamic State and other terrorist organizations . . . based on the principles of the UN Charter."

"We hope," said Putin, "that the international community will be able to develop a comprehensive strategy of political stabilization, as well as social and economic recovery, of the Middle East."

Within days, Russia was bombing IS and Jaysh al Fateh positions, as well as providing air cover for a re-energized SAA. Meanwhile, the US was expressing grave concerns that Russian bombs were hitting US-armed and trained "moderate rebels" (hard to avoid when they are fighting with or alongside Jaysh al Fateh) and embattled Turkish President Recep Tayyip Erdogan (routinely mocked in Turkey as a neo-Ottoman "Sultan") was appealing to NATO for help, apoplectic that Russian jets had violated Turkish airspace. "An attack on Turkey is also an attack on NATO," he squealed.

---

59. "Read Putin's U.N. General Assembly Speech."

NATO Secretary-General Jens Stoltenberg assured Turkey that "NATO is there to help and assist them if they need."[60]

History's Crossroads

In 1828, after the Turkish sultan—who had declared jihad—refused to withdraw his troops from the Danubian Principalities, some sixty-five thousand Russian soldiers crossed the Danube into Ottoman territory in defense of persecuted Christians.

The Turks were weak, the Ottoman Empire was fraying at the seams, and during the northern spring of 1829, Russian troops advanced to within a short march of the ancient Byzantine capital of Constantinople (Istanbul). "At this point," writes historian Orlando Figes, "the Russians could have easily seized the Turkish capital and overthrown the Sultan. Their fleet controlled the Black Sea and the Aegean . . . the Turkish forces were in complete disarray."[61]

Tsar Nicolas contacted the Austrian ambassador in St. Petersburg to inform him that the Ottoman Empire was "about to fall" and suggest it would be in Austria's interests to aid Russia in this venture. Austria—Russia's closest ally—declined, reminding Nicholas that the leaders of Europe (which included Russia) had agreed not to support "revolutionary movements." Russia was alone in seeing the Ottoman Empire's Christian *millets* (nations) as repressed and sorely persecuted fellow Christians deserving of liberty, rather than problematic revolutionaries.

Despite being on the doorstep of Constantinople with the collapse of the Ottoman Empire imminent, Tsar Nicholas—unwilling to risk war with Europe—withdrew his troops. He settled instead for the Treaty of Adrianople, which, amongst other things, secured autonomy for Greek Christians under Russian protection.[62] The Christians of Anatolia, Mesopotamia, and the

---

60. "NATO Says Will Help Turkey Against Russia If Needed."
61. Figes, *The Crimean War*, 39.
62. Ibid., 38–41. The Treaty of Adrianople was imposed by the Russians on the Turks in September 1829. It secured autonomy for Greek Christians under Russian protection and opened the Straits to commercial shipping. Western Europe responded by heightening Russophobia and accusing Russia of exploiting the persecution of Eastern Christians as a pretext for imperialist expansion. To undermine the Russians, Britain backed a Greek independence movement. In 1831, the pro-Russia Greek leader, former Russian Foreign Minister Ioannis Kapodistrias, was assassinated, resulting in the decline of his pro-Russia party. The political momentum shifted to the British-backed separatists. In 1832, in the Convention of London, the modern Greek state was created with Britain's choice of sovereign.

Levant would have to endure another century of persecution, *dhimmitude* and bloody Islamic resistance at the cost of well over three million Christian lives—Greeks, Armenians, and Assyrians—before the collapse of the Ottoman Empire in World War I and the dissolution of the caliphate in 1924.

In 1917, Russia was, to use the language of Russian dissident Alexander Solzhenitsyn, taken into "Communist captivity."[63] Over the next seventy years, at least twelve million mostly Russian Orthodox Christians perished on account of their faith;[64] some sources estimate that the number could be as high as twenty million. Invisible to the world, they were abandoned and betrayed by the World Council of Churches which stood silent,[65] playing politics,[66] as priests, nuns, pastors, and deacons were incarcerated, tortured, and executed; as churches and monasteries were seized, bombed, and bulldozed; and as masses upon masses of believers were deprived of their children, driven into labor camps, or shot dead by fundamentalist atheists and Marxists determined to eliminate faith from the land.[67]

During those days, God raised up Christian advocacy groups—for example, Voice of the Martyrs, Open Doors, Friends of the Martyr Church, Aid to the Church in Need—to raise awareness of the plight of the persecuted. Soviet Communism died, but the Russian church lived. Now, as the West abandons Christianity, Russia is experiencing something of a religious awakening.

Today, nearly two hundred years since Russian troops were poised to liberate Constantinople and some one hundred and sixty years since French (Catholic) and British (Protestant) troops sided with the Muslim Turks against Orthodox Russia (protector of Eastern Christians) in the Crimean War, traumatizing East-West relations, Russia is back—defending its interests as a rational world power and vowing to make the protection of persecuted Christians a key focus of its foreign policy.[68]

In 1829 and 1853, Tsarist Russia was dealing with an ascendant, industrialized Western Europe, which it had respected as an ally. Today, post-Soviet Russia is dealing with a declining, morally confused West that is riddled with Russophobia and Cold War hostility.

---

63. Solzhenitsyn, "A World Split Apart."

64. See "Martyred in the USSR" (film newsletter) and Glazov, "Martyred in the USSR."

65. See Appendix 1: Christian Solidarity: The Sound of Silence.

66. Emerson Vermaat, *The World Council of Churches and Politics.*

67. "Communism abolishes eternal truths, it abolishes all religion, and all morality, instead of constituting them on a new basis . . ." (Marx and Engels, *Manifesto of the Communist Party*).

68. Ibrahim, "Russia Declares 'Holy War' on Islamic State."

Today, some twenty-five years since Russians emerged battered, broken, and traumatized from seventy years of "communist captivity" and fifteen years since Russia was unable to defend its interests or aid its allies in the Balkans, Russia is back and it is not backing off.

How much blood will be spilled may well depend on how long it takes the American-led West to get over its Russophobia and identify the real enemy.

A House Divided

Islam divides the world into two houses: the Dar al Islam (House of Islam) and the Dar al harb (House of war). For too long now, the Dar al harb has allowed itself to be divided: West versus East with Islam in the middle, exploiting tensions and playing one side off against the other.

Today, however, the Islam that divides East and West is not the old Turkish "sick man" of the nineteenth century. Today's Islam—reformed and revived Islam— is ascendant, international, and a global existential threat. Islam is back with US- and Soviet-trained commanders, strategists, intelligence agents, administrators, engineers, scientists, and information technology specialists. Islam is back with US- and Soviet-made weaponry and friends with nuclear weapons. Islam is back with every intention of destroying civilization and plunging us into a new dark age.

The defining battle of the twenty-first century—an expanding and existential, civilizational battle—is only just beginning. It will be a long war, destined to get a lot worse yet. It is war which must be fought both militarily and philosophically, for one without the other will not suffice; and for this, free speech is absolutely essential.

The cradle of civilization, Mesopotamia, is merely ground zero—the epicenter. This is why it is absolutely imperative that Christians, and indeed all in the Dar al harb, understand and respond rightly to the Christian crisis in the Middle East—for this battle will come to a theatre near you.

> "Every kingdom divided against itself is laid waste, and no city or house divided against itself will stand" (Jesus, Matthew 12:25). If ever there was a time for solidarity in the Dar al harb, it is now. We cannot undo the past but we can learn from it.

The days ahead are going to be very dark and very difficult indeed.
But that does not mean Christians should be without hope.

— 12 —

"After Saturday Comes Sunday" for the Nation of the Cross

Friday

TRY TO IMAGINE HOW terrifying and appallingly awful that first "Good Friday" must have been for those who had believed and invested so much in Jesus.[1]

For the followers of Jesus, that Friday—the day of the cross—was the day everything spun out of control. It was a horrific day in which all their hopes, dreams, and aspirations were violently, profoundly, and humiliatingly dashed, smashed, and obliterated. What were they to make of it? How could that weak, submissive, defenseless victim of injustice be the Messiah? That beaten, lacerated, bleeding, and broken victim of savagery who just meekly submitted "like a lamb that is led to the slaughter,"[2] how could he be Israel's Savior?

So was Jesus a fraud or a madman? It certainly appeared that his followers been deceived, conned, led astray like fools who would now be laughed at and pitied as victims of a ridiculous scam. Or worse, had the Messiah indeed come and failed? Had the Christ been defeated? Had God's eternal plan of redemption come unstuck? Had the world and devil triumphed over God's anointed?

---

1. I must say here I am indebted to the late Alan E. Lewis's seminal work, *Between Cross and Resurrection: A Theology of Holy Saturday.*

2. See Isa 52:13–53:12 (the suffering servant, described as "like a lamb that is led to slaughter", written around 700 BC). See also Ps 22 (the Psalm of the Cross, written around 1000 BC).

After Friday Comes Saturday

To make things worse—after Friday came Saturday. Yes, life would go on. Humiliation, confusion, sadness, darkness, and profound emptiness, even anger seemed destined to continue without relief. As far as Jesus' followers could see, everything had changed and that Saturday was to be first day of the rest of their lives without Jesus.

That the disciples were so unprepared for the horror of Friday and the silence of Saturday is a testimony to the human capacity for denial. Jesus had forewarned the disciples three times—in Matthew 16:21-23, Matthew 17:22-23, and Matthew 20:17-19. The latter reads: "And as Jesus was going up to Jerusalem, he took the twelve disciples aside, and on the way he said to them, 'See, we are going up to Jerusalem. And the Son of Man will be delivered over to the chief priests and scribes, and they will condemn him to death and deliver him over to the Gentiles to be mocked and flogged and crucified, and he will be raised on the third day.'"

For the disciples, who were thinking in purely human, worldly, and materialistic terms, such a horrendous scenario was utterly incomprehensible. The idea that God's anointed should suffer and die was not only nonsensical, it was so reprehensible that the disciples refused to entertain it[3] and opted instead for denial. Such is the chasm between "the things of God" and "the things of man."[4]

Just as the deadly cross of Friday extinguished life, the deathly silence of Saturday devoured hope. What were his faithful disciples to make of it? What were his followers to do?

On Friday, before breathing his last, Jesus had declared: "It is finished."[5]

On Saturday, as confusion and despair reigned, Jesus' followers must surely have responded: "It is finished indeed!"

But it wasn't—was it?

---

3. Islam, too, rejects the idea that God would allow his prophet to suffer and be killed in such a humiliating way. According to Islam, Jesus was not crucified. Rather, it was someone who looked just like him. "And [for] their saying, 'Indeed, we have killed the Messiah, Jesus, the son of Mary, the messenger of Allah.' And they did not kill him, nor did they crucify him; but [another] was made to resemble him to them. And indeed, those who differ over it are in doubt about it. They have no knowledge of it except the following of assumption. And they did not kill him, for certain" (Q.4:157, http://quran.com/4/157).

4. In Matthew 16:21-23, after Jesus forewarned the disciples of his death, Peter rebuked him, saying, "Far be it from you, Lord. This shall never happen to you." To which the Lord replied, "Get behind me Satan! You are a hindrance to me. For you are not setting your mind on the things of God, but on the things of man."

5 "When Jesus had received the sour wine, he said, 'It is finished,' and he bowed his head and gave up his spirit" (John 19:30).

After Saturday Comes Sunday

While Jesus' work was indeed finished,[6] the story of the cross was not yet over. For after Saturday came Sunday, and what happened on Sunday changed everything—so much so that history revolves around it. The body of Jesus, who had claimed to be the Messiah, the Son of God, was not in the tomb. Jesus had risen from the dead![7]

§

In February 2015, Catholic writer, Fr. Robert Barron, used the occasion of the twenty-one martyrs of Libya and IS' "Message Signed with Blood to the Nation of the Cross" to reflect on the "startling distinctiveness of the cross."[8]

"In the time of Jesus the cross was a brutal and very effective sign of Roman power," writes Barron. "Imperial authorities effectively said, 'If you cross us (pun intended), we will affix you to a dreadful instrument of torture and leave you to writhe in agonizing, literally excruciating (*ex cruce*, from the cross) pain until you die . . .'"

Barron explains how the cross was essentially used as state-sponsored terrorism, and totalitarian despots would line the road with crucified rebels to dissuade would-be revolutionaries.

"From the crucified Jesus, all of the disciples, save John, fled, precisely because they wanted with all their hearts to avoid his dreadful fate," writes Barron. "After Good Friday, the friends of Jesus huddled in terror in the Upper Room, petrified that they might be nailed up on Calvary as well. The disciples on the road to Emmaus were, understandably, heading out of

---

6. The Savior's "work" involved living a sinless life before being slain as a spotless "lamb" whose blood would save all who placed themselves under it—as was the case in the first Passover (Exod 12). So was Jesus sinless? Could he be God's sacrificial lamb? The answer is in the resurrection. For the law of God states, "the penalty for sin is death" (Rom 6:23). But because Jesus had never sinned, there was no penalty to pay. Because death had no claim on him, God raised him from the dead. The resurrection is proof that Jesus was sinless and his blood could be offered on behalf of others, to atone for their sins. The good news is that forgiveness of sins—which rescues us from the consequences of sin (that being eternal death)—is possible (and *only* possible) through the blood of Jesus Christ, who forgives the sins of all who believe and put their trust in him. Forgiveness of sins results in reconciliation with God—that is, the created being is reconciled to their Creator. And when the time arrives for death and judgement, the forgiven believer can rest assured that the price has already been paid—by Jesus on the cross.

7. The account can be found in the final chapters of the Gospels: Matt 26–28, Mark 14–16, Luke 22–24, and John 18–21.

8. Barron, "A Message in Blood."

Jerusalem, away from danger, and they were utterly convinced that Jesus' movement had come to naught. In a word, the cross meant the victory of the world and the annihilation of Jesus and what he stood for.

"And this is why it is surpassing strange that one of the earliest Apostles and missionaries of the Christian religion could write, 'I preach one thing, Christ and him crucified!'"[9]

The cross became the central theme of Christianity precisely because, as Barron explains, God raised Jesus from the dead, "proving thereby that God's love and forgiveness are greater than anything in the world. This is why [Paul's] exaltation of the cross is a sort of taunt to Rome and all of its brutal descendants down through the ages: 'You think that scares us? God has conquered that!' And this is why, to this day, Christians boldly hold up an image of the humiliated, tortured Jesus to the world. What they are saying is, 'We are not afraid.'"

Barron notes that with their last words—"My Lord, Jesus Christ"—the twenty-one martyrs of Libya asserted "the kingship of Jesus, but what a strange kingship! . . . the one who trumps Caesar doesn't lead an army, but embodies the divine forgiveness."

The Cross as Revelation

As the great theologian Martin Luther realized, the cross is far more than an historic event (i.e., Friday through Sunday, crucifixion through grave to resurrection). The cross is even more than what it achieved (i.e., forgiveness, atonement, salvation). The cross is revelation—that is, the cross reveals something to us of what God is like and how God works.[10]

The cross reveals that the God of the Bible does not sit on a comfortable heavenly throne, far, far away, high in the clouds, firing lightening blots or long-range missiles at his enemies. While he is indeed *the* supreme superpower, that is not his way.

---

9. The Apostle Paul, in his first letter to the church in Corinth, wrote: "And I, when I came to you, brothers, did not come proclaiming to you the testimony of God with lofty speech or wisdom. For I decided to know nothing among you except Jesus Christ and him crucified. And I was with you in weakness and in fear and much trembling, and my speech and my message were not in plausible words of wisdom, but in demonstration of the Spirit and of power, so that your faith might not rest in the wisdom of men but in the power of God" (1 Cor 2:1–5).

10. This "theology of the cross" was the subject of Martin Luther's Heidelberg Disputation of 1518. For a study, see Forde, *On Being a Theologian of the Cross*.

Rather, the God of the Bible comes and enters hostile territory himself so that he might subvert evil, defeat it from within, and redeem it by working it for good in fulfillment of promise.

Defeat sin through sin? Conquer death by dying? Who'd have thought it?

Well, God did. God thought it.

> For my thoughts are not your thoughts, neither are my ways your ways, declares the Lord. For as the heavens are higher than the earth, so are my ways higher than your ways and my thoughts than your thoughts (Isa 55:8–9).

Echoing Martin Luther, Professor Carl R. Trueman of Westminster Theological Seminary explains how, through the cross, "evil is now utterly subverted to the cause of good." For, "If the cross of Christ, the most evil act in human history, can be in line with God's will and be the source of the decisive defeat of the very evil that caused it, then any other evil can also be subverted to the cause of good."

"Indeed," continues Trueman,

> when it is grasped that the death of Christ, the greatest crime in history, was itself willed in a deep and mysterious way by the triune God, yet without involving God in any kind of moral guilt, we see the solution to the age-old problem of absolving an all-powerful God of responsibility for evil. The answer to the problem of evil does not lie in trying to establish its point of origin, for that is simply not revealed to us. Rather, in the moment of the cross, it becomes clear that evil is utterly subverted for good. Romans 8:28[11] is true because of the cross of Christ: if God can take the greatest of evils and turn it to the greatest of goods, then how much more can be take the lesser evils which litter human history, from individual tragedies to international disasters, and turn them to his good purpose as well.[12]

For Christians, the cross is a beacon of hope reminding us that appearances can be deceptive. The cross reminds Christians that even when darkness and confusion reign, and it seems like God is dead and world has won, and the situation appears out of control and utterly hopeless—it is not!

---

11. 'And we know that in all things God works for the good of those who love him, who have been called according to his purpose' (Rom 8:28).

12. Trueman, "Luther's Theology of the Cross."

For deep in the darkness, God is there, doing his work: subverting evil and redeeming it for good in fulfilment of promise.

God Is At Work in the Dar al Islam

As author David Garrison explains in his groundbreaking book,[13] God is at work in the House of Islam.

After citing John 3:8—"The wind blows where it pleases. You hear its sound but you cannot tell where it comes from or where it is going. So it is with everyone who is born of the Spirit", Garrison draws back the curtain on what is arguably one of the most exciting phenomena of our times. Defining a "movement of Muslims to Christ" as at least one thousand baptized new believers and/or one hundred new church plants within a two-decade period, Garrison explains that there were no known voluntary movements of Muslims to Christianity during the first twelve centuries of Islam. Then, in the late 19th century, there were two: one in Indonesia led by Javanese evangelist Radin Abas Sadrach Surapranata, resulting in 10,000–20,000 *Kristen Jawa* (Christian Javanese), and one in Ethiopia led by Shaikh Zakaryas, resulting in at least 7,000 *Adadis Krestian* (New Christians).[14]

The twentieth century saw eleven movements of Muslims to Christ, occurring in Algeria, Bulgaria, Albania, West Africa, Iran (2), Bangladesh (2), and Central Asia (3).[15]

"By the close of the 20th Century," writes Garrison,

> 1,368 years after the death of Muhammad, there had been a total of 13 movements of Muslim communities to faith in Jesus Christ.
>
> It is this long history of frustration, a history that has seen tens of millions of Christians absorbed into the Muslim world that makes the current events all the more striking. In only the first 12 years of the 21st century, an additional 69 movements to Christ of at least 1,000 baptized Muslim-background believers or 100 new worshipping fellowships have appeared. These 21st-century movements are not isolated to one or two corners of the world. They are taking place throughout the House of Islam: in sub-Saharan Africa, in the Persian world, in the Arab world, in Turkestan, in South Asia and in Southeast Asia. Something is happening – something historic, something unprecedented.
>
> A wind is blowing through the House of Islam.[16]

---

13. Garrison, *A Wind in the House of Islam*.
14. Ibid., Chapter 1.
15. Ibid.
16. Ibid., 18.

God Is At Work Amongst Persians

The Persian church is today one the fastest growing churches in the world. This growth is occurring not only in the diaspora—amongst whom the movement of God's Spirit is palpable—but even inside Iran, where Christian witness is illegal and the exercise of faith can be extremely costly.

Repressive Islam does not sit comfortably with traditional Persian culture; there is enormous tension between them, and virtually all the unrest that occurs in Iran is an expression of that profound struggle. A revival of Islam brought the Ayatollah to power. But as Persian culture revives, Iranians are abandoning Islam, often scornful of its negative and destructive impact.[17]

Islam has not brought Iranians any of the things it promised. Birth rates have plummeted to below replacement rate—from seven children per female in 1979 to 1.6 in 2012. As David Goldman notes, it "remains a conundrum to demographers. Never before in recorded history has the birth rate of a big country fallen so fast and so far."[18] (The implications of this are enormous.[19]) Meanwhile, domestic violence, prostitution, and drug abuse are endemic,[20] as Iranians succumb to despair. Youths in particular are rebelling, including by posting photos and video footage to social media showing themselves removing their headscarves[21] or dancing[22]—an act so offensive that in November 2014, it earned six young Iranians ninety-one lashes and jail time (with sentences suspended for three years).[23]

Goldman notes elsewhere, "Iran, the first Muslim country to approach universal adult literacy, is by far the least religious, despite its theocratic regime. When the regime falls, as it eventually must, we will discover that there are no more Muslims in Iran than there were Communists in the Soviet

---

17. The same phenomenon is occurring in other places where Arab imperialism has resulted in the forced Islamization and Arabization of indigenous culture. For example, church growth in North Africa can be partly attributed to the revival of Berber culture, which has triggered a desire for indigenous languages and opened the door for a movement away from Islam. In response to the prayers of many, God entered their darkness and paved the way for a work of grace amongst the Berber people.

18. Goldman, "STDs and Strategy in Iran."

19. For starters, it means that if Iran is to achieve its ambitions, it must do it now, while it still has plenty of men of fighting age.

20. Goldman, "Sex, Drugs and Islam."

21. "The Women in Iran Taking Off the Hijab."

22. Siciliano, "Iranian Woman Dances on Tehran's Metro in Protest Against Laws."

23. "Iran: Happy Video Dancers Sentenced to 91 Lashes and Jail."

Union. Iran's mosque attendance rate is the lowest in the Muslim world at less than 30% by one estimate and much lower by other estimates."[24]

While many urban, educated Iranians are simply apostasizing to atheism, the ancient Persian cult of Zoroastrianism—a pre-Islamic, monotheistic, highly ethical, works-based religion[25]—is making a comeback, especially amongst nationalist youths. Others, meanwhile, are finding life-transforming truth, joy, peace, and blessed grace in the gospel of Jesus Christ.

Mass baptisms of five, ten, twenty or more diaspora Persians now occur routinely in the West, where demands for Farsi-language theological training and worship music are also on the rise. But in April 2013, a mass baptism service took place at a swimming pool in a secret location in the heart of the Middle East. Elam Ministries believes this mass baptism of 246 new believers—228 Iranians, 17 Afghans, and one Pakistani—was possibly the largest mass baptism of Persians since the fourth century. What's more, it was *historic*, in that never before have so many Muslim Background Believers been baptized together.[26]

God Is At Work Amongst Arabs

In 2001, the founder of an Arab-language ministry confessed to me that when he started the ministry in the early 1990s, he never actually expected to see converts: these were, after all, Arabs! He only went ahead because he knew he had to obey the clear and unambiguous call of God.

By 2001, ten years of ministry had turned his world upside down: Arabs were embracing Jesus Christ in numbers he would never have imagined. "Now," he said excitedly, "I'm just waiting for the dam to burst!" What's more, every stereotype he'd ever entertained had been demolished. Saudi men, he said, were coming to faith in Jesus through the preaching of Coptic women! (Incomprehensible!) These converts then took a holiday or business trip where they were secretly baptized before returning to Saudi Arabia as secret Christians. (Remarkable!) They know that if their faith is discovered, they will be killed—often by their own family in what is known as an "honor killing." When 26-year-old Fatima al-Mutayri's conversion became known to her family, they cut out her tongue and then beat and

24. Goldman, "Why Can't Muslims Laugh at Mohammed?"

25. Zoroastrianism dates back to the sixth century BC, to the time of kings Cyrus and Darius and the first Persian Empire. For a good yet simple overview of this belief system—which is monotheistic and highly ethical—see http://www.bbc.co.uk/religion/religions/zoroastrian/. See also Choksy, "How Iran persecutes its oldest religion."

26. "Joy at Iranian Baptisms."

burned her to death.²⁷ Fatima had been blogging under a false name, writing about the difference knowing Jesus Christ was making to her life. When she was murdered, the Saudi blogosphere lit up with shock and revulsion. Saudi youths can be more open-minded than you might think, which is why Saudi authorities keep them under close surveillance when they travel or study overseas.

So determined are the Saudi authorities to avoid the *fitna* (strife) they believe could arise if Saudis ever got the idea they could be Christian, they will pursue converts to the ends of the earth,²⁸ even issuing Interpol Red Notices for them.²⁹ They then make their lives exceedingly miserable, with the aim of discouraging Saudi nationals from following in their footsteps. Yes, even in the kingdom of Saudi Arabia—the Land of the Two Holy Mosques—the authorities are increasingly being forced to confront the reality of Saudi Christianity.

God At Work Across the Whole Middle East

Remember the admission of Yusuf al-Qaradawi, "If they [Muslims] had gotten rid of the punishment [usually death] for apostasy, Islam would not exist today"?³⁰ Remember the words of my Coptic missionary friend, "If there was ever true religious freedom in the Muslim world, it would not be long before there was barely a Muslim left"?³¹ Well, one cannot help feel that an earthquake has struck Mesopotamia and the whole Middle East is undergoing a massive shake-up, resulting in the weakening of Islam's repressive structures.³²

---

27. Saudi Christian Fatima al-Mutayri became a martyr for Jesus Christ in July 2008 (http://www.jesus-for-all.net/christian_books/pdf_234.pdf). See also Hakeem, "Saudi Man Kills Daughter for Converting to Christianity"; Kendal, "Saudi Christian Blogger Arrested" (includes Fatima's case).

28. For cases, see Religious Liberty Prayer Bulletin, label Saudi Arabia.

29. Kendal, "Apostasy, Fitna and Abuse of Interpol."

30. Quoted in the opening of chapter 3.

31. Ibid.

32. Consider: "For thus says the Lord of hosts: Yet once more, in a little while, I will shake the heavens and the earth and the sea and the dry land. And I will shake all nations, so that the treasures of all nations shall come in, and I will fill this house with glory, says the Lord of hosts . . . I am about to shake the heavens and the earth, and to overthrow the throne of kingdoms. I am about to destroy the strength of the kingdoms of the nations, and overthrow the chariots and their riders" (Hag 2:6–7, 21–22). "This phrase, 'Yet once more,' indicates the removal of things that are shaken—that is, things that have been made—in order that the things that cannot be shaken may remain" (Heb 12:27; cf Isa 2:6–21).

In November 2013, United Bible Societies reported that while global Scripture distribution rose by six percent through 2012, it escalated markedly in "persecution hotspots."[33]

The highest increase was in war-torn Syria, where despite the intense fighting, Scripture distribution rose from 14,000 in 2010, to 19,000 in 2011 (the year of the "Arab Spring" uprisings), to 163,000 in 2012 as the state descended into civil war.

The year 2012 also saw a substantial increase in Scripture distribution in neighboring war-ravaged Iraq, with more than 66,000 items distributed—an increase of 132 percent over the previous year.

Similarly in Egypt, Scripture distribution rose by 25 percent during 2012, with more than 2.8 million Scriptures distributed amidst massive unrest and upheavals.

The Middle East is breaking down, causing security to dissolve in a sea of bloody chaos and bringing Christians face-to-face with genocide (again). But, despite all appearances and contrary to all reason, the situation is far from hopeless. For deep in the darkness of this man-made chaos, amidst the evil, hardship, confusion and suffering, is the Spirit of the Lord Jesus Christ. For the God of the cross is a God who comes, a God who enters hostile territory himself so he might subvert evil, redeem it for good in fulfillment of promise, and build his church.[34] Yes, the Lord is there, feeding his flock, carrying his lambs close to his heart, gently leading those with young, and strengthening all who wait on him (Isa 40:11, 31). "Come," he says to the lost and broken, "salvation is free" (Isa 55:1–7). "Here I am," he says to a nation not called by his name—"Here I am!" (Isa 65:1).

With outstretched arm he invites us to join him. "Take up your cross," he says, "step out in faith, and follow me to 'Gethsemane, and Golgotha and the tomb,'[35] to the sad, dark, chaotic and dangerous places where my best redemptive work is done."

As noted at the conclusion of chapter one:

> It is possible that Christians and Christianity could be eliminated from the Middle East.

---

33. "Scripture Distribution Increases in Persecution Hotspots."

34. "I will build my church, and the gates of hell shall not prevail against it" (Jesus, in Matthew 16:18).

35. Commenting on Jesus' response to the hasty scribe in Matt 8:18–22, Arab Christian commentator Ibn Sa'id remarked that this would-be disciple "does not understand that 'follow' means Gethsemane, and Golgotha and the tomb" (cited in Keener, *The Gospel of Matthew*, 274).

And the only thing necessary for this to be achieved is that
we do nothing.

Which begs the question: will the church do something? The Lord is already there, and "by grace through faith" is not only God's paradigm for personal salvation (Eph 2:8–9), it is God's paradigm for everything. So will the church step out in faith, with aid, advocacy, and intercessory prayer for the Christians of the Middle East?

The Blood of the Martyrs

Some Christians refuse to engage with the persecuted church on the misunderstanding that persecution is good for church growth.[36] "The blood of the martyrs is the seed of the church," they say, quoting Tertullian as they back away, not wanting to interfere. If truth be told, Tertullian's words have not only caused a good deal of confusion, they have also been exploited to justify inaction.

While there certainly was persecution in Carthage (Tunis) at Tertullian's time (around AD 200), it was nothing compared to what would come from the seventh century with the armies of Muhammad and the arrival of Islam. Had Tertullian been right, then with all that martyrs' blood poured out in Carthage, churches should have sprung up like mushrooms. But that is not what happened. In fact, the church in Carthage was essentially annihilated, and the blood of the martyrs simply sank into the sands.

In truth, Tertullian might not have thought through his statement. For as Jesus makes clear in his parable of the sower, the seed of the church is the gospel—the word of God—and we are called to scatter that seed.[37]

As a passionate gardener with half an acre of terraced cottage gardens, I can assure you that no amount of labor, "Blood and Bone" (fertilizer), and irrigation will make poppies grow if you fail to scatter the seed.

I believe "the blood of the martyrs" works very much like "Blood and Bone", and the sweat of the laborers and the tears of the intercessors work very much like irrigation: they prepare the soil.

As the blood of the martyrs is poured out across the Middle East, might it not be reasonable to expect that the God of the cross, the God who is there, might be keen to subvert this evil and redeem it for good by making hearts receptive to the gospel? What we need is more sweat and more tears:

---

36. In terms of cause and effect: while persecution does not produce church growth (not directly anyway), church growth always produces persecution.

37. The parable of the sower is found in Matt 13.

more sacrificial giving, more intelligent strategic advocacy, more passionate intercessory prayer, and of course, more urgent and intentional scattering of the seed.

Unprecedented?

Though some people insist that the Christian crisis in the Middle East is *unprecedented*, it is not![38]

What is *unprecedented*, however, is the church's ability to respond. For with today's information and communication technologies, any local church can be aware of a crisis taking place on the other side of the world, often as it unfolds, and respond immediately—*for the saving of many lives.*

Never before in the history of the world has it been so possible for the now globally aware and globally connected church to demonstrate who we are and what we believe. As a people of faith who believe God can be trusted, we are living in an age of *unprecedented opportunity*.

One Sunday in Tel Isqof

Tel Isqof is an Assyrian Christian village 35 km north of Mosul in the far north of Nineveh. On August 7, 2014, IS jihadists seized the village, sending some seven thousand Assyrian Christians, fleeing for their lives, north into Dohuk in Iraqi Kurdistan. The Kurdish *pershmerga* launched a counteroffensive, and by August 17, it had driven the jihadists out (and thoroughly looted the village[39]). Though Tel Isqof had been liberated, it was still exceedingly dangerous, far too dangerous to return to as IS fighters who still controlled the surrounds routinely attempted forays into the town.

On Sunday November 9, 2014, something happened in Tel Isqof that was certainly symbolic and possibly even prophetic. Fr. Paul Thabit Mekko, a displaced Assyrian priest holed up in Arbil, tells what happened:

> A group of young men, now refugees in Kurdistan, wanted to go there [to Tel Isqof] with a priest for a few hours, with the intent to open the church, ring the bells and celebrate mass. After the liturgy they returned to the north, to the places where they are currently living as refugees. It was a way of saying that we do not

---

38. Most of those who insist that the Christian crisis in the Middle East is "unprecedented" are either ignorant of history and/or trying to justify their utter cluelessness and pathetic responses.

39. "Christian Houses Looted Also by the Kurdish Peshmerga Militias."

abandon our lands, and we hope to return to our homes and our churches soon."[40]

Just as IS silenced the bell and removed the cross in order to make a statement, those young Assyrian Christian men rang the bell and restored the cross to its rightful place atop the dome of the church overlooking the Nineveh Plain in order to make a statement of their own—a statement of faith.

Father Rani Hanna, the parish priest in Tel Isqof, now visits the church daily, "to set an example for his people."[41] An example of what? Of courage? (For IS controls the countryside.) Of religiosity? No! Fr. Rani is setting an example of staying, of returning, of valuing heritage, of retaining the Christian presence, and of duty to country. He knows, however, that Christians cannot return until IS is defeated, security is restored, and freedom is realized. Watching Fr. Rani's December 2015 YouTube appeal to Assyrian youths, one cannot help but notice that though Tel Isqof appears dead, the church—its cross restored—is alive: clean, neat, functioning as a house of prayer, and ready for the day when Christians will return.[42]

Surely God has preserved an Assyrian remnant precisely because he intends to restore them to their lands, in what will be a reverse exodus.

For it is promised:

> In that day there will be a highway from Egypt to Assyria, and Assyria will come into Egypt, and Egypt into Assyria, and the Egyptians will worship with the Assyrians.
> In that day Israel will be the third with Egypt and Assyria, a blessing in the midst of the earth, whom the Lord of hosts has blessed, saying, "Blessed be Egypt my people, and Assyria the work of my hands, and Israel my inheritance" (Isa 19:23–24).

What a promise! No wonder so much of the Assyrian church leadership is pressing ahead with an eye to the future. On Sunday September 27, 2015, St. John the Baptist Cathedral in Ankawa, Arbil, Iraqi Kurdistan, buzzed with anticipation as the Assyrian Church of the East consecrated its one hundred and twelfth patriarch. What's more, despite having existed as a headquarters in exile in America since the massacres of 1933, the headquarters of the Assyrian Church of the East is now making plans to return to Iraq.[43]

---

40. "A Mass Celebrated Again in the Nineveh Plain."
41. Fr. Rani Hanna From Tel Isqof, Dec 9, 2015. https://www.youtube.com/watch?v=2z7z1FyQ-kI
42. Ibid.
43. "Assyrian Church of the East Elects New Patriarch."

Amongst his first acts as Patriarch, His Holiness Mar Gewargis III Sliwa reopened St. George Assyrian church in Dora, Baghdad. The church had been vandalized in April 2007 and firebombed a month later. Of the twenty thousand Assyrians who once lived in Dora, only a few hundred remain—a reality that is both tragic and traumatizing. Yet on Monday November 2, 2015, Dora's remnant Christians flooded into the beautifully rebuilt church, overjoyed by its resurrection.[44]

After Saturday Comes Sunday

Yes, the Christian crisis in the Middle East is nightmarish. No, it is not a momentary infliction that will soon pass, for this crisis has decades, even centuries of momentum behind it. Yes, the world has changed and the situation could get a lot worse yet. However, precisely because *after Saturday comes Sunday*, the church can look into this crisis, call it what it is—"horrendous, evil, devastating, appalling"—and still find God at work within it.

> God moves in a mysterious way his wonders to perform;
> He plants his footsteps in the sea and rides upon the storm
> —William Cowper, 1779.

So: Just because Muslims deliver *"Ba'd as-sabt biji yom al-ahad"* ("After Saturday comes Sunday") as a threat, it doesn't mean Christians have to receive it that way. For despite its genocidal overtones, the threat loses all its power to terrorize when translated by way of the cross. Not only does the cross turn this threat on its head, it turns it back on the one who delivered it. Sunday holds no terror for Christians. It is not Christianity that is under threat, it is Islam!

If Muslims chanting, *"Ba'd as-sabt biji yom al-ahad"* ("After Saturday comes Sunday") really understood the significance of Sunday, and why it is that Christians rejoice and worship on Sundays and all that Sunday reveals, they'd be less inclined to hasten the day!

And if more Christians understood it—I mean *really* understood and *believed* it, then I dare say more Christians would step out in faith and follow the Redeemer into those chaotic, dark places where Christians suffer and grieve. It is not a thing to be feared. Indeed, I am certain there could be no greater joy than to be there, at the tomb, when the dawn of Sunday breaks.

44. "Twice Attacked Church Reopens in Baghdad, But is it Too Late for Assyrians?"; "Support is Flooding in for an Assyrian Church's Reopening in Baghdad."

— Appendix 1 —

Christian Solidarity: The Sound of Silence

> Silence in the face of evil is itself evil: God will not hold us guiltless. Not to speak is to speak. Not to act is to act
> —Dietrich Bonheoffer.[1]

IN MAY 2015, ONE of Australia's most well-known secular conservative commentators, journalist Andrew Bolt, criticized the Australian church for its "indefensible" silence in the face of the Christian crisis in the Middle East.

> It is religious persecution on a horrific scale, involving massacres, bombings, slavery, beheadings and mass rape.
>
> So why don't our churches protest against this slaughter of their own?
>
> Yes, Christians are now the prime target of unbelievably barbaric attacks in the Middle East and Africa, yet Australia's bishops, ministers, priests, church "social justice" units and Christian aid groups—usually so vocal—are now near mute ... even our own churches in Australia—normally so keen to defend every other faith—seem unwilling to defend their own.
>
> The only press release issued lately by the Uniting Church that discusses the Middle East criticises not the murder of Christians by Muslims but the alleged meanness of Jews to Muslims, drawing attention to a "critique of the policies of the Government of Israel."
>
> The Baptists' web page of "articles and statements" includes criticisms of government policies on boat children in detention, illegal immigrants and global warming—all part of the Left's

---

1. Though disputed, this quote is commonly attributed to German Lutheran pastor and theologian, Dietrich Bonhoeffer (1906 – 1945), a founding member and leader in the Confessing Church movement, which boldly resisted Nazism. Bonhoeffer was arrested and imprisoned on April 5, 1943, and was executed by hanging on April 9, 1946. See "Bonhoeffer: Timeline."

catechism—but it says absolutely nothing about the murder and rape of fellow believers.

Melbourne's Anglican diocese has a list of news items on its web page that has nothing about the Middle East since October and then it criticised not the Islamic State's persecution of Christians but Israel's treatment of Palestinians.[2]

As Bolt noted, the left-leaning secular media is routinely silent about the persecution of Christians, but there are reasons for this:

> This week *The New York Times* ran a long feature on the mass rape and deliberate impregnation of women by Boko Haram without once mentioning the victims were Christians.
>
> On three successive days after the slaughter of the Kenyan university students, ABC television news reports did not mention the killers were Muslims or dead students Christian. Sure, such media outlets are militantly secular, even actively anti-Christian.[3]
>
> Being of the Left, they also tend not to defend a principle but a side and are therefore unwilling to legitimise warnings from conservatives that some Islamic followers menace our freedoms, particularly the freedoms of women, gays and Christians.

"But what," Bolt asks, "can explain the silence of the churches?"[4]

The Sound of Silence

There are many reasons why Christian individuals and local churches are silent on the matter of the horrendous, escalating persecution being suffered by their fellow believers. Not the least of which is the difficulty this subject poses for the peddlers of prosperity and those who like their Christianity "lite" with perpetual celebration and no strings attached. While these are serious issues—reflecting on Christian spirituality, maturity, and identity—worthy of a chapter or even a book in their own right, I have chosen to focus here on another issue, one that has political consequences: the disastrous resurrection of the failed strategy of "Quiet Diplomacy."

---

2. Bolt, "Churches' Silence Just Indefensible."

3. This is precisely why Christians wanting news pertaining to international Christianity must support and subscribe to Christian advocacy and media organizations; for secular media has little interest in the persecution of Christians—you will not learn anything there.

4. Bolt, "Churches' Silence Just Indefensible."

In their rush to jump on the political bandwagon, and make a name for themselves as political players, many influential Christian leaders and denominational heads have found themselves on a particular political path, the cost of which is a vow of silence. Though the signpost says "to dialogue", the route goes by way of a covenantal agreement in which the Christians must promise not to criticize the persecutors. To agree to such a demand, one must exercise great faith in politics while clinging to hope that the sought-after end (religious freedom) will justify their morally questionable means (the betrayal and abandonment of the persecuted).

Instead of engaging with politics in a prophetic way—speaking truth into power while trusting in the Lord (as did the prophets of old), those who opt for Quiet Diplomacy will appease hostile powers at the expense of the persecuted trusting that their diplomacy and the political process will combine to deliver the desired end. What these Christian leaders fail to see, is that while they are busy congratulating themselves for the coup of scoring dialogue with corrupt, lying dictators, terrorists, and other persecutors, those persecutors are also busy congratulating themselves for the coup of scoring a vow of silence from influential Christian leaders.

I am firmly of the opinion that despite the fine intentions and noble goals of its Christian protagonists, Quiet Diplomacy does not work and invariably makes difficult situations worse. I believe it is a non-solution and an inappropriate response built on misplaced faith and flawed theology, fuelled only by the hope that the end will justify the means. God will never honour such a strategy, for "without faith it is impossible to please him" (Heb 11:6). In God's economy, means matter—and the betrayal and abandonment of his beloved children is something he will not abide.[5]

The Cost of Quiet Diplomacy

Christian leaders who engage in Quite Diplomacy do so at virtually no cost to themselves. To the contrary, many reap great gains from their expeditions into the halls of power and photo opportunities with world leaders and recognized terrorists. When it comes to Quiet Diplomacy, the price is paid by others: the cost to the persecuted is enormous.

What's more, silence is merely the entry fee, the cost of a seat at the table. The price for continuing dialogue goes up over time: from withholding

---

5. My first book, *Turn Back the Battle: Isaiah Speaks to Christians Today*, was written to challenge the strategy of Quiet Diplomacy. It applies Isaiah 1—39 to the times in which we live to propose a biblical response to persecution and existential threat. It is a response that rejects such "covenants with death" (Isa 28:9–22).

criticism, to being obliged to deliver propaganda and engage in public relations on behalf of persecutors (which explains why so many influential Christian leaders have become avid apologists for Islam or for the Chinese Communist Party, etc.), to ultimately being obliged to function as informants so that "troublemakers" might be reined in.

A Case Study from History

When the Communist Party-controlled, state-sanctioned Russian Orthodox Church (ROC) joined the World Council of Churches (WCC) in 1961—that is, during the Cold War, at a time when Christians in Soviet territories were suffering severe persecution, the WCC enacted a protocol establishing that appeals for WCC intervention could not be acted upon, nor could reports be published, without the consent of the relevant WCC member churches.

The protocol essentially gave the Soviet communists' proxies in the ROC the right to veto appeals from the persecuted church so as to protect their own interests. It also indicated that the WCC was prepared to pursue ecumenism and expansion at any cost—including at the cost of faithful, persecuted believers.[6]

In 1975, Russian Orthodox priest Fr. Gleb Yakunin and layman Lev Regelson wrote an open letter to the Fifth WCC Assembly in Nairobi, Kenya. The letter was published in the Assembly's newsletter, *Target*.

Entitled "Two Russians Appeal for WCC Action on Behalf of Persecuted Christians," the letter was essentially a plea to bring persecution to international attention. It included the request that the WCC help get permission for exhausted persecuted Christians to emigrate "somewhere they would be allowed to work and observe their religion in peace."[7]

Along with protesting WCC silence, Yakunin and Regelson called for Christian solidarity and true unity on the basis of our identity as bearers of the cross. Written in 1975, this extraordinary letter is as relevant today as ever:

> The world has not heard the World Council of Churches raising its authoritative voice when the Russian Orthodox Church was half destroyed ... no indignant protest was heard from the WCC even when religion was completely crushed in Albania—and

---

6. For a study of the WCC during this era, see Emerson Vermaat, *The World Council of Churches and Politics*.

7. "Two Russians Appeal for WCC Action on Behalf of Persecuted Christians."

the WCC still remained silent even after a priest was shot to death in Albania for having baptized a baby ...

To that end, they implored the WCC to take the lead and initiate a program to aid "those Christians who are victims of persecution anywhere in the world":

> We are deeply aware that many Christians are deeply concerned about the suffering of their brethren and wish to help them with all their hearts, but often they do not know how to proceed ...
>
> As convinced as we are that only at the foot of the Cross of Golgotha a passion of love may be born that can truly overcome the strife between individual denominations and their alienations and prepare Christian hearts for genuine unity.
>
> Since Christians are not united even on the opinion concerning the significance of bearing the Cross in the modern world, we presume that the doubts about the spiritual quality of the ecumenical movement may be banished only if confession of the Cross in the original sense of the Gospel—as trials and tribulations for the sake of Christ's Name—become the basis for Christian unity.

They wrote of their sense of betrayal and abandonment by the "official leadership of the Russian Church which denied [in 1930, after the mass executions of clergy and lay believers] that persecution was taking place at all and which lied before the whole world that those who appeared to be suffering martyrs for their faith were, in reality, just political offenders."

They noted that after Stalin's death in 1953, the Soviet regime adopted a "reduce tensions" policy in which the state-sanctioned ROC was exploited as foreign policy tool:

> In 1961 the Russian Orthodox Church joined the World Council of Churches. For the Russian Church that year was marked by an increasing wave of anti-religious terror and by forcibly closing of churches, monasteries and theological schools everywhere. Protestant churches were subjected to no less brutal persecution at the same time ... More than 10,000 Orthodox churches were closed on the territory of USSR from 1959 to 1965.
>
> The believers of the Russian Church never harbored any special illusions about the membership of the Moscow Patriarch in the World Council of Churches; that act was sanctioned by the government during the period of extremely brutal persecution of religion and obviously advanced the government's own

strategic aims, quite remote from any consolidation of Christian positions in the modern world.

Nevertheless, the Orthodox believers still hoped that Christian solidarity and determination to achieve genuine unity would prove stronger than the influence of anti-Christian forces; they hoped that the WCC would provide a powerful support to its new member, initiate an international movement for the defense of the persecuted and invite all Christians to join in prayers for the suffering church.

But, as Yakunin and Regelson note, that is not what happened. Rather,

> the matter of religious persecution failed to take its due place—although it ought to become the central theme of Christian ecumenism...
>
> It is now our most imperative task, to restore in the whole Christian community all over the world this spirit of the first Christians who revered the confessors of faith: such a respect must be the most important ecumenical act and then the hearts' warmth could melt away any denominational alienation!

The letter triggered heated debate as well as division between those who believed the WCC should publically promote religious liberty and justice while facilitating aid and prayer for the persecuted, and those who advocated "selective silence" and "quiet diplomacy." Though many delegates were deeply distressed, others were greatly irritated, seeing the appeal as a threat to their political activity.

In Moscow, Soviet authorities moved quickly to neutralize the letter, labelling it a threat to the ecumenical movement. In what was nothing other than blackmail, the state-sanctioned ROC threatened to withdraw from the WCC if the WCC did not discard the letter.

The following year (1976), Fr. Gleb Yakunin established the Christian Committee for the Defense of the Rights of Believers in the USSR, to document the persecution of religious believers. Meanwhile, WCC delegates at the October 1976 Montreux Colloquium were appeasing and reconciling with the Soviet communists, lobbying for the establishment of "Christian-Marxist dialogue."

In 1979, Fr. Gleb Yakunin (45) and Lev Regelson (40) were arrested on charges of "anti-Soviet agitation and propaganda." Regelson pled guilty and was released. Unrepentant, Fr. Gleb Yakunin (who was married with three children) was sentenced to five years in prison followed by five years' internal exile in Yakutsk, 8,400 km northeast of Moscow in remote arctic Siberia.[8]

The WCC's response: silence!

History Repeats

The parallels between the WCC's response to Christians suffering under Soviet communism during the Cold War and the response of many Christian denominations and international organizations to Christians suffering persecution today—in particular, those suffering under Islam—are unmistakable and undeniable.

> What has been is what will be, and what has been done is what will be done, and there is nothing new under the sun. Is there a thing of which it is said, "See, this is new"? It has been already in the ages before us—Ecclesiastes 1:9–10.

The church needs to wake up to the fact that the world is not going to save the church; and that's okay, for God never intended that it should. From Genesis onwards, the Bible reveals—through teaching, prophecy, and typology—that God intervenes and saves his people by grace through faith. Consequently, it is absolutely imperative that the church steps out in faith.[9]

The silence of the churches is not only indefensible, it is absolutely disastrous.

---

8. Mikhail Gorbachev amnestied Gleb Yakunin in March 1987. He was allowed to return to Moscow and died on Christmas Day, December 25, 2014, aged 80 years.

9. See Appendix 2: God's Human Instruments: Just Do It!

— Appendix 2 —

God's Human Instruments: Just Do It!

> Theological truth has no point of contact with the world. This does not mean that we doubt whether the Holy Spirit (and he alone) can establish contact; but it means that we have to recognize that throughout the course of history God uses material means—in other words, *he acts by his Spirit through human instruments*—Jacques Ellul.[1]

WE CAN BE GOD'S "human instruments", channels through which the Spirit intervenes in love and mercy. God's word is full of instruction. What's required of us is obedience: that we step out in faith and *just do it!*[2]

Speak Up

> Speak up for those who cannot speak for themselves
> ... defend the rights of the poor and needy
> —Proverbs 31:8–9, NIV.

Silence renders sufferers invisible (which is exactly what their persecutors want); speaking up, however, gives them form and presence. Christians who are impoverished, displaced, and without means; Christians who have been silenced through imprisonment, intimidation, and threat; Christians who have been buried under a pile of propaganda, or pushed deep into the fog of war out of sight and out of mind, rely on our voice to make their plight known. So speak up and shatter the silence!

---

1. Ellul, *The Presence of the Kingdom*, 11. Italics added.
2. 'JUST DO IT.' is a trademark of the Nike shoe company and one of the core components of its brand. I once heard Malaysian evangelist Pastor Daniel Ho say, "I believe in *Nike* evangelism; just do it!" I have never forgotten that.

- Talk to family, friends, neighbors and colleagues—over dinner, while walking, via social media—wherever and whenever the opportunity arises (or wherever and whenever you can make an opportunity arise).
- Write letters to the editor for publication in local, national and international—as well as denominational—newspapers, journals and magazines.
- Phone in and contribute to talk-back radio.
- Add your presence to peaceful demonstrations, rallies, and prayer vigils. The bigger the prayer vigil, the more likely it is to attract media attention that will further amplify the message.[3]
- Join a Christian advocacy group and participate in their advocacy campaigns.
- Write as a concerned individual, to your local Member of Parliament (MP).

Letters to the editor—that is, letters written for publication—should be under 250 words; anything longer will not be published or might be edited down into something you no longer recognize. When responding to news that is current, use email, for it is immediate, and the earlier in the day you send it, the better. Do not include attachments or hyperlinks, as these may result in your email being rejected.

When writing to an MP or diplomat, your letter must be polite but never patronizing or ingratiating. Hostile, demanding, lecturing letters are not well received and will likely be filtered out at the secretary's desk. Letters need to be concise and to the point: one or two pages—no more—with a decent font, decent spacing, and plenty of white space so it is easy on the eye. Use dot points, stay on track, keep focused. Busy MPs and diplomats do not have time for rambling philosophical arguments, they simply want to know what concerns you and what you would like to see done. If you feel you have a lot to say, then consider drip feeding: send short letters at regular intervals. A letter that is long, complex, or verbose will probably not be read

---

3. In August 1998, in a five-second sound bite on the evening news, it was reported that traffic had been diverted in Sydney that afternoon as the Coptic community marched in silence to protest the arrest and torture (under Egypt's emergency laws) of a thousand Coptic Christians in el-Kosheh, Upper Egypt. The subject was the silent protest and its impact on Sydney traffic, not that whole Christian families were being tortured by corrupt, sectarian, Arab Egyptian security personnel in a campaign of injustice and systematic ethnic-religious persecution against the indigenous people of Egypt. God used what was a shameful piece of reporting to call me into fulltime ministry facilitating prayer for the persecuted church.

at all, and will also likely be filtered out at the secretary's desk. Include your contact details and keep any replies.

The contact details of MPs are published on government websites. Although contacting them by email is acceptable, emails are easy to delete and risk being diverted to junk email folders. For a whole lot of reasons, hard copy—good old ink on paper, bearing your signature, and travelling by "snail mail" to be received by hand—is better.

If all Christians were to write routinely to their local MP, I imagine it would greatly improve the quality of partyroom and parliamentary debate—and the outcome. Swamping the foreign minister is but one form of advocacy; flooding the party room is another—one I suspect might be more effective.

Finally and most critically, all speaking and writing must be undergirded, driven and sustained by prayer. Pray that God will open the doors, direct your paths, give you the words, and bless your efforts. For: "Unless the Lord builds the house, those who build it labor in vain" (Ps 127:1).

> A time comes when silence is betrayal—Martin Luther King Jr.[4]

Don't let anything put you off; *just do it!* Speak, speak, speak!

Give Generously

> If a brother or sister is poorly clothed and lacking in daily food, and one of you says to them, "Go in peace, be warmed and filled," without giving them the things needed for the body, what good is that? So also faith by itself, if it does not have works, is dead—James 2:15–17.

Having fled Islamic jihad, hundreds of thousands of Christians are this day displaced, traumatized, and destitute. They have lost their homes, their savings, and their livelihoods. Many have lost everything but the clothes on their backs. Because they avoid the Muslim-dominated UN camps, preferring to seek sanctuary amongst fellow Christians to avoid discrimination and persecution, the burden of care falls not to the UN but to the local church. Across the Middle East, local churches are providing displaced Christians with warm clothes, shelter, food, infant milk formula, clean water,

---

4. 'Silence is Betrayal.'

sanitation, pharmaceuticals, medical care, and education. Though willing to be God's hands, they depend on funds coming in from God's givers.

In these days of escalating persecution, ethnic-religious cleansing, and genocide, churches should be funding both mission *and* aid to the persecuted church. For far too long, mission and persecution have been separated, with mission viewed as gospel outreach which necessitates funding, and persecution viewed as a human rights issue which warrants political activism. This is a false dichotomy. Mission and persecution are two sides of the one coin; they are inseparable. Both warrant political activism (for religious freedom to witness and believe) and both require financial aid (to expand and survive). We must stop separating these issues. After all, what is the persecuted church if not a frontline witness?

Numerous Christian aid and advocacy groups, Christian charities of every denomination, and even former and currently serving missionaries, are delivering aid to persecuted and existentially imperiled Christians through secure, trusted, and well-established channels. But, just as with giving to mission, it is wise to *only* give or send money to well-established, recognized agencies or people whom you know and trust to avoid falling prey to scammers.

I have no intention of providing a list of agencies that deliver aid to the persecuted, for to list is to limit. What's more, there are simply too many—national and international, denominational and non-denominational—and I would hate to overlook any one of them, for they are all champions. Rather, I advise individuals and churches to seek the Lord in this. Ask the Lord to direct you—to open the door and lead you in the way he wants you to go. God will honor this prayer, I guarantee it. For it is promised: "If any of you lacks wisdom, let him ask God, who gives generously to all without reproach, and it will be given him" (Jas 1:5). So ask and keep asking, in faith that the Lord will answer. As for me, I totally trust the Lord in this. Putting this in God's hands ensures that all needs will be covered.

> For I was hungry and you gave me food, I was thirsty and you gave me drink, I was a stranger and you welcomed me, I was naked and you clothed me . . . Truly, I say to you, as you did it to one of the least of these my brothers and sisters, you did it to me (excerpts from Jesus' teaching on the final judgment, Matt 25:35–46).

So consider Christ, and *just do it!* Give, give, give!

Pray

> For we do not wrestle against flesh and blood, but against the rulers, against the authorities, against the cosmic powers over this present darkness, against the spiritual forces of evil in the heavenly places. Therefore take up the whole armor of God . . . praying at all times in the Spirit, with all prayer and supplication. To that end keep alert with all perseverance, making supplication for all the saints—Ephesians 6:12–18.

A spiritual battle against spiritual forces necessitates the use of spiritual weapons. And though the weapons of Ephesians 6—truth, righteousness, preparedness to witness, faith, assurance of salvation, the word of God, and prayer—might not seem like much, they "have divine power to destroy strongholds."[5] Furthermore, the one to whom we pray is "*Baal Perazim*: the Lord who bursts through. He is *Yahweh Sabaoth*: the Lord of hosts and commander of heaven's armies."[6]

Far from being a benign religious duty, a traditional formality, or an "inappropriate interruption" (yes, I have heard intercessory prayer described that way!), true intercessory prayer is:

- "Advocacy to the highest authority."[7]
- Serious business in the courts of the Lord.
- Spiritual warfare.
- Radical faith in action.

We must have a higher view of the serious business of intercessory prayer!

We Are Called to Pray for the Persecuted

"Let brotherly love continue . . . Remember those who are in prison, as though in prison with them, and those who are mistreated, since you also are in the body" (Hebrews 13:1, 3).

---

5. "For though we walk in the flesh, we are not waging war according to the flesh. For the weapons of our warfare are not of the flesh but have divine power to destroy strongholds" (2 Cor 10:3–4).

6. Kendal, *Turn Back the Battle*, 213.

7. Ibid., 110. Quote: "And in this increasingly hostile world, the embattled and besieged, persecuted church of Jesus Christ needs our prayers, for *intercessory prayer is advocacy to the highest authority*."

Suffering, anxious, persecuted believers are exceedingly vulnerable to spiritual attack. "Your adversary the devil prowls around like a roaring lion, seeking someone to devour" (1 Pet 5:8). And who better to stalk than a grief-stricken, confused, utterly exhausted, wounded believer? When we intercede, we interpose ourselves between the lion and his prey. Forget the glorified images of great heroes of the faith; persecuted believers need all the prayer support they can get.

We are Called to Pray for the Persecutors

"You have heard that it was said, 'You shall love your neighbor and hate your enemy.' But I [Jesus] say to you, Love your enemies and pray for those who persecute you, so that you may be sons of your Father who is in heaven. For he makes his sun rise on the evil and on the good, and sends rain on the just and on the unjust" (Matt 5:43–45a).[8]

We need to pray that persecutors will be restrained, that they will come under conviction of sin, and that the God of all grace will open their hearts to receive the gospel. We also need to pray that the Holy Spirit will enable the persecuted to love and pray for those who persecute them. This is really important, for grace is not only a powerful witness, it is a powerful healer.

We are Called to Pray for World Leaders

"First of all, then, I urge that supplications, prayers, intercessions, and thanksgivings be made for all people, for kings and all who are in high positions, that we may lead a peaceful and quiet life, godly and dignified in every way. This is good, and it is pleasing in the sight of God our Savior, who desires all people to be saved and to come to the knowledge of the truth" (1 Tim 2:1–4).

> The king's heart is a stream of water in the hand of the Lord;
> he turns it wherever he will—Proverbs 21:1.[9]

---

8. See also Luke 6:27–28 ("bless those who curse you, pray for those who mistreat you") and Rom 12:14 ("Bless those who persecute you; bless and do not curse").

9. Consider Esth 6:1: "On that night [the night before Haman was to have Mordacai hanged] the king could not sleep. And he gave orders to bring the book of memorable deeds, the chronicles, and they were read before the king" (Esth 6:1). And what was read to the king in his moment of restlessness changed the course of history—in answer to the prayers of many.

Virtually all Christian aid and advocacy groups that serve the persecuted church also provide resources for prayer. Some send printed newsletters and prayer calendars, and virtually all send news and prayer requests via email. Further to this, Christian media organizations now exist for the purpose of reporting the religious (Christian) news the secular media ignores; some even specialize in reporting persecution.

Every week I publish a Religious Liberty Prayer Bulletin (RLPB) designed purely to facilitate informed and strategic intercessory prayer. The RLPB is issued mid week via email; this ministry is totally independent and non-denominational, and the service is absolutely free (absolutely no fundraising is involved). Most weeks the RLPB will cover one situation, incident, or threat; supply four paragraphs of explanation, context, and analysis; list three or four strategic prayer points with scriptural basis; and include a 130-word summary for use in small groups, church bulletins, or electronic mailings. The last RLPB of each month provides updates and a roundup of prayer needs not featured in the weekly RLPBs, any one of which could be used in a church bulletin or email.[10]

I also maintain a site of Critical Prayer Requests (CPR) for states where Christians are persecuted. While the RLPB zooms in, the CPR zooms out to give a wide-angle overview. This site is revised and updated at least quarterly, and it includes numerous Scriptures to aid and underpin intercessory prayer.[11]

The information is out there; these days, it is actually quite easy to be very well informed for the purpose of intercessory prayer.

> Satan dreads nothing but prayer. His one concern is to keep the saints from praying. He fears nothing from prayerless studies, prayerless work, prayerless religion. He laughs at our toil, mocks our wisdom, but trembles when we pray—Samuel Chadwick.[12]

Satan *will* seek to distract you; resist him and *just do it!* Pray, pray, pray!

---

10. To subscribe to the Religious Liberty Prayer Bulletin, visit the blog http://rl-prayerbulletin.blogspot.com.au/, sign up, and then confirm. Emails are sent via Feedburner. Alternatively, for a text-only version, send an empty email to join-rlpb@hub.xc.org. This is a totally free service.

11. See Critical Prayer Requests (CPR), http://criticalprayerrequests.blogspot.com.au/.

12. Quoted by Sanders, in the introduction to *World Prayer*, 12.

Reforming Worship: An Appeal to Church Leaders

Persecution and hardship are increasing globally. For Christian worship to remain relevant and purposeful, it must reflect and address this reality. This does *not* mean we replace our joy with angst and our celebration with mourning. It does mean, however, that we need to make room in our worship for lament (after all, the situation is truly lamentable), the serious business of intercessory prayer, and the absolutely necessary work of preparing believers for dark days and testing times.

It would be unreasonable to expect such reform to happen overnight, for it usually requires a change in church culture—especially in churches that have grown insular during an extended period of comfort and security.

What follows is a proposed strategy for church leaders desirous of facilitating cultural change within their church to the end that worship might be reformed:

- Commission a member of the congregation to serve as an "Ambassador for the Persecuted Church." The ambassador should be willing and able to provide up-to-date information, as well as direction and advice regarding advocacy, aid, and prayer for the persecuted. For most churches, the choice will be obvious, and it will simply sanction and formalize a ministry that already exists, albeit on the margins.

- Have the ambassador submit one prayer need to the church office each week or fortnight for publication in the church newsletter and/or weekly mailing.

- Regularly encourage the congregation, small group leaders, and those who lead intercessory prayers during gathered worship to make use of that material in their prayers, Bible studies, and discussions.

- Lead from the front: model the engagement and behavior you wish to facilitate.

- Set aside the International Day of Prayer (IDOP) for the Persecuted Church (early November, annually)[13] for a full and creative service totally devoted to the issue of persecution.

Such reform will broaden global awareness, deepen prayer focus, generate perspective, and prepare believers to face trial—all with very little effort on anyone's part.

---

13. See "Critical Prayer Requests."

Expect some resistance, as not everyone welcomes change. Be aware that many of those who resist the call to "Bear one another's burdens"[14] do so out of fear that the burdens of the persecuted might prove onerous and oppressive, compounding the burdens they already bear. However, I can assure you that the opposite is actually true. Christians who obey Christ in this respect will find that the burdens of the persecuted do not compound their own burdens; rather, they actually displace them.

And while some resistance is to be expected, at least initially, I can assure you that when you give attention to the plight of those who are persecuted on account of Jesus' name, the Spirit of God will animate those in whom he dwells. For who are these persecuted believers? They, along with us, are his bride—the beloved of his soul. Consequently, such reform can only be that for which the Holy Spirit yearns.

Reject fear, obey the Lord, step out in faith—*just do it!*

---

14. "Bear one another's burdens, and so fulfill the law of Christ [i.e. the law of love]" (Gal 6:2).

Bibliography

"125 Killed in Bloody Two Days for Iraq." *Gulf Times,* April 25, 2013. Online: http://www.gulf-times.com/region/216/details/350346/125-killed-in-bloody-two-days-for-iraq.

"21 New Martyrs of Libya Icon—S100." Legacy Icons. Online: http://www.legacyicons.com/products/21-martyrs-icon.

Abdallah, Wissam. "Syria's Ancient Sites Under Attack." *Al-Monitor*, March 8, 2015. Online: http://www.al-monitor.com/pulse/culture/2015/03/syria-antiquities-looting.html#.

Abel Sadah, Ali. "Anbar Province Headed Toward Isolation." Al-Monitor, February 3, 2014. Online: http://www.al-monitor.com/pulse/originals/2014/02/anbar-province-iraq-military-operations-isolation.html#.

Abi Ali, Firas. "Capture of Palmyra Increases Likelihood of Sudden Syrian Army Withdrawal from Damascus to the Alawite Coastal Homeland." IHS Jane's Intelligence Review, May 20, 2015. Online: http://www.janes.com/article/51596/capture-of-palmyra-increases-likelihood-of-sudden-syrian-army-withdrawal-from-damascus-to-the-alawite-coastal-homeland.

Abi Raad, Doreen. "Syrian Crisis Part of Western Geopolitical Strategy, Says Patriarch." Catholic News Service, May 13, 2013. Online: http://www.catholicnews.com/data/stories/cns/1302115.htm.

Abouzeid, Rania. "Bouazizi: The Man Who Set Himself and Tunisia on Fire." *TIME,* January 26, 2011. Online: http://content.time.com/time/magazine/article/0,9171,2044723,00.html.

al-Ali, Rami. "ISIS Rules in Raqqa." Al-Monitor, February 26, 2014. Online: http://www.al-monitor.com/pulse/security/2014/02/syria-isis-raqqa-quasi-government-opposition.html#.

al-Assad, Bashar. "Syria Will Remain Free." January 10, 2012. Online: http://syrianfreepress.wordpress.com/2012/01/10/syria-will-remain-free-president-bashar-al-assad-speech-on-january-10-2012-full-english-text/.

Al-Shishani, Murad Batal. "Jabhat al-Nusra's New Syria Strategy." Al-Monitor, January 14, 2013. Online: http://www.al-monitor.com/pulse/ar/politics/2013/01/jabhat-al-nusras-new-strategy-in-syria.html#.

Alfoneh, Ali. Review of *The Twilight War: The Secret History of America's Thirty-Years Conflict with Iran* by David Crist. Middle East Quarterly, Spring 2013. Online: http://www.meforum.org/3538/the-twilight-war.

"Algerian Dies in Self-Immolation, Echoing Tunisia." *Al-Arabiya,* January 16, 2011. Online: http://www.alarabiya.net/articles/2011/01/16/133710.html.

Amos, Deborah. "A Smuggler Explains How He Helped Fighters Along 'Jihadi Highway.'" NPR, October 7, 2014. Online: http://www.npr.org/blogs/parallels/2014/10/07/354288389/a-smuggler-explains-how-he-helped-fighters-along-jihadi-highway.

"Anyone Notice the Persecution of Mideast Christians?" Letters, *Wall Street Journal*, October 17, 2011. Online: http://online.wsj.com/news/articles/SB10001424052970204002304576627234243229722

Arraf, Jane. "The Oct. 31 Attack on a Baghdad Church—the Worst in Recent Memory—Has Spurred a Fresh Exodus among Iraq's Christian Community, Already Decimated by the War." Christian Science Monitor, November 9, 2010. Online: http://www.csmonitor.com/World/Middle-East/2010/1109/In-Iraq-Christians-fear-they-could-be-wiped-out-like-Jews-before-them.

Ashkar, Hisham. "The Battle for Qusayr and the Fate of Saint Elias Church." Al-Ahkbar, May 19, 2014. Online: http://english.al-akhbar.com/node/19828.

"Assyria: Assyrian Universal Alliance Asks Australian Government For Help." Letter to the Australian Prime Minster by Hermiz Shahen, Deputy Secretary General, Assyrian Universal Alliance, December 12, 2011. Online at UNPO (Unrepresented Nations and Peoples Organisation): http://www.unpo.org/article/13600.

"Assyrian Church of the East Elects New Patriarch," Assyrian International News Agency, September 18, 2015. Online: http://www.aina.org/news/20150918141220.htm.

"Bahrain." *World Report 2012*, Human Rights Watch, 535–541. Online: http://www.hrw.org/sites/default/files/reports/wr2012.pdf.

Baianonie, Mohamed. "Adhan (The Call to Prayer)." How Do I Pray? Online: http://islam1.org/how_to_pray/times.htm.

Ballout, Mohammed. "US Strike on Syria Would Help Jihadists, Not Secular Opposition." Al-Monitor, August 27, 2013. Online: http://www.al-monitor.com/pulse/security/2013/08/us-military-strike-syria-regime-jihadists.html#.

Banco, Erin. "Syrian Rebel Group Jaysh Al Fatah Captures Ariha, Takes All of Idlib Province from Regime." International Business Times, May 29, 2015. http://www.ibtimes.com/syrian-rebel-group-jaysh-al-fatah-captures-ariha-takes-all-idlib-province-regime-1944273.

Barron, Robert. "A Message in Blood: ISIS and the Meaning of the Cross." February 26, 2015. Online: http://www.wordonfire.org/resources/article/a-message-in-blood-isis-and-the-meaning-of-the-cross/4677/.

Barry, Ellen. "Russians and Syrians, Allied by History and Related by Marriage." *The New York Times*, July 1, 2012. Online: http://www.nytimes.com/2012/07/02/world/middleeast/for-russia-syrian-ties-complicated-by-marriage.html?_r=0.

Beaumont, Peter. "Smuggled Video Testimony Documents Harsh Rule of Syrian Islamist Group." *The Guardian*, February 19, 2014. Online: http://www.theguardian.com/world/2014/feb/19/smuggled-video-testimony-harsh-rule-of-syrian-islamista-raqqa.

Bekdil, Burak. "How Turkey Fights the Islamic State." Gatestone Institute, July 27, 2015. Online: http://www.gatestoneinstitute.org/6205/turkey-fights-islamic-state.

Berger, Judson. "Mob Attacks on Iraqi Christian Businesses Raise Security Concerns." Fox News, December 9, 2011. Online: http://www.foxnews.com/politics/2011/12/09/mob-attacks-on-christian-businesses-raise-security-concerns-as-iraq-enters-new/.

Bhadrakumar, M. K. "Hopeful Signs of a Course Correction on Syria." Asia Times online, September 19, 2015. Online: http://atimes.com/2015/09/hopeful-signs-of-us-course-correction-on-syria/.
Bhalla, Reva. "Making Sense of the Syrian Crisis." Stratfor Global Intelligence, May 5, 2011. Online: http://www.stratfor.com/weekly/20110504-making-sense-syrian-crisis#axzz37gmGbqlH.
Bible Society of Egypt Newsletter. February 19, 2015. Online: http://us6.campaign-archive1.com/?u=017b6b7c5bf6d7468fcc6aedc&id=ea8fa5435c&e=9694d06650.
Black, Edwin. *Banking on Baghdad: Inside Iraq's 7,000-year History of War, Profit, and Conflict.* New Jersey: John Wiley & Sons, 2004.
Black, Ian. "Fear of a Shia Full Moon." *The Guardian*, January 26, 2007. Online: http://www.theguardian.com/world/2007/jan/26/worlddispatch.ianblack.
———. "Saudi Arabian Security Forces Quell 'Day of Rage' Protests." *The Guardian*, March 12, 2011. Online: http://www.theguardian.com/world/2011/mar/11/saudi-arabia-police-quell-protests.
Blair, David. "Iraq Invasion Anniversary: The Last Christians in Baghdad." *The Telegraph*, March 17, 2013. Online: http://www.telegraph.co.uk/news/worldnews/middleeast/iraq/9935960/Iraq-invasion-anniversary-the-last-Christians-in-Baghdad.html.
"Block the Jihadist Highway." Editorial, *The Australian*, August 26, 2014. Online: http://www.theaustralian.com.au/opinion/editorials/block-the-jihadist-highway/story-e6frg71x-1227036506847.
Bodansky, Yossef. "Did the White House Help Plan the Syrian Chemical Attack?" Global Research, September 1, 2013. Online: http://www.globalresearch.ca/did-the-white-house-help-plan-the-syrian-chemical-attack/5347542.
———. *High Cost of Peace: How Washington's Middle East Policy Left America Vulnerable to Terrorism.* New York: Prima, 2002.
———. "Sarajevo, 1995 and Damascus, 2013: The Use of Mass Attack Deception to Decide Wars." World Tribune, August 22, 2013. Online: http://www.worldtribune.com/2013/08/22/sarajevo-1995-and-damascus-2013-the-use-of-mass-attack-deception-to-decide-wars/.
———. "Syria's Multi-Layered Wars." *Defense & Foreign Affairs Strategic Policy*, issue 2, 2012.
———. "The Khorasan Pledge." *Defense & Foreign Affairs Strategic Policy*, April 2014, in *Focus on Defense and International Security*, ISPSW Strategy Series, issue 270, April 2014. Online: http://www.isn.ethz.ch/Digital-Library/Publications/Detail/?id=179342.
———. "The Release of Abu-Musab al-Suri." *Defense & Foreign Affairs Strategic Policy* issue 1, 2012. Excerpt available online: https://www.questia.com/magazine/1P3-2599595781/the-release-of-abu-musab-al-suri.
———. *The Secret History of the Iraq War.* New York: ReaganBooks/HarperCollins, 2005.
———. "Washington's Deal with Iran," *Defense & Foreign Affairs Strategic Policy*, issue 1, 2008.
Bodansky, Yossef and Forrest, Vaughn S. "The Truth About Gorazde." Task Force on Terrorism and Unconventional Warfare, House Republican Research Committee, US House of Representatives, Washington D.C., May 4, 1994. Online: http://serbianlinks.freehosting.net/gorazde.html.

BIBLIOGRAPHY

Bolt, Andrew. "Churches' Silence Just Indefensible," *Herald Sun*, May 21, 2015. Online: http://www.heraldsun.com.au/news/victoria/churches-silence-just-indefensible/story-fnpp4dl6-1227361920703.

"Bonhoeffer: Timeline." Public Broadcasting Service, January 12, 2006. Online: http://www.pbs.org/bonhoeffer/timeline.html/.

Borger, Julian and Inzaurralde, Bastien. "West 'Ignored Russian Offer in 2012 to Have Syria's Assad Step Aside'." *The Guardian*, September 15, 2015. Online: http://www.theguardian.com/world/2015/sep/15/west-ignored-russian-offer-in-2012-to-have-syrias-assad-step-aside.

Bradley, Matt. "Clashes Between Christians, Police Rock Cairo." *Wall Street Journal*, October 10, 2011. Online: http://online.wsj.com/news/articles/SB10001424052970203499704576621184220609012.

Brode, Daniel; Farhat, Roger; and Nisman, Daniel. "Syria's Threatened Christians." *The New York Times*, June 28, 2012. Online: http://www.nytimes.com/2012/06/29/opinion/syrias-threatened-christians.html?_r=0.

"Bush Makes Historic Speech Aboard Warship." CNN, May 2, 2003. Online: http://edition.cnn.com/2003/US/05/01/bush.transcript/.

"Brother of Egyptian Christians Murdered by Islamic State Prays for Killers Live on SAT-7." SAT-7 (UK), February 18, 2015. Online: Onhttp://www.sat7uk.org/announcements/brother-of-egyptian-christians-murdered-by-islamic-state-prays-for-killers-live-on-sat-7.

"Brother of Two Christian Victims of ISIS Calls in to SAT-7 Live Programme 'We Will Sing'." SAT 7-ARABIC, February 18, 2015. Online: https://www.youtube.com/watch?v=-yCmnyzYeW8.

Byrne, Aisling. "A Mistaken Case for Syrian Regime Change." Asia Times online, January 5, 2012. Online: http://www.atimes.com/atimes/Middle_East/NA05Ak03.html.

―――. "Covering Syria: The Information War." Asia Times online, July 12, 2012. Online: http://www.atimes.com/atimes/Middle_East/NG12Ak01.html.

―――. "Syria: The Information War." Interview with Al Mayadeen TV, Lebanon, February 2012. Online: https://www.youtube.com/watch?v=ayGIMb_oYwY.

Calderwood, Imogen. "Slaughter in the Roman Amphitheatre: Horrific Moment ISIS Child Executioners Brutally Shoot Dead 25 Syrian Regime Soldiers in Front of Bloodthirsty Crowds at Ancient Palmyra Ruin." *Daily Mail (UK)*, July 5, 2015. Online: http://www.dailymail.co.uk/news/article-3149469/Slaughter-amphitheatre-ISIS-executioners-brutally-shoot-dead-25-Syrian-regime-soldiers-bloodthirsty-crowds-ancient-Palmyra-ruin.html.

Cartalucci, Tony. "US-Backed Terrorists Murder US Ambassador in Libya." Global Research, September 12, 2012. Online: http://www.globalresearch.ca/us-backed-terrorists-murder-us-ambassador-in-libya/5304206.

Casper, Jayson. "How Libya's Martyrs Are Witnessing to Egypt." *Christianity Today*, February 23, 2015. Online: http://www.christianitytoday.com/ct/2015/february-web-only/how-libyas-martyrs-are-evangelizing-egypt.html.

Casper, Jayson. "Libya's 21 Christian Martyrs: 'With Their Blood, They Are Unifying Egypt'." *Christianity Today*, February 18, 2015. Online: http://www.christianitytoday.com/ct/2015/february-web-only/libya-21-christian-martyrs-with-their-blood-unify-egypt.html.

Cervellera, Bernardo. "Syria: Melkite Patriarch on Fears of a Future of Chaos and Fundamentalism." Interview with Gregory III Laham, Melkite Patriarch of Damascus. *AsiaNews*, April 29, 2011. Online: http://www.asianews.it/news-en/Syria:-Melkite-Patriarch-on-fears-of-a-future-of-chaos-and-fundamentalism-21428.html.

Cetingulec, Mehmet. "Islamic State Urges Turkish Businessmen to Return to Iraq." Al-Monitor, July 28, 2014. Online: http://www.al-monitor.com/pulse/originals/2014/07/cetingulec-iraq-isis-mosul-turkey-zeybekci-interview-mosul.html.

"Chaldean Church Mourns Fr. Ragheed Ganni and His Martyrs, The." AsiaNews, April 6, 2007. Online: http://www.asianews.it/news-en/The-Chaldean-Church-mourns-Fr.-Ragheed-Ganni-and-his-martyrs-9443.html.

Cheterian, Vicken. "Libya's Rebel Leader with a Past." *La Monde*, May 8, 2012. Online: http://mondediplo.com/2012/05/08libya.

Choksy, Jamsheed K. "How Iran Persecutes its Oldest Religion." CNN, November 14, 2011. Online: http://edition.cnn.com/2011/11/14/opinion/choksy-iran-zoroastrian/.

"Christian Houses Looted Also by the Kurdish Peshmerga Militias," Fides, November 19, 2014. Online: http://www.fides.org/en/news/36790-ASIA_IRAQ_Christian_houses_looted_also_by_the_Kurdish_Peshmerga_militias#.VSiWGPmUdNo.

"Christians in Iraq on the Run." *Aid to the Church in Need*, August 11, 2014. Online: http://members4.boardhost.com/acnaus/msg/1407729972.html.

"Chronology of Libya's Disarmament and Relations with the United States." Arms Control Association. Online: https://www.armscontrol.org/factsheets/LibyaChronology.

Chulov, Martin. "Baghdad Church Siege Survivors Speak of Taunts, Killings and Explosions: Attack Prompts Worldwide Condemnation and Leaves Iraq's Beleaguered Christian Community in Despair." *The Guardian*, November 2, 2010. Online: http://www.theguardian.com/world/2010/nov/01/baghdad-church-siege-survivors-speak.

———. "Christian Worshippers Killed in Baghdad Church Raid." *The Guardian*, November 1, 2010. Online: http://www.theguardian.com/world/2010/oct/31/christian-worshippers-killed-baghdad-raid.

———. "Iraq Prison System Blamed for Big Rise in Al-Qaida Violence." *The Guardian*, May 23, 2010. Online: http://www.theguardian.com/world/2010/may/23/iraq-prison-al-qaida-violence.

———. "Saudi Arabian Troops Enter Bahrain as Regime Asks for Help to Quell Uprising." *The Guardian,* March 15, 2011. Online: http://www.theguardian.com/world/2011/mar/14/saudi-arabian-troops-enter-bahrain.

Chulov, Martin and Mahmood, Mona. "The Houla Massacre: Reconstructing the Events of 25 May." *The Guardian*, June 2, 2012. Online: http://www.theguardian.com/world/2012/jun/01/houla-massacre-reconstructing-25-may.

"Churches in Mosul Are Used as Prisons by Jihadist of the Caliphate." Fides, December 2, 2014. Online: http://fides.org/en/news/36879-ASIA_IRAQ_Churches_in_Mosul_are_used_as_prisons_by_jihadist_of_the_Caliphate#.VKeHPCuUdNo.

Clarke, Michelle A. "The Disappearance, Forced Conversions and Forced Marriages of Coptic Christian Women in Egypt." N.d. Online: http://chrissmith.house.gov/uploadedfiles/copt_hearing_clark.pdf.

Cockburn, Patrick. "An Obvious First Step – Close the Jihadis' Highway." *The Independent*, August 24, 2014. Online: http://www.independent.co.uk/voices/comment/an-obvious-first-step—close-the-jihadis-highway-9687899.html.

Coghlan, Jo. "In Response to Houla Massacre Australia Expels Syrian Diplomats." International Policy Digest, May 29, 2012. http://www.internationalpolicydigest.org/2012/05/29/in-response-to-houla-massacre-australia-expels-syrian-diplomats/.

"Colonel Gaddafi Dead: David Cameron Says He Is 'Proud of UK's Role in Libya.'" Huffington Post (UK), October 20, 2011. Online: http://www.huffingtonpost.co.uk/2011/10/20/david-cameron-on-the-deat_n_1021851.html.

"Confirming Russia's Expanded Presence in Syria," Stratfor Global Intelligence, September 10, 2015. Online: https://www.stratfor.com/analysis/confirming-russias-expanded-presence-syria.

Copley, Gregory R. (ed.). "Early Warning. Here Comes the Cavalry." *Defense & Foreign Affairs Strategic Policy*, issue 3, 2008.

Copley, Gregory R. "Libya, Africa, and the Mediterranean After Qadhafi." *Defense & Foreign Affairs, Strategic Policy*, issue 8, 2011.

———. "Why the Islamic Caliphate May Presage Change." *Defence & Foreign Affairs Strategic Policy*, issue 7, 2014.

———. "Zahedi Memoir Taps Archives, Corrects Record on the Iranian People's Rejection of Mossadegh." World Tribune, January 16, 2013. Online: http://www.worldtribune.com/2013/01/16/zahedi-memoir-taps-archives-corrects-record-on-the-iranian-peoples-rejection-of-mossadegh/.

Crist, David. *The Twilight War: The Secret History of America's Thirty-Year Conflict with Iran*. New York: Penguin, 2012.

Critical Prayer Requests (CPR). Online: http://criticalprayerrequests.blogspot.com.au/.

Dabiq, The Clarion Project. Online: http://www.clarionproject.org/news/islamic-state-isis-isil-propaganda-magazine-dabiq.

Dagher, Sam. "Bombs Hit School Buses in Northern Iraq." *The New York Times*, May 2, 2010. Online: http://www.nytimes.com/2010/05/03/world/middleeast/03iraq.html?_r=0.

Darwish, Nonie. "If They [Muslims] Had Gotten Rid of the Punishment for Apostasy, Islam Would Not Exist Today." Gatestone Institute, February 5, 2013. Online: http://www.gatestoneinstitute.org/3572/islam-apostasy-death.

Dawood, N. J. (trans). *The Koran*. London: Penguin Books, 2000. Online: http://quran.com.

"Denied Dignity: Systematic Discrimination and Hostility toward Saudi Shia Citizens." Human Rights Watch, September 3, 2009. Online: http://www.hrw.org/news/2009/09/02/saudi-arabia-treat-shia-equally.

"Despite Pleas from Iraqi Leaders, Christians Say They Won't Go Home." Catholic News Service, April 23, 2010. Online: http://www.catholicnews.com/data/briefs/cns/20100423.htm.

Dettmer, Markus, and Schindler, Jörg. "Islamic State is a Diversified Criminal Operation." Interview with terror expert Louise Shelley, Spiegel Online, January 6, 2015. Online: http://www.spiegel.de/international/business/terror-expert-shelley-speaks-of-islamic-state-business-model-a-1011492.html.

"Disappearance, Forced Conversions, and Forced Marriages of Coptic Christian Women in Egypt, The." Christian Solidarity International (USA) and the

Coptic Foundation for Human Rights (Switzerland), November 2009. Online: http://www1.umn.edu/humanrts/research/Egypt/The%20Disappearance,%20 Forced%20Conversions,%20and%20Forced%20Marriages.pdf.

"Displaced Iraqi Christians Ponder an Iraq without Christians." *Morning Star News*, December 29, 2014. Online: http://morningstarnews.org/2014/12/displaced-iraqi-christians-ponder-an-iraq-without-christians/.

Dragovic, Denis. "Migrant Crisis: Best Solution is Aid for Turkey, Lebanon and Jordan." *The Australian*, September 8, 2015. Online: http://www.theaustralian.com.au/in-depth/europes-migrant-crisis/migrant-crisis-best-solution-is-aid-for-turkey-lebanon-and-jordan/story-fnws9k7b-1227516720372.

Durie, Mark. "A Message Signed with Blood to the Nation of the Cross." Lapidomedia, February 20, 2015. Online: http://www.lapidomedia.com/message-signed-with-blood-to-nation-cross.

———. "Isa, the Muslim Jesus." Answering Islam. N.d. Online: http://www.answering-islam.org/authors/durie/islamic_jesus.html.

———. "Islam's Second Crisis: The Troubles to Come." Middle East Forum, February 13, 2014. Online: http://www.meforum.org/3750/islam-second-crisis.

———. "Sex Slavery and the Islamic State." Middle East Forum, July 3, 2015. Online: http://www.meforum.org/5361/islamic-state-sex-slavery.

———. *The Third Choice: Islam, Dhimmitude and Freedom*. Melbourne, Australia: Deror Books, 2010.

Eckel, Mike. "Battle-Tested Chechens Drive Islamic State Gains." Voice of America, September 26, 2014. Online: http://www.voanews.com/content/syria-chechens-islamic-state-iraq/2462711.html.

Edry, Ronny. "Israel and Iran: A Love Story?" Ted Talks, September 2012. Online: https://www.ted.com/speakers/ronny_edry.

"Egypt: The Distance Between Enthusiasm and Reality." Stratfor Global Intelligence, February 13, 2011. Online: http://www.stratfor.com/weekly/20110213-egypt-distance-between-enthusiasm-and-reality#axzz37DLqJ8oo.

"Egyptian Man Dies after Setting Himself Alight." BBC, January 19, 2011. Online: http://www.bbc.com/news/world-middle-east-12214090.

"Egyptian, Mauritanian Set Themselves on Fire." *Al-Arabiya*, January 17, 2011. Online: http://www.alarabiya.net/articles/2011/01/17/133833.html/.

"Elizabeth Kendal's Message in Solidarity with Syrian and Iraqi Christians." Rally, Religious Liberty Monitoring, August 3, 2014. Online: http://elizabethkendal.blogspot.com.au/2014/08/elizabeth-kendals-message-in-solidarity.html.

Ellul, Jacques. *The Presence of the Kingdom*. Colorado Springs: Helmers & Howard, 1989.

Emerson Vermaat, J. A. *The World Council of Churches & Politics*. New York: Freedom House, 1989.

"End of Sykes-Picot, The." Al-Hayat Media Center, video, August 2014. Online: https://archive.org/details/TheEndofSykesPicot_201408; http://www.liveleak.com/view?i=d43_1404046312.

"Era of Iranian Hegemony in the Middle East Is Upon U, The." Middle East Media Research Institute (MEMRI), Special Dispatch Series No. 1817, January 21, 2008. Online: http://www.memri.org/bin/articles.cgi?Page=archives&Area=sd&ID=SP181708.

Erdbrink, Thomas. "In the Shadows of Shrines, Shiite Forces Are Preparing to Fight ISIS." *New York Times*, June 26, 2014. Online: http://www.nytimes.com/2014/06/27/world/middleeast/in-the-shadows-of-shrines-shiite-forces-are-preparing-to-fight-isis.html?_r=0.

Escobar, Pepe. "Exposed: The Arab Agenda in Syria." Asia Times online, February 4, 2012. Online: http://www.atimes.com/atimes/Middle_East/NB04Ak01.html.

Escobar, Pepe. *Globalistan: How the Globalized World is Dissolving Into Liquid War*. Ann Arbor, MI: Nimble Books LLC, 2006.

"Exporting Jihad: Foreign Fighters from the North Caucasus and Central Asia and the Syrian Civil War." Chatham House, September 23, 2015. Online: https://www.chathamhouse.org/event/exporting-jihad-fighters-north-caucasus-and-central-asia-and-syrian-civil-war.

Fagge, Nick. "Syria Rebels 'Beheaded a Christian and Fed Him to the Dogs' as Fears Grow over Islamist Atrocities." *Daily Mail*, December 31, 2012. Online: http://www.dailymail.co.uk/news/article-2255103/Syria-rebels-beheaded-Christian-fed-dogs-fears-grow-Islamist-atrocities.html.

"Fierce Clashes Pit Syrian Kurds against Jihadists." Middle East Online, January 18, 2013. Online: http://www.middle-east-online.com/english/?id=56533.

Figes, Orlando. *The Crimean War: A History*. New York: Picador, 2010.

"Food and Fuel Supply to Aleppo Restored." Armenpress (Armenian News Agency), October 14, 2014. Online: http://www.dailystar.com.lb/News/Middle-East/2013/Oct-07/233819-in-northern-push-syrian-troops-reopen-key-road.ashx.

"Forced Marriages & Forced Conversions in the Christian Community of Pakistan." *Movement for Solidarity and Peace in Pakistan*, April 7, 2014. Online: http://www.msp-pk.org/forced_marriages_forced_conversions_in_the_christian_community_of_pakistan_msp_report.

"Forcibly Islamized Armenians get Baptized in Turkey." PanARMENIAN.Net, May 16, 2015. Online: http://www.panarmenian.net/eng/news/192217/.

Forde, Gerhard O. *On Being a Theologian of the Cross: Reflections on Luther's Heidelberg Disputation, 1518*. Grand Rapids MI: William B. Eerdmans, 1977.

Foster, Peter. "Barack Obama's Faustian pact with Vladimir Putin over Syrian Chemical Weapons Brings Despair to Allies." *Telegraph*, September 14, 2013. Online: http://www.telegraph.co.uk/news/worldnews/middleeast/syria/10309943/Barack-Obamas-Faustian-pact-with-Vladimir-Putin-over-Syrian-chemical-weapons-brings-despair-to-allies.html.

Foxe, John. *Foxe's Book of Martyrs*, edited by W. Grinton Berry. Grand Rapids, Michigan: Baker, 1978, 7.

Fregosi, Paul. *Jihad*. New York: Prometheus Books, 1998.

Friedson, Felice. "Vicar of Baghdad Says Nothing Short of US Ground Troops Will Halt ISIS," *The Media Line*, October 21, 2014. Online: http://www.jewishjournal.com/live_from_the_arab_spring/article/vicar_of_baghdad_says_nothing_short_of_us_ground_troops_will_halt_isis.

Furness, Hannah. "BBC News Uses 'Iraq Photo to Illustrate Syrian Massacre.'" *Telegraph*, May 27, 2012. Online: http://www.telegraph.co.uk/culture/tvandradio/bbc/9293620/BBC-News-uses-Iraq-photo-to-illustrate-Syrian-massacre.html.

Gaddafi, Muammar. Interview, Russia Today, March 28, 2011. Online: https://www.youtube.com/watch?v=gVcefsgO4zM.

BIBLIOGRAPHY

Gallagher, Sean. "Iraqi Archbishop: Plight of Fleeing Christians Has Challenged His Faith," Catholic News Service, August 25, 2015. Online: http://www.catholicnews.com/services/englishnews/2015/iraqi-archbishop-plight-of-fleeing-christians-has-challenged-his-faith.cfm.

Garrison, David. *A Wind in the House of Islam*. Monument, CO: WIGTake Resources, 2014.

Gavlak, Dale and Ababneh, Yahya. "Exclusive: Witnesses of Gas Attack Say Saudis Supplied Rebels with Chemical Weapons." August 29, 2013. Online: http://www.mintpressnews.com/witnesses-of-gas-attack-say-saudis-supplied-rebels-with-chemical-weapons/168135/.

Glazov, Jamie. "Martyred in the USSR, Militant Atheism in the Former Soviet Union." *Frontpage Magazine*, March 18, 2013. Online: http://www.frontpagemag.com/fpm/181392/martyred-ussr-militant-atheism-former-soviet-union-jamie-glazov.

Gold, Dore. *Hatred's Kingdom: How Saudi Arabia Supports the New Global Terrorism*. Washington, DC: Regnery, 2003.

———. "The Iranian Nuclear Program and Regional Instability." Rubin Centre in Research and International Affairs, July 16, 2015. Online: http://www.rubincenter.org/2015/07/the-iranian-nuclear-program-and-regional-instablity/.

Goldman, David (a.k.a. "Spengler"). "Sex, Drugs and Islam." Asia Times online, February 24, 2009. Online: http://www.atimes.com/atimes/Middle_East/KB24Ako2.html.

———. "STDs and Strategy in Iran." Asia Times online, January 30, 2015. Online: http://www.atimes.com/atimes/Middle_East/MID-02-300115.html.

———. "Take Putin at His Word: Social Disintegration in the Middle East is the Issue." Asia Times online, September 30, 2015. Online: http://atimes.com/2015/09/take-putin-at-his-word-social-disintegration-in-the-middle-east-is-the-issue/.

———. "Why Can't Muslims Laugh at Mohammed?" Asia Times Online, May 5, 2015. Online: http://atimes.com/2015/05/why-cant-muslims-laugh-at-mohammed/.

———. "World Bows to Iran's Hegemony." Asia Times online, March 5, 2015. Online: http://www.atimes.com/atimes/Middle_East/MID-01-040315.html.

Gregorios III. "Appeal to Syria's Young People." August 13, 2015. Online: https://melkite.org/patriarchate/appeal-to-syrias-young-people.

Gunter, Joel. "Alan Kurdi Death: A Syrian Kurdish Family Forced to Flee." BBC News, September 4, 2015. Online: http://www.bbc.com/news/world-europe-34141716.

Güsten, Susanne. "Christians Squeezed Out by Violent Struggle in North Syria." *The New York Times*, February 13, 2013. Online: http://www.nytimes.com/2013/02/14/world/middleeast/christians-squeezed-out-by-violent-struggle-in-north-syria.html?pagewanted=all.

Gyapong, Deborah. "Leader Says West Must Stop Syrian and Iraq Wars So Refugees Can Stay Home." B.C. Catholic, September 10, 2015. Online: http://www.bccatholic.ca/canadian/5498-syriac-catholic-patriarch-visits-ottawa.

Hakeem, Mariam. "Saudi Man Kills Daughter for Converting to Christianity." *Gulf News*, August 12, 2008. Online: http://gulfnews.com/news/gulf/saudi-arabia/saudi-man-kills-daughter-for-converting-to-christianity-1.124541.

Halabi, Alaa. "Syria's Ever-shifting Battle Lines." Al-Monitor, August 9, 2015. Online: http://www.al-monitor.com/pulse/politics/2015/08/syria-battlefield-army-opposition-hama-ziyadiya.html#.

Hassan, Hassan. "Syria's Revitalized Rebels Make Big Gains in Assad's Heartland." *Foreign Policy*, April 28, 2015. Online: http://foreignpolicy.com/2015/04/28/syrias-revitalized-rebels-make-big-gains-in-assads-heartland/.

Hauslohner, Abigail. "The Dictator in His Cage: Hosni Mubarak Goes on Trial in Egypt." *TIME*, August 3, 2011. Online: http://content.time.com/time/world/article/0,8599,2086688,00.html.

Haykal, Husein. *The Life of Muhammad*. Translated by Isma'il Raji al-Faruqi. Kuala Lumpur: Islamic Book Trust, 1976.

Hersh, Seymour M. "Whose Sarin?" *London Review of Books*, vol. 35, no. 24, December 19, 2013. Online: http://www.lrb.co.uk/v35/n24/seymour-m-hersh/whose-sarin.

———. "Military to Military." *London Review of Books*, vol. 38, no. 1, January 7, 2016. Online: http://www.lrb.co.uk/v38/n01/seymour-m-hersh/military-to-military.

Hillenbrand, Carole. "Legacy of the Crusades." In *Crusades: The Illustrated History*, edited by Thomas F. Madden. London: Duncan Baird, 2004.

"History of the Nestorian Church." N.d. Online: http://www.nestorian.org/history_of_the_nestorian_church.html.

"Houla Massacre: 108 dead, Says UN." *The Sydney Morning Herald*, May 28, 2014. Online: http://www.smh.com.au/world/houla-massacre-108-dead-says-un-20120528-1zdlp.html.

"How a Fruit Seller Caused Revolution in Tunisia." CNN, Arabic staff, January 16, 2011. Online: http://edition.cnn.com/2011/WORLD/africa/01/16/tunisia.fruit.seller.bouazizi/.

"How an 11-year-old Survived Houla Massacre." The Associated Press, May 30, 2012. Online: http://www.cbc.ca/news/world/how-an-11-year-old-survived-houla-massacre-1.1177439.

Hughes, Dana and Radia, Kirit. "Syria's Guilt in Chemical Attack 'Clear to the World', Kerry Says." ABC News (America), August 26, 2013. Online: http://abcnews.go.com/International/syrias-guilt-chemical-attack-clear-world-kerry/story?id=20072589.

Hurtas, Sibel. "How Some Armenians Are Reclaiming Their Christian Faith." Al-Monitor, June 1, 2015. Online: http://www.al-monitor.com/pulse/originals/2015/06/turkey-armenians-disguised-muslims-recover-true-identity.html#.

Ibrahim, Raymond. "Russia Declares 'Holy War' on Islamic State." Frontpage Magazine, October 7, 2015. Online: http://www.frontpagemag.com/fpm/260372/russia-declares-holy-war-islamic-state-raymond-ibrahim.

"Internet World Stats: Usage and Population Statistics." N.d. Online: http://www.internetworldstats.com/africa.htm.

"IOCC Assists Syrian Families Escaping Bloodshed In Idlib." International Orthodox Christian Charities, March 31, 2015. Online: http://www.iocc.org/news/3-31-15-iocc-assist-syrian-families-idlib.aspx.

Iqbal, Anwar. "1,000 Minority Girls Forced in Marriage Every Year: Report." Dawn (Pakistan), April 8, 2014. Online: http://www.dawn.com/news/1098452/1000-minority-girls-forced-in-marriage-every-year-report.

"Iran: Happy Video Dancers Sentenced to 91 Lashes and Jail." BBC, September 19, 2014. Online: http://www.bbc.com/news/world-middle-east-29272732.

"Iraq: Christians Prepare for Christmas under Siege." Independent Catholic News, December 11, 2011. Online: http://www.indcatholicnews.com/news.php?viewStory=19478.

"Iraq: Danger as Sectarian War Looms." *Religious Liberty Prayer Bulletin*, May 1, 2013. Online: http://rlprayerbulletin.blogspot.com.au/2013/04/rlpb-208-iraq-danger-as-sectarian-war.html.

"Iraq's al-Qaida Threatens To 'Destroy the Cross.'" *Jerusalem Post*, September 18, 2006. Online: http://www.jpost.com/Middle-East/Iraqs-al-Qaida-threatens-to-destroy-the-cross.

"Iraq's Forgotten Conflict." Heart And Soul, BBC Radio, April 25, 2010. Online: http://www.bbc.co.uk/programmes/p0074who.

"Iraqi Christians Flee after Isis Issue Mosul Ultimatum." BBC, July 18, 2014. Online: http://www.bbc.com/news/world-middle-east-28381455.

"Is Growing Beards Mandatory in Islam?" Answering Christianity. N.d. Online: http://www.answering-christianity.com/growing_beards.htm.

"ISIS in Mosul Marks Christian Homes: Patriarch Issues Urgent Appeal." Assyrian International News Agency (AINA), July 19, 2014. Online: http://www.aina.org/news/20140719115241.htm.

"ISIS Issues New Rules for Mosul." Assyrian International News Agency, June 14, 2014. Online: http://www.aina.org/news/20140613202148.htm.

"ISIS Seizes Armenian Church in Raqqa." *Daily Star* (Lebanon), December 5, 2013. Online: http://www.dailystar.com.lb/News/Middle-East/2013/Dec-05/239954-isis-seizes-armenian-church-in-raqqa.ashx.

"ISIS, the Inside Story." *The Guardian*, December 11, 2014. Online: http://www.theguardian.com/world/2014/dec/11/-sp-isis-the-inside-story.

"ISIS Urges Militants to March to Baghdad." Al-Arabiya, June 12, 2014. Online: http://english.alarabiya.net/en/News/2014/06/12/ISIS-militants-plan-to-march-on-Baghdad.html.

"Islamic State Destroying Another Ancient Archaeological Site In Iraq." *The Japan Times*, March 8, 2015. Online: http://www.japantimes.co.jp/news/2015/03/08/world/islamic-state-destroying-another-ancient-archaeological-site-iraq/#.VP1FHPmUdNo.

Jenkins, Philip. *The Lost History of Christianity: The Thousand-Year Golden Age of the Church in the Middle East, Africa, and Asia—and How It Died*. New York: HarperOne, 2008.

"Jesuit Priest Abducted in Syria," Ankawa.com, May 22, 2015. Online: http://english.ankawa.com/?p=14929.

"Jews in Islamic Countries: Iraq." Jewish Virtual Library, updated 2013. Online: http://www.jewishvirtuallibrary.org/jsource/anti-semitism/iraqijews.html, accessed August 2015.

"Jews in Islamic Countries: Syria." Jewish Virtual Library. Online: http://www.jewishvirtuallibrary.org/jsource/anti-semitism/syrianjews.html, accessed August 2015.

"Jihadists 'Killed, threatened Christians' in Syrian Town of Maalula." Agence France-Presse, September 11, 2013. Online: http://www.news.com.au/world/jihadists-killed-threatened-christians-in-syrian-town-of-maalula/story-fndir2ev-1226716527428.

"Joe Biden Forced to Apologise to UAE and Turkey over Syria Remarks." *The Telegraph*, October 6, 2014. Online: http://www.telegraph.co.uk/news/worldnews/middleeast/unitedarabemirates/11142683/Joe-Biden-forced-to-apologise-to-UAE-and-Turkey-over-Syria-remarks.html.

"Joint Comprehensive Plan of Action." US Department of State. N.d. Online: http://www.state.gov/e/eb/tfs/spi/iran/jcpoa/.

Jones, Sophia. "ISIS Boasted Of These Christians' Deaths. Here Are The Lives They Lived." Huffington Post, February 19, 2015. Online: http://www.huffingtonpost.com/2015/02/18/isis-christians-killed-_n_6703278.html.

Joscelyn, Thomas. "Al Qaeda and Allies Form Coalition to Battle Syrian Regime in Idlib." Long War Journal, March 24, 2015. Online: http://www.longwarjournal.org/archives/2015/03/al-qaeda-and-allies-form-coalition-to-battle-syrian-regime-in-idlib.php.

———. "Al Qaeda in Iraq, Al Nusrah Front Emerge as Rebranded Single Entity." Long War Journal, April 9, 2013. Online: http://www.longwarjournal.org/archives/2013/04/the_emir_of_al_qaeda.php.

———. "Analysis: Zawahiri's Letter to Al Qaeda Branches in Syria, Iraq." Long War Journal, June 10, 2013. http://www.longwarjournal.org/archives/2013/06/analysis_alleged_let.php.

———. "Jihadist Coalition Claims Control of Idlib." The Long War Journal, March 28, 2015. Online: http://www.longwarjournal.org/archives/2015/03/jihadist-coalition-claims-control-of-idlib.php.

———. "Videos Show Joint Al Nusrah, Free Syrian Army Attacks in Ancient Village." Long War Journal, September 6, 2013. Online: http://www.longwarjournal.org/archives/2013/09/videos_show_joint_ex.php#.

"Joy at Iranian Baptisms." Evangelicals Now, August 1, 2013. Online: https://evangelicalsnow.wordpress.com/2013/08/01/joy-at-iranian-baptisms/.

Kamill, Emad. "NGO report: 93,000 Copts Left Egypt Since March." *Egypt Independent*, September 25, 2011. Online: http://www.egyptindependent.com/news/ngo-report-93000-copts-left-egypt-march.

Keener, Craig S. *The Gospel of Matthew: A Socio-Rhetorical Commentary*. Grand Rapids, MI: William B. Eerdmans, 2009.

Kendal, Elizabeth. "Apostasy, Fitna and Abuse of Interpol." Religious Liberty Monitoring, September 10, 2012. Online: http://elizabethkendal.blogspot.com.au/2012/09/apostasy-fitna-and-abuse-of-interpol.html.

———. "August Update." *Religious Liberty Prayer Bulletin*, August 28, 2013. Online: http://rlprayerbulletin.blogspot.com.au/2013/08/rlpb-225-august-update-incl-syria.html.

———. "Christian Crisis in the Middle East." Religious Liberty Prayer Bulletin, September 9, 2015. Online: http://rlprayerbulletin.blogspot.com.au/2015/09/rlpb-326-christian-crisis-in-middle-east.html.

———. "EGYPT: 'More Radicalised Than We Realised': Islam, Dhimmitude and the Maspero Massacre." *Religious Liberty Monitoring*, October 19, 2011. Online: http://elizabethkendal.blogspot.com.au/2011/10/egypt-more-radicalised-than-we-realised.html.

———. "Erodgan, Ergenekon, Europe and the Islamisation of Turkey." *Religious Liberty Monitoring*, October 3, 2012. Online: http://elizabethkendal.blogspot.com.au/2012/10/erodgan-ergenekon-europe-and.html.

———. "Iraq & Egypt: Al-Qaeda Declares War on Christians." *Religious Liberty Prayer Bulletin*, November 17, 2010. Online: http://rlprayerbulletin.blogspot.com.au/2010/11/082-iraq-al-qaeda-declares-war-on.html.

———. 'Iraq: Can Sovereignty Guarantee Security?' *Religious Liberty Monitoring*, May 28, 2004. Online: http://elizabethkendal.blogspot.com.au/2004/05/iraq-can-sovereignty-guarantee-security.html.

———. "IRAQ: Christians Flee the Killing Fields." *Religious Liberty Prayer Bulletin*, August 13, 2014. Online: http://rlprayerbulletin.blogspot.com.au/2014/08/rlpb-273-iraq-christians-flee-killing.html.

———. "Iraq: Propaganda versus Reality." *Religious Liberty Prayer Bulletin*, December 13, 2011. Online: http://rlprayerbulletin.blogspot.com.au/2011/12/138-iraq-propaganda-versus-reality.html.

———. "ISIS Takes the War Back to Iraq." *Religious Liberty Monitoring*, June 11, 2014. Online: http://elizabethkendal.blogspot.com.au/2014_06_01_archive.html.

———. "Libya-Egypt: A Call to Jihad Against Copts." *Religious Liberty Prayer Bulletin*, February 17, 2015. Online: http://rlprayerbulletin.blogspot.com.au/2015/02/rlpb-297-libya-egypt-call-to-jihad.html.

———. "Plight of Assyrian Captives." *Religious Liberty Prayer Bulletin*, October 13, 2015. Online: http://rlprayerbulletin.blogspot.com.au/2015/10/rlpb-331-syria-plight-of-assyrian.html.

———. "Raqqa, Syria: Christians in the Lions' Den," *Religious Liberty Prayer Bulletin*, March 5, 2014. Online: http://rlprayerbulletin.blogspot.com.au/2014/03/rlpb-250-raqqa-syria-christians-in.html.

———. "Religious Freedom and Realpolitik." *Religious Liberty Monitoring*, June 2, 2013. Online: http://elizabethkendal.blogspot.com.au/2013/06/religious-freedom-and-realpolitik.html.

———. 'Religious Freedom in an Age of Realpolitik.' *Religious Liberty Monitoring*, October 26, 2014. Online: http://elizabethkendal.blogspot.com.au/2014/10/religious-freedom-in-age-of-realpolitik.html.

———. "Saudi Christian Blogger Arrested." *Religious Liberty Monitoring*, January 27, 2009. Online: http://elizabethkendal.blogspot.com.au/2009/01/saudi-christian-blogger-arrested.html.

———. "SYRIA: Appealing for the Lord's Intervention," *Religious Liberty Prayer Bulletin*, Aug 12, 2015. Online: http://rlprayerbulletin.blogspot.com.au/2015/08/rlpb-322-syria-appealing-for-lords.html.

———. "Syria: Christians' Plight Lost under Mountain of Propaganda." *Religious Liberty Prayer Bulletin 167*, July 11, 2012. Online: http://rlprayerbulletin.blogspot.com.au/2012/07/rlpb-167-syria-christians-plight-lost.html.

———. "SYRIA: False Narratives and Propaganda." *Religious Liberty Monitoring*, January 9, 2012. Online: http://elizabethkendal.blogspot.com.au/2012/01/syria-false-narratives-and-propaganda.html.

———. "SYRIA: Who is Deploying Chemical Weapons?" *Religious Liberty Monitoring*, August 28, 2013. Online: http://elizabethkendal.blogspot.com.au/2013/08/syria-who-is-deploying-chemical-weapons.html.

———. "Syria: Situation Critical." *Religious Liberty Prayer Bulletin*, April 15, 2015. Online: http://rlprayerbulletin.blogspot.com.au/2015/04/rlpb-305-syria-situation-critical.html.

———. "The Humanitarian/Moral Intervention: An Exercise in Duplicity." *Religious Liberty Monitoring*, September 5, 2013. Online: http://elizabethkendal.blogspot.com.au/2013/09/the-humanitarianmoral-intervention.html.

———. "The Insufferable Plight and Bleak Future of Iraq's Indigenous Assyrian-Chaldean Christians." *Religious Liberty Monitoring*, May 5, 2010. Online: http://elizabethkendal.blogspot.com.au/2010/05/insufferable-plight-and-bleak-future-of.html.

———. "The Syria Crisis: Cutting Through the Propaganda." *Religious Liberty Monitoring*, July 10, 2012. Online: http://elizabethkendal.blogspot.com.au/2012/07/syria-crisis-cutting-through-propaganda.html.

———. "The UN, Saudi Arabia and International Human Rights." *Religious Liberty Prayer Bulletin*, September 22, 2015. Online: http://rlprayerbulletin.blogspot.com.au/2015/09/rlpb-328-un-saudi-arabia-international.html.

———. *Turn Back the Battle: Isaiah Speaks to Christians Today*. Melbourne, Australia: Deror Books, 2012.

———. "Upper Mesopotamia: Christians at the Mercy of ISIS." *Religious Liberty Prayer Bulletin*, June 17, 2014. Online: http://rlprayerbulletin.blogspot.com.au/2014/06/rlpb-265-upper-mesopotamia-christians.html.

———. "Why Andijan Changed Everything." Religious Liberty Monitoring, March 23, 2007. Online: http://elizabethkendal.blogspot.com.au/2007/03/uzbekistan-why-andijan-changed.html.

Kern, Soeren. "Britain's Female Jihadists." Gatestone Institute, September 21, 2014. Online: http://www.gatestoneinstitute.org/4714/britain-female-jihadists.

"Kessab Targeted by Al-Qaeda Front Groups in Cross-Border Attack from Turkey." Armenian Weekly, March 23, 2014. Online: http://www.armenianweekly.com/2014/03/23/kessab-targeted-by-al-qaeda-front-groups-in-cross-border-attack-from-turkey/.

"Key Judgments From a National Intelligence Estimate on Iran's Nuclear Activity." The New York Times, December 4, 2007. Online: http://www.nytimes.com/2007/12/04/washington/04itext.html?pagewanted=all&_r=0.

Khan, M. A. *Islamic Jihad: A Legacy of Forced Conversion, Imperialism, and Slavery*. Bloomington, Indiana: iUniverse Inc., 2009.

"Kidnappers Behead Priest in Mosul." World Watch Monitor, October 12, 2006. Online: https://www.worldwatchmonitor.org/2006/10-October/newsarticle_4579.html/.

Kimball, Roger. *The Long March*. San Francisco: Encounter Books, 2000.

Kozak, Christopher. "Russian Deployment to Syria; Putin's Middle East Game-Changer." ISW Intelligence Summary: September 13–19, 2015. Institute for the Study of War. Online: http://understandingwar.org/russian-deployment-syria-putins-middle-east-game-changer.

Krause-Jackson, Flavia. "Syrian Christians Say 'Arab Spring' Changes Could Hasten Extinction." Bloomberg, May 13, 2011. Online: http://www.bloomberg.com/news/2011-05-12/syrian-christians-say-arab-spring-changes-could-hasten-extinction.html.

———. "Syrian Christians Say 'Arab Spring' Changes Could Hasten Extinction."

Landes, Richard. "Islamism is Winning the Cognitive War—Thanks to Manipulative and Gullible Journalists." *The Telegraph*, April 4, 2013. Online: http://blogs.telegraph.co.uk/news/richardlandes/100210522/islamism-is-winning-the-cognitive-war-thanks-to-the-media/.

Lee, Adrian. "Migrant Crisis: The Truth about the Boy on the Beach Aylan Kurdi." Express, September 15, 2015. Online: http://www.express.co.uk/comment/

expresscomment/604590/Migrant-crisis-the-truth-about-the-boy-the-beach-Aylan-Kurdi.

"Letter from Aleppo: 20 Years a Bishop—Fighting for His Faithful to Stay in Syria." Aid to the Church in Need, September 24, 2015. Online: http://www.churchinneed.org/site/News2?page=NewsArticle&id=8679&news_iv_ctrl=1001.

Lev, David. "Aleppo: Syrian Rebels 'Cut Off' Regime Troops." Israel National News, August 26, 2013. Online: http://www.israelnationalnews.com/News/News.aspx/171303#.VMl4gWjLcrp.

Lewis, Alan E. *Between Cross & Resurrection: A Theology of Holy Saturday*. Grand Rapids: Wm. B. Eerdmans, 2001.

"Like Russia, Chechnya is Being Increasingly Drawn into Syrian Conflict," *The Jamestown Foundation*, Eurasia Daily Monitor, vol. 12, issue 182, October 8, 2015. Online: http://www.jamestown.org/programs/edm/single/?tx_ttnews%5Btt_news%5D=44467&cHash=760602bbff179e2cb5f467154705ab59#.ViAfNfkrLIU.

Linde, Steve. "Judy Feld Carr Secretly Rescued Syrian Jews." *Jerusalem Post*, June 18, 2012. Online: http://www.jpost.com/Jewish-World/Jewish-Features/Judy-Feld-Carr-secretly-rescued-Syrian-Jews.

Loveluck, Louisa. "Christians Flee Iraq's Mosul After Islamists Tell Them: Convert, Pay or Die." *The Telegraph*, July 19, 2014. Online: http://www.telegraph.co.uk/news/worldnews/middleeast/iraq/10977698/Christians-flee-Iraqs-Mosul-after-Islamists-tell-them-convert-pay-or-die.html.

Loveluck, Louisa and Samaan in Al-Our, Magdy. "Egyptian Christians Wait for News of Loved Ones Kidnapped by Isil." *The Telegraph*, January 23, 2015. Online: http://www.telegraph.co.uk/news/worldnews/africaandindianocean/egypt/11364924/Egyptian-Christians-wait-for-news-of-loved-ones-kidnapped-by-Isil.html.

Lund, Aron. "Are Saudi Arabia and Turkey about to Intervene in Syria?" Carnegie Endowment for International Peace, April 24, 2015. Online: http://carnegieendowment.org/syriaincrisis/?fa=59904.

Lund, Aron. "Who and What Was Abu Khalid al-Suri?" Carnegie Endowment, February 24, 2014. Online: http://carnegieendowment.org/syriaincrisis/?fa=54618.

Mackay, John L. *Jonah, Micah, Nahum, Habakkuk, Zephaniah. God's Just Demands*. Focus on the Bible Commentary Series. Fearn, Great Britain: Christian Focus, 2008.

Madden, Thomas F. "The Crusades Then and Now." *Augustine Institute*, 2011–2012, Archbishop's Lecture Series. Online: http://vimeo.com/33043624.

———. "The Real History of the Crusades." *Christianity Today*, May 6, 2005. Online: http://www.christianitytoday.com/ct/2005/mayweb-only/52.0.html.

Malek-Yonan, Rosie. "Genocide Unfolding: Death of a Catholic Assyrian Archbishop in Iraq." Assyrian International News Agency, March 18, 2008. Online: http://www.aina.org/guesteds/20080318055924.htm.

Malek-Yonan, Rosie. "Genocide Unfolding: Death of a Catholic Assyrian Archbishop in Iraq." Assyrian International News Agency (AINA), March 18, 2008. Online: http://www.aina.org/guesteds/20080318055924.htm.

Malik's Muwatta. Book 45, Numbers 45.5.17 and 45.5.18. Online: http://www.usc.edu/org/cmje/religious-texts/hadith/muwatta/045-mmt.php.

"Mapping the Global Muslim Population." Pew Forum Research, October 7, 2009. Online: http://www.pewforum.org/2009/10/07/mapping-the-global-muslim-population/.

"Martyred in the USSR: Militant Atheism in the Former Soviet Union." Film newsletter. N.d. Online: http://martyredintheussr.com/about.html.

Marx, Karl, and Engels, Frederick. *Manifesto of the Communist Party, 1848.* Online at http://www.anu.edu.au/polsci/marx/classics/manifesto.html.

"Mass Celebrated Again in the Nineveh Plain, A." Fides, November 11, 2014. Online: http://www.fides.org/en/news/36732-ASIA_IRAQ_A_Mass_celebrated_again_in_the_Nineveh_Plain#.VQpQ7I6UdNo.

Mauro, Ryan. "The Islamic State Seeks the Battle of the Apocalypse." The Clarion Project, November 18, 2014. Online: http://www.clarionproject.org/analysis/dabiq-islamic-state-wants-battle-end-days.

McCoy, Terrance. "Why Hamas Stores its Weapons inside Hospitals, Mosques and Schools," *Washington Post*, July 31, 2014. Online: http://www.washingtonpost.com/news/morning-mix/wp/2014/07/31/why-hamas-stores-its-weapons-inside-hospitals-mosques-and-schools/.

McElroy, Damien. "Repent or Die: Al-Qaeda Forces Announce Rules for Iraqi Territory They Now Control." *The Telegraph* (UK), June 12, 2014. Online: http://www.telegraph.co.uk/news/worldnews/middleeast/iraq/10895007/Repent-or-die-al-Qaeda-forces-announce-rules-for-Iraqi-territory-they-now-control.html.

McGrath, Alister E. *What was GOD doing on the Cross?* Eugene, Oregon: Wipf & Stock, 1992.

McRoy, Anthony. "Shia Eschatology in Contemporary Islamic Politics." In *Islam and the Last Days: Christian Perspectives on Islamic Eschatology*, edited by Brent J. Neely and Peter G. Riddell. CSIOF Occasional Papers No. 4, 2013–2014.

Mepham, David. "Nato Must Investigate the Civilian Casualties of its Libyan Campaign." *The Guardian*, May 15, 2012. Online: http://www.theguardian.com/commentisfree/2012/may/14/nato-civilian-casualties-libyan-campaign.

Merriam Webster Unabridged Dictionary. Online at http://unabridged.merriam-webster.com/.

Miles, Hugh. "Saudi Arabia: Eight of King Salman's 11 Surviving Brothers Want to Oust Him." *The Independent*, October 24, 2015. Online: http://www.independent.co.uk/news/world/middle-east/saudi-arabia-power-struggle-between-king-salman-and-mohammed-bin-salman-could-bring-down-the-a6706801.html.

Miller, Elhanan. "Syrian Christians Sign Treaty of Submission to Islamists." Times of Israel, February 27, 2014. Online: http://www.timesofisrael.com/syrian-christians-sign-treaty-of-submission-to-islamists/.

Mortada, Radwan. "Khorasan Pledge Splits Al-Qaeda." Al-Akhbar, April 23, 2013. Online: http://english.al-akhbar.com/node/19516.

"Mosul Christians Tell of ISIS Force' Iraqi Takeover." World Watch Monitor, June 12, 2014. Online: https://www.worldwatchmonitor.org/2014/06/article_3181068.html/.

"Mother of 3 Year-old Assyrian Girl Kidnapped By ISIS." Assyrian International News Agency (AINA), August 28, 2014. Online: http://www.aina.org/news/20140828181542.htm.

Mroue, Bassem. "Syrian Army Reopens Key Road to Aleppo." *Daily Star (Lebanon)*, October 7, 2013. Online: http://www.dailystar.com.lb/News/Middle-East/2013/Oct-07/233819-in-northern-push-syrian-troops-reopen-key-road.ashx.

Naama, Kamal. "Militants Kill Five Iraqi Soldiers, Sunni Protesters Form 'Army.'" Reuters, April 27, 2013. Online: http://www.reuters.com/article/2013/04/27/us-iraq-violence-idUSBRE93Q08120130427.

Nasr, Vali. *The Shia Revival: How Conflicts within Islam Will Shape the Future*. New York: W.W. Norton & Company, 2006.

"NATO Says Will Help Turkey Against Russia If Needed." Reuters, October 12, 2015. Online: http://www.reuters.com/article/2015/10/12/us-mideast-crisis-turkey-nato-idUSKCN0S61DU20151012.

Neff, David. "PLO Chairman Yasser Arafat's First Appearance at the United Nations." Washington Report on Middle Eastern Affairs, November/December 1994. Online: http://www.wrmea.org/1994-november-december/plo-chairman-yasser-arafat-s-first-appearance-at-the-united-nations.html.

Noble Qur'an, The. Online at http://quran.com/.

Nordland, Rod, and Rubin, Alissa J. "Massacre Claim Shakes Iraq." *The New York Times*, June 15, 2014. Online: http://www.nytimes.com/2014/06/16/world/middleeast/iraq.html?_r=0.

Norton-Taylor, Richard. "Gaddafi Seen as Ally in War on Terrorism." *The Sydney Morning Herald*, August 9, 2002. Online: http://www.smh.com.au/articles/2002/08/08/1028157991952.html.

Nuland, Victoria. "Terrorist Designations of the al-Nusrah Front as an Alias for al-Qa'ida in Iraq." US Department of State, Washington DC, December 11, 2012. Online: http://www.state.gov/r/pa/prs/ps/2012/12/201759.htm.

O'Bagy, Elizabeth. "Syria Update: The Fall of Al-Qusayr." Institute for the Study of War, June 6, 2013. Online: https://www.understandingwar.org/backgrounder/syria-update-fall-al-qusayr.

"Obama and Maliki Back Iraq Post-war Future." BBC, December 13, 2011. Online: http://www.bbc.com/news/world-middle-east-16134259.

"Obama, Maliki Meet over Iraq Future." Press TV (Iran), December 12, 2011. Online: http://edition.presstv.ir/detail.fa/215331.html.

"Obama Warns Syria Not to Cross 'Red Line.'" CNN, August 21, 2012. Online: http://edition.cnn.com/2012/08/20/world/meast/syria-unrest/.

"Oops, BBC: Iraq Photo to Illustrate Houla Massacre?" *Russia Today*, May 28, 2012. Online: http://rt.com/news/bbc-iraq-syria-houla-400/.

Parasiliti, Andrew. "Former UN Syria Envoy Says Iran Plan on Syria 'Worth Discussing.'" Al-Monitor, May 18, 2014. Online: http://www.al-monitor.com/pulse/originals/2014/05/brahimi-syria-envoy.html#.

Parsons, Chris. "I Put My Brother's Blood all over Me and Acted Like I was Dead." *Daily Mail*, June 1, 2012. Online: http://www.dailymail.co.uk/news/article-2152843/I-brothers-blood-acted-like-I-dead-In-gut-wrenching-heartbreaking-Syrian-boy-11-relives-slaughter-parents-siblings.html.

"Persian Gulf Oil & Gas Exports Fact Sheet." Marcon International, Inc. N.d. Online at http://www.marcon.com/marcon2c.cfm?SectionListsID=93&PageID=771.

Philipose, Thomas. "What Made a Non Believer Chadian Citizen Die for Christ, Along with His '20 Coptic Christian Friends'?" Bombay Orthodox Diocese, February 22, 2015. Online: http://bombayorthodoxdiocese.org/what-made-a-non-believer-chadian-citizen-die-for-christ-along-with-his-20-coptic-christian-friends/.

Pickthall, Muhammad M. *The Meaning of the Glorious Qur'an*. Online at quran.com.

Pleitgen, Frederik. "Author's Journey Inside ISIS: They're 'More Dangerous Than People Realize.'" CNN, January 4, 2014. Online: http://edition.cnn.com/2014/12/22/world/meast/inside-isis-juergen-todenhoefer/; video online: https://www.youtube.com/watch?v=1ucAqS4Qodg (part 1); https://www.youtube.com/watch?v=430W_imRQXw (part 2).

Pollard, Ruth. "ISIL Twitter Terror: Gruesome Iraq Photos and Candid Selfies of Jihadist Group Members." *The Age*, June 15, 2014. Online: http://www.theage.com.au/world/isil-twitter-terror-gruesome-iraq-photos-and-candid-selfies-of-jihadist-group-members-20140615-zs898.html.

———. "ISIL's New Rules for Captured City of Mosul." *The Sydney Morning Herald*, June 13, 2014. Online: http://www.smh.com.au/world/isils-new-rules-for-captured-city-of-mosul-20140613-zs783.html.

Pontifex, John. "Charity Gives Urgent Help after Exodus of Christians from Homs." Aid to the Church in Need, March 27, 2012. Online: http://members4.boardhost.com/acnaus/msg/1332805831.html.

"President al-Assad's July 26, 2015, Speech," PresidentAssad.net, accessed August 26, 2015. Online: http://www.presidentassad.net/index.php?option=com_content&view=article&id=1454:president-al-assad-s-july-26th-2015-speech&catid=319:2015&Itemid=496.

"Protesters in Syria, Yemen Take to Streets, Inspired by Gadhafi Death." Associated Press, October 22, 2011. Online: http://www.haaretz.com/news/middle-east/protesters-in-syria-yemen-take-to-streets-inspired-by-gadhafi-death-1.391375.

Putin, Vladimir V. "A Plea for Caution From Russia." *The New York Times*, September 11, 2013. Online: http://www.nytimes.com/2013/09/12/opinion/putin-plea-for-caution-from-russia-on-syria.html?pagewanted=all&_r=0.

"Qaeda, Allies Advance on Syrian Regime Bastion: Monitor," *Daily Mail (UK)*, April 25, 2015. Online: http://www.dailymail.co.uk/wires/afp/article-3053811/Qaeda-fighters-advance-regime-northwest-Syria.html.

Qur'an Dilemma, The: Former Muslims Analyze Islam's Holiest Book, vol. 1. Seattle, Washington: Water Life Publishing, 2011. Online: http://thequrandilemma.com/.

Rashwan, Nada Hussein. "Maspero Survivors Finally Testify: Army Shot at Unarmed Demonstrators Without Provocation." Ahram online, October 13, 2011. Online: http://english.ahram.org.eg/~/NewsContentP/1/24102/Egypt/Maspero-survivors-testify-army-shot-at-unarmed-dem.aspx.

"Read Putin's U.N. General Assembly speech," *Washington Post*, September 29, 2015. Online: https://www.washingtonpost.com/news/worldviews/wp/2015/09/28/read-putins-u-n-general-assembly-speech/.

"Reconsidering the Houla Massacre—OpEd." *Eurasia Review*, June 11, 2012. Online: http://www.eurasiareview.com/11062012-reconsidering-the-houla-massacre-oped/.

"Religious Leaders Say Isis Persecution of Iraqi Christians Has Become Genocide." Ankawa.com, August 9, 2014. Online: http://english.ankawa.com/?p=11919.

Religious Liberty Prayer Bulletin. Online at http://rlprayerbulletin.blogspot.com.au/.

"Remarks by President Obama to the United Nations General Assembly," September 28, 2015. Online: https://www.whitehouse.gov/the-press-office/2015/09/28/remarks-president-obama-united-nations-general-assembly.

Remnick, David. "Going the Distance: On and Off the Road with Barack Obama," *The New Yorker*, January 27, 2014. Online: http://www.newyorker.com/magazine/2014/01/27/going-the-distance-2?currentPage=all.
"Report of the Head of the League of Arab States Observer Mission to Syria for the Period from 24 December 2011 to 18 January 2012." League of Arab States Observer Mission to Syria, January 27, 2012. Online: http://www.columbia.edu/~hauben/Report_of_Arab_League_Observer_Mission.pdf.
"Report on the Protection of Civilians in Armed Conflict in Iraq: 6 July–10 September." United Nations agencies. Online: http://www.ohchr.org/Documents/Countries/IQ/UNAMI_OHCHR_POC_Report_FINAL_6July_10September2014.pdf.
Reuter, Christoph. "The Iranian Project: Why Assad Has Turned to Moscow for Help." Spiegel Online, October 6, 2015. Online: http://www.spiegel.de/international/world/syria-leader-assad-seeks-russian-protection-from-ally-iran-a-1056263.html.
"Revenge for the Muslimat Persecuted by the Coptic Crusaders of Egypt." *DABIQ*, issue 7, 2015, 30–32. Online: http://media.clarionproject.org/files/islamic-state/islamic-state-dabiq-magazine-issue-7-from-hypocrisy-to-apostasy.pdf.
"Revival of Slavery Before the Hour, The." *Dabiq*, issue 4, 2014, 14–17. Online: http://media.clarionproject.org/files/islamic-state/islamic-state-isis-magazine-Issue-4-the-failed-crusade.pdf.
Rezk, Tony. "Loving Your Enemies." February 17, 2015. Online: http://tonyrezk.blogspot.com.au/2015/02/loving-your-enemies.html.
Roberts, Hannah. "ISIS Threatens to Send 500,000 Migrants to Europe as a 'Psychological Weapon' in Chilling Echo of Gaddafi's Prophecy that the Mediterranean 'Will Become a Sea of Chaos.'" *Daily Mail*, February 19, 2015. Online: http://www.dailymail.co.uk/news/article-2958517/The-Mediterranean-sea-chaos-Gaddafi-s-chilling-prophecy-interview-ISIS-threatens-send-500-000-migrants-Europe-psychological-weapon-bombed.html.
Robinson, Dan. "Obama, Maliki Hail 'New Chapter' for Iraq Without US Troops." Voice of America, December 11, 2011. Online: http://www.voanews.com/content/obama-maliki-hail-new-chapter-for-iraq-without-us-troops-135449683/149460.html.
Rosenthal, John. "German Intelligence: Al-Qaeda all over Syria." Asia Times online, July 24, 2012. Online: http://www.atimes.com/atimes/Middle_East/NG24Ak02.html.
Roggio, Bill. "Al Qaeda in Iraq Claims Credit for Tikrit Jailbreak." Long War Journal, October 12, 2012. Online: http://www.longwarjournal.org/archives/2012/10/al_qaeda_in_iraq_cla_3.php.
———. "ISIS Announces Formation of Caliphate, Rebrands as 'Islamic State.'" Long War Journal, June 29, 2014 http://www.longwarjournal.org/threat-matrix/archives/2014/06/isis_announces_formation_of_ca.php.
———. "ISIS Seizes Border Crossing in Western Anbar." Long War Journal, June 21, 2014. Online: http://www.longwarjournal.org/threat-matrix/archives/2014/06/isis_seizes_border_crossing_in.php.
———. "ISIS Takes Control of Mosul, Iraq's Second Largest City." *Long War Journal*, June 10, 2014. Online: http://www.longwarjournal.org/archives/2014/06/isis_take_control_of.php.

———. "Syrian National Coalition Urges US to Drop Al Nusrah Terrorism Designation." Long War Journal, December 12, 2012. Online: http://www.longwarjournal.org/threat-matrix/archives/2012/12/syrian_national_coalition_urge.php.

Roy, Francois-Alexandre. "Regime Change in Syria: A True Story." Asia Times online, July 6, 2012. Online: http://www.atimes.com/atimes/Middle_East/NG06Ak01.html.

Rubin, Barry, and Schwanitz, Wolfgang G. *Nazis, Islamists, and the Making of the Modern Middle East*. New Haven: Yale University Press, 2014.

"Russian Deployment in Syria: Putin's Middle East Game Changer." Institute for the Study of War, September 17, 2015. Online: http://www.understandingwar.org/backgrounder/russian-deployment-syria-putin%E2%80%99s-middle-east-game-changer.

Ryan, Yasmine. "How Tunisia's Revolution Began." *Al-Jazeera*, January 26, 2011. http://www.aljazeera.com/indepth/features/2011/01/2011126121815985483.html.

———. "The Tragic Life of a Street Vendor." *Al-Jazeera*, January 20, 2011. http://www.aljazeera.com/indepth/features/2011/01/201111684242518839.html.

Sadeghi, Saheb. "Why Iran and Russia Aren't As Closely Aligned on Syria As You Might Think." Al-Monitor, November 10, 2015. Online: http://www.al-monitor.com/pulse/originals/2015/11/iran-russia-syria.html.

Sahih Bukhari. 'Hadith of Bukhari', Internet Sacred Text Archive. Online: http://www.sacred-texts.com/isl/bukhari.

Sanders, Oswald. *World Prayer: Powerful Insights from Four of the World's Great Men of Prayer*. Littleton CO: Overseas Missionary Fellowship, 1999.

Satherley, Jessica. "The Last Jews of Baghdad: Just SEVEN Remain (and They Fear for Their Lives after Being Named by WikiLeaks)." *Daily Mail*, November 29, 2011. Online: http://www.dailymail.co.uk/news/article-2067252/Last-SEVEN-remaining-Jews-Baghdad-named-WikiLeaks—leaving-lives-danger.html.

Satloff, Robert. "King Abdullah II: 'Iraq is the Battleground—The West against Iran'." Middle East Quarterly, Spring 2005, 73–80. Online: http://www.meforum.org/688/king-abdullah-ii-iraq-is-the-battleground.

Scot, Daniel. *Critique of Learning From One Another: Bringing Muslims Perspectives into Australian Schools*, 2nd edn. Stafford, Qld, Australia: Ibrahim Ministries International, 2013.

———. *Windows into the Qur'an*. Stafford, Qld, Australia: Ibrahim Ministries International, 2011.

"Scripture Distribution Increases in Persecution Hotspots." United Bible Societies, November 23, 2013. Online: http://www.unitedbiblesocieties.org/news/scripture-distribution-increases-in-persecution-hotspots/.

Serbian Orthodox Diocese of Raska-Prizren. "Crucified Kosovo: Desecrated and Destroyed Orthodox and Serbian Churches and Monasteries in Kosovo and Metohia (June 1999–May 2001)." 3rd edn. Life of the Orthodox Church. Online: http://www.kosovo.net/ckos/page_01.htm.

Shahen, Hermiz. "Assyria: Assyrian Universal Alliance Asks Australian Government For Help." Letter to the Australian Prime Minster. UNPO (Unrepresented Nations and Peoples Organisation), December 12, 2011. Online: http://www.unpo.org/article/13600.

Shaikh, Zaki, and Rosenbaum, Andrew Jay. "Russia Increases Weapon Orovisions to Syria." Al Bawaba, September 18, 2015. Online: http://www.albawaba.com/news/russia-increases-weapon-provisions-syria-745168.

Shayesteh, Daniel. *The House I Left Behind: A Journey from Islam to Christ*. Melbourne, Australia: Deror Books, 2012.

Shelley, Louise. "Blood Money: How ISIS Makes Bank." Foreign Policy, November 30, 2014. Online: http://www.foreignaffairs.com/articles/142403/louise-shelley/blood-money.

Shelton, Tracey. "The Death of Gaddafi." Global Post, October 24, 2011. Online: http://www.globalpost.com/dispatch/news/regions/middle-east/111024/gaddafi-sodomized-video-gaddafi-sodomy. (Warning: disturbing, graphic images.)

Sherlock, Ruth. "Syrian Christians: 'Help us to stay—stop arming terrorists.'" *Telegraph*, November 22, 2014. Online: http://www.telegraph.co.uk/news/worldnews/middleeast/syria/11247798/Syrian-Christians-Help-us-to-stay-stop-arming-terrorists.html.

———. "Syrian Christian Towns Emptied by Sectarian Violence." Telegraph, August 2, 2013. Online: http://www.telegraph.co.uk/news/worldnews/middleeast/syria/10218869/Syrian-Christian-towns-emptied-by-sectarian-violence.html.

———. "Syrian Rebels Defy US and Pledge Allegiance to Jihadi Group." *Telegraph*, December 10, 2012. Online: http://www.telegraph.co.uk/news/worldnews/middleeast/syria/9735988/Syrian-rebels-defy-US-and-pledge-allegiance-to-jihadi-group.html.

Sherlock, Ruth, and Malouf, Carol. "Inside an ISIL Town: 'Raqqa is Being Slaughtered Silently.'" *Telegraph*, August 23, 2014. Online: http://www.telegraph.co.uk/news/worldnews/middleeast/syria/11052984/Inside-an-Isil-town-Raqqa-is-being-slaughtered-silently.html.

"Shiite Question in Saudi Arabia, The." International Crisis Group, Middle East Report No. 45, September 19, 2005. Online: http://www.crisisgroup.org/en/regions/middle-east-north-africa/iraq-iran-gulf/saudi-arabia/045-the-shiite-question-in-saudi-arabia.aspx.

Shoebat, Walid and Barrack, Ben. "Evidence: Syrian Rebels Used Chemical Weapons (Not Assad)." Shoebat Foundations, August 27, 2013. Online: http://shoebat.com/2013/08/27/evidence-syrian-rebels-used-chemical-weapons-not-assad/.

Siciliano, Leon. "Iranian Woman Dances on Tehran's Metro in Protest against Laws." *Telegraph*, November 26, 2014. Online: http://www.telegraph.co.uk/women/11255717/Iranian-woman-dances-on-Tehrans-metro-in-protest-against-laws.html.

"Silence is Betrayal (MLK Anti-war Speech)." Sott.net, March 30, 2011. Online: http://www.sott.net/article/226559-Silence-is-betrayal-MLK-anti-war-speech.

Sindawi, Khalid. "The Shiite Turn in Syria." Hudson Institute, June 23, 2009. Online: http://www.hudson.org/research/9894-the-shiite-turn-in-syria-.

Sisto, Christine. "A Christian Genocide Symbolized by One Letter." National Review Online, July 23, 2014. Online: http://www.nationalreview.com/article/383493/christian-genocide-symbolized-one-letter-christine-sisto.

Smith, Chris. "Plight of Coptic Christians in Egypt." Friday, 22 July 2011. Online: http://chrissmith.house.gov/news/documentsingle.aspx?DocumentID=253570.

Sokol, Sam. "Amid Civil War, Syria's Remaining Jews to Celebrate High Holy Days." *Jerusalem Post*, September 2, 2013. Online: http://www.jpost.com/Jewish-World/

Jewish-Features/Amid-civil-war-Syrias-remaining-Jews-to-celebrate-High-Holy-Days-325004.

Solzhenitsyn, Alexander I. "A World Split Apart." Commencement Address Delivered at Harvard University, June 8, 1978. Online: http://www.orthodoxytoday.org/articles/SolzhenitsynHarvard.php.

"Speech by Yasser Arafat." Le Mond Diplomatique, November 17, 1974. Online: http://www.monde-diplomatique.fr/cahier/proche-orient/arafat74-en.

Spencer, Richard. "Assad's Forces Defeated on Roads North and South." Telegraph, June 9, 2015. Online: http://www.telegraph.co.uk/news/worldnews/middleeast/syria/11663774/Assads-forces-defeated-on-roads-north-and-south.html.

———. "Iraq Crisis: The Streets of Erbil's Newly Christian Suburb Are Now Full of Helpless People." *The Telegraph*, August 8, 2014. Online: http://www.telegraph.co.uk/news/worldnews/middleeast/iraq/11022879/Iraq-crisis-The-streets-of-Erbils-newly-Christian-suburb-are-now-full-of-helpless-people.html?fb.

———. "Militant Islamist Group in Syria Orders Christians to Pay Tax for Their Protection." *Telegraph*, February 27, 2014. Online: http://www.telegraph.co.uk/news/10666204/Militant-Islamist-group-in-Syria-orders-Christians-to-pay-tax-for-their-protection.html.

Spyer, Jonathan. "Islamic State Defeat in Kobani Will Be Hard to Replicate." Middle East Forum, January 20, 2015. Online: http://www.meforum.org/4998/islamic-state-defeat-in-kobani.

Spyer, Jonathan, and Al-Tamimi, Aymenn Jawad. "Iran and the Shia Militias Advance in Iraq." Middle East Forum, December 2014. Online: http://www.meforum.org/4927/how-iraq-became-a-proxy-of-the-islamic-republic.

Stenhouse, Paul. "What Is Going On in Syria?" Quadrant online, vol. LVI, no. 4, April 2012. Online: http://quadrant.org.au/magazine/2012/04/what-is-going-on-in-syria/.

Stern, Jessica, and Berger, J.M. *ISIS: The State of Terror*. New York: HarperCollins, 2015.

Stewart, Scott. 'The Jihadist Trap of Here and Now.' Stratfor Global Intelligence, June 25, 2015. Online: https://www.stratfor.com/weekly/jihadist-trap-here-and-now.

"Support is Flooding in for an Assyrian Church's Reopening in Baghdad." Albabawa, November 3, 2015. Online: http://www.albawaba.com/loop/support-flooding-assyrian-churchs-reopening-baghdad-763142.

"Syria in Crisis: The Muslim Brotherhood in Syria." Carnegie Endowment. N.d. Online: http://carnegieendowment.org/syriaincrisis/?fa=48370&reloadFlag=1.

"Syria: Murder and Abduction of Christians, Idlib." Middle East Concern, April 1, 2015. Online: http://www.meconcern.org/index.php/en/prayer-requests/871-syria-murder-and-abduction-of-christians-idlib.

"Syria: President Assad Admits Army Strained by War," *BBC*, July 26, 2015. Online: http://www.bbc.com/news/world-middle-east-33669069.

"Syria's President Assad – Should He Resign?" The Doha Debates, December 25, 2011. Online: http://www.thedohadebates.com/external/uploads/doha/polling/YouGovSirajDoha%20Debates-%20President%20Assad%20report.pdf.

"Syrian Christians Threatened: Join Anti-Government Uprising or Leave." Barnabas Fund, May 11, 2011. Online: http://www.barnabasfund.org/syrian-christians-threatened-join-anti-government-uprising-or-leave.html.

"Syrian Patriarch Says Middle East Christians Feel Abandoned by West." Catholic News Service, June 18, 2014. Online: http://www.catholicsentinel.org/main.asp?SectionID=2&SubSectionID=34&ArticleID=25508.

"Syrian Rebels Crucified: Islamic Extremists Execute Two Men in the Most Public Way for 'Fighting against Muslims.'" *Daily Mail*, April 30, 2014. Online: http://www.dailymail.co.uk/news/article-2616694/Horrifying-scenes-Syria-Islamic-extremists-CRUCIFY-two-fighting-against-Muslims.html.

Tabler, Andrew. "Catalytic Converters." *The New York Times*, April 29, 2007. Online: http://www.nytimes.com/2007/04/29/magazine/29wwlnphenomenon.t.html?_r=1&.

Takeya, Ray. "What Really Happened in Iran: The CIA, the Ouster of Mosaddeq, and the Restoration of the Shah." *Foreign Affairs*, July/August 2014. Online: http://www.foreignaffairs.com/articles/141527/ray-takeyh/what-really-happened-in-iran.

Talbi, Karim, and Ketz, Sammy. "In Syria, Russia Chasing Chechens Once Again." AFP, Ocober 7, 2015. Online: http://news.yahoo.com/syria-russia-chasing-chechens-once-again-074337140.html.

"Testimony of Samuel Tadros." US House Committee on Foreign Affairs Subcommittee on the Middle East and North Africa, May 20, 2015. Online: http://docs.house.gov/meetings/FA/FA13/20150520/103497/HHRG-114-FA13-Wstate-TadrosS-20150520.pdf.

Tiedmann, R. G. "China and Its Neighbours." In *A World History of Christianity*, edited by A. Hastings, 369–70. London: Cassell, 1999.

"Tortured by Extremists—Now Caring for Refugees." Interview, Aid to the Church in Need, October 2015. Online: http://www.acnuk.org/data/files/Faces_of_Persecution.pdf.

Trofimov, Yaroslav. *The Siege of Mecca: The 1979 Uprising at Islam's Holiest Shrine*. New York: Anchor Books, 2008.

Troper, Harold. *The Rescuer: The Amazing True Story of How One Woman Helped Save the Jews of Syria*. Toronto: Lest, Mason & Begg Ltd., 2007.

Trueman, Carl R. "Luther's Theology of the Cross." New Horizons, October 2005. Online: http://www.opc.org/new_horizons/NH05/10b.html.

"Twice Attacked Church Reopens in Baghdad, But is it Too Late for Assyrians?" Assyrian International News Agency, November 3, 2015. Online: http://www.aina.org/news/20151102212136.htm.

"Two Russians Appeal for WCC Action on Behalf of Persecuted Christians." Open letter, *Target*, November 25, 1975. World Council of Churches, Library and Archives, Geneva, Switzerland.

"Two Thousand Kessab Armenians Find Safety in Latakia (Update)." Armenian Weekly, March 23, 2014. Online: http://www.armenianweekly.com/2014/03/23/activist-rebels-robbing-homes-desecrating-churches-in-kessab/.

"Up to 1000 Christian Families Flee Iraq's Second City." World Watch Monitor, June 10, 2014. Online: https://www.worldwatchmonitor.org/2014/06/article_3178590.html/.

"US Casts Doubt on Claim Syrian Rebels May Have Used Sarin Gas." *The Guardian*, May 7, 2013. Online: http://www.theguardian.com/world/2013/may/06/syria-us-no-evidence-rebels-sarin.

Van Biema, David. "The Last Jews of Baghdad." *TIME*, July 27, 2007. Online: http://content.time.com/time/world/article/0,8599,1647740,00.html

Van Wilgenburg, Wladimir. "The Rise of Jaysh Al-Fateh in Northern Syria." Jamestown Terrorism Monitor, vol. 13, issue 12, June 12, 2015. Online: http://www.jamestown.org/programs/tm/single/?tx_ttnews%5Btt_news%5D=44027&cHash=0b4ad2f6b4306e9ef3cc7f6f8d8db310#.VgiSIfmqqko.

"Victory over ISIS Found in the Last Words Uttered by Christians." Christian Concern, February 20, 2015. Online: http://www.christianconcern.com/our-concerns/international-persecution/victory-over-isis-found-in-last-words-uttered-by-christians.

"Video Mocking IS Causes Riots in Egypt." World Watch Monitor, April 27, 2015. Online: https://www.worldwatchmonitor.org/2015/04/3824434.

Wagner, Laura. "Putin Defends Russian Military Support for Syrian Regime." National Public Radio, September 15, 2015. Online: http://www.npr.org/sections/thetwo-way/2015/09/15/440578356/putin-defends-russian-military-support-for-syrian-regime.

"Way of Fatima, The." N.d. Online at http://www.jesus-for-all.net/christian_books/pdf_234.pdf.

Williams, Lauren. "IS Makes Gains in Palmyra Despite Government Reinforcements." Middle East Eye, May 16, 2015. Online: http://www.middleeasteye.net/news/makes-gains-palmyra-despite-government-reinforcements-1099378079.

Williams, Lauren. "Why Palmyra Matters for ISIS," Lowy Interpreter, May 25, 2015. Online: http://www.lowyinterpreter.org/post/2015/05/25/Why-Palmyra-matters-for-ISIS.aspx.

Ward, Stephen. *Immortal: A Military History of Iran and Its Armed Forces*. Washington DC: Georgetown University Press, 2009.

Waterman, Shaun. "Syrian Rebels Used Sarin Nerve Gas, Not Assad's Regime: U.N. Official." *Washington Times*, May 6, 2013. Online: http://www.washingtontimes.com/news/2013/may/6/syrian-rebels-used-sarin-nerve-gas-not-assads-regi/.

"We Came, We Saw, He Died: What Hillary Clinton Told News Reporter Moments after Hearing of Gaddafi's death." *Daily Mail*, October 21, 2011. Online: http://www.dailymail.co.uk/news/article-2051826/We-came-saw-died-What-Hillary-Clinton-told-news-reporter-moments-hearing-Gaddafis-death.html.

Weiss, Michael and Hassan, Hassan. *ISIS: Inside the Army of Terror*. New York: Reagan Arts, 2015.

"What Does History Tell Us About How Islam Began?" Trinity Channel, May 20, 2015. Online: https://www.youtube.com/watch?v=tMpSOmjxy6E.

"What is the Future for Iraq's Christians? Canon Andrew White, the Anglican Vicar of Baghdad, Speaks to John Humphrys." BBC Radio, July 26, 2014. Online: http://www.bbc.co.uk/programmes/p023n73x (7 minutes).

"Why They Died, Civilian Casualties in Lebanon During the 2006 War." Human Rights Watch, September 5, 2007. Online: http://www.hrw.org/reports/2007/09/05/why-they-died.

Wigram, William Ainger. *Our Smallest Ally*, London: Society for Promoting Christian Knowledge, 1920. Online: http://digital.slv.vic.gov.au/dtl_publish/pdf/marc/16/832978.html.

Witherington, Ben III. *The Acts of the Apostles: A Socio-Rhetorical Commentary*. Grand Rapids, MI/Cambridge, UK: William B. Eerdmans, 1998.

"Woman Who Saved Syria's Jews, The." *The Daily Beast*, March 17, 2014. Online: http://www.thedailybeast.com/articles/2014/03/17/the-woman-who-saved-syria-s-jews.html.

"Women in Iran Taking Off the Hijab, The." BBC, May 12, 2014. Online: http://www.bbc.com/news/blogs-trending-27373368.

Wood, Graeme. "What IS Really Wants." *The Atlantic*, March 2015. Online: http://www.theatlantic.com/features/archive/2015/02/what-isis-really-wants/384980/.

Worth, Robert F. "In Syrian Villages, the Language of Jesus Lives." *New York Times*, April 22, 2008. Online: http://www.nytimes.com/2008/04/22/world/middleeast/22aramaic.html?adxnnl=1&adxnnlx=1400151908-9Z5lojrWEJioCD7iNvhj8Q.

Wright, Robin and Baker, Peter. "Iraq, Jordan See Threat To Election From Iran." *Washington Post*, December 8, 2004. Online: http://www.washingtonpost.com/wp-dyn/articles/A43980-2004Dec7.html.

Wyer, Sam. "The Islamic State of Iraq and the 'Destroying the Walls' Campaign." Institute for the Study of War, September 21, 2011. Online: http://www.understandingwar.org/sites/default/files/ISWSecurityUpdate_Islamic-State-Iraq.pdf.

Ye'or, Bat. *The Decline of Eastern Christianity Under Islam: From Jihad to Dhimmitude*. Fairleigh Dickinson University Press, 1996.

———. *Islam and Dhimmitude: Where Civilizations Collide*, Lancaster (UK): Fairleigh Dickinson University Press, 2002.

"Yemen President Ali Abdullah Saleh Appears on TV." BBC, July 7, 2011. Online: http://www.bbc.co.uk/news/world-middle-east-14072324.

"Yusuf al-Qaradawi: Killing of Apostates is Essential for Islam to Survive." YouTube, February 5, 2013. Online: https://www.youtube.com/watch?v=huMu8ihDlVA.

Zen, Eretz. "US VP Biden: We Couldn't Convince Our Mideast Allies to Stop Supporting Extremists in Syria." YouTube. October 3, 2014. Online: https://www.youtube.com/watch?v=wo4YE5zRmc8.

Zimmermann, Augusto. *Western Legal Theory: History, Concepts and Perspectives*. Chatswood, Australia: LexisNexis Butterworths, 2013.

"Zoroastrianism." BBC, 2014. Online: http://www.bbc.co.uk/religion/religions/zoroastrian/.